T0418996

Managing Security

This textbook is designed to be used by those tackling the complex and challenging issues of security sector reform (SSR).

The questions of 'What is security?' and 'How can governments deliver it in the most efficient and effective manner?' are central to this volume. The text explores the ways in which security might be achieved, providing readers with the guiding principles of governance and management. Principles are illustrated through reference to the experiences of countries engaged in reform of their security institutions, allowing the reader to identify continuities and discontinuities in the process of change within the security sector. Written by practitioners for practitioners, the book provides readers with a framework with which to assess and respond to first-, second-, and third-generation issues within SSR. All chapters include an introduction to the topic, empirical case studies, and exercises to encourage readers to reflect upon their own experiences of governing and managing security.

This book will be of much interest to students of security studies, defence management and defence policy, as well as to practitioners in the field of security management.

Laura R. Cleary is the Director of Oakwood International Security, UK. She has three decades of experience as an academic, author, and consultant specialising in security governance and management.

Roger Darby is an academic, author, consultant, and practitioner with over 20 years' experience in international development, higher and continuing education, and with business, education, and training expertise. He holds a number of appointments as a visiting professor in the UK and overseas.

Cass Military Studies

For more information about this series, please visit: https://www.routledge.com/Cass-Military-Studies/book-series/CMS

Managing Security
Concepts and Challenges

Edited by
Laura R. Cleary and
Roger Darby

Routledge
Taylor & Francis Group

LONDON AND NEW YORK

First published 2022
by Routledge
4 Park Square, Milton Park, Abingdon, Oxon OX14 4RN

and by Routledge
605 Third Avenue, New York, NY 10158

Routledge is an imprint of the Taylor & Francis Group, an informa business

British Library Cataloguing-in-Publication Data
A catalogue record for this book is available from the British Library

Library of Congress Cataloging-in-Publication Data
Names: Cleary, Laura Richards editor. | Darby, Roger, 1952– editor.
Title: Managing security : concepts and challenges / edited by
Laura R. Cleary, and Roger Darby.
Description: Abingdon, Oxon; New York : Routledge, 2022. |
Series: Cass military studies | Includes bibliographical references and index.
Identifiers: LCCN 2021020666 (print) | LCCN 2021020667 (ebook) |
ISBN 9780367683511 (hardback) | ISBN 9780367683504 (paperback) |
ISBN 9781003137061 (ebook)
Subjects: LCSH: National security—Textbooks. | Security sector—Textbooks.
Classification: LCC UA10.5.M36 2022 (print) | LCC UA10.5 (ebook) |
DDC 355/.03—dc23
LC record available at https://lccn.loc.gov/2021020666
LC ebook record available at https://lccn.loc.gov/2021020667

ISBN: 978-0-367-68351-1 (hbk)
ISBN: 978-0-367-68350-4 (pbk)
ISBN: 978-1-003-13706-1 (ebk)

DOI: 10.4324/9781003137061

Typeset in Times New Roman
by codeMantra

This book is dedicated to our students:
those in the past, who taught us so much,
those of the future, from whom we have much to learn.

Contents

Contributors

Dr Kogila Balakrishnan is the Director for Client and Business Development (East Asia) at WMG, University of Warwick. Formerly, the Under Secretary Department of Defence Industry at the Malaysian Ministry of Defence, she is currently an Adjunct Professor at the Malaysian National Defence University and a member of the advisory board for the Journal of Defence Analysis and Security.

Dr Tim Burnett is a Senior Lecturer in Economics at Aston Business School. His research focusses on management and competition in regulated industries which are subject to high rates of technological development.

Dr David Chuter worked for thirty years for two governments, international organisations and think tanks, and is now an independent author, lecturer, consultant and translator based in France. He lectures at Sciences Po in Paris and has written four books and many articles on security questions.

Prof Laura R. Cleary is the Director of Oakwood International Security. She has three decades of experience as an academic, author and consultant specialising in security governance and management. Her research on aspects of security sector reform has contributed to British and other governments' policy formation and strategic planning.

Dr Gemma Collantes-Celador is a Senior Lecturer in International Security at Cranfield University. Concerned with issues pertaining to security, conflict and development, her research has been published in the *International Journal of Human Rights, International Peacekeeping, Conflict, Security & Development* as well as in a number of edited volumes.

Dr Roger Darby is an experienced consultant, academic, researcher and author, with over 20 years' experience in international development, security and governance, higher and continuing education. He has worked throughout East and Southeast Asia, Africa, the Middle East, South America, and Europe.

Dr Lorraine Dodd is a Cranfield University Associate and a highly respected international contributor to studies in Defence and Security organisations as complex adaptive systems. Her research explores the multi-perspective approach in agile organisations. Her teaching covers critical systems thinking, Strategic Leadership and Management, Programme and Project Management, and Cyber Security.

Mr Jeremy Hilton is a Senior Lecturer in Complex Systems at Cranfield University at the Defence Academy of the UK. His research focuses on integrating systems thinking approaches to enhance organisational success and resilience. Key Publication: A multifaceted evaluation of the reference model of information assurance & security (2016)

Dr John McCormack is a Senior Lecturer in Strategic Project Management at Cardiff Metropolitan University. He teaches courses addressing the operationalisation of Strategy, Project Management and Change Management. His research focuses on behaviour and operational effectiveness, with special emphasis on public-private sector management practices.

Mr David Turns is a Senior Lecturer in International Law at Cranfield University. He has extensive experience of providing education for military lawyers, civil servants and humanitarian aid workers. Author of 60+ publications, including 'The law of armed conflict (international humanitarian law)' in MD Evans, *International Law* (OUP 5th ed., 2018).

Dr Anicée Van Engeland is Associate Professor in International Security and Law at Cranfield University. Her main areas of research and practice are human rights law, humanitarian studies and governance, with a focus on the Muslim world, and Islamic law. She regularly advises governments, international organisations, NGOs and civil society on Islam, security and conflict.

Dr Bryan Watters is Associate Professor of Defence Leadership and Management at Cranfield University. He is a Head of Centre, director of an MSc and academic director of the UK MOD's Senior Strategic Leadership Programme. Following a successful career in the British Army achieving the rank of brigadier, Bryan completed a PhD at Leeds University Business School.

Dr Edith Wilkinson is a Lecturer in the Cranfield Forensic Institute of Cranfield University. Currently, her focal area for research includes Risk, Crisis and Resilience. Edith recently published a chapter on 'Resilience and Deterrence: Exploring Correspondence between the Concepts' in Filippidou A. (2020) *Deterrence: Advanced Sciences and Technologies for Security Applications* (Springer).

Dr Ifti Zaidi is a Senior Lecturer in Leadership and Strategy at Cranfield University. His area of interest is applied leadership at the nexus of security and management. He is Course Director of Cranfield University's fully online Leadership and Security MSc, and academic director for the UK MOD's Strategic Leadership Programme.

Preface

In 2006, Laura Cleary and Teri McConville edited a book entitled *Managing Defence in a Democracy*. That volume was the result of the work they and others had undertaken in support of the UK MOD's Defence Diplomacy mission, now referred to as Defence Engagement. Through the provision of education, the UK government sought to exercise its soft power and to facilitate security sector transformation in post-conflict and post-authoritarian states.

The name of the mission and the content of the courses delivered to support it have changed over time, but the aim has remained essentially the same: to facilitate a discussion on how security can best be achieved. It has long been apparent to those engaged in the delivery of these programmes, many of whom are contributing to this volume, that regardless of whether one resides in a developed or developing country, the challenges of providing security are common across all states.

There have been significant changes in the political, economic, social, technological, legal, environmental and security dimensions since that 2006 publication. *Managing Security: Concepts and Challenges* is our attempt to take stock of those changes as well as reflect upon what we have learned from engaging with students across Africa, Asia, Eastern and Central Europe and Latin America. In reflecting on not just the principles of security sector reform, but the practice of reform within security institutions we have sought to identify the concepts and principles that matter, clarify those that often cause confusion in the field, and highlight the challenges that are commonly encountered but also the ways in which they can be overcome. A key theme of this book is the constancy of change, but we stress throughout that the requirement for and management of change needs to be understood within the context in which it is occurring. There is no single best way of conducting change within the security sector, but there are certainly better ways of approaching it then have been experienced in the past. The aim of this book is to enable readers to determine what 'better' might look like.

In practical terms, one of the aims of this book is to develop the security literacy of its readership. Those in uniform may think that they fully understand the concept of security, but often the way in which they conceive of and articulate that concept is different to the way in which their civilian counterparts do. We are endeavouring, therefore, to create a common understanding of security, its core principles and practices, so that those engaged in its provision can work effectively together to set the agenda for their nation's security in the 21st century.

We would like to thank all of the authors who contributed to this volume. Their depth of knowledge, expertise and skill is unparalleled. Their input is a tribute to their continuing professionalism and commitment to their subject fields as well as their own personal development and that of their students. We salute you.

Finally, to our past, present, and future students, we hope you continue to engage with and benefit from the continuing debate on the role of security in an uncertain future. While we believe this volume contributes to that discussion do not underestimate the value of your contribution.

Laura R. Cleary and Roger Darby

Acknowledgements

This book is the by-product of a series of conversations and a question. The conversations occurred over a number of years and in a variety of locations around the world. They were held with colleagues and with students and they centred on security: what it is, how to achieve it, and why it remains so elusive. The question was posed by Roger Darby in the spring of 2019 when he asked, 'Don't you think it is time for us to write a book on managing security?' The answer was 'yes'.

We are grateful, and relieved, that the editorial board at Routledge agreed with the answer to that question. We would like to thank Andrew Humphrys and Bethany Lund-Yates, our editors, for their encouragement, advice, understanding and patience as we endeavoured to bring this project to a successful conclusion during the course of an 'unusual' year. They are true professionals, and it has been a pleasure to work with them. We would also like to thank the four anonymous reviewers who looked at the initial proposal for this book. Their constructive criticism proved a useful benchmark during the editing process.

Our contributing authors also deserve mention. We recognise that the past 12 months have not provided the ideal conditions in which to gather one's thoughts and put pen to paper. There have been professional and personal challenges along the way. This book is all the more remarkable because of that, and should be viewed as a testament to sheer grit and determination. Thank you for your perseverance, your insights, and your camaraderie. Distance has not impacted the quality of conversations that we have had.

Finally, we would like to thank Joan Richards, Vanessa Sinclair and Christina Cleary. They have assisted in proofreading, when our eyes would no longer focus; in formatting, when software packages refused to do what we wanted them to do; in calming our nerves as the deadline approached; and, perhaps more importantly, they have provided us with a steady supply of tea and coffee. Their services have been invaluable. Thank you for getting us over the finish line. You may be family, but we still owe you one.

Abbreviations

AI	Artificial intelligence
AMO	Ability-motivation-opportunity framework
APM	Association for Project Management
ARMSCOR	Armaments Development and Production Corporation
ASEAN	Association of Southeast Asian Nations
BA ICO	British Airways / The Information Commissioner's Office (UK)
CADMID	Concept, Assessment, Demonstration, Manufacture, In-Service, Disposal/ Termination
CHOD	Chief of Defence
CMR	Civil-military relations
CPTPP	Comprehensive and Progressive Agreement for Trans-Pacific Partnership
CSFs	Critical success factors
CSOs	Civil society organisations
DARPA	Defense Advanced Research Projects Agency, USA
DFID	Department for International Development
DIP	Defence Industrial Policy
DIS	Defence Industrial Strategy
DLOD	Defence Lines of Development
DOTMLPF	Doctrine, organization, training, materiel, leadership and education, personnel and facilities
DPA	Dayton Peace Agreement
DTI	Department of Trade and Industry, UK
ECCO	European Club for Countertrade and Offsets
ECtHR	European Court of Human Rights
EEZ	Exclusive Economic Zone
EPRDF	Ethiopian People's Revolutionary Democratic Front
EU	European Union
FAA	Functional area analysis
FCO	Foreign and Commonwealth Office
FDIs	Foreign direct investments
FNA	Functional needs analysis
FSA	Functional solution analysis
GICA	Global Industrial Cooperation Association
HCW	Healthcare workers
HQs	Headquarters

HRM	Human resource management
ICC	International Criminal Court
ICJ	International Court of Justice
ICP	Industrial Collaboration Programme
ICTY	International Criminal Tribunal for the Former Yugoslavia
IFIs	International financial institutions
IHL	International Humanitarian Law
IHRL	International Human Rights Law
IM	Information management
INGOS	International non-governmental organisations
IPMA	International Project Management Association
IOs	International organisations
IoT	Internet of things
IPR	Intellectual property right
ISO	International Organization for Standardization
JCIDS	Joint Capabilities Integration and Development System
KAIN	Indonesia's Committee for High Technology and Strategic Industries
KLA	Kosovo Liberation Army
KM	Knowledge management
KSF	Kosovo Security Forces
LDF	Lesotho Defence Forces
LOAC	Law of Armed Conflict
LTTE	Liberation Tigers of Tamil Eelam
MOD	Ministry of Defence
MONUSCO	United Nations Organization Stabilization Mission in the Democratic Republic of the Congo
MTCR	Missile Technology Control Regime
NATO	North Atlantic Treaty Organization
NCSC	The National Cyber Security Centre, UK
NPM	New public management
NSC	National Security Council
NSS	National security strategy
OAS	Organisation of American States
OECD	Organisation for Economic Co-operation and Development
OEMs	Original equipment manufacturers
OPSEC	Operations security
OVF	Offsets value framework
P3M	Project, Program and Portfolio Management
PAC	Public accounts committee
PESTLE	Political, Economic, Social, Technological, Legal and Environmental
PfD	Partnership for Development
PFP	Partnership for Peace
PIS	Polish Law and Justice Party
PMI	Project Management Institute
POW	Prisoner of war
PSOs	Public sector organisations
PTSD	Post-traumatic stress disorder

RBV	Resource-based view
R2P	Responsibility to Protect
RoC	Relative opposing capabilities
ROE	Rules of Engagement
RUSI	Royal United Services Institute
SADC	South African Development Community
SALW	Small Arms and Light Weapons
SCP	Situational Crime Prevention
SDSR	Strategic Defence and Security Review (UK)
SHRM	Strategic Human Resource Management
SIHRM	Strategic International Human Resource Management
SIDS	Small island developing states
SMEs	Small to medium enterprises
SOMILES	SADC Mission to the Kingdom of Lesotho
SSD	Security sector development
SSG	Security sector governance
SSM	Security sector management
SSR	Security sector reform
SST	Security sector transformation
SM	Strategic management
SWOT	Strengths, Weaknesses, Opportunities and Threats
TEZ	Total exclusion zone
TM	Talent management
TOV	Triple offsets value
TPP	Trans Pacific Partnership
UN	United Nations
UNDP	United Nations Development Program
UNSC	United Nations Security Council
UNSCR	United Nations Security Council Resolution
VUCA	Volatile, uncertain, complex and ambiguous world
VSM	Viable system model
WGA	Whole-of-government approach
WSA	Whole-of-society approach
WTO	World Trade Organization
WWA	Whole-of-world approach

1 Introduction

Change within context

Laura R. Cleary and Roger Darby

Introduction

Terrorism, environmental and man-made disasters, mass migration, intra- and inter-state violence, cyber-attack, hybrid warfare, attacks against critical national infrastructure, organised crime, social and political atomisation, pandemic. For over a decade these are the risks that have been regularly identified in corporate, national and global risk assessments and referenced within national security policies. While the risks identified would appear common across the world, their probability and impact on individual states have proven variable, as has been the ability of governments to effectively manage those risks. Effective risk management requires an understanding of the overall risk appetite, the capacity to assess risk in terms of probability and consequence, and the desire and ability to mitigate, or respond to, those risks (Rice & Zeigart, 2018). In essence, an effective government takes political risk seriously, approaches it systematically and provides leadership from the top (Rice & Zeigart, 2018).

Reflect for a moment on the different national responses to the Covid-19 pandemic which began in the winter of 2019. Those countries that responded best, and were able to limit the infection and mortality rates, were those that clearly understood the risk appetite across the social, business and political spheres, and had achieved this understanding through systematic analysis of the nature of the risk. Leadership was displayed through means of clear political direction and coherent and consistent communications. Examples include New Zealand, the Republic of Georgia, South Korea, Uruguay and Germany. Those that failed to respond effectively, countries such as the United States, the United Kingdom, Italy and Brazil displayed a number of similar traits: a certain degree of arrogance evidenced in the attitude that 'it couldn't possibly happen here'; a failure to adhere to their own risk assessments by taking corrective action; an inability to formulate and adopt rational policies due to polarised domestic politics; a lack of agility in terms of response; and, flamboyant, but generally poor, leadership. In essence, they succumbed to what Michael Lewis has termed the 'fifth risk', bad project management (Lewis, 2018). In seeking to deliver public goods, government is necessarily engaged in the business of project management across multiple domains, variable dimensions and fluctuating time scales. Failure to manage projects effectively raises questions about the capacity of government and the quality of governance, which, in turn and over a longer time frame, will undermine the security of individuals and states.

So, the question arises, how can we ensure the most effective, efficient and economic provision of security? The answer is dependent upon the responses to a series

DOI: 10.4324/9781003137061-1

of integral questions. How does the state conceptualise its security? What are the perceived risks to attaining that vision? For whom does the state wish to provide security? What is the best way of doing so? More importantly, who is ultimately responsible for its provision? These may appear to be simple questions, but the answers are frequently complex and liable to change over time. These are the questions that our students ponder on a daily basis. Therefore, they are the questions with which *Managing Security: Concepts and Challenges* is ultimately concerned.

An alternative approach

When we first started to scope this project in 2019 – which feels like a lifetime ago – we were motivated by two desires. First, we wanted to take stock of the work we had been doing to support the UK Ministry of Defence's (MOD) Defence Engagement mission. In 1998, as part of a Strategic Defence Review, the MOD established Defence Diplomacy, now referred to as Defence Engagement, as one of eight military missions. A component of that mission was the development of an educational outreach programme through which politicians, civil servants, military and security personnel from developing democracies could be educated in the governance and management of security. Having been actively engaged in the design and delivery of that global programme for close to 20 years we felt it was time to pause, reflect and renew our approach to our subjects and the way in which we disseminate knowledge. Second, we also wanted to consider more deeply the issues with which our students are increasingly concerned. The topics addressed within this book are the ones in which our students and their sponsors are most interested. Little did we know when we began our deliberations in 2019 that these questions would gain added urgency in 2020 as a result of both a global pandemic and crises of governance.

Historically, our students have been mid- to senior level officials, military and civilian, from countries undergoing a significant transition, be that from conflict or authoritarianism. These are the individuals grappling with the challenges of building a better future for their country. It is those individuals for whom this book primarily is intended. Our aim is that this text serves as a handbook to those tackling the complex and challenging issues of transformation within the security sector, as opposed to transformation of the security sector.

We draw a distinction between reform within the security sector and reform of the security sector for particular reasons. Security sector reform (SSR), also referred to as security sector governance (SSG), management (SSM), transformation (SST), and development (SSD), was initially predicated upon the belief that 'countries with unprofessional and unaccountable security forces, weak justice systems and inappropriate levels of military expenditure are particularly susceptible to violent conflict' (Short, 2002). In the 1990s, the donor community believed that there was an opportunity to tackle these issues and reform security institutions, thereby preventing conflict and promoting sustainable development.

Over time, however the rationale for SSR changed. Before 9/11 SSR was viewed primarily as an element of conflict resolution; post-9/11 it was meant to address both conflict prevention and resolution. This emphasis on 'upstream engagement' arose as a result of the belief that 'risks' to national and international security, e.g., terrorism, drug trafficking, mass migration, proliferation of Small Arms and Light Weapons (SALW), arose within 'fragile', 'failing' and 'failed' states. The promotion of SSR as an antidote to state fragility has not met with universal acclaim. More recently, in an attempt to strip it of any pejorative connotations, SSR has been equated with any effort to make a security sector more effective, transparent, accountable, and affordable (FBA, 2020). Meaning that SSR can occur in both developed and developing states.

Those institutions, agencies and ministries deemed to constitute the security sector include:

- **The security forces** (armed forces, police, paramilitary and intelligence services)
- **The relevant ministries and offices** within the executive branch charged with managing and monitoring security forces (ministries of defence, finance, internal and foreign affairs, national security councils, and budget and audit offices)
- **Informal security forces**
- **The judiciary and correction systems**
- **Parliamentary oversight committees**
- **Private sector**
- **Civil society** (academia, NGOs, media, etc)
- **External actors** (donors, alliances, IGOs and NGOs).

According to the OECD-DAC (2005), SSR is the term used to describe the transformation of those named previously, addressing their roles, responsibilities and actions, ensuring that they are consistent with democratic norms and sound principles of good governance, and are working together to ensure a well-functioning security framework.

While the interpretations of SSR have changed over time, the general prescriptions for how that reform should be conducted have not. There are, however, inherent flaws in the way in which we have thought about and promoted SSR. First, the initial construction of SSR, with its emphasis on conflict resolution through the application of democratic norms, values, institutions and practices, stemmed from a liberal normative framework (Chandler, 2010), which has become discredited. The initial outreach in the early 1990s to the states of the former Warsaw Pact Organization was couched in terms of 'if you structure your institutions in this way and adopt these practices you can be part of our club' (be that NATO or the EU). For some countries, like those in the Baltic region concerned that Russia might still pose an existential threat, there was a desire to adopt a 'prescribed template' or NATO standard. Buoyed by their apparent success in the region, the international donor community sought to try something similar in other parts of the world, for example in Sierra Leone, Liberia and East Timor, but this led to an overly technocratic approach to reform.

Second, with its emphasis on whole-of-government approaches to reform, the SSR literature applies a pseudo-systems approach to change. For example, while there is recognition that governments are complex operating systems and that there are intense interactions between actors within those systems and with the broader environment, there is a failure to acknowledge the many other components of dynamic complexity. We would argue that systems thinking is applied only in part because all too often those advising on how to reform the security sector underestimate the significance of inter-ministerial relationships across government, neglect feedback loops, assume change is linear, ignore history, prefer adoption of methods over adaptation, focus on the symptoms of a problem rather than the cause, and as a result become frustrated by policy resistance.[1]

Which brings us back to our students and the issues they are seeking to resolve. While the countries our students represent may be undergoing SSR, the students themselves are not necessarily coordinating that programme, but trying to initiate or manage change in one ministry, department or sub-unit. While they may be acutely aware of what is occurring within the sector as a whole, they are trying to focus on the specific task at hand.

While there are several publications that address security sector transformation in specific countries or regions, they tend to be either a review of what has been achieved to date or address a specific element of reform, e.g., defence institution building or the establishment of law and justice. Our approach is different. We are focusing on the ways in which security *might* be achieved, providing readers with guiding principles of governance and management, examples of how those principles have been applied in practice in countries engaged in a similar process of reform, and key issues that practitioners may wish to consider as they initiate and implement change. What sets this text apart is the firm belief that improvements in the quality of security can only be achieved through equal and commensurate improvements in the quality of governance and management.

There are four key themes that run through this book: 1) change is a constant; 2) context matters; 3) conceptual clarity is crucial; and 4) experiential learning is valuable. It is worth setting out here what we mean by these.

Change is a constant

The catalysts for reform can be big or small. They may include a changed security environment, be that the end of war as was the case in Kosovo in 1999, or its commencement as in the case of Ukraine in 2014; it may be a change of government as in Ghana in 2001; or it may be the simple recognition that the old ways of behaving and operating are no longer effective or appropriate, as has been the case in Bangladesh. Catalysts are variable as are the justifications for change. Reform of the security sector may be viewed as a necessary requirement for the prevention of conflict, the consolidation of democracy or the enhancement of the professionalism of the security services. It could be one of these reasons or all of them, but it is important to recognise that the specific catalyst and justification for the reform will shape the process and method of change and influence the extent and duration of support for it. Ukraine provides a useful example through which to illustrate this point. Between 1991 and 2014 there was limited change to the armed forces beyond their reduction in size. No effort was made to address the structure of those forces, their doctrine, training, procurement or logistics systems (Cleary, 2016). In 2014 following the overthrow of the Yanukovych government, Russia's invasion of Crimea and the outbreak of civil war in Eastern Ukraine, there was a strong and sustained grassroots demand for change. That has manifested itself in a variety of ways ranging from reform of the medical logistics system, introduction of an e-procurement system to reduce the risk of corruption, the initiation of reforms of the police and border service and the reconstitution of the Ukrainian Navy. Although not always visibly joined up or observable from outside the system, change is occurring in pockets and it has developed its own momentum. Change may be initiated quickly, but to measure its extent and depth we need to adopt a long-term perspective.

Context matters

It is argued in this book that understanding and managing context is key. Furthermore, students who use this book in differing country contexts should be cognizant of the interplay and influence including historical, institutional, regulatory, cultural, military and security traditions. We contend that culture and cross-cultural management in the defence and security sector are pivotal to understanding and applying the concepts and practices propounded in it. For example, the importance of effective communication, an understanding of traditions, norms and customs within and between defence and security organisations and stakeholders such as civilian communities in which the sector engages, provide a necessary introduction to the following chapters in this volume.

Example 1.1: Georgia

In the case of the Republic of Georgia, a senior civil servant in the MOD expressed his frustration with the NATO advisors with whom he was engaged. He stated that those advisors were normally deployed for a six months tour in Georgia. Although they had a reasonable understanding of how their own defence and political systems worked, they had no familiarity with Georgian politics, bureaucratic structures, cultures or procedures, nor did they appreciate the varied legacy of Georgia having been part of the Soviet Union for 70 years. As a result, that civil servant spent more time educating the advisors than he did receiving advice.

Over the 30 years we have taught on defence and security courses and have been actively engaged in SSR, we have come to realise that the concepts at the heart of discipline and practice are frequently contested or mediated through important cross-cultural lenses. We would divide those challenging concepts into four categories:

1. Those that mean different things in different languages; words such as: policy, strategy, doctrine, management, administration, control and logistics.
2. Words that are not easily translatable, e.g., accountability, civil and civilian, and employee engagement.
3. Those concepts that are often understood in a pejorative sense, such as good and bad governance and control, specifically when preceded by the word 'civilian'. Or when language is culture-bound for example in defining the difference between a 'terrorist' or a 'freedom fighter'.
4. Those ideas related to the management of essential finite resources to support civil-military relations (CMR) which are not immutable, nor prescriptive but generally essential to effective, efficient and economic SSR, e.g., knowledge creation, capture and transfer, and performance management.

Historical, strategic, political, institutional, social and cultural contexts also have a bearing on how change is initiated and executed within the security sector. Experience has shown that too many policy makers and security advisors lack a detailed and nuanced understanding of the cross-cultural contexts in which they are operating, as the example of the Georgian civil servant referenced previously makes evident. Too often

SSR programmes are formulated on the donor's, rather than the recipient's analysis of the strategic context. As a result, those programmes are structured in such a way as to further the security and foreign policies of the donor and their impact and effectiveness is measured in accordance with the donor's accountability guidelines, which may not be understood or shared by the target country. As Warren Liu, former Vice President of KFC in China has argued, strategic success is in large part dependent on individuals having a deep and broad understanding of the context(s) in which they are operating (Liu, 2008). That intuitive knowledge (and cultural understanding) will be held by those working within the institution undergoing reform; and they know which and when the levers of power and influence can be pulled.

Example 1.2: Ukraine

Recently whilst delivering training to an advisory mission in Ukraine, we were forcibly struck by how European security advisors' interpretations of what constituted the civilian security sector limited their ability to engage with individuals within that sector. Although Ukraine has initiated a number of reform programmes across the whole of its security sector since 2014, and in doing so has incorporated certain Western concepts pertaining to oversight and control into its legislation, those concepts are not necessarily understood in a consistent fashion by the politicians, bureaucrats and uniformed personnel responsible for implementation of the reform programmes. As a result, pre-existing institutional structures, cultures and practices continue to prevail. In the Ukrainian case that means that the civilian security sector still behaves a lot like its uniformed counterpart. The advisors with whom we spoke admitted their frustration with what they viewed as limited progress in reform. They were, however, comparing the system in 2019 with that of 2014, when they should have been comparing it to the system of 1991, when Ukraine achieved its independence from the Soviet Union. What the advisors failed to appreciate was that 'doing and undoing have fundamentally different time constants' (Sterman, 2002: p.6).

Conceptual clarity is crucial

It is a common refrain that the military speaks its own language. That may be true in the sense that the concepts they employ and the acronyms on which they rely are different to those that their civilian counterparts use, but it is also true that their language is not universal across all militaries. Therefore, in the course of an SSR programme the norms, values and practices which one may be trying to impart are often lost in translation. The following two examples illustrate the point:

Example 1.3: Common language

Over 15 years ago Laura Cleary, one of our editors, was invited to participate in a workshop being held for senior military and civilian personnel from the UK's MOD and Department for International Development (DFID). The purpose of the workshop was to familiarise the respective organisations on how they each viewed and sought to deliver security cooperation programmes, thereby allowing them to work in a more collaborative fashion in the future. While there was a good level of discussion, it quickly became apparent that the two delegations were speaking at cross purposes. The two words that were causing confusion were policy and strategy. When the military spoke of policy, they were referring to the highest-level document through which political direction was given. Strategy was deemed a subordinate document, the purpose of which was to detail how the policy objectives should be implemented. For the DFID representatives, however, strategy was the higher-level document in which goals were articulated and policy outlined how those goals would be achieved. If that level of confusion can exist between just two ministries in one government, imagine the discord that can exist across either the whole of government or between ministries of one nation seeking to engage with their opposite numbers in another country in order to support reform.

Example 1.4: Cultural references

In another instance a decade ago, a British Colonel was delivering a Defence Engagement programme in Serbia, and was lecturing on leadership. He came from a system that was based on the principle of delegated authority, and thus believed that leadership could be displayed at different times by different rank levels. He asked the 15 participants, all of whom were male and of the rank of Major or Lieutenant Colonel, whether they considered themselves leaders or commanders. Two students said that they were commanders, 12 said they were followers, and one said, to much laughter from his comrades, that he was merely a drone. The British Colonel and his students had very different cultural reference points which inhibited meaningful discussion.

In the chapters that follow, our authors' objective is to explain and simplify the terminology that they employ. In doing so, we want to increase the security literacy of our readers; however, we also want to identify those principles that help to improve the practice of security. Reflecting on several decades of experience in the field, we have tried to concentrate on those issues which practitioners are focused on or even challenged by. One of those issues is what is actually meant by civil, civilian and democratic control. We would like to address our interpretation of this concept here, because doing so will help to frame our approach to the subjects addressed within this volume.

The conceptual framework of SSR is derived from CMR, which itself is reflective of a liberal philosophical tradition. Historically, the focus of CMR has been on the prevention of tyranny through the subordination of the armed forces to civilian and democratic control. Only more recently has the focus shifted away from prevention of tyranny to improving the effectiveness of the armed forces and by extension the security services (Brooks & Stanley, 2007). Nevertheless, emphasis still tends to be placed on civil, civilian and democratic control of those services.

In teaching CMR across Asia, Africa, Eastern and Central Europe and Latin America, we have found that these words are not easily translatable, therefore the concepts are not accurately understood, which means that their application tends to be piecemeal. In a number of languages there is no distinction between civil and civilian. Furthermore, democracy, and by extension democratic control, are increasingly contested worldwide. Indeed, the word 'control' when preceded by 'civil', 'civilian' or 'democratic' is often viewed negatively by those in the security services because they question the wisdom of submitting to 'civilians' (politicians and civil servants) who are often perceived as being uneducated, unscrupulous, corrupt, unprofessional and generally ignorant of how and why defence and security services operate the way they do.

Based on our experiences, we have adjusted the way we approach the subject of CMR. In this book civil control, civilian *management* and democratic *management* are viewed as distinct but related concepts. We would argue that while a state may adhere to one component, the failure to adhere to the other two may cause disharmony within civil-security relations.

We define civil control, sometimes referred to as civil supremacy, as the allegiance that the security services owe to the civis, the state (Chuter, 2000: p.27). This concept implies an allegiance to a group larger than the government of the day; it is an allegiance to the citizen body in its entirety. The question of allegiance should be addressed in the constitution, in legislation establishing and regulating the security services, in doctrine and in training. Generally, we have found that if civil control is equated with allegiance to society then it is not contested.

With respect to civilian and democratic management our starting point is the question posed by Yagil Levy (2016): when we talk of civilian control, are we seeking to control the military or the process of militarisation? Control of the military, or of the wider security services, relates to operational aspects of their performance (e.g., doctrine, deployment and resources). Control of the process of militarisation refers to controlling the mechanisms that legitimise the use of force. In our view it is this latter aspect that civilians should seek to manage. However, we reject the use of the word 'control' in this context, preferring instead to speak of 'management'.

We recognise that across the security sector the term 'management' has been, at least, a contested concept and at worst, a pejorative expression. Some have long held the view that public sector organisations have been merely administered rather than managed (Hood, 1995). Nevertheless, we argue that management is no longer simply an organisational activity but a global issue. It is a complex process which is cultural, social, economic, political and informational and through it we can recognise that our accepted theories as well as practices are culturally shaped and relative.

Effective management requires expertise and specialised skills that can be learned. There is a strong argument to suggest a key skill that is required to practice management is to learn how to undertake *critical inquiry* (Linstead et al., 2004). To learn how to learn and be able to do this not just from books but from practice and to go on to inspire this in others, is what is being promoted throughout this text. The effective use of such skills and expertise in defence and security organisations is key to enabling the transfer of knowledge from other sectors and applying it to enhance services.

The work of a Frenchman, Henri Fayol (1916), widely regarded as the founder of the classical school of management, provides us with the essence of management. He argued that management consisted of five key functions:

1. **Planning:** setting objectives or goals that will focus the activities of everyone within the organisation.
2. **Organising:** establishing appropriate structures within an organisation, and marshalling necessary resources so that objectives can be achieved.
3. **Commanding or Leading:** guiding others towards their objectives.
4. **Coordinating:** uniting and combining the efforts of all parts of an organisation in the achievement of mutual goals. To achieve this requires linking various activities.
5. **Controlling:** establishing standards and applying them to the attainment of the goal.

To further support students in understanding the need for a *critical perspective* when learning about management, this text follows four key processes of inquiry, adapted from Alvesson and Deetz (2000: p.8):

1. Identify and challenge assumptions.
2. Develop an awareness of the context in which management ideas have evolved historically, culturally and socially.
3. Always seek alternative ways of seeing situations, interpreting what is going on, understanding why a *(security)* organisation is configured the way it is, and speculating about the way the organisation could be managed differently and in ways that disrupt routines and established order.
4. Finally, be appropriately sceptical about what you hear and read about management.

Based on this, we argue that by replacing the word control with management it is possible to have a more meaningful conversation about who actually governs security and how. In CMR theory, the subordination of the security services to civilian control is justified on the basis that civilians, be they elected or working for those who are, have a legal authority and are uniquely accountable under the law and to the electorate. That is the theory, however, while those individuals may have a legal authority, they are not in all cases accountable. As we have seen in a number of countries, the inability, or unwillingness, to hold officials to account has a deleterious effect on security and civil-security relations. By employing the term management, we hope to have a more meaningful conversation about decision-making and decision-implementation processes.

Civilian management, therefore, relates to more than just the appointment of a civilian minister of defence or interior; it refers to the totality of decisions taken by civilians across government which have a bearing on the policy, oversight and capability of the security services. As will be discussed in subsequent chapters, effective civilian management requires an investment in building the capacity and professionalism of the civilian contingent and may require a review of how information is handled and decisions are made. Ultimately, civilian management is about people and the decisions they make.

Democratic management, in turn, is about the process through which those decisions are made and implemented. We recognise that civilian governments are not necessarily democratic, and that there is no guarantee that civilian policymakers will make good decisions or implement policy in such a way as to result in the effectiveness of the security services. We also acknowledge that democratic management may be viewed as a contested process, not as a fixed attribute of existing democracies. This is because of the contested nature of democracy itself, as will be discussed in Chapter 3, and because some of the largest 'democratic deficits', or shortfalls in governance, are to be found in the security sector (Luckham, 1996). As a result, it is necessary to build institutional mechanisms through which political direction can be given and oversight conducted (Bruneau & Matei, 2008), as well as to develop a culture in which professionalism and accountability are the norms rather than the exceptions. Those institutional mechanisms are the subject of Chapters 4 through 9 and Chapter 13. Ultimately, we are concerned with how to improve the capacity of all those who work within the security sector and those who would seek to manage the process of securitisation.

Experiential learning is valuable

Many of the authors contributing to this volume started off as academics before they became practitioners, although a couple made the journey in reverse. What unites all of us is a belief that education is important, and that reflective learning is crucial for individual and institutional growth. In writing this book we are taking stock of the many and various reform programmes in which we have been engaged and reflecting on what has or has not worked, and why. It is our hope that by sharing these observations and asking and posing questions, we will encourage the reader to reflect on their own experiences and draw their own conclusions about how security in their country might be improved. As Edith Wilkinson and Laura Cleary argue in Chapter 2, a resilient organisation or a resilient society is one that learns from experience, both good and bad. Since we hope to contribute to the resilience and security of societies, we therefore encourage reflective learning.

Managing security: an overview

Managing Security: Concepts and Challenges is artificially divided into two sections: governance and management. As the reader will have already deduced, we believe that equal attention must be afforded to each discipline if the quality of security is to be improved. Although we have attempted to treat topics in a discrete fashion, certain concepts and themes are common throughout and our authors will be alluding to arguments made by co-contributors to demonstrate the interconnectedness that exists in practice.

In the following chapter Edith Wilkinson and Laura Cleary explore what it means to be secure and resilient. Given that the two terms are frequently used in tandem, their aim is to determine what being resilient actually means and what it entails. They consider issues of agency, risk management, adaptive capacity and capability; topics that are explored in subsequent chapters. Advocating a layered approach to living with risk and uncertainty, they propose a conceptual framework for the resilience of security institutions, and thus national resilience. The proposed model places a novel emphasis on institutional and political cultures; the aim being to embrace whole-of-society approaches (WSAs) to security.

The theme of holistic response is explored further by Laura Cleary and Gemma Collantes-Celador in Chapter 3 as they review the principles, practices and actors associated with security governance. They adhere to the argument posited by Jeff Haynes (2006: p.17) that governance has 'two key aspects: It 1) describes the process of governmental decision-making, and 2) the manner by which decisions are put into practice (or, in some cases not put into practice)'. They explore how recent trends in domestic politics (e.g., populism) and global security (e.g., transnational crime, terrorism, cyber and the environment), increase the requirement for, and the challenges of, ensuring good governance. They propose that while common principles of governance should exist, the socio-political context in which they are applied will determine the actors and practices, making the outcomes unique to the country studied.

David Turns and Anicée Van Engeland contend that the law forms an integral part of that socio-political context. In Chapter 4 they examine the significance and application of law in the governance, human rights, deployment and conduct of armed and security forces. The authors are concerned with how the law informs and constrains the activities of the security services as those services seek to provide the ultimate public good.

Building on the conceptual and legal frameworks of governance, David Chuter explores in Chapter 5 the practicalities of governing. He examines the role of policy as a means to provide direction to, and ensure coordination of, security institutions and agencies. He begins by attempting to clarify what policy is, and how it relates to strategy, concepts and doctrine, in a context where the rhetoric employed has become confused, with some terms (such as 'strategy' and 'policy') being used interchangeably. He concentrates on what needs to be done, examining how policy should be formulated, communicated and implemented.

In Chapter 6, Laura Cleary returns to a number of themes addressed in Chapter 3, looking at the interplay between trust, legitimacy, transparency and accountability and how all can be enhanced. Central to this review is the understanding that the way in which a society defines and values accountability informs the institutional arrangements that are devised to ensure it.

Chapter 7 acts as a segue between the sections on governance and management. The explicit purpose of the chapter is to explore the types of security structures that exist at all levels from policy-making to ground-level implementation, and how they are best organised and staffed. Their coordination and overall tasking, through mechanisms such as National Security Committees, is also addressed. Although certain pragmatic judgements are offered about effectiveness, David Chuter stresses the need for structures and processes to take account of local needs and cultures. He makes the argument that an appropriate degree of coordination is required for effective provision of security.

In Chapter 8, Ifti Zaidi and Bryan Watters promote the view that strategic management is one of the most vital requirements for success in contemporary organisations. He argues that the viability of public, private and non-governmental organisations is dependent upon the pursuit of strategies that enable them to generate value in the goods and services they provide to their customers and stakeholders. Zaidi explores the role of the strategic manager and the factors that they need to consider if they want their organisations to be successful.

Roger Darby, in Chapter 9, explores the concept of strategic management in greater detail through reference to the management of a critical resource: people. In applying the resource-based view (RBV) to the management of people, he highlights crucial issues such as the employment relationship and employee engagement, both of which are essential for the effective management of security. In relationship to these, he explores the evolving nature of the psychological contract or military covenant, which adapt in accordance with changes in the situational context. An important question addressed in this chapter for security institutions is whether there is a single, identifiable way of managing human resources which is universally appropriate or if there is a need for an alternative contingent approach more suited to local situational context.

Situational and organisational context are key themes explored in Lorraine Dodd, Jeremey Hilton and Roger Darby's treatment of cyber resilience and security in Chapter 10. The ability to understand and anticipate your organisation's part in an increasingly complex operating environment plays a key role in its continued survival. It is argued that the utility of the key asset of knowledge and the management of this vital resource, plays a major role in the success or failure of this necessary objective. The chapter argues that systemic risk and cyber threats challenge existing paradigms for managing data, information and knowledge and it suggests that a more radical approach to gaining and sharing knowledge is a requirement to remaining agile in the fast-moving, technologically advanced wider defence and security sector.

Management of finance and economics in security implies acquiring both tangible and intangible assets. For John McCormack and Tim Burnett in Chapter 11, acquisition is the process of investing in the technologies, goods and services, which are required for a nation to deliver its national security objectives. In their treatment of this subject, they acknowledge the bearing that political, institutional, economic, social, and technological factors have on the decision-making process when determining what to acquire and how.

Kogila Balakrishnan in Chapter 12 argues that one economic advantage provided to transitional states is the use of Offsets, which is often seen as the 'dark horse' of defence. Offsets are often used by governments (e.g., Malaysia and Indonesia) to justify defence value leading to economic development and prosperity. However, as the author argues, as much as offsets policy is crucial to secure national technological and industrial prowess, the implementation of offsets itself is highly questionable and open to corruption. She argues that offsets become potentially crucial, as state political systems increasingly shift from interdependence to independence, favouring nationalism and self-sufficiency (e.g., Turkey). In its present form offsets policy, and the associated governance structure, often fail to deliver maximum value to stakeholders unless there is a culture of change, transparency and innovation in management practice.

The theme of strategic leadership in Chapter 13, is identified by Bryan Watters and Ifti Zaidi as playing a fundamental role in determining the direction of travel and the nature of governance and management of security institutions. The authors clarify the increasing dichotomies in literature where there is a blurring of the line between leadership and strategic management; particularly when leadership is qualified with the adjective 'Strategic'; and argue that management and leadership constitute distinctly different systems of action. The relevance of Adaptive Leadership theory is discussed and it is argued this approach provides a useful framework for coping with an increasingly unpredictable world where deliberate, long-term, planning for organisational development and change needs to be supplemented with emergent approaches to deal with strategic shocks and to keep both the organisation and stakeholders on course towards achieving a shared vision.

Each of these chapters addresses the concept of change at some level, whether it is changes to conceptual frameworks or to practice. In Chapter 14, Roger Darby considers the theories of change most pertinent to the defence and security sectors, and in so doing highlights the tension between planned and emergent change, particularly within countries in development and transition. He argues that if change is indeed a constant then those working across the security sector need to become more adept at its management.

In the final chapter, Laura R. Cleary and Roger Darby draw a conclusion that is *Janus-like* in its structure. They reflect on those aspects of security sector reform that appear to have been constant and contemplate how the concept and practice of security may continue to evolve. They argue that the symbiotic relationship between governance and management will and must continue even in the face of major challenges involving: shifting global power, finite tangible and intangible resources, contradictory legal and ethical positions, countervailing ideology and unpredictable human behaviour, in a myriad of different *situational contexts*. This chapter concludes by providing an agenda for discussion about the future of security governance and management in the 21st century.

Note

1. John D Sterman provides an excellent overview of dynamic complexity. He suggests that dynamic complexity arises because systems are tightly coupled, constantly changing, governed by feedback, non-linear, history dependent, self-organising, adaptive, characterised by trade-offs, counter-intuitive and policy resistant.

References

Alvesson, Mats & Deetz, Stanley (2000) *Doing Critical Management Research*. London: Sage. DOI:10.4135/9781849208918

Brooks, Risa A. & Stanley, Elizabeth A., eds. (2007) *Creating Military Power: The Sources of Military Effectiveness*, Stanford, CA: Stanford University Press. DOI:10.11126/Stanford/9780804753999.001.0001

Bruneau, Thomas C. & Matei, Floriana Cristiana (2008) 'Towards a new conceptualisation of democratization and civil-military relations', *Democractization 15* (5). DOI:10.1080/13510340802362505

Chandler, David (2010) *International Statebuilding: The Rise of Post-Liberal Governance*, London: Routledge. DOI:10.4324/9780203847329

Chuter, David (2000) *Defence Transformation*, Pretoria: Institute for Security Studies.

Cleary, Laura R. (2016) 'Ukraine'. In: Andrew M. Dorman, Thomas O'Brien and Matthew Craig, eds., *Security Sector Horizon Scanning, 2016 – Eastern Europe and Central Asia*, London: Crown Copyright, pp. 201–259.

Fayol, Henri (1916) Administration Industrielle et Générale, trans. C. Storrs (1949) as *General and Industrial Management*, London: Pitman.

Folke Bernadotte Academy (2020) *Security Sector Reform for Practitioners*. Available at https://fba.se/en/about-fba/publications/security-sector-reform-for-practitioners/ [Accessed: 5 January 2021].

Haynes, Jeff (2006) 'The principles of good governance'. In: Laura R. Cleary & Teri McConville, eds., *Managing Defence in a Democracy*, Abingdon: Routledge.

Hood, C. (1995) 'Contemporary public management: A new global paradigm?' *Public Policy and Administration*, *10* (2), pp.104–117. DOI:10.1177/095207679501000208

Levy, Yagil (2016) 'What is controlled by civilian control of the military?', *Armed Forces and Society*, *42* (1), pp. 75–98. DOI:10/1177/0095327X14567918

Lewis, Michael (2018) *The Fifth Risk*, London: Allen Lane.

Linstead, S., Fulop, L., Lilley, S. & Banerjee, B. (2004) *Management and Organization: A Critical Text*, Basingstoke: Palgrave Macmillan, pp. 497–500.

Liu, Warren K (2008) *KFC in China: Secret Recipe for Success*, Singapore: John Wiley and Sons.

Luckham, Robin (1996) 'Faustian bargains: Democratic control over military and security establishments'. In: R. Luckham & G. White, eds., *Democratization in the South: The Jagged Wave*, Manchester: Manchester University Press.

OECD-DAC (2005) *DAC Guidelines: Security System Reform and Governance*, Paris: OECD Publications. DOI:10.1787/19900988

Rice, Condoleezza & Zeigart, Amy (2018) *Political Risk: Facing the Threat of Global Insecurity in the Twenty-First Century*, London: Weidenfeld & Nicolson.

Short, Clare (2002) 'Preface'. In: *Security Sector Reform Strategy*, London: Crown Copyright.

Sterman, John D (2002) 'Systems dynamics: Systems thinking and modelling for a complex world', *Massachusetts Institute of Technology Engineering Systems Division Working Paper Series ESD-WP-2003–01.13*. Available from https://dspace.mit.edu/handle/1721.1/102741 [accessed 19 August 2021]

2 If you can't be secure, be resilient

Edith Wilkinson and Laura R. Cleary

Introduction

We begin our discussion of security and resilience by offering a 'health warning': over the following pages the reader will encounter more questions than answers. Our aim within this chapter is not to tell the reader what to think, but to help identify issues for consideration when developing security capabilities. We acknowledge that the concepts of security and resilience are both contested (Buzan, 1991; Walklate et al., 2014). We also accept that neither security nor resilience are fixed attributes of a society. They are 'multilayered, multifaceted' (Walklate et al., 2014: p.419), in variable evidence over time, and rarely the sole responsibility of any one entity.

Over the last 30 years, the concepts and practice of security and resilience have become intertwined, as is evident by the policy pronouncements of both states and intergovernmental institutions alike (see for example the Unites States of America, 2015; HM Government, 2015; European Union, 2016; Association of Southeast Asian Nations, 2018). It has been suggested that the change in government focus from state to non-state-based threats (Vasilache, 2019), the emergence of an 'all-hazards' approach to risk management (Walklate et al., 2014), the promotion of the liberal peace-building agenda (De Coning, 2018), and subsequent concerns over its efficacy have resulted in a reconsideration of whether and how security can be provided.

This issue became evident, indeed inescapable, during the course of 2020. As we write this chapter, a global pandemic continues to exact its toll on lives, public health services, economies and political systems. COVID-19 dramatically exposed the fault lines of our societies. The acknowledgement of the fragility of our systems has amplified interest in the concept of resilience and in its relationship with the State and with security.

In Chapter 1, Cleary and Darby presented five questions with which this book is concerned. In conceptualising security through its congruence to resilience, this chapter offers insights to some of those questions, while asking additional ones. The exploration of the security and resilience nexus revolves around two questions which are explored in this chapter:

- If security is elusive can societies become resilient instead?
- What does that mean and what would that actually entail?

In seeking to address these questions we will be highlighting certain themes that are integral to the book as a whole: agency, adaptive capacity, capability, risk and change

DOI: 10.4324/9781003137061-2

management. It is through the treatment of these subjects that we engage with the issue of who is ultimately responsible for individual and collective well-being.

It is argued within this chapter that resilience is not solely about how one prepares and responds to a crisis. It is about whether we choose to learn from crises, what we choose to learn, and how we apply that knowledge to the prevention or mitigation of future crises. Ultimately, resilience is about the capacity to learn and adapt; only then can individuals, institutions and states become more resilient and secure.

Defining security and resilience

While the questions posed above might appear to be simple ones, the answers are frequently complex, and liable to change over time. When lecturing on security we often begin our sessions by asking our students to define the concept.

What does it mean to be secure? No matter where in the world the class is being held the responses are fairly consistent. Security is described as a 'feeling of safety', as 'freedom from fear, want or threat', as the 'institutions and/or process through which that perception of safety and condition of freedom are achieved'. As our discussions continue our participants often acknowledge their concern that their institutions and processes are no longer capable of providing security to the standard demanded by the public. There are a variety of reasons for why this might be the case, ranging from a consistent lack of policy direction and investment to the development of sclerotic bureaucratic structures, but certainly one of the reasons has to be a heightened sense of subjectivity as a result of the globalisation of information and the prevalence of 'competing truths'. Back in 1991, Buzan memorably described security as 'an essentially contested concept' (Buzan, 1991). He argued that, although security can be objectively defined as freedom from fear, from want, and from threat, freedom itself is relative, thus a sense of security is ultimately subjective in nature. Therefore, responses to the question of 'what is security' are as varied as the states and institutions tasked with providing it.

Since the end of the Cold War in 1989 we have witnessed a rapid evolution in the discourse and practice of security. During the Cold War, the state was viewed as the referent object of security (Buzan, 1991). The focus of government policy, evidenced in institutional arrangements and budget allocations, was on the defence of territory, be that from invasion or nuclear annihilation. From the perspective of the United States and the Soviet Union, internal unrest in proxy states was either to be encouraged or suppressed depending on whose ally they were. That approach began to change in the last decade of the 20th century. Triumphalist claims regarding the 'end of history' and the supremacy of democracy over communism (Fukuyama, 1992) appeared, warranted given the headlong rush to overthrow authoritarian regimes across Latin America, Eastern Europe and Africa throughout the 1980s and 1990s. The 'new world order' proclaimed by US President George H. W. Bush in 1990 would be one in which democratic and Pacific states would take collective action within regional and international organisations to resolve global concerns (Bush, 1990). In the absence of existential threats to national security, governments sought 'peace dividends' by downsizing or right-sizing their armed forces, and either redirecting the money previously spent on defence to other public sector organisations or reducing the rate of tax. These structural adjustments both gave rise to, and were subsequently underpinned by, the belief that a singular focus on the state as the referent object of security was no longer appropriate (Owen, 2004). Academic discourse and international policy increasingly emphasised the importance of the individual as both an agent and object of security.

The term 'human security' was coined by the United Nations Development Programme (UNDP) in 1994 and was quickly embraced within the policies of nations and the strategies and programmes of international organisations. As the term implies, a human-centred, rather than a state-centred, approach to security is advocated, with emphasis being placed on those elements which allow individuals to survive and thrive (UNDP, 1994). Whether the concept is understood in narrow terms as 'freedom from fear' (e.g., direct violence, displacement) or in a broader sense as 'freedom from want' (e.g., food, poverty and access to education), it is the individual desiring that freedom (Owen, 2004; Sharpe et al., 2020). The individual, however, cannot achieve that freedom on their own or in isolation; a combination of top-down and bottom-up approaches that place an emphasis on both protection and empowerment is required (Sharpe et al., 2020: p.468). Therefore, the notion of state security has not been abandoned; indeed, in some parts of the world it remains the dominant concern, but in the West an attempt has been made to place the concept in broader context. Preservation of state security became the means to the end of securing individuals and communities (Pettman, 2005). Debate continues as to whether human security is truly the dominant paradigm as states continue to serve as the primary actor in the international environment. However, the rhetorical opening has at least provided an opportunity for neglected concerns and marginalised voices to surface (Cleary, 2016). We are individually and collectively confronted by a host of risks and threats, some the result of the change in the security discourse, others the inevitable consequence of globalisation.

It is worth exploring the distinction drawn between the concepts of 'risk' and 'threat'; while the concepts are complementary, they are not synonymous. Risk is typically defined in terms of probability and consequence and need not be associated with a named agent, whereas threat is defined as existing when an actor or group of actors has the capability and intention to inflict a negative consequence on another actor or group (Rousseau, 2007; Davis, 2000). Consequently, the way in which we seek to manage risks may be very different to the way in which we respond to threats. Yee-Kuang identified the 2002 US National Security Strategy (NSS) as a 'watershed' document in terms of the conceptualisation of security as risk management; in his estimation, that NSS 'crystallised the proactive calculus of risk. Declaring the obsolescence of a "reactive posture" of containment and deterrence, it plumped instead for anticipatory actions even if uncertainty [remained] as to the time and place of the enemy's attack' (Yee-Kuang, 2006: p.25). From that point onwards until 2015 policy documents produced by the US, the United Kingdom, and other NATO states and Partnership for Peace (PFP) members were notable for the absence of named enemies and the similarities of the risks identified. As will be detailed below, the adoption and advocacy of a risk management approach to security led a number of countries to frame reform of their own security institutions and those of other countries in terms of resilience (see Example 2.1).

Example 2.1: Reframing Security: the case of Armenia

Since the Republic of Armenia achieved independence from the Soviet Union in 1991 it has published two National Security Strategies (NSS); one in 2007, the second in 2020.

In its assessment of its security context, Armenia's 2020 NSS highlights a number of risks at the geo-strategic, regional, national, and societal levels that present challenges to the sovereignty and/or territorial integrity of the state, but it also identifies countries as posing specific existential threats to the state.

The long-standing dispute with Azerbaijan over the territory of Artsakh, or Nagorno-Karabakh, (erupting violently in 2016 and again in 2020) has, perhaps unsurprisingly, led the Armenian government to place an emphasis on modernising its armed forces, developing its military-industrial complex, and ensuring the political oversight of both. The 2020 NSS, however, additionally 'aims to enhance resilience through a nationwide approach to planning and maintaining national security' (Republic of Armenia, 2020: p.2). The broadening of the idea of security is noteworthy – the NSS now suggests that the resilience of the defence and security sector, as well as that of the economic, food and health sectors, needs to be enhanced if Armenia's long-term security is to be guaranteed.

What does it mean to be resilient? Identifying a definition which fits the purpose of our discussion is challenging; it needs to reflect the complexity of our societies, the dense interconnections that characterise them, the ever-evolving nature of threats faced and, in turn, the endeavours for coherent and collective response to disturbances. David Omand, a retired British senior civil servant who served as the Security and Intelligence Co-ordinator for the Cabinet Office proposes that,

> national resilience, [is] in other words our ability to detect, prevent and, if necessary, to handle disruptive challenges. The depth and breadth of our resilience governs our ability as a nation to face shocks and disruption and to be able to maintain or to restore normal life as quickly as possible.
>
> (Omand, 2004)

However, like security, resilience is a contested concept, with individuals, communities, businesses, governments and regional and international organisations attributing different meanings to it. The range of definitions for resilience reflects the variety of objects modern societies have wanted to protect (Edwards, 2009). At various points in time and in different contexts, resilience has been understood as implying stability, durability and adaptability in the face of shock and disruption (Giroux & Prior, 2012).

Like security, resilience, is viewed both as an outcome, something that we wish to create, and as a process, something that we carry out. An evolution in the characterisation of the resilience concept from an outcome-oriented to a more process-oriented understanding is noticeable (Manyena, 2006). Yet, 'resilience-as-outcome', inherent within objects, individuals or societies, is more often one for which capacity needs to be actively developed, which in turn leads us to an understanding of 'resilience-as- process'.

Accordingly, the plethora of interpretations of what the concept entails makes it difficult to operationalise strategies for resilience. Many societies, however, appear to agree that resilience is important as it governs a nation's ability to face shocks and disruption and to maintain or to restore normal life as quickly as possible (Omand, 2010). The policy approaches, are, at times, imperfectly defined, and yet they have in common a recognition of the diverse nature of risk against which Resilient Nations must organise and with which they must cope. For many Western governments (such as the UK) resilience is understood as an approach to integrate and coordinate a range of aspects of emergency management, including processes of assessment, prevention, preparation, response and recovery so as to provide guidance to existing entities such as buildings, systems and networks (UK Cabinet Office, 2013). Before we can develop the capacity for resilience, however, we need to have a reasonable understanding of what we need to be resilient in the face of, which is where the assessment of risk comes to the fore.

Risk approach to national security

Risk-based strategies are at the heart of implementation of resilience. Conceptual frameworks offered in the literature have steered organisations and governments alike towards the deployment of technocratic approaches to resilience. These rely on a comprehensive assessment process to analyse the likelihood and consequences of potentially disruptive events. Risk management promises manageability and control and offers a ubiquitous decision-making framework for the most intricate situations (Power, 2004).

Among the array of material, textbooks and manuals, an international standard (ISO 31000, 2018) stands out as a repository for best practice in risk management. It defines it as a set of 'coordinated activities to direct and control an organization with regard to risk'. The standard describes a systematic process, which, through the execution of a set of iterative activities allows the effective managing of risks at various levels within organisations. Risk management is conceived as a continuous cycle carried out to improve organisational processes, policies, practices and, in turn, learning.

To begin with, risk management requires a framework to clarify how its activities and functions are embedded within the governing structures of the organisation (i.e., the commitment made by top management, the support from stakeholders, the oversight mechanisms, the resources available, and so on). Integration of risk management necessitates statements on mandate, accountability, and roles and responsibility of those involved in the process. Establishing this framework seeks to align strategy and culture of the organisation with its view on risk.

It follows, that the risk management process *per se* is implemented through phases of a risk management cycle.[1]

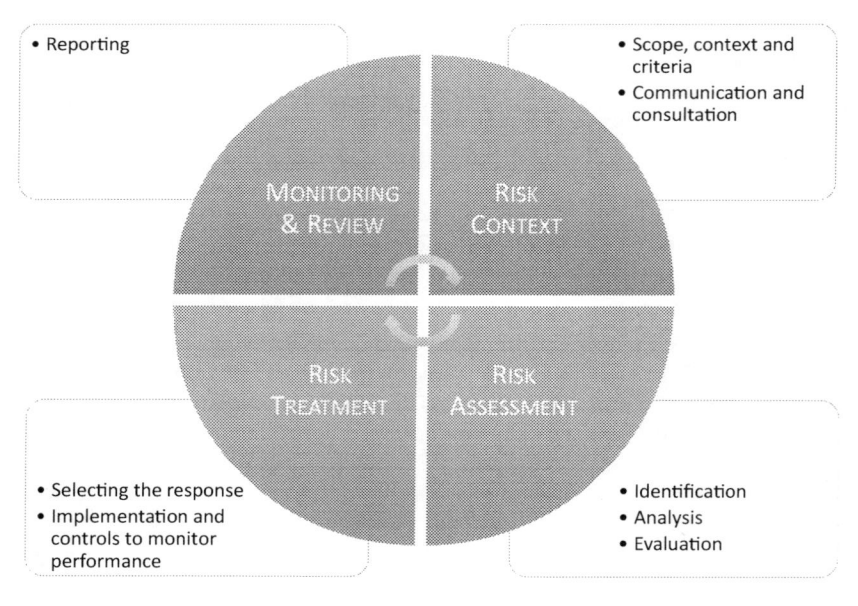

• Reporting

• Scope, context and criteria
• Communication and consultation

MONITORING & REVIEW

RISK CONTEXT

RISK TREATMENT

RISK ASSESSMENT

• Selecting the response
• Implementation and controls to monitor performance

• Identification
• Analysis
• Evaluation

Figure 2.1 The Risk Management Cycle
Source: Authors

The Risk Management Cycle depicted above was adapted from ISO 31000 (2018) and BS 31100 (2008); it highlights the generic phases in the risk management process which are as follows.

Setting the risk context

This phase concentrates on establishing the scope, context and criteria of the risk management focus (including whether to envisage risks at the strategic, operational, programme or project levels) and determining internal and external factors which influence the management of risks. Determining the organisation's strategic objectives is key at this stage. In doing so, the organisation will also require the determination of programmes which need to be protected as well as the tasks that need to be performed successfully to achieve the strategic objectives.

Relevant stakeholders, those essential to the understanding of the risk, able to promote awareness of it, and to support decision-making need to be found and placed at the heart of communication and consultation approaches. In addition, as the context is clarified, some ground rules and activities may be established. These include for instance: selecting appropriate tools and techniques, determining a schedule for the process and considering questions of risk appetite.

Assessing risks

This phase is concerned with the identification of risks, their analysis and their evaluation. These three activities are not always combined under the banner of 'risk assessment'; yet they feature in the standards considered in this iterative order. Identifying risks consists in uncovering, characterising, and listing elements of risk which can affect the organisation's ability to achieve its objectives. The careful selection of sources of up-to-date information and approaches to identify risks is essential and it is the pre-cursor to the detailed and accurate description of the found risks. Approaches to the identification of risks are numerous: ranging from conventional management tools such as Horizon Scanning, SWOT (strengths, weaknesses, opportunities and threats), PESTLE (political, economic, sociological, technological, legal and environment) analyses to more risk-oriented instruments such as the Delphi technique or structured 'What if?' workshops.

Subsequently, risk analysis consists of the systematic use of information (be it historical data, theoretical models, expert opinions, or stakeholders' insights) to determine the probability and impact of the risk. The analysis process considers the nature of the risk from multiple aspects: uncertainties, risk sources, events, scenarios, controls and their effectiveness. The outcome of the analysis will usually be quantitative whereby consequences and their likelihood are assigned values (although qualitative approaches may also be employed).

The risk evaluation that follows aims to combine, aggregate analysed risks, and compare levels of risk with the risk appetite. This prioritisation process seeks to pave the way for subsequent decisions and treatment options. At this stage, visualisation tools such as risk matrices are used to communicate the outcome of the risk assessment to internal as well as external stakeholders.

Treating risks

Treatment comprises selecting from a set of options available to address risks and then implementing the measure selected. There are numerous treatments of risk – Figure 2.2 shows some archetypal options.

Avoid (or terminate)

> Decision not to become involved in or to withdraw from the activity that gives rise to the risk.

Accept (or tolerate)

> Decision to accept a risk (without risk treatment or during the course of an iterative or lengthy treatment).

Reduce and/or mitigate

> Decision to implement measures to modify risks (taken in isolation or in combination to lower probability and impact of risks).

Share the risk

> Decision to transfer to another party through sub-contracts, partnerships or insurance.

Take risk (or seize opportunities)

> Decision to exploit opportunities and to increase the likelihood of positive outcomes.

Figure 2.2 Options for the Treatment of Risk
Source: Authors.

Acceptance of risk can give rise to much discussion within an organisation or a society. This option could be chosen 'because no further worthwhile actions can be devised and the risk is within the risk appetite, or it might be because the only remaining responses are unacceptable for some reason' (BS 31100, 2008: p.30). It can also be associated with the retention of risk which implies retaining the residual risk (including the gains or losses it brings about) without planning for further action or response to it. Reduction or mitigation involve measures to modify risks through actions to control the source, alter the likelihood or dampen consequences. Whilst the option to share the risk involves a contractual redistribution of the risk with other parties (covering burden of loss or benefit of gain). Lastly, there is the option to take risks in order to realise a positive outcome. This positive outlook on risk is founded on the appreciation of opportunities, and produces responses intended to result in desirable consequences.

Once the treatment options have been selected, their implementation requires planning (implementing risk management decisions is referred to as risk control). The arrangements for implementing mitigation measures normally describe the sequence of actions, the resources required, the list of those who are responsible and accountable, and the performance measures expected in the control of the risk. The implementation plan refers to the review processes to track individual risks and the effectiveness of the measures in place.

Monitoring and review

In this phase, the necessary information is gathered, compiled and communicated to the relevant stakeholders. Risk reports capture and document risk information. In turn, reports allow the characterisation of the actual residual risk – which should then be assessed in the subsequent iteration of the cycle. The importance of risk reports should not be underestimated as they provide valuable insights on underlying causes, nature and manifestations of risk as well as the effectiveness of treatments. Consistent reporting can than feed into the review of risks in search of continual improvement of processes.

National risk assessments have become ubiquitous strategies to support a country's overall resilience. Risk analyses have become a universal guide to decision-making, covering phases of anticipation of disruptions through to preparedness, emergency planning and response as well as recovery. Policy makers within governments in many nations use the risk framework to inform them:

> The outcomes have been that national risk assessments have helped to give perspective to the risks facing nations, and to elevate national resilience as a policy priority. As objective, dispassionate, inventories of what would have to be reckoned with in a disaster they have helped to make the case for investment in resilience in an increasingly competitive national security field, and informed the optimal allocation of scarce resources.
>
> (OECD Publishing, 2017: p.57)

However, the risk approach has detractors. Adams (2002) argues that risk management is a 'balancing act', or 'risk thermostat', in which 'perceptions of risk are weighed against the propensity to take risk' (Adams, 2002: p. 15). Yet, institutionalisation of risk management emphasises practices of risk reduction (Adams, 2002), and if precaution is applied systematically it tends to deny possibilities of seizing worthwhile opportunities, process or activity (Sunstein, 2003). In addition, one should recognise that cost-benefit calculations, which underpin risk analyses, are constrained by the limits of quantification. This point was made by Slovic, Fischhoff and Lichtenstein in 1979. They noted that psychology matters greatly to the comprehension of risk and people's reactions to it. If managers and decision-makers are to manage risk effectively, they need to understand what shapes the perception of risk. Whilst risk assessments bring systematic reasoning and evidence, 'hard facts go only so far and then human judgement is needed to interpret the findings and determine their relevance for the future' (Slovic, et al., 1979: p.14).

Exercise 2.1

When performing a PESTLE analysis in relation to the impact of COVID-19 on security, one could focus an assessment of risks by concentrating on the TECHNOLOGICAL dimension.

By and large, the global pandemic has altered the risk context; examples include:

- Negative effect on raw material supply and the electronics value chain, potentially leading to disruptions in the manufacturing of weapon systems and platforms;
- Increased use of cloud-based services and teleconferencing software; this, in turn, raises concerns over the routine access to IT capability, the security of end-to-end communications and the increase in cybersecurity risks;
- Changes to the ways in which employers (including governments) manage the workload, well-being of and communication with their staff. Some people have been disturbed by disinformation circulating on sharing platforms, whilst others have strongly perceived the impingement of new working conditions on their lives.

Although the identification of risks relevant to security sectors is incomplete, it presents a start-point to the risk assessment process. Can you add details to the analysis of risks relevant to the security sector of your country? Can you the perform the next steps in the risk cycle?

Adaptation for security

Although national risk assessments have facilitated the resilience of nations, the culture of control these approaches denote does not fully embrace the evolutionary understanding of resilience[2] highlighted in Holling's notions of 'adaptive cycles' and 'panarchy':

> A management approach based on resilience ... would emphasize the need to keep options open, the need to view events in a regional rather than a local context, and the need to emphasize heterogeneity. Flowing from this would be not the presumption of sufficient knowledge, but the recognition of our ignorance; not the assumption that future events are expected, but that they will be unexpected
> (Holling, 1973: p.21).

Holling's (1973) seminal work inspired much of the social ecological literature upon which the concept of resilience is based (Brand & Jax, 2007). He introduced the notion that the resilience of a system was, in fact, its dynamic capacity to remain in its current 'basin of attraction' – also referred to as its 'stability domain'. Since then, ecologists have directed discussion and thinking in terms of Complex Adaptive Systems. In this framework, another set of assumptions was brought into consideration: that multiple stability domains exist, and that disruption or stress will move systems from one basin to another (such movement can also be referred to as 'regime shift'). Acknowledgment of regime shifts subsequently leads to an increased interest in the associated 'thresholds' or tipping points. When critical levels of 'driver' variables are reached, the 'normal' functioning of the system is no longer possible or sustainable. Beyond the tipping point, abrupt changes are triggered, and systems head towards alternative system states (Chapin et al., 2009). This has significant importance as some of these thresholds can be irreversible, but are not necessarily detectable.

These issues brought about another trend in resilience thinking that diverged from the idea of stability and single equilibrium: the management of adaptive capacities. At the heart of which is the question: 'how much adaptation needs to (and can realistically) be administered to prevent a system or its parts switching into an alternative state or dynamic stability?' (Davoudi et al., 2012: p.326). In the Social Sciences, debates emerged as to what was a return to normality and whether it was desirable. In its colloquial use, the term resilience implies stability, but recently the increasing prevalence of the social-ecological school of thought has resulted in an understanding of resilience centred on periodic cycles of change.

For Holling, 'the adaptive cycle therefore embraces two opposites: growth and stability on the one hand, change and variety on the other' (Holling, 2001: p.395). Adaptive cycles depict (metaphorically) the perpetual fluctuations of systems between periods of exploitation, crisis, learning and renewal (Carpenter et al., 2001). The dynamics of this cycle combine across temporal and spatial scales in the idea described as 'panarchy' (Gunderson & Holling, 2002). Gunderson and Holling invented this word as a reaction to the rigid and top-down connotation of hierarchies. In doing so, they acknowledge and refer to the evolutionary hierarchies of nested adaptive cycles operating at different temporal and spatial scales. Dynamic in nature, panarchies imply that a critical change in one cycle at one level can cascade up or down to other levels of the hierarchy through interaction and feedbacks.

The implications for the concept of resilience of 'adaptive cycles' and 'panarchy' are considerable. Through them, scholars have inferred a system's approach to resilience – which, in turn led them to differentiate between 'specified' and 'general' resilience (Folke et al., 2010). Specified approaches to resilience tend to focus on specific adversities or risks and prescribe protection or mitigation against one or a range of specific scenarios. In so doing, they seek to answer the question in terms of the 'resilience of what to what' (Carpenter et al., 2001). Illustrations of such specified approaches permeate various disciplines interested in resilience. For instance, in psychology this involves individuals' response to stress, trauma or mental illness, and so on; in disaster studies it consists of building defences in communities prone to local risks (be they flooding, drought or other natural hazards); in economics and management studies it relates to a business-centric outlook contained within 'Business Continuity Management' (Giroux & Prior, 2012). Thus, for many of these traditions, resilience has come to mean a practice of planning for adversity with risk management at its heart. Often, the stated aim for research is to investigate how to: anticipate and mitigate or reduce risk; improve responses if the risk materialises; and speed up recovery so as to allow systems to stay functioning (Davoudi et al., 2012).

Example 2.2: COVID-19 as an illustration of 'panarchy'

Post-traumatic stress disorder (PTSD) is a recognised psychiatric disorder that may occur in people who have experienced or witnessed a traumatic event.

The COVID-19 pandemic has been classified as a 'traumatic event of exceptional magnitude that transcends the range of normal human experience with exposure to risk of death' (Dutheil et al., 2020: p.1). Recent studies of healthcare workers (HCW) on the frontlines of COVID-19 treatment have noted increasing susceptibility to acute stress and PTSD. They have been confronted by unprecedented demands, professionally and personally, as they endeavour to manage a disease with unclear aetiology and pathology, no cure, until recently no vaccine, and a high mortality rate (Ibid.). For many healthcare providers there is an urgent requirement to review the support and care given to those who are in the caring profession.

Amongst other things, COVID-19 has highlighted the dependency relationship between the resilience of individuals and the resilience of systems.

The security-resilience nexus: living with uncertainty

So, what does this all mean for our understanding and pursuit of security? Managers of risk, be it to achieve security or resilience, face a fundamental problem of uncertainty – in the face of which their knowledge is incomplete, inadequate, or lacking in some way. Yet, risk management thrives on data and systematic gathering and analysis of information. Boin and Lodge (2016) suggest that it is time for public institutions, including security institutions, to adopt designs that will help them deal more effectively with today's complex threats and ensuing crises. The model depicted in Figure 2.3 presents a layered approach to Security Sector Resilience. Derived from work dealing with complex adaptive systems, our model categorises three layers, or domains of uncertainty, and the corresponding coping strategies. We acknowledge that the current trends in security and resilience, based overwhelmingly on the management of risk, offer a specified approach to resilience. In the interest of embracing change, we suggest this alternative perspective.

The first tier of such a Resilience approach applies to the 'foreseeable domain' where risks are to some extent known and controllable (Kaplan & Mikes, 2012). It is characterised by the development of strategies that answer the question 'resilience of what to what'. Some control is possible because at this domain level there is a degree of predictability.

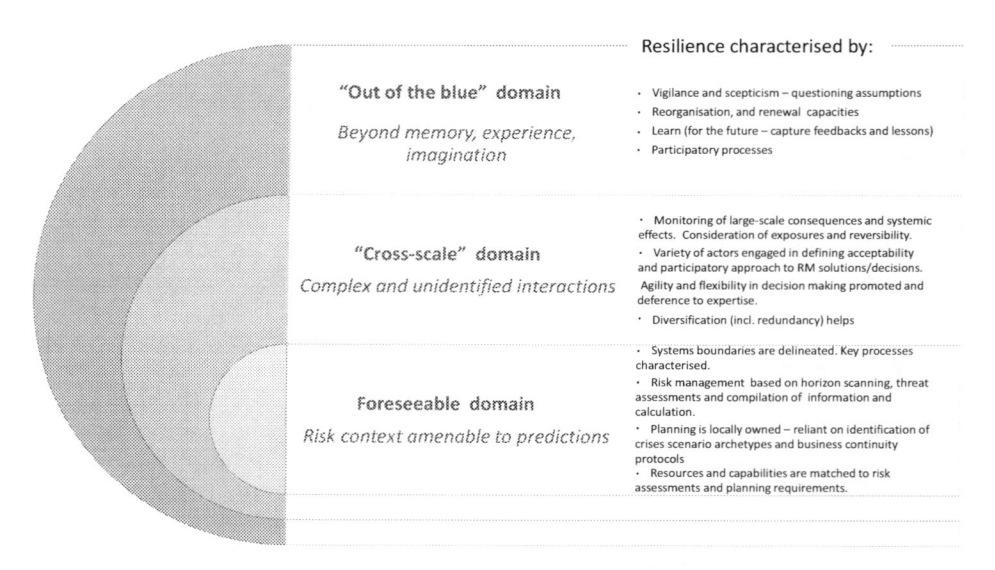

Figure 2.3 Layered Approach to Resilience of the Security Sector
Source: E. Wilkinson.

Not all issues will be foreseeable, there will be 'local surprises'. Broader observation and gathering of historical information can help to fill the knowledge gap (Gunderson, 2003). Risk management processes are applicable, but the ignorance of underlying causes or longer-term developments may not allow this type of event to disappear altogether. Adaptations (although limited in their scope) will be possible, but overall, the efforts at this level are geared to maintaining the status quo (Davidson-Hunt & Berkes, 2003). The key lines of security sector resilience activities will be around prevention (through horizon scanning, risk assessment and planning), the development of capabilities, rules-based compliance, and monitoring the effectiveness of measures. Goble et al. (2017) suggest that management strategies to deal with the knowledge gap of this tier consist in the reframing or redefining of the risks in recognition, for instance,

> that the original presentation of the hazard was arbitrarily narrow and it is better viewed as embedded in a more inclusive set of problems that should be dealt with all together or the hazard might have a different look when the passage of time is taken into account. Reframing may bring in information from other contexts or alter the questions that are posed.
>
> (Goble et al., 2017: p.50)

The second tier of a layered Resilience approach applies to the domain of 'complex and unidentified interaction'. In this domain, cross-scale interactions and complexity dominates. Risk management approaches have limited effect as the nature of the risks cannot be well anticipated and, combined with system's complexity, there is an imperfect understanding of the effectiveness of responses. Although some factual information may exist about the risk problems, interpretations vary on predictions, tolerability and management priorities. Thus, the participation and engagement of appropriate stakeholders is necessary for a sound risk governance framework (Renn, 2017). In addition, proposed interventions need to adopt an adaptive stance by attempting to learn from experience (i.e., interventions are designed to produce knowledge and learning). The heart of the development of a portfolio of adaptive responses is obtaining information on how situations might evolve over time and on what works (Goble et al., 2017). In this domain, the impact of an event is likely to spread between different parts of the system with non-envisioned interactions emerging. Lack of understanding or visibility of interconnections leading to contagion and loss of control are likely to be the dominant challenges in the coordination of any response. Typically, a range of stakeholders will need to contribute to resolving issues. (Davidson-Hunt & Berkes, 2003). Thus, resilience will be provided by improved decision-making based on enhanced institutional flexibility and agility. At times, authority and decisions will need to shift towards those with expertise to allow errors to be spotted and dealt with prior to harmful or needless escalation. Diversity and redundancy are part of the resilience portfolio at this level.

The third of these resilience layers applies to the 'out-of-the-blue' domain, where predictions are precluded due to the sheer fact that no exposure exists to the surprises in this domain. The magnitude of disruption will call for different questions to arise: 'Resilience for whom?' and even 'Why Resilience?' At this level, however, resilience will be characterised by capacity to reorganise and renew. In this context, persistence (in terms of efficiency of return to a previously known status or equilibrium) may not be as important as dynamics (referring to the capacity to change) (Gunderson, 2003).

The ability to learn for the future is fundamental to resilience at this level. In short, lesson capture, experimentation and similar activities will be the predominant tools to allow learning beyond present scale (i.e., beyond the here and now). This domain requires a form of 'vigilance' - not simply relating to emerging risks but also in relation to viable strategies. Goble et al. (2017) explain that vigilance involving a mix of scepticism and questioning of existing assumptions can be seen as a pre-requisite to the search for novel strategies. For them, social 'trust and credibility' is equally important as it is threatened by high uncertainty. Institutions can manage this erosion through enhanced participation of major stakeholders and their engagement in decision-making or negotiation processes.

Exercise 2.2

Using the layered approach to resilience model, how would you categorise the risks that your country or your security sector institutions face? Do they reside in one domain or several? Are current approaches likely to enhance resilience? If not, what needs to change?

Conclusion

In this chapter we have argued that, beyond our ability to manage risks, the security of our systems is contingent upon the flexibility of our management structures, our willingness to share information vertically *and* horizontally, a recognition of the 'high permeability of institutional boundaries to external environments', as well as an acknowledgement that across state and society there are 'multiple centres of learning' that require active engagement with stakeholders (Goble et al., 2017: p.52). Over the last two decades alone there have been numerous events that have highlighted the interconnectedness of our societies. We only need to think of the impacts of any one of the following: conflicts such as those in Iraq (2003–2011), Syria (2011 to present), or Ukraine (2014 to present) to name only a few; the 2008 global financial crisis; or epidemics such as Ebola (2013–2016) to become conscious of the way in which events, responses and outcomes have the ability to affect us all. The COVID-19 pandemic is simply the latest and loudest alarm bell to ring.

Over the same time frame, recognising the myriad ways in which globalisation has made the security of any one nation dependent upon the decisions taken by its own government, as well as those taken by other states, non-state actors, international organisations and multinational corporations, there has been a concerted effort to promote whole-of-government and whole-of-society approaches to security. Increasingly, there have been calls for whole-of-world approaches (WWA) to contend with the current and future pandemics, and global warming. The success of any of those approaches requires dialogue and collaboration in order to determine and share the risk and to balance it over time. That will require changes in institutional and political culture. Far too many ministries and security services remain 'stovepiped', hoarding information and knowledge. They simply do not know how to share it. The atomisation of responses to security challenges results in the diminishment of trust in and credibility of government. In the following chapters, our co-authors will return to the themes of governance, policy formation, security architecture, strategic, knowledge, and change management (see Chapters 3, 5, 7, 8, 10 and 14). We need to adapt to survive. From the perspective of one West African civil servant in 2018, that means that resilience should be the ultimate goal of security sector reform.

Note

1. Although there are differing standards for managing risks, they share common principles. This chapter uses established risk management standards (ISO 31000:2018, ISO/IEC Guide 73:2002 and BS 31100:2008) which are relevant to the context of governance and management of risks across an organisation (ISO Guide, 2002).
2. In their collection of papers Davoudi et al. explain that 'evolutionary resilience challenges the whole idea of equilibrium and advocates that the very nature of systems may change over time with or without an external disturbance […]. In this perspective, resilience is not conceived of as a return to normality, but rather as the ability of complex socio-ecological systems to change, adapt, and, crucially, transform in response to stresses and strains' (2012, p.302).

Questions to consider

1. Where does the responsibility for risk assessment reside within your government system?
2. How is that risk assessment employed in the process of policy formation *and* policy implementation?
3. Does your nation pursue a specified or general approach to resilience?

Suggested further reading

Gunderson, L.H. & Holling, C.S., eds. (2002) *Panarchy: Understanding Transformations in Systems of Humans and Nature*, Washington DC: Island Press.
Omand, D. (2010) *Securing the State*, London: Hurst & Co.

References

Adams, J. (2002) *Risk*, Abingdon: Routledge.
Association of Southeast Asian Nations (2018) 'Joint Declaration of the ASEAN Defence Ministers on Strengthening Cooperation, Building Resilience' 12th ASEAN Defence Ministers' Meeting, 19 October 2018. Available at https://asean.org/joint-declaration-asean-defence-ministers-strengthening-cooperation-building-resilience/?highlight=Resilience [Accessed: 27 January 2021].
Boin, A. & Lodge, M. (2016) 'Designing resilient institutions for transboundary crisis management: A time for public administration', *Public Administration*, 94 (2), pp. 289–298. DOI:10.1111/padm.12264
Brand, F.S. & K. Jax. (2007) 'Focusing the meaning(s) of resilience: Resilience as a descriptive concept and a boundary object', *Ecology and Society*, 12 (1), p. 23. Available at http://www.ecologyandsociety.org/vol12/iss1/art23/ [Accessed: 1 February 2021].
British Standard - European Standard (BS 31100) (2008) *Risk Management: Code of Practice*, London: British Standards Institution (BSI). DOI: https://doi.org/10.3403/30191339
Bush, George H.W. (1990) 'Speech to the Joint Houses of Congress 11 September 1990'. Available at https://www.c-span.org/video/?c4528359/user-clip-george-bush-defines-world-order [Accessed: 25 January 2021].

Buzan, B. (1991) *Peoples, States and Fear: An Agenda for International Security Studies in the Post-Cold War Era*, 2nd ed., Boulder, CO: Harvester Wheatsheaf.

Carpenter, S., Walker, B., Anderies, J. M. & Abel, N. (2001) 'From metaphor to measurement: Resilience of what to what?', *Ecosystems*, *4* (*8*), pp. 765–781.

Chapin III, F.S., Folke, C. & Kofinas, G.P. (2009) *'A Framework for Understanding Change' in Principles of Ecosystem Stewardship*, New York: Springer, pp. 3–28.

Cleary, Laura R. (2016) 'Half-measures and incomplete reforms: The breeding ground for a hybrid civil society in Ukraine', *Southeast European and Black Sea Studies*, *16* (*1*), pp. 7–23. DOI:10.1080/14683857.2016.1148410

Davidson-Hunt, I.J. & Berkes, F. (2003) 'Nature and society through the lens of resilience: Toward a human-in-ecosystem perspective'. In: *Navigating Social-ecological Systems: Building Resilience for Complexity and Change*, Cambridge: Cambridge University Press, pp. 53–82.

Davis, James W. (2000) *Threats and Promises: The Pursuit of International Influence*, Baltimore, MD: Johns Hopkins University Press.

Davoudi, S., Shaw, K., Haider, L.J., Quinlan, A.E., Peterson, G.D., Wilkinson, C., Fünfgeld, H., McEvoy, D. & Porter L. (2012) 'Resilience: A bridging concept or a dead end?', *Planning Theory & Practice*, *13* (*2*), pp. 299–333. DOI:10.1080/14649357.2012.677124

De Coning, C. (2018) 'Adaptive peacebuilding', *International Affairs*, *94* (*2*), pp. 301–317. DOI:10.1093/ia/iix251.

Dutheil, F., Mondillon, L. & Navel, V. (2020) 'PTSD as the second tsunami of theSARS-Cov-2 pandemic', *Psychological Medicine*, *1–2*. DOI:10.1017/S0033291720001336

Edwards, C. (2009) *Resilient Nation*, London: Demos.

European Union (2016) *Shared Vision, Common Action: A Stronger Europe, A Global Strategy for the European Union's Foreign and Security Policy*. https://eeas.europa.eu/sites/eeas/files/eugs_review_web_0.pdf [Accessed: 8 February 2021].

Folke, C., Carpenter, S., Walker, B., Scheffer, M., Chapin, T. & Rockström, J. (2010) 'Resilience thinking: integrating resilience, adaptability and transformability', *Ecology and Society, 15* (*4*). Available at http://www.ecologyandsociety.org/vol15/iss4/art20/ [Accessed: 25 February 2021].

Fukuyama, Francis (1992) *The End of History and the Last Man*. London: Penguin Books. DO I:10.1177/03058298920210010701.

Giroux, J. & Prior, T. (2012) 'Factsheet: Expressions of resilience: From "bounce back" to adaptation'. Zurich: Risk and Resilience Research Group, Center for Security Studies (CSS).

Goble, R., Kasperson, R.E. & Ratick, S. (2017) 'How can we best deal with the unexpected?'. In: *Risk Conundrums: Solving Unsolvable Problems*, Abingdon: Routledge, pp. 47–61.

Gunderson, L.H. (2003) 'Adaptive dancing: Interactions between social resilience and ecological crises'. In: *Navigating Social-ecological Systems: Building Resilience for Complexity and Change*, Cambridge: Cambridge University Press, pp. 33–52.

Gunderson, L.H. & Holling, C.S., eds., (2002) *Panarchy: Understanding Transformations in Systems of Humans and Nature*, Washington DC: Island Press.

Holling, C.S. (1973) 'Resilience and stability of ecological systems', *Annual Review of Ecology and Systematics*, *4* (*1*), pp. 1–23.

Holling, C.S. (2001) 'Understanding the complexity of economic, ecological, and social systems', *Ecosystems*, *4* (*5*), pp. 390–405.

HM Government (2015) *National Security Strategy and Security and Defence Review: A Secure and Prosperous United Kingdom*. London: Crown Copyright. Available at https://assets.publishing.service.gov.uk/government/uploads/system/uploads/attachment_data/file/478933/52309_Cm_9161_NSS_SD_Review_web_only.pdf [Accessed: 8 February 2021].

International Standards Organisation (ISO 31000) (2018) 'Risk management – guidelines. International Organization for Standardization – ISO'. Geneva, Switzerland. Available at https://www.iso.org/obp/ui/#iso:std:iso:31000:ed-2:v1:en [Accessed: 17 February 2021].

International Standards Organisation (ISO Guide 73) (2002) 'Risk Management—Vocabulary. International Organization for Standardization – ISO', Geneva, Switzerland. Available at https://www.iso.org/obp/ui/#iso:std:iso:guide:73:ed-1:v1:en [Accessed: 17 February 2021].

Kaplan, R. & Mikes, A. (2012) 'Managing risks: A new framework', *Harvard Business Review*. Available at https://www.nsf.gov/oirm/bocomm/meetings/spring_2018/Managing_Risks_A_New_Framework.pdf [Accessed: 26 February 2021].

Manyena, S.B. (2006) 'The concept of resilience revisited', *Disasters, 30 (4)*, pp. 434–450.

OECD Publishing (2017) *National Risk Assessments-A Cross Country Perspective*. Paris: OECD Publishing. DOI:10.1787/9789264287532-en

Omand, D. (2004) 'National resilience priorities for UK Government'. Speech of 19 May 2004. London: Royal United Services Institute (RUSI). Available at https://rusi.org/commentary/national-resilience-priorities-uk-government-sir-david-omand [Accessed: 26 February 2021].

Omand, D. (2010) *Securing the State*, London: Hurst & Co.

Owen T. (2004) 'Human security – conflict, critique and consensus: Colloquium remarks and a proposal for a threshold based definition', *Security Dialogue, 35 (3)*, pp. 373–385. DOI:10.1177/0967010604047555

Pettman, R. (2005) 'Human security as global security: Reconceptualising strategic studies', *Cambridge Review of International Affairs, 18 (1)*, pp. 137–150. DOI:10.1080/09557570500059878

Power, M. (2004) 'The risk management of everything: Rethinking the politics of uncertainty'. London: Demos. Available at https://www.demos.co.uk/files/riskmanagementofeverything.pdf [Accessed: 16 February 2021].

Renn, O. (2017) 'Risk governance: Concept and application to systemic risk'. In: *Risk Conundrums: Solving Unsolvable Problems*, Abingdon: Routledge, pp. 243–259.

Republic of Armenia (2020) *National Security Strategy of the Republic of Armenia: A Resilient Armenia in a Changing World*. Available at https://www.gov.am/en/National-Security-Strategy/.

Rousseau, David L (2007) 'Identity, power and threat perception: a cross-national experimental study', *Journal of Conflict Resolution, 51 (5)*, pp. 744–771. DOI:10.1177/0022002707304813

Sharpe, Albie, Razee, Husna & Zwi, Anthony B. (2020) 'Did human security forget the humans? Critically assessing evaluations of interventions with a human security dimension in Sri Lanka', *Conflict, Security & Development, 20 (4)*, pp. 467–495. DOI:10.1080/14678802.2020.1800954

Slovic, P., Fischhoff, B. & Lichtenstein, S. (1979) 'Rating the risks', *Environment, 21 (3)*, pp. 14–39.

Sunstein, C.R. (2003) 'Beyond the precautionary principle', *University of Pennsylvania Law Review, 151 (3)*, pp. 1003–1058. Available at https://core.ac.uk/reader/194863940 [Accessed: 15 February 2021].

UK Cabinet Office (2013) 'Resilience in society: Infrastructure, communities and businesses'. Available at https://www.gov.uk/guidance/resilience-in-society-infrastructure-communities-and-businesses [Accessed: 24 February 2002].

UNDP (1994) *Human Development Report 1994*, New York and Oxford: Oxford University Press. Available at http://hdr.undp.org/sites/default/files/reports/255/hdr_1994_en_complete_nostats.pdf [Accessed: 24 April 2020].

United States of America (2015) *National Security Strategy*. Available at https://obamawhitehouse.archives.gov/sites/default/files/docs/2015_national_security_strategy_2.pdf [Accessed: 25 January 2021].

Vasilache, A. (2019) 'Security in the sovereignty governmentality continuum', *Cambridge Review of International Affairs, 32 (6)*, pp. 681–711. DOI:10.1080/09557571.2019.1632797

Walklate, S., McGarry, R. and Mythen, G. (2014) 'Searching for resilience: A conceptual excavation', *Armed Forces and Society, 40 (3)*, pp. 408–427. DOI:10.1177/0095327X12465419

Yee-Kuang Heng (2006) *War as Risk Management*, London: Routledge. DOI:10.4324/9780203970072

3 Governance

Concept and challenges

Laura R. Cleary and Gemma Collantes-Celador

Introduction

For over a decade, journalists, academics, international non-governmental organizations (INGOs) and international financial institutions (IFIs) have been charting the retreat of democracy. Autocratization may not be what individuals and societies aspire to, but it is certainly what a growing number of the world's population are experiencing (Repucci, 2020). Whether we refer to these regimes as 'electoral autocracies', 'illiberal' or 'hybrid' democracies, it is clear we are experiencing a democratic recession.

While this trend is concerning, it is not unexpected. As Samuel Huntington (1993) argued, each wave of democratization is followed by a reverse wave. What is of concern on this occasion is not that new democracies are faltering, but that long-established ones are more hollow than we thought. As Lührman and Lindberg (2019: p.1095) have argued, in the past democratic breakdowns used to be 'sudden events' – a coup d'état for example – now democracies 'erode gradually and under legal disguise'. While coups still happen, as evidenced by events in Mali in 2012 and 2020, in Thailand in 2014 and in Myanmar in 2021 the more prevalent trend is the rise of populism; the division of societies into opposing camps of 'us' and 'them' and the election of demagogues who further exacerbate those perceived divisions in order to retain power. There has long been concern over the rhetoric employed by Hungarian Prime Minister Viktor Orban and his Fidesz party, the efforts of the Polish Law and Justice (PIS) government to roll back civil liberties, and Indian Prime Minister Narendra Modi's predilection for playing identity politics. The real crisis for democracy, however, appeared to arrive in 2016, heralded first by the UK's Brexit referendum in June of that year, followed in November by the election of Donald Trump to the US Presidency. If populism could take root in such well-established democracies what hope was there for other states?

This is a particularly pertinent question for those engaged in Security Sector Reform (SSR) given that the aim of such sector-wide change programmes is to facilitate, among other things, the transition to and subsequent consolidation of democracy. The SSR agenda is predicated on a series of assumptions. First, that the Westphalian state with a Weberian bureaucracy is the ideal type (Abrahamson, 2016; Hickey, 2012). Second, that governance, be that classed as 'good' or 'good enough', is associated solely with liberal democracy (Hills, 2013). Third, that 'good governance' can be achieved through the 'promotion of a particular set of institutional forms' (Hickey, 2012: p.1233), frequently drawn from Anglo-American and European institutions. Finally, and based on the above, reform of the security sector should result in the promotion of

DOI: 10.4324/9781003137061-3

the norms and practices of civilian and democratic management of the security sector if stability and peace are to be guaranteed (Garcia, 2014).

We find some of these assumptions problematic, because promoting a single model runs the risk of achieving the opposite of what we desire: insecurity rather than security. The quality of governance may improve with the initiation and consolidation of democracy, but it is important to acknowledge that governance is not the sole purview of democratic systems. Inferring a causal link between the integrity of the state, its institutional design, and the nature of its government (e.g., autocratic, democratic or something in between) with the standard of governance limits the space for meaningful conversations about whether governance needs to be improved and if so how. In theory, if not in practice, it has long been recognised that states evolve, or are constructed, to serve their varying constituencies in different ways. The state's functionality will be determined by a range of political, economic, social, cultural, and historical factors. Failure to fully acknowledge this leads to the adoption of technocratic approaches to reform, the result of which may actually be a less responsive, less legitimate form of governance (Tull, 2019; Burt, 2016). We therefore posit that while principles of governance should be immutable, the way in which they are individually and collectively applied is variable and dependent, again, upon socio-cultural factors and prevailing interests.

The chapter begins with a discussion of the relational nature of governance and the associated concepts of legitimacy and trust, before examining how the principles of governance may be applied within the security sector. The chapter concludes by exploring the challenges of improving security sector governance.

Governance, legitimacy and trust

What is governance? It is a straightforward question, with a less than straightforward answer. There are a plethora of international organisations, non-governmental organisations and states interested in assessing the quality of governance and promoting ways to improve it, yet those same actors tend to describe an ideal representation of governance rather than define it in precise terms. Governance has been variably described by various international organisations as the 'rules, processes and behaviours', the 'system of values, policies, and institutions' and the 'traditions and institutions' (cited in UNDP, 2004: p.2) through which 'power' (DFID, 2019; APRM & AGA, 2019: p.16) and 'authority' (DFID, 2019: p.4) are exercised in order to manage a country's affairs. Good governance, in turn, tends to be associated with the ideal of liberal democracy and the efficient, effective, and accountable management of public resources (USAID, 2013; APRM & AGA, 2019).

In reviewing these definitions and interpretations of governance two points become evident. First, that governance is ultimately about exercising legitimate authority and utilising resources to get things done; and, second, that actors' preferences as to who should exercise that authority and how varies, although the principal focal point appears to follow a state-centric approach. The tendency to associate governance, and specifically good governance, with the attributes of liberal democracy begs some questions: what is happening in countries that are not classed as 'free' or 'liberal' democracies? Is there an absence of governance? The answer is no. Even in those states that have been classed as 'weak', 'failing' or 'failed', (Chandler, 2010; Rotberg, 2003) a form of governance is apparent. Those states classed as 'functioning' are separated from those deemed to be 'failing' by a threefold variable that comprises the extent to which the citizenry views that form of governance as legitimate; the governing actors and institutions treat each other as legitimate participants in the process of government; and the international community concurs with that internal assessment of legitimacy.

Within this book we adhere to Haynes' (2006: p. 17) minimalist definition: 'governance describes the process of governmental decision-making and the manner by which decisions are put into practice (or, in some cases not put into practice)'. The process of decision-making and implementation will occur at various levels within a state and society and will be influenced by factors that are culturally, institutionally, and contextually dependent. No two governance systems will be the same even if there are similarities in terms of institutional frameworks.

While we recognise that no system of government is perfect, we eschew the labels of 'good' or 'good enough' governance. As the literature details, the categorisation of states in terms of 'good' and 'bad' governance has had a demotivating effect on those inclined towards reform, but it also has resulted in a very technocratic approach to change (Abrahamsen, 2016; Hickey, 2012; Schroeder, Chappuis & Kocak, 2014). States are encouraged to change their laws, policies, institutions, internal processes and employment practices in their pursuit of democracy, but these changes do not necessarily result in modifications to the culture (political or organisational), mindsets or behaviours which are required to make that democracy self-sustaining. Too many SSR programmes have succumbed to the trap inherent within the McKinsey 7S model. Articulated in 1980 by Robert Waterman, Thomas Peters and Julian Phillips, the 7S model highlights the key factors that need to be addressed if organisational change is to prove successful. Those factors are:

- Strategies (H)
- Structures (H)
- Systems (H)
- Staff (S)
- Skills (S)
- Styles (S)
- Shared Values (S)

Hard factors (H) are ones over which senior managers, or politicians in the case of the security sector, have full control and where change can be made relatively quickly. These are the elements most frequently changed in pursuit of quick wins, with the expectation that the other elements, defined as soft (S), will fall into place on their own. Unfortunately, this is rarely the case and it is in these areas that problems associated with the delivery of change frequently arise.

Example 3.1: Reform of the UK Security Sector

In November 2019, the Conservative Party won a decisive victory in the national election. They had contested the election promising to 'Get Brexit Done' and 'Unleash Britain's Potential'. Once in power the government proceeded to implement the elements of its manifesto which, in the Party's view, would contribute to the attainment of the second aim. This involved large-scale restructuring of the state institutions. Over the next

12 months the government merged the Foreign and Commonwealth Office with the Department for International Development, reduced the overseas aid budget, downplayed the role of the National Security Council and National Security Advisor (Edward and Goodman, 2020); and launched a broadside at the civil service (Payne and Parker, 2020), claiming in each case that the institutions were not fit for a 21st century Britain. Institutional reform was initiated without reference to strategy, with the formulation of the national security strategy delayed by COVID-19, and with limited regard for procedures or systems and scant articulation of the skill sets required to make the new institutional arrangements effective (Payne and Parker, 2020). In seeking to justify reform of the decision-making and implementation processes, thus enhancing the responsiveness of state institutions to political will, the government called into question the legitimacy and trustworthiness of the existing structures, systems, and staff. Deliberately undermining institutions in this way makes it far more difficult to govern in the longer term.

The above case study illustrates the relational characteristics of governance. Ultimately, governance relates to the nature of government, here understood as the system by which a community is governed; the capacity of government; the relationship between government and civil society; the rule of law and the guarantee of rights and freedoms (human, civil, and economic). Essentially, governance relates to the legitimacy of government.

This raises another question: what is legitimacy? At the heart of any relationship between a figure of authority and the subject of that authority is a question: why? Why should I follow you? Why should I obey the government? Why should I obey the rules or the law? We may choose to submit to an individual or a government's authority because we are coerced into doing so. Alternatively, we may perceive that there is a benefit in so doing or because we *trust* that the actor is working in our best interests.

Trust is integral to how we perceive the legitimacy of an actor and the quality of governance. There is sufficient evidence to demonstrate that trust levels serve as a barometric indicator of satisfaction or dissatisfaction with a government's policies and performance (Ball et al., 2019). In our day-to-day relations and in our interactions with government we invest our trust at different levels and for diverse reasons. These varying levels of trust were captured in an article which appeared in the *Harvard Business Review* in 2003. Robert Galford and Anne Drapeau presented a typology which depicted three levels of trust in business organisations: strategic, personal, and organisational. Their model, with modest amendments, has relevance when considering levels of trust in government.

Ball et al. (2019) have argued that there is a distinction to be drawn between trust and trustworthiness. Trust is only experienced at an interpersonal level, based on

Table 3.1 Three Levels of Trust

Strategic Trust	The trust that ... [citizens] have in the people running the show to make the right strategic decisions.
Personal Trust	The trust that employees [or public servants] have in their own managers.
Organisational Trust	The trust that people have in a ... [ministry]. Are the processes well designed, consistent and fair?

Source: Authors adapted from Galford and Drapeau (2003)

assessment of actions that have taken place. In this sense, trust can be won or lost because of individual deeds. Trustworthiness, on the other hand, can be experienced between individuals and other social entities, such as institutions, and relates to a willingness to act. Trustworthiness is founded upon three principal components:

- Competence: whether the institution is perceived to be able to deliver its objectives
- Benevolence: whether the institution is perceived to be concerned about the welfare and integrity of the community, as opposed to acting out of self-interest
- Integrity: whether the institution is perceived to act in an ethical way and not abuse its power.

In some societies, efforts are made to inculcate within children an understanding of and respect for those services engaged in the delivery of public safety, the police and fire services. Representatives of these services are invited into schools to instruct children on what can be done collectively to combat crime and protect lives. The principle is that by developing knowledge and understanding you engender trust. That principle is sound, but what we have seen in several countries is that inconsistency in messaging, actions, and standards impacts significantly on the perceived trustworthiness of an institution. The killing of George Floyd in May 2020 by a Minneapolis policeman may have been the pre-curser for the Black Lives Matter movement in the United States, but the rapid spread of that movement around the world was evidence not just of institutionalised racism but of a perceived lack of institutional trustworthiness. When trust is absent, the legitimacy of institutions is negatively impacted and the quality of governance declines. In extreme cases government may be unable to govern through consent because the population refuses to accept the authority of or obey the government. It is in such instances, when it appears impossible to span the 'chasm between governed and governors' (Kaltwasser, 2012: p.194), that expressions of what is known politically as 'people power' arise. Since 2017, the Carnegie Endowment for International Peace has monitored the number of public protests worldwide. By 29 January 2021 they had registered 230 significant anti-government protests. In some cases, these resulted in the resignation or dismissal of the political leadership as in Algeria, Bolivia, Georgia, Iraq, Kazakhstan, and Mali in 2019 (Carnegie Endowment for International Peace, 2021). Throughout 2020 and 2021, demonstrations occurred against austerity measures and the continuation of COVID-19 restrictions, but there were also significant protests in Hong Kong, Belarus, Thailand, and Myanmar demanding the end to autocratic rule.

Exercise 3.1: Assessing levels of trust

Reflecting upon your own government system, assess the levels of strategic, personal and organisational trust. Do individual and institutional actors display competence, benevolence and integrity? Provide examples.

Improving security sector governance

The concepts of trust, legitimacy and governance are integral to our considerations of the security sector, for the simple reason that in a number of countries around the world the 'security' services (e.g., the police, gendarmerie, armed forces, and intelligence services) are perceived as the source of *insecurity* rather than security. It is for this reason that states engage in and promote SSR. Security Sector Governance (SSG) 'encompasses the rules, systems and processes of making and implementing decisions in the agencies with an authorised use of force' (Ghimire, 2017: p.1416). Thus, SSG is the object of the reform process.

One of the cornerstones of the SSG agenda has been the belief that by asserting the principles of governance and subordinating the security services to civil, civilian, and democratic control, it is possible to increase the trust in and legitimacy of those services. Given the centrality of these beliefs it is worth reviewing those principles of governance and their relationship to the concepts of control and management.

As noted above, institutions and states describe governance in different ways, which means in turn that their articulation of the principles of governance also varies. Nevertheless, there is a degree of consistency when describing the ideal of 'good governance'. Haynes (2006) has grouped the principles and practices of governance into eight major characteristics:

- Participation
  - Participation involves all groups in society;
  - Participation can either be direct or through legitimate intermediate institutions or representatives;
  - Participation also implies, on the one hand, the existence of a diverse but cohesive civil society and, on the other, general freedoms of association and expression.
- Rule of law
  - The rule of law is said to exist when 'all persons and authorities within the state, whether public or private should be bound by and entitled to the benefit of laws publicly made, taking effect (generally) in the future and publicly administered in courts' (Bingham, 2011: p.8);
  - Governance requires fair legal frameworks that are impartially enforced by an independent judiciary and police force, with a minimal opportunity for corruption;
  - Internationally recognised human rights are given full protection, including those of religious and ethnic minorities (see Chapter 4).
- Transparency
  - Accepted and implemented rules and regulations govern how decisions are taken, put into practice and enforced;
  - Information should be accessible to those engaged in decision-making, implementation and oversight, as well as to those who will be affected by those decisions and their enforcement;
  - Limitations on accessing or sharing that information may be imposed when concerns regarding national security arise. The release or censure of information should be determined by law.
- Responsiveness
  - Institutions and processes aim to serve all stakeholders within a reasonable time frame.
- Consensus-orientation, equity and inclusiveness
  - Ensuring that all members of society feel they have a stake in governance: no one is excluded;

- Guaranteeing that all groups, especially the most vulnerable, have clear opportunities to try to maintain or improve their societal and developmental positions;
- Mediating among different interests in society to reach a broad consensus regarding what is in the best interest of the whole community and how to achieve it;
- Developing a long-term perspective for sustainable human development and how to attain it.
- Effectiveness and efficiency
  - Processes and institutions produce results that meet the needs of society while maximising resources at their disposal;
  - A sustainable use of natural resources and the protection of the environment.
- Accountability
  - Governmental institutions, as well as private sector and civil society organisations, must be accountable to the public and to their institutional stakeholders;
  - Organisations and institutions are generally accountable to those who will be affected by decisions or actions.

These principles are incorporated into the concepts of civil control and civilian and democratic management in the following ways.

Civil control

As noted in Chapter 1, we define civil control, or civil supremacy, as the allegiance that the security services owe to the citizenry. This implies an allegiance to a group larger than the government of the day; it is an allegiance to the citizen body in its entirety. The question of allegiance should be addressed in the constitution, in legislation establishing and regulating the individual security services (e.g., the armed forces, police, gendarmerie and intelligence agencies), in doctrine and training. The concept of civil control embodies the principle of the rule of law. As will be discussed in Chapter 4, the security ministries, agencies, and personnel should be both 'bound by and entitled to the benefit of laws publicly made' (Bingham, 2011: p.8). There is a requirement for the law to be promulgated and for personnel to be indoctrinated in it. When security actors are perceived to be operating in accordance with the legal framework, trust in and the legitimacy of those institutions increases.

Example 3.2: Civil control and police in Bosnia and Herzegovina

The history of policing in Bosnia is one characterised by participation and/or consent to harassment, intimidation and disproportionate force during the Communist era, and criminal activities and human rights abuses, under cover of ethnic/nationalist agendas, during the 1992–1995 war and immediately after. Following the signing of the Dayton Peace Agreement (DPA), police reform became a priority. The DPA's failure to address ethnic divisions had allowed ethnic capture of key institutions, like the police. The aim, supported by the international community, has since been to develop effective, inclusive, and responsive police services that follow best international democratic policing practices. For example, the 2004–2008 police restructuring process sought to re-orient the state-police-citizenry relationship by placing legislative and budgetary police competencies at the state level, fighting political interference in police operational matters, and establishing local police areas that are responsive to technical, not political, necessities. The process fell short of intended outcomes, with the alignment of civil control of policing with the needs of the citizenry remaining in need of attention (Collantes-Celador, 2009).

Civilian management

With respect to civilian management, we start with a modified version of the question posed by Yagil Levy (2016). When we talk about civilian management of the security services what do we want civilians to manage? Do we want them directly engaged in operational issues (e.g., doctrine, deployment and resources), or do we want civilians to manage the process of securitisation, referring here to decisions over the activation of the mechanisms that legitimise the use of those security agencies (e.g., law, policy, and finances)? We agree with Levy that the focus of activity should be on the latter, but we diverge from him by choosing to talk about management rather than control. As discussed in Chapter 1, management encompasses several functions, of which control is but one. As will be discussed below, effective management of the security sector requires expertise and specialised skills that can be learnt, and it also requires the development of partnerships between stakeholders. It is our contention that by employing the term management rather than control we create the space for a wider range of inputs in decision-making for security.

Given the breadth of activity that needs to occur to employ the security services effectively, we should view civilian management as more than simply the appointment of civilians to ministerial positions. As defined above, governance is understood as the process of decision-making and the manner those decisions are put into practice (or not). Civilian and democratic management are concerned with the questions of who makes decisions and how. Therefore, civilian management refers to the appointment of civilians to positions of responsibility in governance and management of the security services. We are concerned with the totality of decisions taken within the Presidential or Prime Ministerial office, within the ministries of Foreign Affairs, Defence, Interior, Justice and Finance, and within Parliament that have a bearing on how security agencies seek to deliver the ultimate public good – security.

If we understand civilian management in this holistic way, we can place the promotion of inter-agency cooperation or whole-of-government approaches (WGAs) to security in context. WGA has been adopted by countries in response to the increasingly uncertain and complex security environment discussed in Chapter 2. There has been a growing awareness that if states are to respond effectively to existing and emerging security challenges they will require a coordinated institutional response. Gone are the days when one security ministry or agency could operate in isolation from others.

The introduction of civilian management of the security sector may require changes in the way in which information and knowledge is handled and transmitted as well as a review of decision-making and management practices, as discussed in Chapter 10. At issue are questions such as the following:

- Who has the right to see what? When?
- Are clearance and classification systems consistent across the security sector thereby enabling meaningful discussion and effective decision-making?

- Who has the authority to make decisions?
- Do formal or informal mechanisms exist through which information and knowledge is channelled, decisions are made and communicated?
- How are decisions implemented?
- Are legislators vetted? Are they given the opportunity to familiarise themselves with parliamentary procedure before assuming their seats on oversight committees?

There is no guarantee that civilian policy makers will make good decisions or implement policy in such a way as to result in the effective provision of security. Therefore, investment in the development of their capability is required. Do the civilians who populate the ministries have a general level of security literacy and specific knowledge of the particularities of managing the use of the armed forces, the police, or intelligence services, for example? Can they analyse the strategic context and based on that analysis take informed decisions about how to employ or resource the security agencies? What training is available to them to improve their performance? Examples 3.3 and 3.4 illustrate both the tensions faced when seeking to apply civilian management and the ways in which some states have sought to overcome them.

Example 3.3: Civil-military relations in Uruguay

Garcia (2014: p.488) has argued that to class as a fully established democracy there must be an effective system of 'civilian checks and balances, ensuring full authority over the armed forces, police and secret services'. How then does Uruguay compare? Classed as one of the strongest enduring democracies in Latin America (Freedom House, 2020), its path towards consolidation has been neither smooth nor uninterrupted. Between 1976 and 1985 Uruguay was subject to military dictatorship, only recommencing the transition to democracy in 1986.

Between 1986 and 2005 few efforts were made to reform defence in Uruguay. The passage of an Amnesty Bill in 1986 precluded investigations into human rights abuses perpetrated by security personnel. In the absence of political will, defence reform was not enforced. As a result, defence doctrine and organic military law remained unchanged and the military retained their dominance of the MOD, continuing to control the flow of information and decision-making (Pion-Berlin and Martinez, 2017).

The situation began to change in 2005 when courts were encouraged to undertake inquiries into human rights abuses and public debates on defence and the role of the armed forces were held. In 2010 the National Defence Law initiated the process of civilianising the Defence Ministry and placed it at the heart of defence policy making. The 2010 law also allowed for the military to contribute to the provision of public security, a role which became more prominent with the implementation of the Border Law in 2020.

While rudimentary legal and institutional frameworks necessary for the assertion of civilian and democratic management have now been established, they do not address sufficiently the *process of militarisation*. Concern has been expressed by civil society and the armed forces themselves as to the legal rights and responsibilities of the military in conducting operations in the border areas, whether the police or military have primacy in border operations and the general rules of engagement. There is concern that a lack of clarity over the military's role coupled with insufficient training and resources will lead to mistakes being made in the field which could undermine the military's reputation, perceived legitimacy and the gains that have been made in rebalancing the civil-military relationship. The armed forces do not believe that the current system allows them the opportunity to express their legitimate concerns or that those concerns will be understood and addressed by civilian authorities. A gap remains between the armed forces and policy makers.

It is by means of civilian management that we begin to address the principles of participation, consensus orientation and transparency. These principles and the others articulated above are brought to fruition when civilian management is combined with democratic management.

Democratic management

If civilian management is ultimately about who has the authority to make decisions, then democratic management is about how those decisions are made and implemented. What are the institutional and procedural mechanisms for providing direction and conducting oversight?

The theory of democratic management recognises that elected governments are not necessarily democratic, and that democratic management is a contested process, not a fixed attribute of existing democracies. This is due to the contested nature of democracy itself, as discussed above, and because some of the largest democratic deficits are to be found in the security sector (Luckham, 1996). In this context, democratic deficits refer to a lack of transparency and accountability.

The solution to this is deemed to rest with the establishment of institutional mechanisms that are sufficient for the provision of direction, the conduct of oversight and the development of professional norms. Those institutional mechanisms will consist of a clear legal basis for action (see Chapter 4), functioning ministries capable of providing political direction and oversight (see Chapter 7), parliamentary committees with authority and competence to conduct oversight of policy and budgets (see Chapter 6), institutions such as a National Security Council capable of both directing and co-ordinating security related activity, the responsibility of civil society organisations and the media to debate security issues and engage in oversight activities, and the establishment of transparent and apolitical recruitment and promotion processes for both uniformed and civilian personnel. The establishment and maintenance of such institutions and norms should enable affirmative responses to the following questions: Do civilians (politicians, civil servants, civil society organisation (CSOs)) keep track of what the defence and security forces do? Are the institutional mechanisms responsive and do they result in efficient and effective governance?

Within the literature, much is made of the requirement for professionalism of the defence and security forces if civilian and democratic management are to be achieved. While we endorse that assertion we would argue, based on experience in the field, that an equal emphasis needs to be placed on enhancing the professionalism of civilians, be they politicians or public servants, operating within the security domain. All too frequently in discussions with uniformed personnel we have heard the refrain that civilians are not trusted because they are perceived as lacking sufficient understanding of security issues and general managerial competence. Further, they are accused of being 'arrogant' when they exercise their legal authority to take decisions but do so without availing themselves of the knowledge and expertise of the uniformed personnel (see the Uruguayan case above). The civilian rejoinder is that they are interested in understanding security and learning about how to improve its governance and management, but they have not been given sufficient opportunity to do so. As for availing themselves of information prior to taking decisions there may be cultural or procedural obstacles to doing so. Ultimately, if we want the quality of security sector governance to improve then we need to invest in it. That requires a commitment of political will, financial and human resources, and time. We need to look beyond simply modifying strategies, structures and systems to the development of staff, skills, styles and values.

Example 3.4: Developing competency for civilian and democratic management

Ghana, like Uruguay, is classed as a beacon of stability and democracy within its sub-region. This status has been hard won and follows decades of political and economic mismanagement. Ghana achieved independence in 1957, but between 1966 and 1981 it experienced six coups d'état. Its democratic transition did not begin properly until 1992. Ghana's approach towards establishing civil control and civilian and democratic management of the armed forces and security services has gone beyond formal legalistic and institutional mechanisms; there has been a concerted effort to develop the competency of civilians working within the security sector.

The first step in improving CMR was the establishment in 2003 of a National Reconciliation Commission to address historic cases of abuse between 1957 and 1993. From 2002 onwards, investment was made into educating and training a wide range of security stakeholders. Ministry of Defence (MOD) civil servants received education in defence, security and public administration; members of Parliament attended SSR workshops and training on conducting oversight; investment was made into the employment and training of parliamentary staff to support the work of the Defence and Interior Committee; training and outreach programmes were provided for CSOs and the media so that they could work more effectively with or review the activities of the armed forces, and the armed forces have been educated to appreciate that they are but one of several institutions responsible for security. It has taken 20 years of concerted effort to improve the quality of Ghana's civil-military relations. Levels of trust between the armed forces, civil servants and politicians have increased as their competency levels have improved, and the trustworthiness of the Ghana Armed Forces has grown significantly as it has demonstrated that it is an apolitical force (PeaceFM. com, 2019).

Governance challenges

In reviewing the literature on governance and reflecting on over 20 years of field work experience in countries engaged in SSR as part of a larger transition from conflict to peace or authoritarianism to democracy, we have concluded that the challenges when improving governance are myriad and complex. During our teaching we have regularly asked our students what they perceive to be the principal governance challenges in their country. Wherever the students are from the answers tend to be similar. Whilst by no means exhaustive, common responses are as follows:

- Constitutional arrangements, specifically the absence of sufficient checks and balances.
- Competitive political processes and rival centres of power.
- Role of oligarchs: limiting political pluralism, monopolising the economy, blocking reform, capturing state institutions.
- Politicians 'speak democracy' but do not 'do democracy'.
- A system of law, but not rule of law.
- Corruption.
- Limited state capacity.
- Weak institutions with poorly defined remits.
- Overly bureaucratic institutions.
- Lack of leadership at appropriate levels.
- Limited resources poorly managed.
- Lack of trust (perceived lack of professionalism).
- Inability or unwillingness to share information.

We recognise that each of these challenges may be experienced differently depending on the country. The solution to these challenges – and many others represented by the above list – often lies with the re-allocation of resources, galvanising political will or enhancing public awareness. The fact that citizens, politicians, security professionals and security sector advisers in many of the countries in which we have worked grapple with these issues does point to some more fundamental concerns, such as inherent tensions in the concept of governance and its constituent principles. One of these pertains to something mentioned earlier in the chapter, when discussing how SSR/SSG agendas are predicated on the assumption that the Westphalian state is the ideal type. We have observed that those states classed as 'weak', 'failing' or 'failed' do demonstrate a form of governance. This begs the question: is the Westphalian state – based on a very specific understanding of state-society-security arrangements – an indispensable enabler of a governance agenda?

In her writings on the police and policing models in post-conflict settings, Alice Hills reflects on the relationship between 'security' and 'order'. She argues that order, not security, is the fundamental factor because it 'implies a degree of predictability, regularity and stability to social and political relationships, institutions and behaviours' (2009: p. 12) based on an 'agreed set of rules' which could be repressive or democratic. Through a study of dynamics in post-conflict cities she argues that order may submerge but will always re-appear and the form it takes is very much dependent on social processes of coercion, subjugation, accommodation and negotiation, rather than on levels of security/insecurity. Hills' work adds weight to criticisms of the concept of 'ungoverned spaces' that has been used to describe the result of 'weak', 'failing' or 'failed' statehood. More importantly, it forces us to question state-centric approaches to governance. In a research paper published in 2015 by the then UK Foreign and Commonwealth Office (FCO) on the relationship between 'ungoverned spaces' and terrorism, it is concluded that 'from a state-centric, Western perspective, we may not recognise, fully understand or necessarily approve of how these different forms of governance [tribal, sectarian, clan-based] work. But different forms of governance do exist in most, if not all, "ungoverned spaces"' (2015: p. 2). The research paper offers a substitute term, 'alternative authority and governance structures in contested spaces' (Clunan, 2010), which are far more complex to engage with than resorting to the explanation of a lack of political will, state capacity or the like. The forces/actors governing those spaces could be malign (e.g., terrorist groups, criminal groups, and the like) but that is not the reality in all such situations as pointed out in the FCO document. The question that should occupy our minds is how to make the principles of governance part of the order-making and order-maintenance process in a given territory – contested or not – even when the Westphalian state is not the prime arbiter on processes of negotiation, accommodation, contestation and subjugation.

There is an additional dimension to this discussion on the role of state-centric approaches in determining the direction, content and implementation of SSR agendas that deserves consideration. As noted in Chapter 2, security is amorphous; the plurality of multidimensional security concerns has inevitably led to a 'complex network of state and non-state actors' (Krahmann, 2003: p.5). The resultant diffusion of power and authority, as noted in the literature, does not necessarily mean the State will disappear, rather that it 'will continue to be the juridical repository of sovereignty, although sovereignty will be much more conditional than before' (Kaldor, 2003: p.583). Kaldor's reflection invites us to consider what it means to be sovereign and independent in decision-making and implementation, including in relation to when, how and why to pursue SSR/SSG agendas, especially against the growing authority of external actors. This situation is often presented as a dichotomous relationship with states; on the one hand, the national state driving a governance-led reform process and, on the other hand, external actors – be those regional, global, state or non-state – imposing such process. Our experience in the field shows the response tends to lie somewhere in the middle, but it does raise important questions about legitimacy, effectiveness and authority, cornerstone ideas when explaining governance, particularly when considering areas of limited statehood, including in the security field, 'characterised by weak state institutions and a multitude of non-state and external governance actors' (Schmelzle & Stollenwerk, 2018: p.461).

Conclusion

Governance is a critical enabler for security, development and democracy, which is why governance reform features so extensively in these other agendas. Prior to initiating reform, however, we must first understand what it is we want to change and why. No system exists in isolation; we must be cognizant of the environment in which it operates. In the case of governance, that means understanding the institutional mechanisms of government but also how a society perceives legitimacy, trust, order and security. These are the critical variables. What we have observed is that a failure to acknowledge that there may be different perceptions of these variables within a society and between and within state institutions often poses the biggest stumbling block to exerting civilian control and civilian and democratic management of the security sector. Ultimately, these concepts are about who has authority and what they are allowed to do with it. In the following chapters, our co-authors will explore in more detail the mechanisms through which that authority is exercised and the ways in which those who do so are held to account. We must conclude with a note of warning. The concept of governance and its constituent principles are ideals, 'difficult to achieve and implement in its totality' (Haynes, 2006: p.17). Macro-dynamics (geopolitical considerations) and micro-dynamics (rise of populism and other regressions of democracy at the national level) are in recent years exacerbating this reality. It is too soon to talk of a 'crisis' of governance, but we must remain vigilant to the debilitating impact these political dynamics can have on SSR/SSG processes.

Questions to consider

1. Where does sovereignty reside within your country?
2. What do you consider to be your country's security sector governance challenges?
3. How might you seek to address those challenges?

Suggested further reading

Haynes, J. (2006) 'The principles of good governance'. In: L. Cleary and T. McConville (eds) *Managing Defence in a Democracy*, pp. 17–31, Abingdon: Routledge.
OECD-DAC (2005) *DAC Guidelines: Security System Reform and Governance*, Paris: OECD Publications. DOI: 10.1787/9789264007888-en

References

Abrahamson, R. (2016) 'Exporting decentered security governance: the tensions of security sector reform', *Global Crime*, *17* (3–4), 281–295. DOI:10.1080/17440572.2016.1197507
African Peer Review Mechanism in collaboration with the African Governance Architecture (APRM & AGA) (2019) *The African Governance Report: Promoting African Union Shared Values*. Available at https://au.int/sites/default/files/documents/36418-doc-eng-_the_africa_governance_report_2019_final-1.pdf [Accessed: 7 December 2020].
Ball, K., Esposti, S.D., Dibb, S., Pavone, V. & Santiago-Gomez, E. (2019) 'Institutional trustworthiness and national security governance: Evidence from six European countries', *Governance*, *32* (103–121). DOI:10.1111/gove.12353
Bingham, T. (2011) *The Rule of Law*, London: Penguin.
Burt, G. (2016) 'Haiti's army, stabilization and security sector governance', *Stability: International Journal of Security & Development*, *5* (*1*), pp. 1–16. DOI: http://dx.doi.org/10.5334/sta.473
Carnegie Endowment for International Peace (2021) *Global Protest Tracker*. Available at https://carnegieendowment.org/publications/interactive/protest-tracker [Accessed 29 January 2021].
Chandler, D. (2010) *International Statebuilding: The Rise of Post-Liberal Governance*, Abingdon: Routledge.
Clunan, A.L. (2010) 'Ungoverned spaces? The need for reevaluation'. In: A.L. Clunan and H.A. Trinkunas, eds., *Ungoverned Spaces: Alternatives to State Authority in an Era of Softened Sovereignty*, Stanford, CA: Stanford University Press.
Collantes-Celador, G. (2009) 'Becoming "European" through police reform: A successful strategy in Bosnia and Hezegovina?', *Crime, Law and Social Change*, *51* (*2*), pp. 231–242. DOI: 10.1007/s10611–10008–9157-x.
DFID (2019) *Governance for Growth, Stability and Inclusive Development: A DFID Position Paper*. Available at https://assets.publishing.service.gov.uk/government/uploads/system/uploads/attachment_data/file/786751/Governance-Position-Paper2a.pdf [Accessed 10 March 2021].
Edward, E. & Goodman, S. (2020) 'Global Britain? Assessing Boris Johnson's major changes to national security and foreign policy', *LSE BPP*, 14 July. https://blogs.lse.ac.uk/politicsandpolicy/johnson-natsec-and-fp/ [Accessed 30 August 2020].

FCO (2015) 'The link between "ungoverned spaces" and terrorism: Myth or reality?', *Research Analysist Paper*, 23 March 2015. Available at https://www.gov.uk/government/publications/the-link-between-ungoverned-spaces-and-terrorism-myth-or-reality [Accessed 10 March 2021].

Freedom House (2020) *Freedom in the World, 2020*. Available at https://freedomhouse.org/report/freedom-world/2020/leaderless-struggle-democracy [Accessed 12 December 2020].

Galford, R. & Drapeau, A.S. (2003) 'The enemies of trust', *Harvard Business Review 02/2003*.

Garcia, D. (2014) 'Not yet a democracy: Establishing civilian authority over the security sector in Brazil – lessons for other countries in transition', *Third World Quarterly, 35 (3)*, pp. 487–504. DOI:10.1080/01436597.2014.893489

Ghimire, S. (2017) 'Optimised or compromised? United Kingdom support to reforming security sector governance in post-war Nepal', *Third World Quarterly, 38 (6)*, pp. 1415–1436. DOI:10.1080/01436597.2016.1233811

Haynes, J. (2006) 'The principles of good governance'. In: L. Cleary and T. McConville, eds., *Managing Defence in a Democracy*, pp. 17–31, Abingdon: Routledge.

Hickey, S. (2012) 'Turning governance thinking upside-down? Insights from the "politics of what works"', *Third World Quarterly 33 (7)*, pp. 1231–1247. DOI:10.1080/01436597.2012.695516

Hills, A. (2013) 'Policing, good-enough governance and development: The evidence from Mogadishu', *Conflict, Security and Development 13 (3)*, pp. 317–337. DOI:10.1080/14678802.2013.811051

Hills, A. (2009) *Policing Post-conflict Cities*, London: Zed Books Ltd.

Huntington, S. (1993) *The Third Wave: Democratization in the Late 20th Century*, Norman, Oklahoma: University of Oklahoma Press.

Kaldor, M. (2003) 'The idea of global civil society', *International Affairs, 79 (3)*, pp. 583–593. DOI:10.1111/1468–2346.00324.

Kaltwasser, C.R. (2012) 'The ambivalence of populism: Threat and corrective for democracy', *Democratization, 19 (2)*, pp. 184–208. DOI:10.1080/13510347.2011.572619

Krahmann, E. (2003) 'Conceptualizing security governance', *Cooperation and Conflict, 38 (1)*, pp. 5–26. DOI:10.1177/0010836703038001001

Levy, Y. (2016) 'What is controlled by civilian control of the military?', *Armed Forces and Society, 42 (1)*, pp. 75–98. DOI:10.1177/0095327X14567918

Luckham, R. (1996) 'Faustian Bargains: democratic control over military and security establishments'. In: R. Luckham & G. White, eds., *Democratization in the South: The Jagged Wave*, Manchester: Manchester University Press.

Lührman, A. & Lindberg, S.I. (2019) 'A third wave of autocratization is here; what is new about it?', *Democratization, 26 (7)*, pp. 1095–1113. DOI:10.1080/13510347.2019.1582029

Payne, S. & Parker, G. (2020) 'The smashing of the British State', *FT Weekend Magazine 10/11 October*, pp. 14–20.

PeaceFM (2019) 'Police top corruption list, Ghana Armed Forces, the president & religious leaders the most trusted – study', 5 December 2019. Available at https://www.peacefmonline.com/pages/local/social/201912/396873.php [Accessed: 5 August 2020].

Pion-Berlin, D. & Martinez, R. (2017) *Soldiers, Politicians and Civilians: Reforming Civil-Military Relations in Democratic Latin America*, Cambridge: Cambridge University Press.

Repucci, S. (2020) 'Democracy and pluralism are under assault', *Freedom in the World 2020: A Leaderless Struggle for Democracy*, Freedom House. Available at https://freedomhouse.org/report/freedom-world/2020/leaderless-struggle-democracy [Accessed 12 December 2020].

Rotberg, R. (2003) *When States Fail: Causes and Consequences*, Princeton: Princeton University Press.

Schmelzle, C. & Stollenwerk, E. (2018) 'Virtuous or vicious circle? Governance effectiveness and legitimacy in areas of limited statehood', *Journal of Intervention and Statebuilding, 12 (4)*, pp. 449–467. DOI:10.1080/17502977.2018.1531649

Schroeder, U.C., Chappuis, F. & Kocak, D. (2014) 'Security sector reform and the emergence of hybrid security governance', *International Peacekeeping*, 21 (2), pp. 214–230, DOI:10.1080 /13533312.2014.910405

Tull, D.M. (2019) 'Rebuilding Mali's army: The dissonant relationship between Mali and its international partners', *International Affairs*, 95 (2), pp. 405–422. DOI:10.1093/ia/112003

UNDP (2004) *UNDP Governance Indicators: A User's Guide*. New York: UNDP. Available at https://www.un.org/ruleoflaw/files/Governance%20Indicators_A%20Users%20Guide.pdf [Accessed 1 December 2020].

USAID (2013) *USAID Strategy on Democracy, Human Rights and Governance*. Available at https://www.usaid.gov/democracy-human-rights-and-governance-strategy [Accessed 1 December 2020].

Waterman, R.H., Peters, T.J. & Phillips, J.R. (1980) 'Structure is Not Organization', *Business Horizons*, pp. 14–26.

4 The legal framework for security

David Turns and Anicée Van Engeland

Introduction

The linkage between peace and security is mediated in international law via the United Nations Charter. Historically, international human rights law (IHRL) has been perceived as an inhibitor of conflict (Sriram, Martin-Orteg, & Herman 2009: p.4; Hathaway, 2007: p.589), while international humanitarian law (IHL) has been used to frame the conduct of conflicts. This dichotomy has been challenged in the past few decades, and it is now widely acknowledged that IHRL also applies in conflicts. As a result, the two legal regimes must be studied together to understand how a government can best engage with the legal framework for security.

From the need to ensure that the relevant legal regime applies to the armed forces depending on their deployment, to classic violations of IHL, the law is everywhere when seeking to achieve security. As a result, the adoption of a legal framework pertaining to security and defence is critical to defining what security might look like. When we reflect on how law contributes to the definition of security, the issue of compliance is raised: abiding by international law, but also domestic laws and regional law, implies that nation states are contributing to the existing regulatory narrative of security. Individuals, institutions and states will choose to comply with the law because they perceive a direct benefit in doing so or because they fear consequences if they do not, i.e., the risk of prosecution. As discussed in Chapter 3, compliance with the law is an indicator of the perceived legitimacy of the judicial system and the overall quality of governance.

In reality, the issues pertaining to human rights and IHL are far more complex due to differences on the ground: in a security and defence environment that is uncertain and complex, each State will have a different experience of the enforcement of human rights and IHL, but compliance is assessed using the same benchmarking instruments and reasoning for all States. Yet, there are major differences in terms of security and defence challenges: some authorities have questioned the applicability of IHRL to occupied territories, while others struggle with the legal regime applicable to armed forces deployed during police operations. While the legal framework often appears to be inflexible, there are options for State authorities to adapt the law to local and regional conditions, making security achievable in theory and in practice. This chapter explores the regulatory framework for security, highlighting pertinent issues within constitutional, human rights and international humanitarian law.

DOI: 10.4324/9781003137061-4

Governance and the rule of law: the role of constitutions

Any attempt at defining security from a legal perspective should begin with the national constitution: it is in this document, the *Grundnorm* (Kelsen, 2005: p.8), that one will find all relevant information pertaining to how a nation perceives security and defence. The preamble of the constitution as well as the first few articles are crucial in that regard: those sections of the constitution indicate what a nation holds as their core values, including views on the preferred form of government and rule of law. This will, in turn, impact the articulation, compliance and enforcement of human rights.

Example 4.1: The German constitution, the soldier as citizen and human rights

The post-WWII German constitution ensures the armed forces' independence vis-à-vis civilian authorities without turning the forces into an elite, a ruling class, a cast-away or a totalitarian instrument to avoid a historical repetition (Abenheim & Halladay, 2012: p.308). Central to this legal construct is the concept of *Innere Führung*: a soldier is a citizen in uniform. The purpose of the *Innere Führung* is to place the soldier back at the heart of the civil-military relationship (Kutz, 2003: p.118). To apply this concept in practice requires proper training: soldiers must be morally armed to understand why they are fighting and what they are fighting for, which demands improved communications between the civilian power and the armed forces. The concept also ensures that the soldier is a responsible citizen in uniform, dedicated to protecting state institutions. Finally, the human rights of German soldiers are protected by an independent Parliamentary Ombudsman to whom all soldiers have access (Nolte & Krieger, 2003: p.365). The concept of *Innere Führung* is interesting for both the way in which it frames relations between civilian and military authorities but also in terms of the institutional mechanisms that guarantee the human rights of military personnel in peacetime. The German constitution combines democracy and human rights in a unique fashion, based on lessons learned from history.

The German example demonstrates the importance of having strong core values in a constitution, with clear guidelines and constitutionalism to support a concept such as the *Innere Führung*. It is how a constitution effectively contributes to maintaining peace and security via human rights, as per the UN Charter. The inclusion of a strong and legitimate constitutional philosophy is key for ensuring compliance of citizens with IHRL. Yet, war remains a reality in the human realm, and human rights do not solely apply in peacetime.

IHRL goes to war

For decades, the norm was to apply international IHRL during peacetime with IHL regulating conflict. Yet, it became clear that IHRL does apply in conflict as well, leading to the creation of the principle of *lex specialis*. While applying IHRL during peacetime is rather straightforward, it has been difficult to assess how it could apply in war: would a citizen be allowed to publish a pamphlet undermining the war effort during conflict in the name of freedom of expression? Would the protection of the right to life extend to civilians, making it necessary to delimit war differently? Such questions have hardly been addressed in practice. Scholars and practitioners have engaged with the theory, producing relevant guidelines for admissible killings (Sassòli & Olson, 2008); analysing the application of the *lex specialis* to different types of modern conflicts (Sassòli, 2011); while others have disagreed with the idea of applying IHRL in war (Oberleitner, 2015). As academic debates flourished, States and citizens were confronted with real-life issues, such as the issue of claims for compensation for property forcibly abandoned.

Example 4.2: The reality of applying IHRL in occupied territories

In 2008, Russia invaded Georgia, leading to the occupation of 20% of the territory. Abkhazia and South Ossetia are now referred to as occupied territories under Georgian law. Russia attacked Ukraine in 2014, seeking to control Crimea, and parts of Donetsk and Luhansk. The Parliament of Ukraine adopted laws referring to the temporarily occupied territories. Specific human rights issues soon emerged in both situations, regarding, for example, compensation for property. The European Court of Human Rights (ECtHR) addressed the issue in *Broniowski v Poland* (Application no. 31443/96) in 2004: the case addresses compensation claims for property forcibly abandoned between 1944 and 1953 in the eastern provinces of pre-war Poland, as a result of boundary changes. The Broniowski family had to leave what is now part of Ukraine, leaving behind their property. Poland compensated those who had been 'repatriated' after agreements were reached with Lithuania, Ukraine, and Belarus. Broniowski inherited the property contract from his mother in 1989. He then claimed that the compensation his family had been entitled to had not been satisfied. The ECtHR held the same view, engaging in an important discussion about class action and the type of remedy to compensate loss of property. The ECtHR went on to build case law on the issue, looking at the Cyprus-Turkey dispute and the Nagorno-Karabakh dispute, focusing on compensation. The Court thereby established the right to compensation, and went on to discuss the creation of a property mechanism (see *Sargsyan v Azerbaijan*, Application no.40167/06, 16 June 2016, para. 238; *Chiragov v Armenia*, Application no. 13216/05, 16 June 2015, para.199). Such case law could be of assistance for Russian, Ukrainian, and Georgian authorities in the future, but also for Armenia and Azerbaijan, as they constitute an opportunity for compliance with the right to remedy while protecting internally displaced people's rights. The question remains whether the Court only sought to make a practical contribution to the law or to create positive obligation for States. The latter suggestion would entail the duty for States to put a remedy mechanism in place to foster compliance.

In countries that have parts of their territories occupied or have disputed borders, the issue of land law and property law is a pressing one to ensure compliance with the right to property, the right to remedy, the protection of private and family life and the principle of non-discrimination.

The debate as to whether IHRL applies in conflict becomes moot in a situation where a conflict has become a 'grey zone': this happens when a conflict is punctuated by long stretches of calm during which there are no attacks, but a military presence is felt or seen. Such complex situations raise questions as to when IHL applies, as it is clear that IHRL remains applicable whether the conflict is 'hot' or 'cold'. Some conflicts span generations and involve elements of IHRL, but also refugee and citizenship laws, mixing domestic, regional, and international laws. Issues such as citizenship law, disappearances, displaced people, and access to justice all fall under a variety of legal systems. It is agreed that IHL should apply when there are sporadic outbursts of violence and a level of protracted violence. There is no indication as to what the threshold could be as the law is not interested in the length of an armed conflict but rather in its conduct and consequences. Hence why IHL will only apply once there has been an outbreak of violence, and IHRL will be applicable before, during and after this outbreak. The International Criminal Tribunal for the Former Yugoslavia (ICTY) theorised this approach in the Tadic case (Case No. IT-94–1-AR72, Appeals Chamber, 2 October 1995, para.70): it stated that there is an armed conflict 'whenever there is […] protracted armed violence between governmental authorities and organised armed groups or between such groups within a State', thereby triggering the enforcement of humanitarian principles. The Rome Statute of the International Criminal Court (ICC) has also addressed the concept of protracted conflict, raising questions pertaining to the creation of a sub-category of conflict, and with the possibility of creating further 'enabling arrangements of IHL' (Lewis, 2019: p.1113). The risk is developing an exceptional legal regime with regard to operational needs at the expense of protection of civilians. Complying with international law is complex when the issue of temporality is raised.

The concomitant application of IHRL and IHL in conflict has been criticised; some practitioners and scholars would prefer coming back to a strict separation between legal regimes according to conflict types. However, in the modern era the hybrid nature of conflict makes it impossible to disassociate applicable legal regimes.

Rules of Engagement (ROE)

ROE are often mistakenly assumed to be law as such: although they must be consistent with both national and international law applicable to the mission, they do not in themselves generally have the force of law and a soldier cannot be prosecuted in court for violating a ROE. Yet, they are seen as legally binding as they effectively constitute military orders (Cooper, 2014: p.208). While this relationship of ROE to law may seem counterintuitive, for practical purposes it should be remembered that, while ROE 'may … impose greater limitations on the actions of a soldier than national or international law would actually permit' (Rowe, 2007: p.329), they can never permit actions which are actually prohibited by rules of national or international law.[1] Control over forces is absolutely vital in any mission, across the full spectrum of military deployments – from non-combatant evacuation operations through peacekeeping operations to full-scale combat operations against hostile forces; it is the exercise of such control that distinguishes professionalised, properly commanded and controlled armed forces from disorderly violent mobs. Consider the typical circumstances of an infantry recruit: they are likely to be little more than 18 years old on average, with relatively little formal education, and equipped with weapons that give the effective power of life or death over other human beings. When confronted with an actually or potentially hostile environment, the chances are that the soldier will also be very scared. The question to be answered is: 'Do I shoot or not shoot?'. The stakes are high here, both in politico-military and in legal terms: the risks of unintended de-escalation or, substantially worse, escalation, are significant. Moreover, the consequences of non-compliance are potentially drastic for the soldier as they will likely face disciplinary and/or criminal investigations. ROE, then, are an essential mechanism for the authority to undertake specific actions, serving at the political-strategic level to set the operational parameters of a given mission and at the military-tactical level to control the soldiers' authorisation to use force, whether lethal or non-lethal. The form which ROE take will vary from one country to another, as will their substantive content based on the context of the operation. Although typically (and ideally) promulgated in advance of an operation, ROE must retain enough systemic flexibility to be changed quickly, following justified requests from commanders as the conditions of an operation and its strategic/tactical context change. Often imagined to be a set of pithy absolute rules with legal authority printed on a card issued to all soldiers, it is important to understand that this is not the case. This description relates to what is really a short, basic summary of the most important rules, in simple language which the average soldier can easily understand, remember and apply in combat. Referred to as 'soldier's cards', these small, laminated documents are small enough to fit into a uniform breast or hip pocket.

The full ROE are generally more expansive and also cover many situations apart from those involving the use of force, for example, use of specific weapons or weapons systems (including riot control equipment), detention or seizure of persons or equipment, 'buzzing' or sonic booms by aircraft, boarding of merchant vessels at sea. ROE have been well described as

> distill[ing] law, strategy and policy into tactical instructions for [military personnel] regarding when and against whom they can use force ... [they are] the most specific and direct manifestation of both law and policy on the ground. In effect, ROE tell [military personnel] how they can accomplish their mission – who they can kill and what they can destroy in the process of mission fulfilment.
>
> (Blank, 2011: pp.1–2)

ROE represent an intersection of three perspectives in the control of armed forces: policy, military operations, and law. At the policy level, they 'provide for the conduct of operations in compliance with national policy' in the strategic sense and ensure political accountability of the military command echelons to their civilian superiors in government. At the military level, they 'assist in the delineation of the circumstances and limitations within which military forces may be employed to achieve their objectives'. At the legal level, they 'provide for the judicious use of force in compliance with international [and national] law' (Mandsager, 2009: pp.1–2). Overall, their utility and effect may be summarised in the word: 'control'. Properly drafted and implemented ROE help to ensure that the application of force – which may result in people being wounded or killed and property being damaged or destroyed – is controlled such that it aligns with policy objectives and is subject to civilian political oversight, achieves the mission's legitimate military objectives while preventing unintended escalation or de-escalation, and is consistent with legal rules at the international and domestic levels (thereby helping to avoid legal liabilities, although the classified nature of ROE still may lead to problems of perception). A now-classic example of the use of ROE in a specific operation is provided by a famous episode of Operation Corporate, the British military campaign to retake the Falkland Islands from Argentine occupation in 1982.

Example 4.3: ROE adaptability

On 29 April 1982 the British submarine *HMS Conqueror*, deployed 35 miles outside the southern limit of the Total Exclusion Zone (TEZ) declared by the UK around the Argentine-occupied Falkland Islands, sighted the Argentine light cruiser *ARA General Belgrano*, the largest warship in the Argentine Navy, assuming her to be returning from patrol to Ushuaia. The ROE originally promulgated for the British Task Force authorised attack on Argentine forces only within the TEZ, as a way of limiting the conflict; but, aware now from British intelligence intercepts of an order to Argentine naval units to seek out and attack the Task Force, and realising the threat posed by *Belgrano* with her 15 6-inch guns, Prime Minister Margaret Thatcher's War Cabinet quickly authorised a change to the ROE so that Argentine forces could be attacked wherever they were encountered. On 2 May, acting under the amended ROE, *Conqueror* torpedoed and sank *Belgrano* with the loss of 323 lives. As a direct result, all Argentine naval units were ordered back to their bases, from which they were not allowed to emerge subsequently; this effectively ceded command of the sea in the operational theatre to the UK, granting the Task Force an enormous strategic advantage which strongly influenced the outcome of the campaign, as it ensured that the Argentine carrier-based aircraft no longer had the range to interdict the seas around the Falklands when the British were landing troops to retake the islands. The change to the ROE had implemented the British strategic policy objective of securing command of the sea and protecting the Task Force as it approached the Falklands, and the tactical military objective of destroying a major enemy naval unit, while complying with the law of armed conflict, according to which *Belgrano* was a legitimate military target, lawfully subject to attack.

ROE are flexible: standing ROE can be 'pulled off the shelf' for any relevant operation, while mission-specific, bespoke ROE are tailored to the needs of a particular operation. They can be used in the full spectrum of military deployments, from civil disturbances through peace support and humanitarian assistance operations to full-scale armed conflicts. They can prohibit a particular activity or permit it, with or without restrictions. Whilst ideally issued in advance of a deployment, they can be changed as circumstances warrant. In the contemporary operational context, ROE are more critical than ever as a tool for the oversight of armed forces within a politico-legal framework. In a world with increasingly destructive firepower, instantaneous worldwide communications and the pluralisation of information sources and media platforms, the careful control of troops on operations is essential to strategic communications and public opinion. Failures in communication, intelligence and understanding or application of promulgated ROE can be catastrophic not only to a particular operation – and any civilians unfortunate enough to be caught up in it – but also to broader perceptions of a mission as a whole, as happened when a 2009 US airstrike, called in by a German commander on two fuel tankers captured by Taliban insurgents near Kunduz, Afghanistan, killed 70–140 civilians (Marchant, 2020: pp.73–76). Future areas of practice to look out for will include ROE for military operations in cyberspace and outer space.

The use of force by States

An essential component of the legal control of State armed forces is ensuring that they are used in compliance with the international law governing the resort to force in international relations (*jus ad bellum*). The increasing awareness of potential legal liabilities on the part of the military chain of command is well illustrated by the disclosure that the British Chief of Defence Staff personally sought assurances from Prime Minister Tony Blair that the proposed Coalition invasion of Iraq in 2003 was lawful (Iraq Inquiry, 2011: pp.2–3). With the incorporation since then of a defined crime of aggression within the ICC Statute, potentially rendering senior political and military leaders liable for the unlawful use of force, military and civilian defence personnel need *a fortiori* to be cognisant of the legal framework in this field. The contemporary *jus ad bellum* is largely regulated by Chapter VII of the United Nations Charter, according to which the threat or use of force is generally prohibited, if it is 'against the territorial integrity or political independence of any state, or in any other manner inconsistent with the Purposes of the United Nations' (UN, 1945: Art.2(4)). The Charter only allows for two possible exceptions, which are relatively clear, but with a partial overlap with customary international law rules established long before 1945, and highly subjective in interpretation; and there are additionally certain other claimed justifications that are controversial or are supported by some States but not by others.

The most straightforward justification for the use of force is if it is undertaken as part of a collective security operation mandated by the UN Security Council (UNSC). The UNSC has the exclusive right to determine 'the existence of any threat to the peace, breach of the peace, or act of aggression' (Article 39 UN Charter). If provisional measures and/or sanctions are deemed inadequate, they may then proceed to 'take such action by air, sea, or land forces as may be necessary to maintain or restore international peace and security' (Article 42 UN Charter). Although it was originally envisaged that such action would be undertaken by the UN's own military forces, which would effectively be 'loaned' by Member States to the organisation under the special agreements foreseen in Article 43 and would then be controlled directly by the UNSC, no such agreements have ever been made. As a result, in a line of precedents stretching back to the authorisation given for the use of force in Korea in 1950 (UNSCs 83 and 84), the original coalition of the willing, the UNSC has evolved a practice of inviting States to contribute to missions wherein the use of force is effectively mandated as a collective security enforcement measure. The verbal cue for such action is for the enabling resolution to contain the formula 'all necessary means' or 'such measures as may be necessary'. Examples of such 'pure' use of force measures authorised by the UN since the Korean War are few and far between, but include the first Gulf War (UNSC 678), anti-piracy operations off the coast of Somalia (UNSCs 1816 and 1851), and enforcement of a 'no-fly zone' over Libya (UNSC 1973). It is also sometimes the case that such wording finds its way into elements of peacekeeping mandates, as in the 2013 creation of a Force Intervention Brigade within the United Nations Organization Stabilization Mission in the Democratic Republic of the Congo (MONUSCO), with the authority to undertake targeted offensive action to neutralise designated non-State actors (UNSCR 2098). It should be noted that peacekeeping missions, although involving the deployment of military forces, are not uses of force as such and do not fall under the Charter regime of Chapter VII.

By far the most important exception to the modern prohibition of the use of force by States, both in theory and in practice, is the right of self-defence. Acknowledged in Article 51 of the Charter, self-defence had existed as a right under customary international law – the law of nations developed over centuries of State practice and *opinio juris*[2] – long before the advent of the contemporary collective security architecture. It may be exercised by a State acting individually, or collectively as part of an alliance or in response to a request for assistance by a State that has been attacked: the best-known example of the former is Article 5 of the 1949 North Atlantic Treaty, while the latter is the basis for British military action against so-called Islamic State in Iraq and Syria since 2014. As the oldest justification for the State use of force and incontrovertibly established in classical jurisprudence (Grotius, 1625: Chapter I, §§II–XVI), nobody denies in principle that a State ultimately always has the right to defend itself; indeed, it is invariably the preferred justification cited by States when resorting unilaterally to force. The difficulties in adjudicating such claims lie in the fact that the criteria for the legality of self-defence differ between the Charter provisions and those of customary law, while perceptions of the applicability of those criteria in any given case are highly subjective, to say the least.

The Charter states:

> Nothing in the present Charter shall impair the inherent right of individual or collective self-defence if an armed attack occurs against a Member of the United Nations, until the Security Council has taken measures necessary to maintain international peace and security…

(Article 51 UN Charter)

The clarity and simplicity of this statement are deceptive: it neither defines what is meant by the phrase 'armed attack', nor stipulates any detailed conditions for the legality of an exercise of the right of self-defence. The International Court of Justice (ICJ) has addressed aspects of the right of self-defence in several high-profile cases over the decades, but the jurisprudence is fragmentary and, in some important respects, inconclusive: thus, there is little consensus in the international community about the application of the right in practice, and States are effectively left to make what argument they can for themselves. Whilst it is clear at least that in order for the right of self-defence to be engaged there needs to be an 'armed attack', which the ICJ has determined is constituted by 'the most grave forms of the use of force' (ICJ, 1986: p.101), Article 51's stipulation 'if an armed attack occurs' – meaning on a plain reading of the text that a State is obliged to wait *until an armed attack has occurred* – is inconsistent with both Article 2(4)'s prohibition of the *threat* or use of force and the longstanding customary law recognition of a pre-emptive aspect to the right of self-defence, such that a State may use force in self-defence by way of a 'first strike' if it believes an armed attack to be 'imminent' (Sofaer, 2003). Imminence in itself is a highly subjective perception, and each instance has to be judged on its own facts; it has been open to increasingly elastic interpretation in recent years, particularly in relation to countering threats from extraterritorial terrorist groups (Bethlehem, 2012; Wright, 2017). Customary law also requires that there be a *necessity* to use force in self-defence, and that any force so used be *proportionate* to the original threat or attack. The parameters of the self-defence concept continue to develop in connection with the potential for armed conflict to occur in cyberspace (Schmitt, 2017: pp.244–251), and will doubtless do so further as the domain for likely conflict expands to outer space, although it is worth noting that there are no new laws in these areas: the existing rules are applied by analogy.

Example 4.4: Anticipatory self-defence

Probably the best-known example of anticipatory self-defence in the post-1945 era, although not claimed as such at the time, was Israel's pre-emptive airstrike against the Egyptian Air Force at the start of the Six-Day War (1967). The question is: how do we judge the legal validity of a 'first strike'? The geo-political context and security environment are everything in such cases. Israel's decision to strike its enemies first was made after a conjunction of strategic developments: namely, Egypt's expulsion of the UN peacekeeping force that had been present in the Sinai since 1956, its blockade of the Straits of Tiran to Israeli shipping, its sending of troops to take up offensive positions on the Israeli frontier, its signing of a military pact with Jordan, escalating incidences of violence along Israel's frontier with Syria, and increasingly bellicose statements by Egyptian President Gamal Abdel Nasser (e.g., 'our basic objective will be to destroy Israel') – all combined to make the Israeli Cabinet conclude that an armed attack was imminent (Shapira, 1971: pp.66–68), an assessment with which most States at the time agreed and subsequently concurred. This precedent in part inspired Pakistan to take similar action, much less successfully, against India in 1971 in connection with the latter's aid to insurgents in Bangladesh.

The other principal justification that is sometimes advanced for the unilateral use of force by States is broadly termed humanitarian intervention. Whilst armed intervention is generally prohibited in international law because of its incompatibility with the fundamental principle of State sovereignty (Article 2(7) UN Charter; UNGA 2131), the suggested right of humanitarian intervention has its origins in the (largely undisputed) right of States to intervene in order to protect *their own nationals* in foreign territory, in situations where the host State is unwilling or unable to exercise such protection – for example, due to a civil war. However, since 1945 the notion of a State unilaterally – that is, without a mandate from the UN or another international organisation – intervening in foreign territory to protect *nationals of another State* from gross human rights violations, is much more controversial. The concept was first posited as a legal right in 1991 when the UK asserted it in the face of the UNSC's refusal to support a no-fly zone over northern Iraq for the protection of Iraqi Kurds against repression by Saddam Hussein's forces (UKHC, 2000: §§30–32), and then received a higher profile in connection with the Kosovo War in 1999 after Blair's famous speech to the Chicago Economic Club in which he posited a doctrine of the international community (Blair, 1999), whereby States could intervene unilaterally in order to put a stop to major humanitarian disasters like genocide or ethnic cleansing. The UK has since continued to invoke humanitarian intervention as justification for military action, most recently in connection with the 2018 airstrikes against chemical weapons facilities in Syria (UK Prime Minister's Office, 2018), but it would be fair to say that it has not attracted wider support in the international community as a whole; indeed, a substantial body of UN Member States have explicitly condemned it as contrary to the Charter and general international law (Group of 77 and China at the UN, 1999: §69).

An attempt has been made to put the concept of humanitarian intervention onto a more consensual, multilateral basis with the UN's adoption of the doctrine of Responsibility to Protect (R2P), originally recommended by the Canadian-established International Commission on Intervention and State Sovereignty. The R2P doctrine asserts that it is each State's primary responsibility to protect its own people – as a corollary of that sovereignty which is the foundation of the international legal order – but, if a State is unable or unwilling to do so, the international community may take diplomatic, humanitarian, *or other* steps to exercise such protection. Formally, the only legal authority for the use of force in such extreme cases remains a mandate adopted by the UNSC under Chapter VII of the Charter, so R2P does not in fact create a new, separate basis for the use of force by States. Despite its adoption by the UN (UNGA 60/1: §§138–139), many States consider it too open to abuse for geo-political reasons, and the only case where it has arguably been used to date is that of Libya (UNSCR 1973); even then, it is notable that the doctrine was not mentioned by name in the resolution authorising the action or in the debates preceding its adoption. It remains doubtful, therefore, that R2P presently constitutes a *legal right*; it is more in the nature of a *political aspiration*.

International Humanitarian Law (IHL)

Since the adoption of the four Geneva Conventions in 1949, members of armed forces have been increasingly aware of the need for familiarity with the rules of IHL, a branch of international law that regulates the conduct of hostilities and provides for the protection of certain specific categories of persons. IHL, also known as the law of armed conflict (LOAC) and, historically, as the laws of war, is a body of law, with roots in the ancient world, which has been vastly expanded and updated since the 1860s. Much of this expansion occurred around the turn of the 20th century and therefore was largely dictated, due to the structure of the world order at that time, by a select group of mostly European States, many of which possessed colonial empires; nevertheless, it bears emphasising that the traditions of honour and chivalry that underlie much of IHL are universal in nature. This has only been reinforced in modern times by the fact that every recognised State in the world is party to the Geneva Conventions.

IHL applies in all armed conflicts, whether declared or not, and applies equally to all parties to an armed conflict: it matters not who is the aggressor, and who the victim of aggression, and the application of IHL does not depend on reciprocity. A number of rules, e.g., those defining combatant status, and consequent prisoner of war (POW) status for captured personnel apply only in international armed conflicts, but a great many others are now considered to apply equally in non-international armed conflicts and thus bind non-State actors equally with States. (Henckaerts & Doswald-Beck, 2005). The treaties – now numbering in excess of 100 – range in their coverage from the very specific (e.g., prohibiting certain types of weapons) to the very general (e.g., the Additional Protocols to the Geneva Conventions); the oldest one dates from 1856, the newest from 2017. Although these instruments contain a multitude of detailed regulations, their essence may be distilled in the following fundamental principles:

- *Military necessity* – operations are permitted for legitimate military aims, i.e. whatever is necessary to defeat the enemy, provided they do not violate substantive rules of IHL;
- *Humanity* – the object of war being the defeat (but not the annihilation) of the enemy, operations must be conducted in such a way as to minimise unnecessary loss of life and destruction of property;
- *Distinction* – attacks are to be directed only at combatants and military objectives, civilians and civilian objects are not to be deliberately attacked but must be spared as much as possible; and

- ***Proportionality*** – deaths of civilians and destruction of civilian property incidental to attacks on lawful military objectives must not be excessive in relation to the military advantage anticipated from those attacks (Convention IV).

Special protections are stipulated for certain classes of object (e.g., hospitals, cultural property) and categories of persons (e.g., wounded and sick, POWs), and the civilian population generally should be spared as much as possible from the effects of military operations. To that end, military commanders are required to exercise precautions in attack, with particular regard to the aforementioned principles of distinction and proportionality (Schmitt, 2010).

In international armed conflicts, everyone has the legal status of being either a combatant or a civilian – the former being defined as members of regular State armed forces, or militia satisfying the criteria of:

- Being under responsible command;
- Having a fixed distinctive emblem;
- Carrying arms openly; and
- Conducting operations in accordance with LOAC (Hague Regulations, 1907: Article.1).

Military objectives are defined as, 'objects which by their nature, location, purpose or use make an effective contribution to military action and whose total or partial destruction, capture or neutralization, in the circumstances ruling at the time, offers a definite military advantage' (Article 52 (2) Protocol I, 1977). These rules, despite appearing relatively clear-cut, are not easy to interpret in the heat of battle and do not in themselves take account of either civilians who directly participate in hostilities, or so-called 'dual-use objects'. Moreover, whilst it is important to appreciate that proportionate loss of civilian life or destruction of civilian objects incidental to an attack on a lawful military objective – colloquially known as 'collateral damage' – is actually permitted under IHL, that is not how the media or the court of public opinion tends to see it. The rules can be remarkably difficult to apply, particularly in the urban environments (often with the civilian population still *in situ*) that form an increasing number of the world's battlefields. Consequently, it is extremely important that soldiers are properly instructed in the rules of IHL and how to apply them, as mandated by the current treaty law, and that commanders take care to prevent and punish violations (Articles 82–87 Protocol I, 1977). Even such precautions, however, face difficulties in the context of modern 'hybrid warfare': the blend of political confrontation and militarised provocations (including in the cyber domain) while never quite crossing the line into open conflict, combined with plausible deniability and the manipulation of media and social media, makes for a fog of war that is even thicker than usual. In these circumstances the law, too, can be twisted and 'reinterpreted' – as in recent reinterpretations of the concept of imminence in the right of self-defence or the misrepresentation of civilian casualties (even humanitarian aid workers, as in Syria) on the battlefield as 'terrorists' – to the benefit of certain already-powerful actors, without having conformed to any conventional international law-making process.

Conclusion

The legal framework by which the governance of security is assured is of critical importance to practitioners in the field. Any State designing a security apparatus should therefore include reflections on constitutional law, IHRL and IHL, a wide-ranging body of law that governs the actions of the State and its security forces at all times. IHRL and IHL both apply across the spectrum of State security activity, from peacetime through internal security and counterinsurgency operations, to situations of non-international and international armed conflict.

Notes

1. For example, ROE prohibiting attacks if any collateral damage is anticipated are acceptable, since collateral damage as such is not illegal; but ROE authorising the killing of survivors from enemy warships sunk in maritime operations are unacceptable, since the deliberate killing of shipwrecked survivors constitutes wilful murder of persons protected by Geneva Convention II (1949), which is a grave breach of that Convention (i.e., a war crime).
2. Literally, 'opinion of law', i.e., the belief that a particular mode of conduct is required as a positive legal obligation.

Questions to consider

1. Should IHL apply to armed forces in peacetime?
2. Should IHL be the primary legal regime during conflict or is IHRL equally relevant?
3. Can the established framework of the jus ad bellum survive the advent of new domains of warfare, such as outer space and cyberspace?
4. How can the application of IHL be operationalised in situations of 'hybrid war'?

Suggested readings

Gray, C. (2018) *International Law and the Use of Force* 4th ed., Oxford: Oxford University Press, DOI: 10.1093/law/9780198808411.001.0001

Fikfak, V. (2019) 'Changing state behaviour: Damages before the European Court of Human Rights', *European Journal of International Law*, *29(4)*, pp. 1091–1125. DOI: 10.1093/ejil/chy064

Lamp, N. (2011) 'Conceptions of war and paradigms of compliance: The 'new war' challenge to international humanitarian law', *Journal of Conflict and Security Law*, *16(2)*, pp. 225–262. DOI: 10.1093/jcsl/krr005

Mačák, M. (2018) *Internationalized Armed Conflicts in International Law*, Oxford: Oxford University Press.

Sari, A. (2020) 'Legal resilience in an era of grey zone conflicts and hybrid threats', *Cambridge Review of International Affairs*, *33(6)*, pp. 846–867. DOI: 10.1080/09557571.2020.1752147

Van Dijk, B. (2018) 'Human rights in war: On the entangled foundations of the 1949 Geneva conventions', *American Journal of International Law*, *112(4)*, pp. 553–582. DOI: 10.1017/ajil.2018.84

References

Abenheim, D. & Halladay, C. (2012) 'Stability in flux: Policy, strategy, and institutions in Germany'. In: F.C. Mattei & T.C. Bruneau, eds., *The Routledge Handbook of Civil Military Relations*, London: Routledge, pp. 304–317.

Bethlehem, D. (2012) 'Self-defense against an imminent or actual armed attack by non-state actors', *American Journal of International Law*, *106 (4)*, pp. 770–777. DOI: 10.5305/amerjintelaw.106.4.0769

Blair, T. (1999) 'Doctrine of the international community', 24 April 1999. Available at https://webarchive.nationalarchives.gov.uk/+/http://www.number10.gov.uk/Page1297 [Accessed 27 August 2020].

Blank, L.R. (2011) 'Rules of engagement: Law, strategy and leadership'. In: *Aspects of Leadership: Ethics, Law and Spirituality*, Marine Corps University 2012, Emory Public Law Research Paper No. 11(168). Available at https://ssrn.com/abstract=1872505 [Accessed 27 August 2020].

Convention (IV) respecting the Laws and Customs of War on Land and its annex: Regulations concerning the Laws and Customs of War on Land. The Hague, 18 October 1907. Available at https://ihl-databases.icrc.org/applic/ihl/ihl.nsf/Treaty.xsp?action=openDocument&documentId=4D47F92DF3966A7EC12563CD002D6788 [Accessed 29 August 2020].

Sriram, C.L., Martin-Ortega, O. & Herman, J. (2009) *War, Conflict and Human Rights: Theory and Practice*. London: Routledge.

Cooper, C.G. (2014) 'Rules of engagement demystified: A study of the history, development and use of ROEs', *Military Law and the Law of War Review, 53 (2)*, pp. 189–246.

Grotius, H. (1625) *The Rights of War and Peace*, Book *II* (2005 ed.), Indianapolis: Liberty Fund, Inc. Available at https://oll.libertyfund.org/titles/grotius-the-rights-of-war-and-peace-2005-ed-vol-2-book-ii [Accessed 24 August 2020].

Group of 77 and China at the UN (1999) *Ministerial Declaration (XXIII) of 24 September 1999*. Available at https://www.g77.org/doc/Decl1999.html [Accessed 27 August 2020].

Hathaway O.A. (2007) 'Why do countries commit to human rights treaties?', *Journal of Conflict Resolution, 51 (4)*, pp. 588–621. DOI: 10.1177/0022002707303046

Henckaerts, J.-M. & Doswald-Beck, L. (eds). (2005) *Customary International Humanitarian Law*, Cambridge: Cambridge University Press & International Committee of the Red Cross.

International Court of Justice (ICJ) (1986) *Military and Paramilitary Activities in and against Nicaragua (Nicaragua v. United States of America), Merits, Judgment*, I.C.J. Reports 1986.

Iraq Inquiry (2011) *Witness statement – Admiral the Lord Boyce*, 7 January 2011. Available at https://webarchive.nationalarchives.gov.uk/20171123123539/http://www.iraqinquiry.org.uk/the-evidence/witnesses/b/admiral-the-lord-boyce/ [Accessed 23 August 2020].

Kelsen, H. (2005) *Pure Theory of Law*, Clark, N.J: Lawbook Exchange Ltd.

Kutz, M. (2003) 'Innere Führung – Leadership and civic education in the German Armed Forces', *Connections, 2 (3)*, pp. 109–124.

Lewis, D. (2019) 'The notion of "protracted armed conflict" in the Rome Statute and the termination of armed conflicts under international law: An analysis of select issues', *International Review of the Red Cross, 101 (912)*, pp. 1091–1115. DOI:10.1017/S1816383120000028

Mandsager, D. (ed.) (2009) *Sanremo Handbook on Rules of Engagement*, Sanremo: International Institute of Humanitarian Law.

Marchant, E.J. (2020) 'Insufficient knowledge in Kunduz: The precautionary principle and international humanitarian law', *Journal of Conflict & Security Law* [online], *25 (1)*, pp. 53–79. DOI:10.1093/jcsl/krz033

Nolte, G. & Krieger, H. (2003) 'Military Law in Germany'. In: G. Nolte, ed., *European Military Law Systems*, Berlin: De Gruyter, pp. 337–426.

Oberleitner, G. (2015) *Exclusivity: The Misconceived Idea of Lex Specialis*, Cambridge: Cambridge University Press.

Protocol Additional to the Geneva Conventions of 12 August 1949, and relating to the Protection of Victims of International Armed Conflicts (Protocol I). Geneva, 8 June 1977. Available at https://ihl-databases.icrc.org/applic/ihl/ihl.nsf/Treaty.xsp?documentId=D9E6B-6264D7723C3C12563CD002D6CE4&action=openDocument [Accessed 29 August 2020].

Rowe, P. (2007) 'The rules of engagement in occupied territory: Should they be published?', *Melbourne Journal of International Law* [online], *8 (2)*, pp. 327–339. Available at https://academic.oup.com/jcsl/article-abstract/25/1/53/5709881?redirectedFrom=fulltext [Accessed 25 August 2020].

Sassòli, M. (2011) 'The role of human rights and international humanitarian law in new types of armed conflicts'. In: O. Ben-Naftali, ed. *International Humanitarian Law and International Human Rights Law*, Oxford: Oxford University Press.

Sassòli, M. and Olson L.M. (2008) 'The relationship between international humanitarian and human rights law where it matters: Admissible killing and internment of fighters in non-international armed conflicts', *International Review of the Red Cross*, 90 *(871)*, pp. 599–627.

Schmitt, M.N. (2010) 'Military necessity and humanity in international humanitarian law: Preserving the delicate balance', *Virginia Journal of International Law*, 50 *(4)*, pp. 795–839.

Schmitt, M.N. (2017) 'Peacetime cyber responses and wartime cyber operations under international law: An analytical vade mecum', *Harvard National Security Journal* [online], 8 *(2)*, pp. 239–282. Available at https://harvardnsj.org/wp-content/uploads/sites/13/2017/02/Schmitt-NSJ-Vol-8.pdf [Accessed 23 August 2020].

Shapira, A. (1971) 'The six-day war and the right of self-defence', *Israel Law Review*, 6 *(1)*, pp. 65–80. DOI: https://doi.org/10.1017/S0021223700002843.

Sofaer, A.D. (2003) 'On the necessity of pre-emption', *European Journal of International Law*, 14 *(2)*, pp. 209–226. Available at http://ejil.org/pdfs/14/2/411.pdf [Accessed 23 August 2020].

UK House of Commons, Select Committee on Defence (UKHC) (2000) *Thirteenth Report of Session 1999–2000*, HC 453. Available at https://publications.parliament.uk/pa/cm199900/cmselect/cmdfence/453/45302.htm [Accessed 27 August 2020].

UK Prime Minister's Office (2018) *Syria Action – UK Government Legal Position*, 14 April 2018. Available at https://www.gov.uk/government/publications/syria-action-uk-government-legal-position/syria-action-uk-government-legal-position [Accessed 27 August 2020].

UN (1945) *Charter of the United Nations*, 26 June 1945. Available at https://www.un.org/en/charter-united-nations/index.html [Accessed 23 August 2020].

UNGA, *Resolution 2131 (XX), Declaration on the Inadmissibility of Intervention in the Domestic Affairs of States and the Protection of their Independence and Sovereignty*, 21 December 1965. Available at https://undocs.org/en/A/RES/2131(XX) [Accessed 27 August 2020].

UNGA, *Resolution 60/1, 2005 World Summit Outcome*, 16 September 2005. Available at https://documents-dds-ny.un.org/doc/UNDOC/GEN/N05/487/60/pdf/N0548760.pdf?OpenElement [Accessed 27 August 2020].

UNSC, *Resolution 83 of 27 June 1950 [S/1511]; Resolution 84 of 7 July 1950* [S/1588]. Available at https://undocs.org/S/RES/84(1950) [Accessed 23 August 2020].

UNSC, *Resolution 678 of 29 November 1990* [S/RES/678]. Available at https://undocs.org/S/RES/678(1990) [Accessed 24 August 2020].

UNSC, *Resolution 1816 of 2 June 2008* [S/RES/1816]. Available at https://undocs.org/S/RES/1816(2008) [Accessed 24 August 2020].

UNSC, *Resolution 1851 of 16 December 2008* [S/RES/1851]. Available at https://undocs.org/S/RES/1851(2008) [Accessed 24 August 2020].

UNSC, *Resolution 1973 of 17 March 2011* [S/RES/1973]. Available at https://undocs.org/S/RES/1973(2011) [Accessed 24 March 2020].

UNSC, *Resolution 2098 of 28 March 2013* [S/RES/2098]. Available at https://undocs.org/S/RES/2098(2013) [Accessed 23 August 2020].

Wright, J. (2017) *Attorney General's Speech at the International Institute for Strategic Studies*, 11 January 2017. Available at https://www.gov.uk/government/speeches/attorney-generals-speech-at-the-international-institute-for-strategic-studies [Accessed 26 August 2020].

5 Policy formation and implementation

David Chuter

Introduction

Governments are elected to do things. Electorates expect them to manage continuing problems, and react to new ones. This is as true of security as anything, and so there is a need for a well thought-out and well-organised system for security policy-making, linked to a clear system for its implementation.

A word on definitions first. There is a ceaseless debate about the meanings of the English words 'policy' and 'strategy', and the two are often used interchangeably, sometimes in the same document. The easiest way to differentiate between them is to refer to the original root of each word. *'Policy'* comes, via Latin and French, from the same Greek root that gives us 'politics', 'politician' and the old-fashioned 'polity', meaning 'state' or 'political unit'. (Indeed, in some European languages, the word for 'politics' is the same as the word for 'policy'.) This suggests that we can usefully confine 'policy' to the aspirations and plans of governments. On the other hand, 'strategy' comes ultimately from the Greek word for 'General', so it is better to reserve it for practical activities by security institutions to *implement* policy. This is how 'policy' will be defined in this chapter.

Example 5.1: Policy and strategy

To take a simple example: both the UK and France have independent national nuclear systems. This is sometimes described as a 'policy', although in fact it is really an example of an implementation of one. The policy objective, in each case, is national autonomy and enhanced status in NATO and the UN, and, in very different ways, some influence over the United States. This is one of the strategies employed in support of that policy. Others include the maintenance of a substantial Intelligence capability, a domestic armaments industry and so forth.

In this context, we should perhaps also distinguish between *doctrine* (from the Latin word meaning 'what is to be taught') which tells security forces, and especially the military, how to go about their business, and *concepts*, which are much more general sets of assumptions about how operations should be carried out. In western usage, both relate to more detailed implementation of policy, and then of strategy, and so are not considered further here. However, it should be noted that, for example, in countries influenced by the former Soviet Union, 'doctrine', has a much wider meaning. Attempts

DOI: 10.4324/9781003137061-5

by the author and others to discuss these issues with students around the world have often fallen victim to such linguistic and interpretation problems.

Of course, the political leadership and its advisors cannot implement policy by themselves. Policy has to be informed and implemented by operational institutions that operate from the strategic level downwards. Likewise, a policy-making Ministry will inevitably be involved in issues of strategy, just as strategic-level institutions (such as a Defence HQ) will advise on what policies are actually feasible and how they may be carried out.

Thus, security policy is not the same as statements or publications by government on security issues. Policy is what governments decide to do, and then carry out, not just what they say. Likewise, the security sector, as a major area of government, cannot avoid being impacted by policies, laws and developments elsewhere. It is unlikely, for example, that pensions in the security sector can be managed in a way that takes no account of a government's pensions policy generally.

Basic principles

To carry out their duties to electors and taxpayers, governments have various operational institutions at their disposal, organised into different sectors. The security sector is one, and will generally include a police service, a prison service, military, customs and border forces, intelligence services, and perhaps others. Like other sectors (for example, health or education), security requires the contributions of a number of organisations, and affects many more, and so it requires policy direction from Ministries, as well as a degree of central coordination. More is said about this in Chapter 7. The operational security institutions themselves have two principal characteristics:

- They are *executive* arms of the state, concerned with turning security policy into practical action.
- They *advise* on the making of policy, but they do not make it themselves, any more than teachers make education policy.

As the previous examples indicate, security policy should not be considered in isolation, but rather as part of a hierarchy of government policies. At the top, obviously, is overall government policy. Below this, are the foreign and interior policies of the state, and below that, one would normally find sectoral policies, including security policy. Finally, there should be individual policies for each part of each sector. The area of *Security Policy* is where the total contribution of the different institutions is planned and coordinated, to support the overall policies of the government. By definition, therefore, security policy questions have implications for more than one part of the security sector. From a very long list, examples may include:

- Security relations with neighbours and others
- Policy towards regional organisations and the UN
- Intelligence priorities and collection
- Cyber defence and security
- Transnational organised crime, trafficking and terrorism

- Peacekeeping and participation in multinational operations
- Security of borders, natural resources and shipping.

This gives us, in principle a simple hierarchy:

- Government Policy
- Foreign and Interior Policy
- Security Policy
- Defence, Police, Intelligence, etc. Policy.

Needless to say, this description is normative, and few if any states manage it perfectly. Indeed, many states have failed to develop a security policy at all, even after much effort. Nonetheless, it represents both a reasonable aspiration and also a reasonable expectation by professionals in the security sector, that government will tell them what it wants the sector to do. The aim should be to develop a proper security policy, which we can define as:

> A Policy for maintaining, coordinating and employing the assets of the security sector so that they contribute optimally to the government's overall foreign and interior policy objectives, whilst respecting the sectoral policies of the government in other areas.

This has to be understood primarily as a hierarchy of status and importance, not of action: that is to say, it is not necessary for each level to wait for the level above to finish its work. In fact, this hierarchy has two important characteristics:

- The levels are not completely distinct from each other.
- Each level is influenced by those below it.

In particular, the formation of higher policy has to take account of what is actually possible. Thus, what we have here is something scientists call a *tangled hierarchy* which is to say that each level affects the others. An example may make this clearer.

Example 5.2: Tangled hierarchy

A stable and prosperous state is frequently criticised by its neighbours because it is reluctant to take part in regional peacekeeping missions. At a regional political summit, the President (accompanied only by the Foreign Minister) is unexpectedly presented with a demand to make a contribution to a forthcoming mission, and, for wider political reasons, agrees to do so. There is no time to get specialist advice. The Ministry of Defence is very concerned when it hears of this agreement, and the Minister and the Chief of Defence (CHOD) explain that there are no forces trained in peacekeeping, and that the military has no experience of foreign deployments. In addition, the defence forces are in the middle of a five-year major reorganisation. The President accepts that what has been agreed will be difficult, but the Minister and the CHOD accept that higher-level political objectives have to take precedence, and agree to do what they can.

This kind of situation – often encountered in real life – illustrates the need for a flexible hierarchy which seeks policy advice from below. In this situation, it would have been wise for the President's Office to have anticipated the demands, and asked the Ministry of Defence what might be feasible. That is how a sensible security policy works in practice, whereas here, a new security policy has effectively been developed on the spot, without a reality check. Precedents like this have a way of determining security policy ever after. So, for example, Ghanaian officials will tell you publicly that participation in international and UN Peacekeeping is part of their security policy. They will tell you privately, however, that it is simply a *practice*, now hallowed by time, which earns money from the UN and ensures that at least a part of the Army – which has played a role in politics in the past – is out of the country.

Practice is complicated

An effective security policy should reflect the government's overall objectives and policies, and should in turn serve as a guide for policies of individual Ministries. Yet practice is more complicated, and there are three particular reasons why this may be so.

First, political power may distort the smooth operation of the hierarchy shown previously. Rather than government policy determining security policy, it may be dominated by it, and the security forces may ultimately dictate wider government policy. This happens for a variety of reasons. In Pakistan, for example, the military sees itself (and to some extent is seen by others) as all that stands between the country and annihilation. So historically the Chief of the Army Staff formed part of a triumvirate, with the President and Prime Minister, to decide major issues of government policy. Likewise, the powerful Inter-Services Intelligence organisation has a long history of interfering in the tabulation of election results to make sure the right people win.

In countries like Algeria or Zimbabwe, on the other hand, the Army has historically had great power and prestige, derived from its origins in the military forces that liberated the country. As a result, there is a striking difference in how security policy is made in Algeria compared with Tunisia, and in Zimbabwe compared with Zambia.

Tradition also may give parts of the security forces special status. In the Iberian tradition, for example, which was exported to Latin America, the military not only had a constabulary role, but were also seen as the ultimate guardians of the security and interests of the country. This kind of distortion can produce a 'securocratic' approach – i.e., problems are seen through a security lens first. This can be true even in very mundane cases. For example, on several occasions, international students were asked whether the military should have a say in school curricula, notably physical training, to ensure that young people were ready for military service. The majority thought they should.

The second possibility is disunity and competition between the different parts of the security sector. This may be because (as in Lebanon) parts of the security sector, like other state organs, may be identified primarily with one specific community. It is often just because the system is large and cumbersome. The prototypical example is the United States which has a large number of very powerful and almost wholly independent security organisations, competing against each other, and operating largely independently. Any form of coherent security policy is agonisingly difficult to establish, and almost impossible to enforce.

Finally, the security sector may be divided against itself. In some cases, this can be positive: the already mentioned Lebanese case, enables each of the major communities to feel that it has a stake in the security sector. In Senegal, on the other hand, there is both a military and a gendarmerie, and the rivalry between the two contributes to the stability of the country, if not necessarily the coherence of its security policy.

Of course, the stability of the country has to be the first priority of any political system, and this involves ensuring the integrity and survival of the political system itself. In a developed democracy, the state and the legitimate government should ideally be able to rely on the security forces for this. But governments which feel themselves under threat, and doubt that they have the security forces under control may well take measures for their own survival, even if they undermine the coherence of the system. (It is better, after all, to be inefficient than dead.) Key units or capabilities may be put in the hands of family or clan members, parallel security systems may be created, and capable military units may be disbanded if seen as a threat: this was the case, for example, in Zaire under President Mobutu (1965–97). Intelligence organisations, vital for the survival of any political system, may deliberately be given overlapping and competing mandates and encouraged to spy on each other: this certainly happened in Saddam Hussein's Iraq, and also appears to be the case within the Assad regime in Syria.

Mechanics

But assuming that the political leadership can count on the loyalty of the security forces, and that these forces are both relatively capable and prepared to work together, what are the mechanics of security policy, and what is it about? First, we need to remember that policy of any kind is a government responsibility. The government typically says what it wants, and its professional advisers provide it with options for making it happen. Other parts of the political system (notably Parliament and the Courts) have separate constitutional roles but they do not make policy. Second, security policy is not made through conferences, or consultations: it is the security component and reflection of the government's strategic objectives, and it is from the government as a whole that guidance should be expected and even demanded. (Of course, the detail and the implementation of security policy may well involve public debate, but that is a different issue.)

Security policy should not be a kind of compromise or least common denominator between what the different security institutions are willing to accept. It needs to be a reflection of wider government policy, driven from the very top. Of course, in practice, different organisations will have different ideas about what can and should be done, and how to respond to crises and challenges, and there will be rivalry and competition. But again, it is the responsibility of the political leadership to keep such debates within limits, and to set up whatever structures are needed to get a proper answer.

Nor should security policy become a kind of grotesque auction, in which different 'threats' are allowed to flourish by different organisations to acquire more influence and larger budgets. Indeed 'threat' as a concept for national security planning is generally unhelpful, and is really an ideological leftover from the security thinking of the 19th and early 20th centuries (see Chapter 2). Whilst there are still countries which do face an articulated military threat from foreign powers with the capability to destroy them (Iran is an obvious case) and others who have to deal with a much larger neighbour (Vietnam and Ukraine for example), most countries are not in that situation. 'Threatism', as it may be called, encourages an unseemly competition in which threats are exaggerated and even invented sometimes, and is not a satisfactory basis for planning.

Security policy questions are fundamentally those where the interests of more than one institution are involved, or where there are wider political and financial impacts to take into account. Whilst there should be nothing in the activities of security institutions that is *inconsistent* with overall security policy, many decisions can safely be left to the institutions themselves. For example, changes to the length and syllabus of military or police training are really management issues for the relevant institutions and Ministries to address. On the other hand, a decision to move away from national service and towards a volunteer force will have profound implications for the security forces as a whole, as well as having many financial, political and procurement consequences. The government as a whole, including even the Pensions Ministry and the Ministry of Foreign Affairs, will need to be involved.

In terms of the actual mechanics of security policy-making, it is useful to divide questions into three types: the Active, the Passive and the Unavoidable. (This distinction is not peculiar to security issues: it is found throughout politics and government.)

Much of politics and government consists of dealing, as best you can, with the *Unavoidable*: 'events' that 'just happen' as the former British Prime Minister Harold Macmillan once put it. An aircraft accident, a corruption allegation, a high-profile legal case, a sudden fall in the value of your currency, an unexpected resignation, a political crisis in your neighbour's country ... the list is almost endless. Little of this can be anticipated in advance, and it is pointless, and probably counter-productive, to try to have very detailed policies to cover every possibility. Almost by definition, what happens will be the one thing you did not expect. However, any good security policy should incorporate some sensible contingency planning, so that you know what *kind* of response you may need to consider.

For example, all governments are interested in the stability of their neighbours. If your neighbour is always having political crises but they are rarely serious, then your security policy reaction to the latest crisis may be limited to making sure that reports from your Embassy and your own analysts are widely distributed. But if the neighbouring country is inherently deeply unstable, and the possibility of violence and even conflict is always present, then you need contingency measures for everything from potential conciliation initiatives to coping with an influx of refugees. The aim of such a policy, once more, is not to have everything planned in advance, but to be as prepared as possible for whatever may happen.

Then there is a category of security problems in which you are a *passive recipient*. A recurrent boundary or natural resources dispute with your neighbour, trafficking and organised crime, superpower initiatives or competition, violent tensions between different communities, positions to choose on controversial issues in regional or international organisations .... once more the list is a very long one. The origins of such problems may lie in the past, or are otherwise beyond your control.

Much of the business of security policy-making is of this kind, and the danger is of confusing these problems with the Unavoidable kind: which is to say, allowing problems to fester for long periods because there is not the time or inclination to consider them properly, consequently you have to deal with individual crises as they occur, rather than with the underlying problem. In the case of a border dispute for example, you might recognise that any resolution is unlikely in the near future, but this should not prevent you developing a security policy concept of how you would *wish* the problem to be resolved, to guide your behaviour in the periodic flare-ups that are inevitable in such a subject. (Such a dispute between Chile and Bolivia was, indeed, resolved by the ICJ in 2018. That between India and Pakistan has remained unresolved since 1947, and it is probably in the interest of neither country that it should be). In that way, short-term crises can be handled in a way that ideally brings you closer to your long-term objective, or at least does not take you further from it.

Less dramatic, but often as important for day-to-day policy-making is the extensive, diffuse and constantly changing popular international security agenda, fixed largely by western governments and NGOs and international organisations, with help from, and sometimes manipulation by, the media. An illustrative list of such topics over the last 25 years would include, amongst others, land mines, small arms and light weapons, child soldiers, sexual and gender-based violence in war, international courts, terrorism, and refugees and migration.

Irrespective of the degree of inherent importance of such topics they insinuate their way onto the security agenda – often in competition with each other – because of the financial and political influence of those promoting them. Whatever nations may privately feel, it is necessary to take note of them and to decide on a response, whether substantive or simply procedural.

Finally, there is the relatively small area of security policy where a country can be properly *active*. Even for large and powerful states, true and unconstrained freedom of action is very rare, but it is possible, even if it amounts to as little as an informed and free choice between options. The danger, however, is that the need to deal with the issues of the day crowds out the process of actually formulating a proactive policy. The result can be to have a security policy (since in practice it is impossible *not* to have one) that is just a series of ad hoc decisions, which eventually leave you far from where you started, in a place you had no intention to go.

One way in which it is easier to have a proactive security policy is through creating effective and well-coordinated institutions, as described in Chapter 7, but even more important perhaps, is the need for a clear consensus about the actual security interests of the country. Such a consensus should not be artificially forced, nor should it be a laborious compromise or a vague slogan. Concepts such as *Ubuntu* (roughly meaning, being human) offered as a basis for security policy by the South African government a few years ago, whilst praiseworthy, are not easy to operationalise.

In countries where there is no real agreement between major players about what the security interests of the country actually are, developing a proper security policy becomes effectively impossible. So, quite elaborate formal 'security policies' may be written, and even published in elegant documents whose principal function is to disguise the fact that no consensus exists on fundamental issues. A useful question to ask those flourishing such documents is precisely *how* their high-level orientations are reflected in planning and the conduct of security policy day to day. Often, the relationship is exactly the reverse: so-called 'security policy' is simply a statement of what is being done, or what is anyway unavoidable, dressed up to look like policy.

Although the list of potential subjects for an active security policy is, like the others, very long, a few indications can be given of possible subjects and how they might be addressed. Suppose, for example, a state has significant natural resources, such as oil and gas, minerals or fish. On the one hand, the state will want to benefit economically from these resources, and will probably invest in their protection. This needs to be done in an organised fashion, and as part of an integrated policy. On the other hand, the state will have neighbours, who might share some of the problems, but might also have competing objectives, notably in issues like fishing. An overall policy on resources, therefore, will have to take into account dimensions ranging from law enforcement and prevention of theft to diplomacy.

Another example might be policy for confronting violent separatism in one part of the country, perhaps based on ethnic or religious differences. Here, it is important to understand the nature of the separatist movement, their degree of support, their degree of international backing, if any, and their links with other problems such as organised crime. From that understanding, it is possible to develop an active policy which combines political, economic and classic security responses. Such problems may not always be as simple as they first appear: for example, separatist movements are seldom united, and may even fight amongst themselves. Likewise, the media and the political elites may be fixated on the (perhaps) limited problem of terrorism, but in the region itself the separatists may be using violence primarily to control or polarise the population. Without a sophisticated understanding of such issues, it is likely that the response will not be well adapted and that there will be the risk of overreacting and treating the problem as entirely one of conflict and law enforcement. As Wilkinson and Cleary argued in Chapter 2, the analysis of the strategic context is an important step in determining policy responses and the capabilities required for execution.

The use of a state's intelligence apparatus is always a general security policy question. Some of the institutional features of intelligence are covered in Chapter 7, but here it is worth stressing the importance for an effective security policy in the careful tasking of intelligence agencies, and the sensible use of their products. These agencies are essentially the providers of sensitive security-related information to enable high-level decisions to be made. They should not be allowed to become separate centres of policy advice, still less of policy-making. Intelligence agencies are also an important part of the international side of security policy. At its simplest, because intelligence is a market, having information and analysis to share buys you useful favours and information from abroad. It also provides a basis for cooperation and, indeed, influencing other countries to your way of thinking.

The same logic broadly applies to other parts of the security sector. The level of expertise in police forces, for example, varies enormously between countries. Developing a capability for criminal intelligence work is not only useful domestically, it provides access to a relatively small international club, and the possibility of influencing others. Indeed, tackling transnational organised crime is by definition an international task, and countries who do it well can expect to increase their international status and influence.

Example 5.3: Police and the Intelligence function

Prior to the 2014 referendum on Scottish independence, the Scottish Government commissioned a number of studies into how an independent Scotland could provide for its own security. One of those studies explored whether and how Scotland should develop its own intelligence capabilities. Three options were explored: 1) continuing access to the rump UK's domestic and foreign intelligence services (MI5 and MI6 respectively); 2) developing independent intelligence capabilities, and, 3) expanding the intelligence functions of Police Scotland (the national, unified Police Service). The third option was viewed as having several merits. Police Scotland already had an intelligence capability based on a long history of policing against sectarianism and serious organised crime, which in turn meant that the Service had well established links with other national police forces and international databases. Further, it would take less time and money to expand upon an existing capability then it would to create two new organisations.

It is probably with defence forces that there is the greatest opportunity to conduct a wider and more sophisticated security policy. First, though, we need to divest ourselves of the reductivist view of defence forces that sees their role in overly simplistic terms – for example 'to fight and win wars' in a work which has unfortunately been influential (Huntington, 1957: p.90). Although even today most constitutions define the role of defence forces merely as the protection of national territory and the nation's interests, it is doubtful whether the roles of defence forces have ever, in practice, been conceived so simply by those who use them. In practice, defence forces, if intelligently used and well trained, can be a major force multiplier for the wider political and security policy objectives of a state (as discussed in Chapter 9). Some simple examples are given below.

International negotiations are like a game of poker: the outcome depends on what cards you have and how skilfully you play. Well-trained and expert defence forces give nations options in the international arena, but they also provide them with negotiating capital. This is most noticeable in the case of nuclear-weapon states, but it applies pervasively. In the UN Security Council or in regional debates, possession of defence forces of a reasonable size, provided they are well-trained and deployable, enable a state to influence debates on security issues. Mandates for international missions, for example, will be disproportionately influenced by states with capable forces and with experience of deploying them abroad. Important command positions will tend to be reserved for states with a history of commanding international missions, or at least armies where the higher levels of command are frequently exercised. Outside these international forums, states are often invited to give views or help define international procedures on the basis of their military capabilities.

Collectively, well-trained and led military forces also can assist international political processes without either threatening or taking part in combat. The obvious example is peacekeeping, where neutral troops can provide reassurance where, for example, demilitarisation protocols are being implemented and thus help a political process along. Sometimes, however, the simple intimidatory presence of well-trained forces – even if never used in anger – can overcome political obstacles which were previously insurmountable.

It is true, of course, that some countries still have land borders with potential enemies, and that there are many unstable parts of the world where large-scale conflict is still a possibility. (Major engagements using sophisticated weapons were fought in Angola up to the turn of the millennium, for example, and large-scale conflicts using some armour and air power are under way in Syria, Libya and Yemen at the time of writing.) Obviously armed forces must be ultimately capable of conducting conventional operations and fighting wars, but this does not have to be the only way of addressing security problems. Indeed, it was not always so in the past. Such a 'capability-based' approach, of course, absolutely requires to be underpinned by a clear policy (See Chapters 8 and 11).

If this discussion seems a little complex, and the range of possible defence tasks very great, it is worth recalling the words of the great Prussian writer Carl von Clausewitz (Clausewitz, 1976). He was concerned that theorists had concentrated too much on technical issues, and wanted to remind people what the purpose of military operations –

'war' in an age which used that term without embarrassment – actually was. It was, he said, an instrument of state policy, to provide further options for continuing with the policies beyond the usual diplomatic and economic means. With due allowances for changed times, and different uses of the military, that remains essentially true today, at all levels.

Avoiding confusion

It remains now to discuss some of the complicating factors that make the real-life implementation of the kind of tidy process described previously more difficult. We can identify three.

First, this discussion has assumed that governments are basically free to try to draw up their own security policies, subject to practical and financial constraints. In practice, of course, this is not the case. At its simplest, the attitudes of donors, neighbours, major allies and international institutions can count for a great deal. Even domestically, however, in a federal system, a local government of a different political complexion may be trying to delay or even reverse decisions taken by central government.

Second, there is the question of relations with *Parliament*. This is a complex issue, and depends very much on the political structure of the country itself. However, in a constitutional democracy, at least, the situation is relatively clear: the government, whose legitimacy comes from the ballot box, makes policy. Parliament (which represents all shades of political opinion) passes laws and votes expenditure, but does not make policy. (Of course, in what are called 'Westminster' systems around the world, the government is the government *because* it controls parliament, so this distinction can be somewhat academic.) At the other extreme, where parliament is both powerful and completely separate from the executive (as is most notably in the United States) it can try to be a second policy-making institution, with disastrous consequences. In general, though, no security policy, however coherent and well-founded, can be implemented if parliament votes against it. This can be a special problem with expenditure and procurement: parliaments are notoriously the most corrupt part of any political system, and a seat on a security-related parliamentary committee is potentially a source of income. Likewise, members of such committees can obstruct and delay initiatives in search of favours or concessions elsewhere.

A linked issue is that of relations with the *Media*. An honest and conscientious media is important if security issues are to be properly debated and the public is to be well informed: it is a shame that in most countries such a media does not exist. Even in an ideal situation, however, policy makers have to recognise that the interests of good government and the interests of the media are basically different. Journalism flourishes on conflict, scandal and failure. Even the most responsible media will look for exciting stories, and will sometimes invent them if they are not readily available. Talking to the media, and explaining the position of government is important, and is a democratic obligation, but it is often a thankless task, and policy makers should understand that their chances of a fair hearing, even from a serious, professional media, will never be very high. The opposite situation – a media that is too dependent on government – may be more convenient for policy-makers, but is less valuable for citizens. Developments in the media over the last 20 years have, in general, exacerbated these problems, without necessarily providing any compensating advantages.

Finally, there are a large number of groups active in the security area who have no formal status but may seek to influence policy and will offer unsolicited advice. Some are described as *non-governmental organisations* (NGOs) and some as *civil society organisations* (CSOs) (see Chapter 3), although these categories often overlap, and there are no generally accepted definitions of either. In transitional environments, informal groups from outside government have played a valuable role in bringing the security forces and opposition political groups together. In a number of cases – especially in Africa in recent years – these relationships have proved fruitful and mutually beneficial, because the two sides have seen their relationship as essentially cooperative. In most societies, however, there will be a profusion of other groups, often funded by foreign governments, asserting that they defend human rights or represent the interests of various sections of society. Some such groups may do good work, or be at least well-meaning, but from the practical perspective they have to be treated essentially as political lobbyists.

In discussing these external actors, we have to remember that we are dealing with politics, not with an academic discussion. Groups currently out of power will seek to extend their influence, where they can. They may adopt fashionable slogans and seek to ally themselves with foreign agents. Likewise, many groups, inside and outside formal politics, see themselves as primarily opposing the government, whatever it may be doing at the time, and so will always criticise the government's policies in public, even if they privately agree with them. As a result, policy makers have to recognise that a true consensus may often not be possible, and would, indeed, probably be meaningless even if it could somehow be reached. It is generally better to stick with a policy in which you have confidence, recognising that there will always be opposition, and that such opposition (just like support) may owe much more to the dynamics of the political process than to the merits of the argument.

A second type of constraint comes from the political history and culture of the country, and the position of its various security forces. Sometimes, this is essentially a question of traditions, which can vary even among close neighbours: Morocco has long contributed to international military operations, whereas its neighbour Algeria has not. It can also be a matter of political expediency: the post-1994 South African government chose a security policy that would be avowedly non-threatening for its neighbours, and began restructuring and re-equipping its forces appropriately. When, against all expectations, the country suddenly found itself required to contribute to peacekeeping operations on the African continent, it lacked the equipment and training to do so easily. Additionally, it can be a matter of history itself: the very different security policies of Japan and South Korea, for example, have roots in history going back more than a century, and in the role that the armed forces played in politics. Also, as these two latter examples show, a country's security policy is often influenced by the attitude of neighbours.

The final type of constraint comes from the wider security context and how that changes and is portrayed. There are fashions in security policy as there are in politics generally, and one of the challenges is to evaluate changing fashions and to see which are genuinely significant. Sometimes, problems might be taken much less seriously than they deserve. An example is the threat from fundamentalist Islamic militant groups outside their traditional operating areas in the Middle East. One expert (Thomson, 2014) correctly predicted such attacks and was ridiculed for so doing. Another, Burke (2015) wrongly predicted they would not. On the other hand, whilst both Artificial

Intelligence (AI) and the use of unmanned vehicles are undoubtedly significant in the long term, excitement over each has probably been excessive in terms of what they can currently perform for most countries. The effective policy maker is one who considers the significance of trends for their own country.

A particularly difficult question, on which we conclude, is the use (and abuse) of information and news. In many ways this is an old story: propaganda is a practice with a long history, instigated by the Catholic Church in the early 17th century, while cyber-warfare, (discussed in Chapter 11) is essentially an updating of traditional technical intelligence gathering and sabotage, both of which go back at least a century. Fake news stories, and leaked documents have an even longer history, although the arrival of the Internet has given them significantly more visibility.

At the most basic level, any government wants to communicate its policies and the reasons for them to its people. In many cases, including security policy, citizens of other countries are also affected. So, all governments will explain and defend their policies, cultivate friendly journalists, emphasise positive features and downplay the negative. This is normal – indeed universal. Whilst opposition forces and unfriendly media will be seeking to do roughly the opposite. Governments will also be trying to promote a favourable image of the country and its policies abroad.

The extent to which this can be done depends partly on which ideas and policies are regarded as potentially acceptable at any one time. This is the famous 'Overton Window', proposed by the political scientist Joseph P. Overton (Mackinac Centre, n.d.). Governments find it very hard to go outside this window, even if circumstances dictate that they obviously should. Accordingly, the security area is one of those where governments make a special effort to control where this window is. The mechanism by which most states try to influence public opinion was originally set out by Walter Lippmann, an influential American journalist writing in the 1920s. Lippmann (1922) argued that modern events were too complicated for ordinary people to understand, and so traditional concepts of democracy were no longer feasible. Thus, he said, it was necessary to 'manufacture consent', for those policies that informed and which expert opinion thought appropriate, while the role of journalism was to act as an intermediary to create this consent on the part of the public. To a greater or lesser extent, this has been the policy of all governments of all political systems on security issues.

In the days of print newspapers and small numbers of terrestrial TV channels, this was perhaps feasible to attempt. But governments, and power elites more generally, began to lose control of the media from the early 1990s, with the advent of satellite television and the deregulation of the electronic media. It thus became easier for outside actors to influence and manipulate news coverage. This first became a real issue during the 1992–1995 conflict in Bosnia, which was the first to be fought out on TV (Gow, Paterson & Preston, 1996). The Bosnian Muslims, in particular, had a highly professional and well-funded media strategy, narrowly aimed at the media, NGO and political classes of major western states, especially the US. However, whilst this strategy created major difficulties for the resolution of the conflict, and promoted much bitterness and division, it could not actually alter the underlying situation – as has generally been true of propaganda initiatives throughout modern history. These days, technology has advanced to the point where convincing propaganda about a security crisis is trivially easy to produce; it is wise to assume that all such material is false until proved otherwise.

A final consideration is the rise of multilingual satellite broadcasting. Most important states now have TV news channels broadcasting in major languages: some, like Al Jazeera and Russia Today have become well-established, and have widened the Overton window, providing access to facts, opinions and personalities not ordinarily encountered from domestic sources. States have started to become sensitive to and even nervous about, these developments, although the security policy consequences are not yet clear. By contrast, the consequences of related initiatives – for example the satellite TV and internet activities of extremist Salafist preachers from the Gulf, have been evident for a while.

Conclusion

Any policy is about what governments do, not what they say. All governments have a security policy of some kind (since few act irrationally or randomly) but the solution is to make it as coherent as possible. This means that it should have its origins in the overall policy priorities of the government, and should in turn provide clear guidance for policy at lower levels. Whilst not everything can be anticipated (and it is doubtful if the attempt is worthwhile) sensible contingency planning means that a policy response to the unexpected is more likely to be effective.

Questions to consider

1. Does your country have an articulated security policy? If so, does government's actual behaviour correspond to the announced policy?
2. Do the various parts of your country's security sector seem to work broadly in the same directions, or are there conflicts, overlaps or contradictions in their activities?
3. Is there any evidence of central direction or coordination of security policy in your country?

Suggested further reading

Cawthra, Gavin (2003) 'Security transformation in post-apartheid South Africa'. In: Gavin Cawthra and Robin Luckham, eds., *Governing Insecurity: Democratic Control of Military and Security Establishments in Transitional Democracies*, London: Zed Books.
Chuter, David (2007) 'From threats to tasks: Making and implementing national security policy', *Journal of Security Sector Management*, 5(2), pp. 1–19.
Cohen, Eliot (2002) *Supreme Command: Soldiers, Statesmen and Leadership in Wartime*, New York: The Free Press.
Heuser, Beatrice (2002) *Reading Clausewitz*, London: Pimlico.

References

Burke, Jason (2015) *The New Threat from Islamic Militancy*, London: The Bodley Head.
Clausewitz, Carl von (1976) *On War*, Princeton, NJ: Princeton University Press.
Gow, James, Paterson, Richard and Preston, Alison (1996) *Bosnia by Television*, London: British Film Institute.

Huntington, Samuel (1957) *The Soldier and the State: The Theory and Politics of Civil-Military Relations*, Cambridge, Massachusetts: The Belknap Press of Harvard University Press. DOI:10.2307/j,ctvjf9wx3.

Lippmann, Walter (1922) *Public Opinion*. Available at http://www.gutenberg.org/ebooks/6456 [Accessed 1 June 2020].

Mackinac Centre for Public Policy (n.d.) *The Overton Window*. Available at https://www.mackinac.org/OvertonWindow [Accessed 1 June 2020].

Thomson, David (2014) *Les Français jihadistes*, Paris: Les Arènes.

6 Accountability

A tangled web

Laura R. Cleary

Introduction

Accountability is one of the eight characteristics of good governance, and is deemed a critical element of civilian and democratic management of defence and security forces (see Chapter 3). Within any security sector reform (SSR) programme, an enormous amount of time, energy and resource is expended on the establishment of institutional and procedural mechanisms through which accountability can be ensured and management of the security services can be exercised. Yet often these technocratic approaches fail to take root, with external observers suggesting that the country undergoing reform lacks a 'culture of accountability' (CESS, 2021; Aldrich & Richterova, 2018). That is, however, an overly simplistic and sweeping judgement to make. Societies understand and value accountability in different ways. If one genuinely wishes to enhance accountability then one needs to reflect upon the way in which accountability is understood and valued, as well as recognise that there are a number of layers, approaches and systems to it.

This chapter is concerned with both the relational and procedural aspects of accountability. It begins by exploring how accountability is defined, arguing that the way in which a society interprets the concept will inform the institutional mechanisms for ensuring accountability. It then looks at the layers, approaches and systems of accountability, and in so doing returns to themes that were addressed in Chapter 3, namely the issues of transparency, trust and legitimacy. Finally, the chapter addresses the most frequently encountered obstacles to ensuring accountability and the ways in which different countries have sought to overcome them.

Defining accountability

The purpose and meaning of accountability are perceived in a variety of ways. For example, reviewing the literature from two different disciplines, Political Science and Management, we see that accountability can be understood as a 'higher order principle to symbolise social progress and democracy' (Alawattage & De-Clerk Azure, 2019: p.2), as a 'system of control' (Ryu & Chang, 2017: p.484; Olsen, 2018: p.79), as the 'management of expectations' (Busuioc & Lodge, 2016: p.91), as a 'requisite for social order' and as a 'perceptual rather than an actual state of affairs' (Hall et al., 2017: p.208).

In over two decades of teaching on the subject it has become apparent that the way in which a society defines accountability will inform the mechanisms through which it seeks to achieve it. In the Slavic languages there is no separate word for accountability;

DOI: 10.4324/9781003137061-6

its meaning is either subsumed within that of responsibility (*otvetstvennost'*) or circumscribed by use of the term 'public finance accountability' (*publichnaya finansovaya podotchetnost'*). The same is true in Spanish and French. In non-technical settings accountability may be translated as *responsabilidad* (SP) or *responsibilité* (FR) (responsibility), but if financial matters are concerned then the phrase employed is *rendicion de cuentas* or *reddition de comptes* (the surrendering of accounts). Such interpretations of accountability tend to result in very limited and formalistic mechanisms for ensuring accountability. Thus, in many of the post-Soviet countries the practice of accountability tends to focus on the ability to provide quantitative evidence: How many bullets were used on operations? How much fuel was consumed? How many arrests were made? In many Hispanic countries, accountability is understood as a responsibility to report. Beyond receiving a report from a ministry there is no inherent requirement for a legislative committee to do anything with that report. No corrective actions are taken and there are few if any tangible consequences for non-performance.

In English, by contrast, a distinction is made between responsibility and accountability. Responsibility can refer to the duties or tasks that one undertakes and to be responsible implies that the individual has some control or authority over the performance of those duties. Accountability advances the concept of responsibility and infers that an individual should be able to explain and answer for their actions, and may be legally obliged to do so. By contextualising accountability in this way, we can begin to engage with three interrelated questions:

- Accountable to whom?
- Accountable for what?
- How is accountability ensured?

In whichever context we are operating, accountability will be defined by a series of relational and procedural stages, be these formal or informal in nature (Jarvis, 2014), as will be illustrated.

Layers of accountability

At first glance the questions posed above appear fairly simplistic and easy to answer, yet it soon becomes apparent that an individual (the account giver) may need to juggle multiple accountabilities to multiple audiences in what has been described as a 'web of accountabilities' (Hall et al., 2017: p.209). The most commonly identified fixed points within that web are individual, social, horizontal and vertical accountabilities, although these layers are not uniformly defined.

Individual accountability

Individual accountability is essentially about ethics and the extent to which an individual adheres to their own moral compass and the ethical standards of society. Busuioc & Lodge (2016) have suggested that accountability is bound up with reputational concerns. Both the holding and giving of account is about advancing one's own reputation vis-à-vis different audiences (Busuioc & Lodge, 2016: p.92). How might this be manifested within a government context? George Hanbury (2004) has made reference to a series of obligations that could serve as instruments to guide civil servants specifically through the ethical problems with which they might be confronted. These include:

- Obligation to the Constitution
- Obligation to the Law
- Obligation to the Nation
- Obligation to Profession and Professionalism
- Obligation to Family and Friends
- Obligation to Self
- Obligation to Middle-range Collectives (interest groups, churches, unions, etc.)
- Obligation to the Public Interest or General Welfare
- Obligation to Humanity
- Obligation to Religion or to God

(Hanbury, 2004: p.191)

Some of these instruments are relevant not only to individual accountability, but to horizontal and vertical forms as well. The idea behind the collective use of these instruments, however, is that we as individuals should be able and willing to give an account to ourselves for our behaviour. We are our own judges in the first instance. This belief is not solely a Western, liberal one; it is reflected in traditional practice in other parts of the world, as is illustrated in Example 6.1.

Example 6.1: Traditional forms of accountability

During the period of Ethiopian feudalism, which spanned millennia and only ended in 1974, it was believed that all individuals were accountable to a higher power. If a subject, you were accountable to the feudal lords and ultimately the emperor. If Emperor, you were accountable to God. All believed in the principle of *yelugnta* or deference to public moral accountability. Before taking any action (spoken or physical) one was supposed to ask, 'What would people think?' The public good had primacy over the will of the individual (Tibebu, 2008: p.356; Cleary, 2016a: p.34). This belief system was abandoned following the overthrow of Emperor Haile Selassie in 1974, the imposition of Ethiopian Socialism by the Derg regime and Ethiopia's descent into a long and violent civil war as individuals and their families struggled desperately to survive.

In the case of Rwanda, the traditional form of accountability is *imihigo* (singular *umihigo*), which can be literally translated as a self-defined policy target one publicly vows to achieve for the greater communal good (Kamuzinzi & Rubyutsa, 2019: p.634). *Imihigo* tended to be exercised at moments of great crisis for a community. The responsibility to achieve what you were supposed to do came from the need to survive together (Ibid.: p. 635). Individuals would take public vows to achieve public good, and face public shame in the case of failure. This traditional approach to accountability was dismissed during the age of European colonialism, with European systems of accountability being imposed. Although Rwanda achieved independence in 1962, it did not immediately abandon European systems of governance. It was not until 2006 that *imihigo* was reintroduced, and that was done specifically to reinvigorate public policy implementation as the country sought to unite and recover following the genocide of 1994. Studies suggest the implementation of *imihigo* is producing positive results in terms of efficiency, effectiveness and accountability (Ibid.).

Social accountability

Social accountability, also referred to as diagonal accountability, 'is about how citizens can exercise control over public authority via direct participation in policy formation and implementation' (Alawattage & De-Clerk Azure, 2019: p.2). The principal actors within this layer of accountability are deemed to be civil society organisations (CSOs) and the media, and the health of a democracy is often measured in terms of the viability, diversity and vitality of those organisations.

The challenge within transitional democracies is often that CSOs are viewed with a high degree of suspicion by those in power and there may be severe legal restraints on who can constitute a CSO, how they are financed and the subjects that they can address. The same constraints apply to the media. It should be noted that the general level of suspicion of CSOs and the media is heightened considerably when they seek to engage in issues of national security, as Example 6.2 illustrates.

Example 6.2: Limiting social accountability

The Ethiopian Constitution of 1995 is the most democratic ever enjoyed by the country. Like many constitutions drafted after 1990 it is front loaded with rights: Articles 14–28 address human rights, while Articles 29–49 are concerned with democratic rights. Although Ethiopian society initially appeared to blossom under this more liberal regime, the onslaught of the Ethiopian-Eritrean War (May 1998–June 2000), the emergence of rival factions within the then ruling Ethiopian People's Revolutionary Democratic Front (EPRDF), and viable opposition parties able to contest the EPRDF's hold on power, resulted in the government restricting liberties enshrined within the Constitution. For example, even though the freedom of the press is guaranteed under Art. 29 of the Constitution, the 1992 *Law on the Press*, which addresses publication of false and offensive information, incitement of ethnic hatred, or libel was frequently invoked by the EPRDF government in order to justify the arrest and detainment of journalists. Further restrictions on freedom of expression and freedom of association were achieved through the *Proclamation for the Registration and Regulation of Charities and Societies* (2009) and the *Anti-Terrorist Proclamation* (2009), which when combined served to fundamentally limit political debate by severely restricting the areas in which civil society organisations could engage and branding most opposition movements as terrorist organisations and those who sought to report on them as sympathisers (Cleary, 2016a: p.35).

The types of restrictions that Ethiopia placed on CSOs and the media are not uncommon, unfortunately. So, while the viability, diversity and vibrancy of civil society may well be an indicator of the health of a democratic polity, social accountability is not necessarily apparent at the start of a democratic transition. Mechkova, Lührmann and Lindberg (2019) have argued that while vertical accountability may be apparent from the start of a democratic transition, social (diagonal) and horizontal accountability take much longer to emerge and are contingent upon progress being made within vertical accountability.

Horizontal accountability

The concept of horizontal accountability is contextually dependent. At a governmental level it refers to the checks and balances between institutions: Can the legislature check the executive? Can the judiciary in turn check the legislature and executive? At an organisational level, horizontal accountability refers to peer accountability, where professionals hold each other accountable for their respect of the ethical code of conduct or their professional standards (Kamuzinzi & Rubyutsa, 2019: p.635). In the context of SSR both of these interpretations of horizontal accountability are relevant.

Consider a country in which the executive has been historically strong and not been subject to any meaningful oversight from the legislature or judiciary. That executive has had direct control over the deployment of the armed forces, police and intelligence services. Recruitment and promotion within those services has been overtly politicised and corruption and brutality have been allowed to flourish. Under a new democratic dispensation, and as part of a SSR programme, efforts may be made to enhance the capacity of the legislature and the judiciary to conduct oversight of the executive, and specifically of the executive's use of the security services. That may require in the first instance changes to legislation in order to grant these institutions the authority to scrutinise government policy. Second, procedures for conduct of oversight will need to be established. What can a parliamentary committee investigate and how? Third, training for those performing the oversight function may be required. Finally, other resources, be those financial, human, or technical, may be necessary in order to ensure the effectiveness of the legislature or judiciary. That is what is required at the strategic level. Within the individual institutions, however, investment also needs to be made into improving the integrity, accountability and professionalism of individual personnel and the service as a whole. Those reforms are, however, contingent upon political will, as a recent study of oversight of intelligence services in Albania, Kosovo and North Macedonia makes clear. A CESS (2021) report found that there was a persistent lack of domestic commitment toward democratic governance and an underdeveloped culture of accountability and oversight in all three countries; that legislative frameworks for oversight were lacking and that there was insufficient institutional and human capacity within oversight bodies to adequately hold intelligence agencies to account (CESS, 2021: pp.2–3). The report recommended that more emphasis would need to be placed on establishing appropriate legislative frameworks and on the depoliticisation and professionalisation of the services.

Vertical accountability

Vertical accountability can also be understood in one of two ways. At the governmental level this form of accountability is related to elections and political parties. The freer and fairer the elections, the more one can say that vertical accountability has evolved (Mechkova et al., 2019: p.41). Within the institutional context, vertical accountability relates to bureaucratic hierarchies and tends to manifest itself through systems of command and control (Ehren et al., 2019: p.3). This approach is compliance oriented, with individuals held accountable for adherence to rules.

It should be evident from the above that these layers are not discrete. An individual, the account giver, may need to demonstrate accountability to multiple audiences all at the same time, and those audiences may be assessing performance in very different ways. As Olsen (2018) has acknowledged, 'governance is embedded in networks across levels of government, institutional spheres and public-private realms and based on informal partnership and dialogue rather than hierarchical command and formal

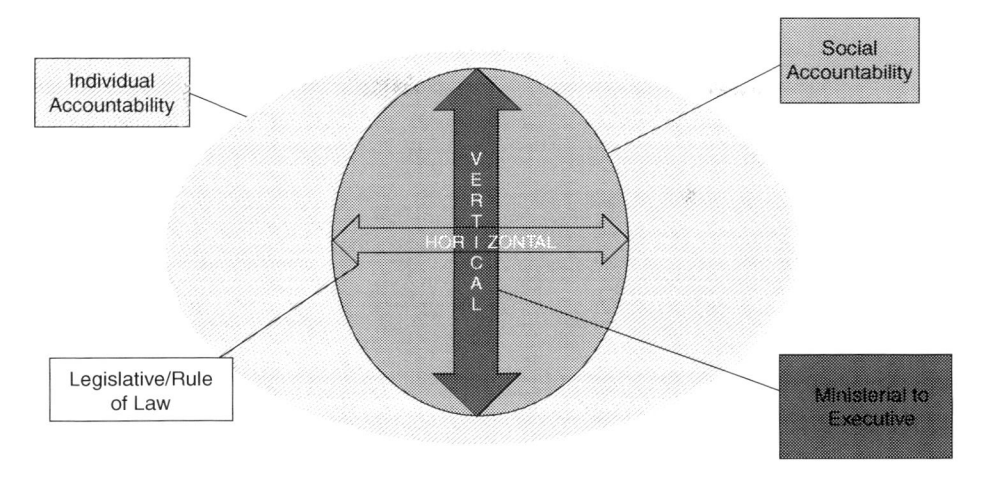

Figure 6.1 Layers of Accountability

control relationships' (Olsen, 2018: p.91). In order to make sense of these relationships we now turn our attention to two different approaches to accountability.

Approaches to accountability

Joy Moncrieffe (2001) identified two forms of accountability: *ex-post facto* and *ex-ante accountability*. Depending on the approach adopted we see the employment of different methods or systems of accountability.

Ex-post facto accountability

This form of accountability refers to holding public officials accountable through the law, various monitoring and sanctioning mechanisms and ultimately through elections. Inherent within this approach is a belief that the policy process is a linear one: problems are analysed, responses reviewed, the best course of action is selected and implemented, and eventually results are evaluated based on evidence, and the approach corrected if required (Ozga, 2020: p.20). This form of accountability is not the responsibility of a sole individual or institution; various actors have a role to play, and they may perform their roles in concert with others. Ultimately, these actors through accountability relations, structures and processes are seeking to assess whether designated resources have been employed for designated purposes (Alawattage & De-Clerk Azure, 2019: p.3). This form of accountability is referred to as 'functional' and tends to be associated with accounting. Table 6.1 illustrates the actors involved and the requirements placed upon them.

Now, clearly, Table 6.1 represents an ideal. We see varying patterns of actor engagement across polities, the result of different institutional arrangements, political cultures, legal frameworks, availability of information, and the perceived legitimacy of

Table 6.1 Account holders and their responsibilities

Actors	Responsibilities
Political Parties	Should be responsible for the vetting of candidates, the development of programmatic platforms and ensuring legislative or voting discipline, which is dependent upon loyalty and cohesion (of both the party in power and in opposition).
Elected Representatives	Willing and able to hold government to account by posing questions on the floor of the legislature. More intense oversight is conducted within parliamentary committees that have the authority to scrutinise policy, budgets and administration.
Public Officials	Should coordinate, maintain and evaluate the activities of government, ensuring that they accord with political, social and economic objectives. This is dependent on the nature of the civil service system and the extent to which the service is effective, transparent and results oriented.
Monitoring and Sanctioning Mechanisms (e.g., Ombudsman and Audit Offices)	Should be 'independent' from the executive and free to investigate cases and make recommendations without fear of outcomes being over-ruled by the executive.
Civil Society Organisations and Media	CSOs and the media have the legal right and the ability to question and challenge undemocratic practices and values, set political agendas and generate a broad consensus on the legitimacy of the constitutional order.
Direct Citizen Assessment	Citizens are given periodic opportunities to express their approval or disapproval of their representatives and the policies implemented in their name.

Source: Author.

the process. If all actors, however, are equally and effectively engaged then we would expect to see three accountability systems in operation:

- Compliance-oriented: where an individual or institution is held accountable for adherence to rules and accountable to the bureaucracy.
- Professional accountability: where an individual demonstrates adherence to professional norms. They are judged by their adherence to standards and are judged by their peers.
- Performance based: the account giver is accountable for deliverables.

(Ehren et al., 2019: p.3).

How might this work in practice? Public officials and parliamentary committees might be focussed in the first instance on compliance. A national audit office, civil society organisations and the electorate would be concerned with government performance. Political parties would be interested in the professional accountability of their members. Each agent and all systems would need to be exercised, however, to ensure a higher standard of governance. Examples 6.3 and 6.4 illustrate the relationship between some of these actors, but they also highlight the constraints faced when seeking to ensure accountability.

Example 6.3: The role of CSOs in Ukraine

Ukraine has been classed as a hybrid democracy. Its institutional framework remains a legacy of the Soviet past, as does the structure and purpose of civil society (Cleary, 2016b: p.15). Prior to EuroMaidan in 2014, Ukrainian civil society was viewed as 'atomised', generally 'apathetic', and unwilling to 'show commitment for any good cause' (Vorbrugg, 2015). The 'Dignity Revolution', which began in the winter of 2013–2014, altered that status. Initially, demonstrations were in response to then President Yanukovych's refusal to sign an Association Agreement with the EU. Mobilised by a belief that an opportunity to join the European community had been denied them, protestors subsequently demanded an end to corrupt and autocratic rule. The EuroMaidan movement became characterised by a sense of distrust, particularly where politicians were concerned. It assumed a traditional role associated with civil society, which is to bear witness against those in authority. This is a role that it has continued to perform, with the slogan 'Remember Maidan' being frequently employed when reforms appear to have stalled or corruption is not being tackled. What is absent, however, is a coherent agenda for reform. CSOs tend to be reactive to issues and events, rather than strategic in terms of how they wish society and politics to develop. CSOs have sought to augment the state's provision of basic services or to assume the responsibility for the provision of those services in full; behaviour which is typical in conflict situations. There is, however, limited engagement with government regarding the formulation of policy. While CSOs have acquired a great deal of expertise since 2014, their efforts are frequently hindered by a lack of financial and human resources. So, while there is a desire to ensure accountability, the opportunity and ability to do so are not always apparent.

Example 6.4: Oversight of intelligence: The role of the media

Intelligence services are often viewed as mysterious, secretive and distinct from the other security agencies. The intelligence function, however, is integral to executive decision-making as it helps leaders acquire and utilise information against competitors (Stout & Warner, 2018: p.519). It is right, therefore, that oversight of the intelligence services be conducted and the services held to account. Intelligence oversight consists of four principal elements: executive (internal), legal, judicial and public (Hildebrand, 2012: p.692). Looking specifically at the role of the media in ensuring public oversight, Hildebrand suggests that news media can act as information transmitters, watchdogs and stimulators for formal scrutinisers (e.g., parliamentary committees), as well as legitimising actors (Ibid: pp.693–699). Regrettably, legislators 'rarely engage in intensive intelligence oversight, unless a major scandal or failure forces them to do so' (Ibid., p.695).

Ex-ante accountability

Moncrieffe (2001) suggests that ex-ante, or positive accountability, allows for a continual check on policies. The process aims to enhance the responsiveness of agents to those whom they are expected to serve, and by these mechanisms improve the quality of representation. This form of accountability is far more difficult to achieve for the simple reason that it is trying to improve performance and ensure accountability during the process of decision-making, rather than after the fact.

This form of accountability can be achieved in the following ways. The first is by taking account of, but not necessarily accepting, sectionalised or partial interests. In simple terms this is about consultation. Which stakeholders does government consult with when formulating policy? For example, when the United Kingdom drafted its Integrated Security, Defence, Development and Foreign Policy Review in 2020 it sought to 'root the review in the best available evidence, analysis and expertise ... taking key partners' and stakeholders' views into consideration ... through a systematic programme of engagement, analysis and challenge' (HM Government, 2021: p.106). The principle is that the more widely a government consults the more likely it will achieve consensus on its final decision. In this instance, the Government consulted with international allies and partners as well as with Parliament, departments of state, the public, experts and practitioners.

The second method is to subject policy choices to deliberation and consultation within the ruling and opposition parties within the legislature. A government may do this by outlining its policy proposals on the floor of the legislature. Alternatively, opposition parties may be briefed by civil servants, or seek to elucidate details from the government through parliamentary questions or by exercising their rights under freedom of information legislation. The idea here is to generate greater transparency in decision-making.

The third way of achieving ex-ante accountability is by means of referenda. This is not to infer that a referendum should be staged for every policy issue, simply for those that may have constitutional implications. The United Kingdom provides a good example, holding two referenda in the space of two years. The first, in 2014, pertained to Scottish independence, the second, in 2016, concerned the UK's continued membership of the EU. Both decisions had constitutional implications, and thus it was right to put these issues to the public. In this instance, the key principle of governance is that of participation. Although referenda should not necessarily be viewed as a tool of last resort, they should be used sparingly and their timing and wording chosen carefully.

Example 6.5: The variable outcomes of referenda

Over the last decade a number of secessionist movements have employed referenda in order to further their agendas, with variable results. In the case of the Scottish referendum in 2014, legislation was passed by the British Parliament which allowed only those individuals residing in Scotland the right to vote in the referendum. The question put to them was a binary one: Should Scotland be an independent country? Yes or no. The No camp won with 55.3% of the vote to 44.7%.

This process was watched with interest by citizens of Ukraine. Following the invasion of Crimea and Eastern Ukraine by Russian forces in 2014, a referendum was organised by the Crimean legislature. Residents were asked whether they wished to join Russia or have greater autonomy in Ukraine. Although approximately 95.5% of voters approved secession, the vote was deemed illegitimate for several reasons. First, the Ukrainian Rada (parliament) had not sanctioned the referendum. Second, voters were not provided with an option to stay within Ukraine. Third, the presence of Russian troops was viewed as a form of intimidation. The vote was therefore condemned nationally and internationally.

In the case of Catalonia, an autonomous region in Spain, the October 2017 referendum was also declared illegal by the Spanish national government. The Catalan parliament, without the consent of the national government in Madrid, held a referendum on 1 October 2017 in which citizens were asked whether Catalonia should become a republic. Of the voters, 90% voted in favour of independence and the Catalan parliament declared this on 27 October. The Madrid government reacted sharply, dissolving the Catalan parliament, sending armed police onto the streets, and arresting local politicians. Where the EU had viewed events in Ukraine in 2014 as a matter of foreign and security policy, and thus worthy of response, the reaction to events in Scotland and Catalonia was that they were domestic matters of Member States.

The final element of ex-ante accountability is not a method, but a principle. Government must understand that it has a duty to explain and justify its actions. This may seem a simplistic and naïve prescription, but it goes to the heart of 'government for the people, by the people'. Ensuring accountability is not simply about establishing certain institutional structures and procedures, but about altering patterns of behaviour. In order to remain vigilant, we need to have a clear aim to which we can work, and we also need to understand that structures have consequences for ethical behaviour (Hanbury, 2004: p.191).

Exercise 6.1

Imagine that you are a member of defence ministry working group tasked with identifying military installations for closure. What information does the working group require? With whom should that group confer? How should they prioritise their response?

On transparency

The ability to ensure accountability, be that ex-post facto or ex-ante, is entirely contingent upon access to relevant information. There is a reason why transparency and accountability are discussed in tandem. Transparency comes in two forms: domestic and international.

Domestic transparency refers to the ease or difficulty with which a country's own legislature plus the media, interest groups, civil society and the public at large, can see what is going on. Ideally, the aim should be to achieve transparency in decision-making, allocation of budgetary resources and administration of the rule of law. One can see that this form of transparency is relevant to ex-post facto accountability, but it also relates back to the principles of governance detailed in Chapter 3 (pp. 000–000).

International transparency refers in turn to the ease or difficulty with which other countries and international organisations can observe a state's affairs. Now, if a country is good at domestic transparency it is highly likely that it will be good at international transparency. The reverse, however, does not necessarily hold true. A country can be very good at international transparency, but very poor at the domestic form. Studies have suggested that where countries are dependent upon support from international financial institutions (IFIs), international development agencies and donor states there is a tendency to prioritise international rather than domestic transparency. This in turn skews the system of accountability towards vertical and functional mechanisms rather than horizontal and social (Alawattage & De-Clerk Azzure, 2019: p.3).

Questions then arise as to whose interests the government serves. As was indicated at the start of this chapter, accountability is defined by the relationships between the account giver and the recipients of those accounts. The varying account holders will have different perceptions of the trustworthiness and legitimacy of the account givers.

Satisfying these various audiences is a time-consuming activity, one in which a 100 per cent success rate is illusory. In a digital age in which critics of government tend to grow exponentially, there has been a tendency for governments to engage in 'fishbowl transparency'. This term refers to the 'proactive release of uncontextualized data' as a means of building public trust (Busuioc & Lodge, 2016: p.95). The uncontextualised release of information may prove as damaging, however, as an unwillingness to provide any information at all. In Chapter 3 (p. 000) the three components of trustworthiness were outlined: competence, benevolence and integrity. These components are relevant to the discussion of transparency. As noted above, the aim of transparency is to reveal how decisions are made, budgets allocated and the rule of law administered; inherent within that agenda is a desire to display competence, benevolence and integrity. To achieve that, however, requires the addition of a fourth component: *consistency*, both in word and deed.

This brings us to the concept and practice of strategic communications. Christopher Paul defines strategic communications as the 'coordinated actions, messages, images and other forms of signalling or engagement intended to inform, influence or persuade selected audiences to support national objectives' (Paul, 2011: p.3). The purpose of strategic communications is to convey policy. The purpose of a strategic communications strategy should be to inform, influence and persuade. We can view strategic communications as a *way* (a course of action or option) and as a means (a resource). It may help to think of this as a two-way process. Government seeks to share 'meaning' as well as elicit feedback from the target audience to inform periodic adaptation and adjustment of policy and strategy. That outcome is dependent, however, on the messaging being relevant, credible, authoritative and consistent.

Obstacles to accountability

As should now be evident from the preceding discussion, accountability processes involve both decision-making and sense-making (Olsen, 2018: p.81). It should also be evident that there are inherent challenges to both. A significant one is failing to understand why we are engaged in the process at all. As noted at the start of this chapter, accountability is often understood in terms of control, which leads to the implementation of compliance-oriented systems with an emphasis on vertical relations (Ehren et al., 2019: p.3). Within this formulation, accountability systems and procedures appear geared solely towards the uncovering of wrong doing. If, however, we conceive of these systems and procedures as a means to improve individual and collective working practices then they can serve to enhance trustworthiness and effectiveness (Ibid., p. 4).

Although enhanced trustworthiness and legitimacy should be the aim, there needs to be recognition that accountability cannot be achieved at all levels of activity at all times. As Olsen has argued, it is difficult to see how 'accountability can be safeguarded when governance is embedded in networks across levels of government, institutional spheres, and public-private realms' (Olsen, 2018: p.91). Ultimately, we must be concerned with all of the following forms of accountability, but recognise that the actions taken to satisfy one type may not be suitable for meeting the requirements of another:

- Individual accountability
- Public accountability
- Parliamentary accountability
- Bureaucratic accountability
- Accountability from professional groups
- Intra-institutional accountability
- Inter-institutional accountability
- Financial accountability
- Managerial accountability

There is also the risk that formal systems of monitoring and accountability may entail very high transaction costs. Individuals and organisations may spend more time justifying the decisions they have made than they do making or implementing those decisions. Demonstrating high levels of accountability may actually diminish effectiveness. In some circumstances it may be simply impossible to demonstrate accountability because of the lack of specificity of the underlying activity.

We should also recognise that linkages between those who are responsible and those who are accountable may not always be apparent or exist. Margaret Hodge identified this issue as one of deep concern in her 2016 book, *Called to Account*. Previously a Member of the British Parliament and Chair of the Public Accounts Committee (PAC), Hodge indicated that the work of the Committee frequently was frustrated because those giving evidence (the account givers) may not have been in post at the time the decisions and actions under review were taken. Hodge campaigned to change parliamentary procedure thereby allowing parliamentary committees to call witnesses who previously had been responsible to give account of their decision-making process.

Hodge and her fellow members of the PAC clearly had an interest in and the capacity to hold government to account. In seeking to ensure ex-post facto accountability, the Committee worked closely with the National Audit Office to augment their knowledge and understanding of the issue under investigation. Frequently, however, we see in many transitional democracies evidence of another challenge. Specifically, that those responsible for ensuring oversight and accountability may lack the capacity to do so. Example 6.3 is illustrative of this point. In a number of countries there is a recognition that parliament must do more to improve its capacity to hold government to account. That requires the appointment of qualified staff, training and time, as was detailed in Example 3.4 in Chapter 3 of this volume (p. 40), which considered how Ghana had approached the issue.

Even with the best will in the world, however, an executive may still seek to override the legislature's efforts to ensure accountability. Indeed, there may well be disharmony between all three branches of government: executive, legislative and judicial. The final days of the Trump presidency in the United States in January 2021 are illustrative of this point. The executive called into question the legitimacy of the electoral process, the professionalism of state and national officials and incited violence against the legislature. The legislature in turn, or at least parts of it, sought to hold the executive to account. There was evidence, however, of collusion between the executive, parts of the legislature, some of the security services and the mob that stormed the

Capitol. Individuals and corporations who viewed themselves as having been injured by the events of 6 January 2021 picked up the burden of ensuring accountability as they sought redress through the court system. America's vaunted check-and-balance system did not appear up to the task. The events of January 2021 and the subsequent impeachment proceedings in February of that year highlighted the tangled web of accountabilities: personal, professional, legal, social, horizontal and vertical.

The events witnessed in the US, regrettably, are not uncommon, and they speak of the inherent difficulty in creating systems that can respond effectively to every eventuality. As the complexity of our domestic political and wider security environments continue to evolve it will grow increasingly difficult for governments to make their choices and positions clear, even in an age in which an abundance of information is available in the public domain. For many countries, secrecy has long been equated with security: the more secretive you are, the more secure you must be. If, however, a state proclaims itself to be a democracy and values the rule of law and accountability then it needs to be more transparent. It must be recognised that a lack of transparency will restrict accountability and may undermine security in the longer term. As events in the United States have illustrated, however, an abundance of transparency does not necessarily equate to higher levels of accountability. A balance, therefore, needs to be struck. If we can have a golden rule then it should be that government should be transparent about why it is not being transparent.

Conclusion

This chapter has argued that accountability should be about more than simply uncovering wrongdoing. It should be about improving individual and collective behaviour and the process of government. Ideally, our 'structures of accountability should mirror structures of power, and where structures of power have changed, the structures of accountability should be adjusted accordingly' (House of Lords Select Committee on the Constitution, 2010: p.8). Our mechanisms for accountability, therefore, should be organic, evolving as our political systems mature. As we seek to make appropriate adjustments to those mechanisms, we should be conscious that accountability is ultimately enhanced by overcoming secrecy. Greater transparency contributes to the development of trust. As was discussed in Chapter 3, the development of trust requires concerted effort and time. A conscious effort must be made to recognise that actors such as the media, opposition parties, and the public, are not necessarily the enemy of the government, but potentially its partners in the provision of security. To turn enmity into partnership requires capacity building so that account givers and recipients can perform their roles effectively. Attention should be given to organisational cultures, professional ethics, and training, topics that will be addressed by Roger Darby in Chapter 9. Ultimately, all those engaged in trying to ensure accountability need to recognise that actions have consequences. As Romeo Dallaire noted in his 2004 account of genocide in Rwanda: 'To properly mourn the dead and respect the potential of the living, we need accountability, not blame' (p.513).

Questions to consider

1. How does the concept of individual accountability in your society relate to the pursuit of social, horizontal and vertical accountability?

2. Does a code of ethics exist for the legislature and the civil service in your country? If yes, how strictly is it applied? If no, what values would you like to see such a code incorporate?

3. Do the laws on secrecy in your country support or hinder efforts to ensure accountability?

Suggested further reading

Cleary, Laura R. (2006) 'Transparency and Accountability'. In: Laura R. Cleary & Teri McConville (eds.), *Managing Defence in a Democracy*, Abingdon: Routledge, pp. 59–77.

Schierkolk, Nazli Yildirim (2018) *International Standards and Good Practices in the Governance and Oversight of the Security Services*, Tbilisi: DCAF, Available at: https://www.dcaf.ch/sites/default/files/publications/documents/TI_EMC_DCAF_Security_Services_Oversight_Best_Practices.pdf [Accessed 24 March 2021].

References

Alawattage, Chandana & De-Clerk Azure, John (2019) 'Behind the World Bank's ringing declarations of 'social accountability': Ghana's public financial management reform', *Critical Perspectives on Accounting*, DOI: 10.1016/j.cpa.2019.02.002

Aldrich, Richard J. & Richterova, Daniela (2018) 'Ambient Accountability: Intelligence services in Europe and the decline of state secrecy', *West European Politics 41 (4)*, pp. 1003–1024. DOI: 10.1080/01402382.2017.1415780

Busuioc, Madalina & Lodge, Martin (2016) 'Reputation and accountability relationships: Managing accountability expectations through reputation', *Public Administration Review 77 (1)*, pp. 91–100. DOI:10.1111/puar.12612.

CESS (2021) *Strengthening Oversight of Intelligence in Albania, Kosovo and North Macedonia: CESS Policy Brief No. 4*, Merijn Hartog & Erik Sportel (eds) Groningen: Centre for European Security Studies.

Cleary, Laura R. (2016a) 'Ethiopia', *Security Sector Horizon Scanning 2016 – East Africa*. Laura R. Cleary, Tracey German & Matthew Craig (eds), Andover: HQ Army.

Cleary, Laura R. (2016b) 'Half measures and incomplete reforms: The breeding ground for a hybrid civil society in Ukraine', *Southeast European and Black Sea Studies 16 (1)*, pp. 7–24. DOI:10.1080/14683857.2016.1148410

Dallaire, Romeo (2004) *Shake Hands with the Devil: The Failure of Humanity in Rwanda*, London: Arrow Books.

Ehren, Melanie, Paterson, Andrew & Baxter, Jacqueline (2019) *'Accountability and Trust: Two Sides of the Same Coin?'*, CIES: Comparative and International Education Conference 2019: Education for Sustainability, San Francisco, CA, 14–18 April 2019.

Hall, Angela T., Frink, Dwight D. & Buckley, M. Ronald (2017) 'An accountability account: A review and synthesis of the theoretical and empirical research on felt accountability', *Journal of Organizational Behaviour, 38*, pp. 204–224. DOI:10.1002/job.2052

Hanbury, George (2004) 'A "pracademic's" perspective of ethics and honor: Imperatives for public service in the 21st Century!', *Public Organization Review: a Global Journal, 4*, pp. 187–204.

Hildebrand, Claudia (2012) 'The role of news media in intelligence oversight', *Intelligence and National Security, 27 (5)*, pp. 689–706. DOI:10.1080/02684527.2012.708521

Hodge, Margaret (2016) *Called to Account: How Governments and Vested Interests Combine to Waste our Money*, London: Little, Brown.

House of Lords Select Committee on the Constitution (2010) *4th Report of Session 2009–2010, The Cabinet Office and Centre of Government*, London: The Stationary Office. Available at: https://publications.parliament.uk/pa/ld200910/ldselect/ldconst/30/30.pdf [Accessed 23 March 2021].

HM Government (2021) *Global Britain in a Competitive Age: The Integrated Review of Security, Defence, Development and Foreign Policy, CP 403*. Available at: https://assets.publishing.service.gov.uk/government/uploads/system/uploads/attachment_data/file/975077/Global_Britain_in_a_Competitive_Age-_the_Integrated_Review_of_Security__Defence__Development_and_Foreign_Policy.pdf [Accessed 16 March 2021].

Jarvis, Mark D. (2014) 'The black box of bureaucracy: Interrogating accountability in the public service', *Australian Journal of Public Administration 73 (4)*, pp. 450–466. DOI:10.1111/1467–8500.12109

Kamuzinzi, Masengesho & Rubyutsa, Jules M. (2019) 'When tradition feeds on modern accountability mechanisms in public policy implementation: The case of "Imihigo" in Rwanda', *Public Performance and Management Review 42 (3)*, pp. 632–656. DOI:10.1080/15309576.2018.1494018

Mechkova, Valeriya, Lührmann, Anna & Lindberg, Steffan I. (2019) 'The accountability sequence: From de-jure to de-facto constraints on governments', *Studies in Comparative International Development, 54*, pp. 40–70. DOI:10.1007/s12116-018-9262-5

Moncrieffe, Joy (2001) 'Accountability: Idea, ideals, constraints', *Democratization 8 (3)*, pp. 26–50.

Olsen, John P. (2018) 'Democratic accountability and the changing European political order', *European Law Journal, 24*, pp. 77–98. DOI:10.1111/eulj.12261

Ozga, Jenny (2020) 'The politics of accountability', *The Journal of Educational Change, 21*, pp. 19–35. DOI:10.1007/s10833-019-09354-2

Paul, Christopher (2011) *Strategic Communication: Origins, Concepts and Current Debates*, Santa Barbara, CA: Praeger.

Ryu, Sangyub & Chang, Yongin (2017) 'Accountability, Political Views and Bureaucratic Behaviour: A Theoretical Approach', *Public Organizational Review, 17*, pp. 481–494. DOI:10.1007/s11115-016-0349z

Stout, Mark & Warner, Michael (2018) 'Intelligence is as intelligence does', *Intelligence and National Security, 33 (4)*, pp. 517–526. DOI:10.1080/02684527.2018.1452593

Tibebu, Teshale (2008) 'Modernity, Eurocentrism, and radical politics in Ethiopia, 1961–1991', *African Identities, 6 (4)*, pp. 345–371.

Vorbrugg, A. (2015) 'Governing through civil society? The making of a post-Soviet political subject in Ukraine', *Environment and Planning D: Society and Space, 33 (1)*, pp. 136–153. DOI:10.1068/d13055p

7 Security institutions

Their function, structure and staffing

David Chuter

Introduction

As discussed in Chapter 5, a security policy is pointless unless it can be implemented, and to be implemented it requires institutions. This chapter looks at typical institutions, where the need arises for them, what they are, how they work, who staffs them and how they can best work together.

Security needs and tasks

It would be easy to begin with a standard list of security institutions (police, military, intelligence services) and then try to lay down individual and collective rules for them. Such an approach, however, is not very helpful. National security institutions have developed over long periods, for different reasons, with different objectives, and to address different issues. Even when the names are similar, institutions in different countries may vary sharply in their origins, composition, status and organisation.

So, it makes more sense, before considering institutions, to look at tasks; which vary over time, and may be approached in different organisational ways. Security tasks are diverse, and the easiest way of visualising them is to borrow the military distinction between tactical, operational and strategic levels of security. It can be said that:

1. *Tactical Level Security* is the security of everyday life. It includes security from robbery or assault in the home, security while walking the streets, security of possessions, even protection from such problems as racial or other harassment or aggressive begging. If security institutions cannot guarantee this basic level of security, others will move in to do it for them.
2. *Operational Level Security* is the security of the larger unit: the town, the region, the group. It ensures the state's monopoly of legitimate violence and political power at the local level, which is to say it involves the suppression of organised criminal gangs, drug dealers or terrorists. It also means that the state controls the ground: citizens are not likely to be threatened by mass political violence or other threats to public order.
3. *Strategic Level Security* is the security of the state itself, and sometimes of an international unit of which it is part. In one sense, it ensures the state monopoly of organised violence, the security of national territory, the protection of frontiers and the control of movement across them. It also involves the wider interests of the state: such things as regional security problems, alliances and membership

DOI: 10.4324/9781003137061-7

of international organisations (IOs), joint operations and training, security and intelligence cooperation, trade and natural resources, among other issues.

Not only is this a very long list, it is obvious that not all its elements will be equally important in all countries. A small island nation and a large, landlocked state will have different security issues to address. A state which is a magnet for economic migration will have a different set of problems from a state which sends workers abroad. A state in a stable region has different concerns from a state in an unstable one. And so on. In turn, these differences produce very different security structures and institutions.

A further complication is that, quite obviously, these three levels overlap, have consequences for each other and are influenced by each other. Thus, security problems at different levels (for example: street drug-dealing and transnational organised crime) have to be dealt with in a holistic fashion, and if not by precisely the same structure, then in closely related ones. Working through the levels in turn gives some idea of what the totality of the security issues are likely to be, and that will help to guide our thinking about required capabilities, and hence which institutions are needed.

The tactical level

The tactical level is normally associated with police services of some kind, and some sort of rudimentary law enforcement system seems to have been a feature of most civilisations. Yet organised, professional police forces are not even two centuries old: by convention the oldest is the London Metropolitan Police, founded in 1828. Many police forces in advanced states today are considerably younger than that. This illustrates one important preliminary point: security began, and to some extent continues even now, as the business of communities and their own institutions. Police forces were largely created in response to the explosive growth of towns and cities in the nineteenth century. Before that time, communities were small and homogeneous, and crime by insiders was thus difficult. The life of a traditional village, with old ladies sitting in the doorways of houses and watching everything that went on, was itself a form of security institution – a tradition not yet dead in certain parts of Asia and Africa. Even half a century ago in most western countries the police would be called only by exception: reprobation, apologies and making amends would be the way in which petty crimes were often treated. With the increasing destruction of historical social bonds, and the massive increase in the scope of criminal law and its application, this is no longer the case.

Nonetheless, neighbours watching each other's cars and houses during absences, people handing in property they have found or participating in anti-crime watch groups are continuing examples of unofficial security structures. The most basic form of tactical level security is therefore crime prevention, as any policeman will happily confirm. Indeed, individual and collective common sense are equally valuable: examples include advice produced by the police urging people not to go into certain areas at certain times, not to obviously carry or wear expensive cameras, telephones or jewellery or to avoid unlicensed taxis. Mundane anti-crime programmes to fit locks and security gates may not have the glamour of projects researching cyber-security challenges, but they probably do a great deal more to ensure the security of ordinary people. At a very different level, information from local communities in recent years has been a valuable aid in fighting Islamic extremism: these communities, after all, are often the first victims.

More recently, steps have been taken towards what criminologists term *Situational Crime Prevention (SCP)*, which is less concerned with criminals themselves, and more with producing situations where crime is difficult, and ideally impossible. SCP encompasses a huge range of measures, but, in common with traditional community-based security, they draw on resources and disciplines well outside what we customarily think of as the professional security sector (Clarke, 1997).

Formal security institutions operating at the tactical level must take account of all these realities. An institution concerned with tactical level public safety is overwhelmingly dependent on public participation and help for its effectiveness. Conversely, an institution of that kind which is corrupt or has little credibility, will be ineffective, and this bad opinion will have an effect on other parts of the institution elsewhere. The actual tasks that can be carried out at tactical level are obviously limited: numerous studies in many countries have shown that patrolling police officers seldom encounter crimes in progress. Reliable communications and transport (which not all police forces have) can enable a wider range of responses, but ultimately the responsibilities at that level are more deterrent and community based.

Most tactical-level security issues are related to public safety. There is, however, another class of issues to do with the protection of places and people representing the state and its agents. Clearly, a state which cannot guarantee the safety of its public buildings and its personnel is not going to be respected. Providing this protection – and being seen to do so – is therefore important politically.

In some cases, the protection is wholly or largely symbolic. A Head of State's residence or a Parliament, for example, may be guarded by troops in ceremonial uniform. Most official buildings will have some form of access control to stop just anybody walking in. Sensitive sites and military headquarters may also have armed guards (though probably not in ceremonial uniform) although again their function is primarily dissuasive.

Arrangements will be rather different where there is an assessed threat to a place or a person. At that point, specially trained individuals capable of using their weapons will be employed. Where the threat is very general (an airport or a tourist site, for example) mobile patrols will be used. Where the threat is to a person, Close Protection teams are employed. In both cases, there will also be tactical control, to organise a response if one is needed, and it is important that the personnel concerned are properly trained, and ideally members of an institution which is experienced in handling weapons and dealing with tactical situations where there is danger to the public.

The operational level

The first institutional characteristic of the Operational level of security is that it coordinates the tactical level. Policemen are not deployed aimlessly or according to how they happen to feel at the time. Guards are not allocated randomly to protect sites or people.

Public security forces need local headquarters to coordinate patrol patterns, respond to emergency calls and direct effort where it is needed. In cities, there will be specialist teams for dealing with serious or complex crimes, and managers to allocate resources where needed. A surprising number of police forces around the world, notably in Africa, lack this kind of capability even today, and their work consists of little else but patrolling.

Example 7.1: Policing in the DRC

In Kinshasa some years ago, a very professional and dedicated police officer recently returned from training overseas said to me that he hoped I would not be a victim of crime while I was there. His colleagues would not be able to respond, since they did not have the resources to do so, and I would have to provide the paper and pen for a statement to be taken. Any possibility of actual investigation of the crime was, of course, out of the question. The officer added that he knew exactly how, in theory, to reduce crime in the area of the city for which he was responsible, but that without any resources he was helpless to do so.

This is also the level at which criminal investigation, and the relatively new activity of criminal intelligence take place: attempting to identify and analyse the activities of criminal groups and look for ways of dismantling them (UNDOC, 2011).

Similarly, groups of soldiers protecting a tourist area will not have been randomly selected, but come from a larger unit which is stationed in the area for a period of time, working to patterns, legal constraints and rules of engagement (see Chapter 4) dictated by a higher command authority and agreed with local political authorities and the police.

Operational-level security problems affect a community as a whole. They may range from organised begging and street crime gangs, to drug dealing, to different forms of trafficking, to protection rackets, to open conflict between political or ethnic groups, up to attempts to actually dispute the state's monopoly of legitimate violence in a city or a district. Groups promoting political Islam have been quietly taking control of parts of the poorer areas of European cities for some years now, often with the cooperation of local politicians for whom they provide a guaranteed electorate, and even cooperating with organised crime from the same communities, which can provide weapons and logistic support (see for example Rougier, 2020).

Example 7.2: Organised crime in context

In every country there has been a tendency for organised crime to be dominated by immigrant or minority groups (Al Capone was the son of Italian immigrants). Such groups tend to be more effective than domestic organised groups because they are based around family and clan links, languages not widely spoken, and links back to the home country, e.g., for trafficking. In addition, many such groups come from countries where their ancestors were marginalised or otherwise had a history of violent resistance to the state, and what we would see as 'criminal' behaviour was considered normal and even praiseworthy. (Most of the Chicago Italian gangsters were from Sicilian families, for example, just as organised crime in France for many years was controlled by Corsicans.) Albanian organised crime groups have been especially successful in controlling organised crime in much of Europe over the last generation, and creating links all over the world (Arsovska, 2015).

Recent examples include Jamaica, as well as battles between immigrant gangs for the control of the drugs trade in several European cities. The key is that they cannot be addressed by individuals or small groups, no matter how skilled, but require careful and systematic operations extending over time and involving significant resources. Dismantling a protection racket, for example, may involve months of patient surveillance, careful establishment of networks and hierarchies, identification and preparation of possible witnesses, targeting of principal suspects, preparation of charges that can be proved and many other activities, which cannot be improvised and take time to carry out.

One important operational-level task is the security of the streets and the safety of the population. This operates at two main levels. The first is that of political violence and demonstrations. Even in the most benign environment, where peaceful demonstrations are normal, they involve significant potential security issues. Routes have to be agreed, traffic has to be stopped, public transport redirected or cancelled, residents and businesses forewarned, emergency medical services organised and some form of liaison established between the organisers and the authorities.

But even a peaceful demonstration on a controversial subject has the potential to escape control. The forces of order may have to cope with counter-demonstrators, or just protesters, who need to be kept away from the main group. Some may go so far as to try to attack the peaceful demonstrators. Other groups (like the Black Blocs widespread in Europe) may infiltrate peaceful demonstrations with the aim of attacking police and destroying property, or of provoking the authorities into over-reaction.

Example 7.3: Undermining legitimate protests

The Black Blocs are not a movement, and have no fixed membership, which make them difficult to identify, let alone infiltrate. They are adherents of a tactic of direct action, especially to destroy property, and they actively seek violent conflict with the authorities. They are distinguished by black clothing and masks, and their tactics are to join peaceful demonstrations in normal clothing, revealing themselves only later. The tactic seems to have begun in Germany in the 1980s, but has most recently been seen in France during the high point of the demonstrations by the *Gilets jaunes* in 2018–19. These demonstrations, largely spontaneous and coordinated by social media, were not centrally organised and so were easy to infiltrate. The demonstrations were intended to be peaceful, but the infiltrators (often numbering in the hundreds, and from all over Europe) ran riot, destroying shops and businesses and conducting running battles with police.

However, in many political cultures, violent and illegal street demonstrations are a normal part of political life. Sometimes they may be just a show of force, to intimidate the government (or the opposition), sometimes they are aimed at other political parties, communities or religious groups, or directly at government or political party HQs, or media outlets. The organisers (since such demonstrations are seldom spontaneous) may have political objectives, which can go as far as the promotion of anarchy from which they think they may benefit, or even the overthrow of the government. In such cultures, it is normal for demonstrators to be paid, and to receive assurances of free medical and legal assistance if they are injured. Indeed, provoking a violent over-reaction from the authorities is a common objective of such demonstrations.

Coping with such events, and keeping the streets safe for ordinary people, is probably the greatest operational level challenge for security institutions. Whichever institutions are involved, empirical evidence suggests that there are two particular characteristics that are essential. One is that the force be properly trained, equipped and led, and should not intervene unless ordered. Surprisingly, this is often not the case.

Such forces require proper protection – without which discipline is impossible – organisation and training to enable them to work together in confusing and dangerous circumstances, and leadership to tell them what they are supposed to be doing and how. They also need both equipment and tactical doctrine for dispersing violent crowds with the minimum of force – something which has proven to be difficult, if not impossible, to guarantee in practice.

Secondly, such forces need a sophisticated doctrine to stop things getting out of control. What seems to work best is the deployment of the lowest level of force appropriate to the situation, but with the capacity to escalate if necessary, above and beyond the ability of the demonstrators to respond. Intimidation, rather than brute force, seems the best way to cope with street violence, but this is difficult and complex to do, and the right training and equipment is required.

The other major operational level challenge, for some states going through transition and development, is making sure that authority of the government is not challenged by criminal or political groups, putting the safety of the local population in jeopardy. In many countries in Europe, for example, parts of cities are under the control of organised crime, and the law of the country is not enforced. In other areas, political, religious or ethnic groups may exert *de facto* control, even imposing their own form of social organisation and political system. Of course, every criminal act, and every violent political act, are challenges to the authority of the state. So long as individual acts can be investigated and the perpetrators brought to justice, the overall authority of the state is not in question. In some circumstances however, a criminal or political group may exert effective control over a district or part of a city: if a state tolerates such a situation for too long, it loses credibility in the eyes of its population.

There is no simple answer to such problems. The areas concerned may have been neglected by the state in the first place, or the communities in the areas may have been historically disadvantaged. Alternatively, foreign powers may be involved (especially in border regions), international criminal syndicates may be active, and religious or other extremists may be stirring things up. Such groups, whether criminal or political, often come from immigrant communities, and it is essential that the communities as a whole (who are often the first victims) should not feel that they themselves are being targeted by the state. At the operational level, capabilities have to be developed to dismantle such groups, and ensure the monopoly of legitimate violence remains in the hands of the state. In addition, the state needs to develop a capability for small-scale and extremely precise operations with limited objectives, such as rescuing hostages, or arresting organised crime bosses in dangerous environments.

The strategic level

The strategic level first involves coordination and direction of the other levels. For example, there has to be a single policy for tackling organised crime and separatist violence, if they are the major problems. Moreover, both subjects will require some sort of consultation or even cooperation, certainly in the region, and possibly beyond. Individual operations will usually require high-level political approval. The strategic level is the most varied and complex, but its activities can be divided into a few basic categories as follows:

1.   It sets national policies to ensure that institutions at the operational and tactical levels all know what they are doing, and are working to the same criteria. It also

looks outward, since many operational level problems cross frontiers, and neighbours and others may be equally affected, or for that matter may be the origin of the problems.

2. The strategic level looks at the security interests of the country as a whole. Classically, this has meant two things. One was ensuring the monopoly of legitimate violence across the whole of the territory in the protection of the political system and the constitutional order. This remains the case today, even in advanced countries: a state which cannot ensure these things will not last very long. The other is the protection of the territorial integrity and interests of the country. There is also the strategic positioning of the state relative to its neighbours, great powers and international organisations. States may wish to cultivate alliances, avoid domination from an external power, or play great powers off against each other. Armed forces may be configured so that they are not perceived as a threat. Alternatively, they may be organised and trained so as to provide a disincentive to aggression, because they can inflict more damage on an invader than that invader is willing to risk. It is at this level that the analysis of the country's strategic context, or security environment, should occur, taking into consideration the political, economic, social, legal, technological and environmental dimensions. At this point, issues pertaining to trade and the economy need to be considered; how can these be secured and what are the implications of long-term economic performance for the capability and affordability of the security services? The assessment and prioritisation of risks will inform individual and collective institutional responses and influence the size, budgets and acquisition programmes of security services (see Chapter 11).

3. The wider security policy of the country is also a major strategic issue. Decisions about membership of regional security organisations, multilateral regimes, contributions to peace missions, police, military and intelligence cooperation, and the national profile within international fora dealing with security are all strategic level issues. Responses to regional crises, decisions about whether to agree to participate in multinational missions, even decisions about how to vote in the UN or what position to publicly take on a sensitive security issue are strategic level issues as well.

Security institutions and roles

It will already be clear that dedicated security institutions are required, and are obliged to operate at a number of different levels, if only to ensure direction and coordination. It is not therefore possible to provide a simple equivalence between the strategic, tactical and operational levels at which security issues are posed, and the levels of institutions which deal with them. We can, however, make an approximate distinction, dividing institutions into those which are *primarily* concerned with policy, those which are *primarily* concerned with command and control, and those (few) which are *primarily* concerned with execution on the ground.

The policy level

This is the highest and most general level of security institutions. It is the level of the political leadership and political direction, and of the institutions which serve central government directly. In practice, it is the level of government ministries, or other bodies headed by political figures directly responsible to Parliament. The number of such bodies is relatively small, in spite of attempts to define the 'security sector' more widely than can really be justified and so increase their number. There are, of course, government Ministries which deal with certain *other types* of 'security' (food security, social security, etcetera) but, even if we should acknowledge the tiresome human security debate, it is clear that such ministries do not deal with security in any way that is useful to include here. There are also other parts of the *political system* which involve themselves in security issues from time to time, such as Parliament and the courts, but the latter are not *part of* the security sector's institutions, except insofar as they are part of (or more properly involved with) all sectors of government, and indeed would still exist if the security sector were one day to magically disappear. To argue otherwise, is to seriously misunderstand the separation of powers in a political system.

Security institutions, for the purposes of this chapter, consist of all those institutions whose *primary* function is the provision of security at various levels. At the policy level, this includes all policy-making institutions headed by political appointees responsible for formulating and implementing government policy. The two most important are usually the defence or armed forces ministry, which is responsible for the country's military, but also other defence capabilities such as science and technology; and the interior ministry, which is responsible for police, prisons, justice, borders and related issues. Other ministries will be involved as well, however, depending on the subject. For example, the finance ministry, in any political system, will be involved in all spending decisions, attempting to ensure that as little as possible is spent. The foreign ministry should always be a major player in security policy affairs, even if the country concerned does not deploy its soldiers abroad. Training programmes, ship visits, security fora, bilateral discussions, and even the views of neighbours and others on your defence policy and forces are all important subjects. Likewise, the trade ministry, the transport ministry, even the education ministry may have some involvement with security issues. The security forces will often have a role in emergencies and disaster management therefore they will need links with organisations responsible for such questions. The main ministerial actors and their roles in security issues are summarised in Table 7.1. It should be noted that as practice differs greatly this summary should be seen as typical, rather than prescriptive.

So, the first question is how the policy function is organised. Here, one complication is that security issues are key issues of state. A president or prime minister will almost always involve themselves in security issues, and their staffs may be large enough to constitute a supplementary, and even rival, power centre for decision-making about security questions. In countries with strong Presidencies, this can make decisions complex and time-consuming, but equally, in weak parliamentary systems with coalitions (ranging from the Netherlands to Lebanon), differences between ministers of different parties can cause decision-making to be just as slow.

A typical government system will discuss security issues in a limited configuration of the Council of Ministers, chaired by the president and/or the prime minister, defence minister, foreign minister, interior minister, finance minister, often the justice minister, and also the minister for intelligence in the countries that have them. Other ministers would attend as needed. Depending on the political system, non-elected officials may also attend. Such a structure may be given a special name – National Security Council, for example – but in practice it will be similar to any specialist ministerial committee. This is the level at which binding political decisions are taken, and policy is agreed. Major decisions about budgets, spending, deployments, organisation, legislation and so forth will be taken, or at least ratified, there.

Table 7.1 Typical Examples of Security Ministries and Responsibilities

Ministry	Main Functions	Secondary Functions
Central Secretariat of President/PM	Coordination of security sector business, meetings and decisions.	May also have a central policy-making and coordination role. May control intelligence assessment.
Interior	Borders, customs, passports and identity cards, strategic police issues, control of entry and movement, prisons, emergency planning.	May also directly control domestic intelligence service. Control of national police force if there is one. May have its own paramilitary public order or border force. May control justice issues, or this may be a separate ministry.
Defence	Making and implementing defence policy. Administration and budgets of the armed forces. Procurement of equipment and services. Research and development. Strategic direction of operations.	May incorporate a national Military HQ. May directly command units in the field. May be an actor in the national economy, disaster relief, etc.
Foreign Affairs	Security policy coordination. Treaties and international agreements. Security cooperation with other countries, foreign/UN deployments, reciprocal training.	May also directly control foreign intelligence service. May be responsible for defence attachés and exchange personnel.
Others	Coastguards, border guards, customs officers and others may come under the control of other ministries (e.g., finance). Intelligence services may be headed by political figures or appointees, although not strictly government departments. Many countries have federal police forces, under the control of elected local political figures.	

Source: Author.

Formal institutions at the policy level will not be very numerous. The important players know each other, and will see each other all the time and be in frequent contact. It would be unusual for a Ministerial Security Committee (let us call it) to meet more than once a week, except in situations of crisis. What is important is the permanent structure that underpins it. Irrespective of the political system, the purpose will always be the same: to prepare decisions as far as possible, to eradicate differences, and to enable decision makers to concentrate on the essential issues. It should also be a forum for making sure that all aspects of a security issue are considered and dealt with together. There is also an obvious need to make sure that decisions that are made are recorded, respected and implemented.

The precise institutional arrangements will depend heavily on the political culture of the country. A highly centralised state may have a large secretariat staff, partly duplicating work done in the ministries, and sometimes dictating policy on behalf of the president or prime minister. At the other extreme, a highly decentralised parliamentary system may have a secretariat which does little more than arrange meetings and issue minutes. In general, also, there will be provision for a more informal and operational committee to meet, especially in moments of crisis, usually chaired by a minister.

Likewise, in a state where power is heavily personalised, ministers will have large, personal staffs loyal to them as individuals. Equally, they will reserve the right to make personnel changes at all levels to make sure that the institutions they are responsible for will carry out their policies loyally. This would apply to the security sector at least as much as anywhere else, and can create overlapping and sometimes conflicting networks of personal loyalty, which can frustrate attempts to get things done. In other political cultures more based on compromise and consensus, such as those in Old Commonwealth countries and parts of Asia, ministers largely work with staffs they have inherited.

There is a fine line to tread as regards working practices, between letting individual ministries get on with their work on the one hand, and alternatively risking them working at cross-purposes, or even against each other. What has been called in recent years a 'whole-of-government' approach (WGA) obviously makes pragmatic sense, insofar as security policy questions naturally cross administrative boundaries. When different Ministries compete with and undermine the policies of others (as happens often in the United States), or where, as frequently, different ministries represent different and competing power-bases, the results are seldom effective. On the other hand, however, WGA can become an invitation to any lobby within government to argue that it has an interest and should be involved: in such cases paralysis can result. The best answer, self-evidently, is a compromise, which ensures that those with a genuine interest are involved, but that decisions are still taken expeditiously. This is easier said than done.

The question is easier to resolve if the different institutions share a broadly similar culture, and so think in broadly the same way. The problem is most acute when security ministries are controlled by technical specialists such as the military and the police. Both have strong and clannish cultures, and there can be rivalry between them. Whilst cultural differences can never be eradicated, they can be minimised if civilian officials are also employed in large numbers, and are expert enough to understand the concerns of their uniformed colleagues, whilst also being able to communicate effectively with civilian colleagues elsewhere in government. Experience suggests, for example, that a civilian official in Defence or the Interior who has the same kind of social and educational background as a diplomat will find it much easier to have a productive relationship, which is obviously good for the management of policy. Although cultural differences will always exist (it would be pointless and counter-productive if military officers were indistinguishable from diplomats) and may also reflect real divergences of interest; they are not insurmountable.

The ministries concerned with security (or the 'power ministries') are in principle just like any other. The observation that policies need institutions to carry them out applies universally: foreign policy requires embassies, education policy requires schools and universities, and health policy requires clinics and hospitals. The police, military, intelligence services, etc. are the implementing or executive institutions that carry out government policies, under the direction of ministers. In all cases, the ministry consists of:

1. an elected political figure or a figure appointed by an elected office-holder, and their staff;
2. advisors responsible for making and implementing policy, dealing with Parliament, negotiating budgets, etcetera;
3. technical experts who advise, but do not make policy.

The first two categories are essentially the same anywhere. The second consists of policy and administrative civil servants, ideally those who have made a career specialty of security issues. (There is a bizarre argument, sometimes encountered, that ministries exist to 'control' the security forces, rather as if the health ministry existed to control dentists. See Chapters 1 and 3 for a discussion of this phenomenon.) Just as in education, for example, where the expert advisers will include educational psychologists, experts on curriculum design, architects, so in the interior ministry, they will be policemen, forensic experts, lawyers, penologists, lawyers and others. In a defence ministry, they will be military officers, intelligence specialists, lawyers, scientists, engineers and others with similar skills.

There are some particular issues in security ministries. The organisation of an interior ministry depends to a considerable extent on whether the country has a national police, or a series of regional or local ones, and, if the latter, how far they are responsible for recruitment, training and promotion. At one extreme, the ministry may have a national police HQ, responsible for everything, and a minister directly concerned with many operational issues. At the other, the ministry as a whole may only set very general guidance, and not be involved in day-to-day police issues at all. It is impossible to say which alternative works better: it entirely depends on the political culture of the country. France, for example, with its centralised Jacobin tradition, has a national police force directly controlled by the interior ministry, and its public order and counter-terrorist capabilities reside there and in the *gendarmerie nationale*. (In recent years municipal police forces, often unarmed, have been created to handle routine issues, as part of a trend towards decentralisation.) In Germany, the previous (Prussian) model of a centralised police force was abandoned after 1945 for political reasons, and the German police are now highly decentralised. Indeed, the only way a counter-terrorist capability could be constructed when one was needed after the 1972 Olympics massacre, was from the one national police unit that did exist, the *Bundesgrenzschutz* (Federal Border Guard Service). It was politically unacceptable for the military to be used in such a capacity.

This conveniently leads to the question of whether the Interior Ministry is responsible for public order and anti-terrorism. This very much depends on the situation of the country and the nature of the problems it faces. Since using untrained policemen in improvised groups to counter unrest is a recipe for disaster, a decision has to be taken to recruit, train and correctly equip such a force, with due attention to the political and legal implications. This implies a special department to cope with such operations, as well as command and control systems and the need for political direction in real time. Likewise, counter-terrorism operations and hostage rescue are not part of core police capabilities, and so specialists have to be carefully selected, trained and equipped, and command and control systems set up to manage operations. Experience suggests that such operations are extraordinarily delicate and risky and the ministry needs to develop a range of capabilities to make the chances of success as great as possible. In both these cases, there is also a deeper institutional judgement to make: how militarised do you want your police force to be? The rule of thumb in most countries is that the police deal with incidents until the level of violence exceeds their ability to cope, at which point the military are invoked. Of course, the more the police are militarised the less need they will have of the military, yet the less they will resemble a traditional police force, as is evidenced in the United States. The less the police are militarised, the more the military will be called on to carry out tasks for which they themselves were not originally intended.

The organisation of a defence ministry depends on several factors, including primarily whether it is actually a proper ministry or not. Practice varies enormously, and in some countries, what is described as a defence ministry is actually an armed forces headquarters with a minister and staff bolted on. This is explicable by the fact that in many countries the military actually pre-dated the modern state, and already had a nationwide command system, but such models are, happily, becoming less common, and there is an increasing move to making defence a ministry like any other, along the lines described above. Nonetheless, the fact that the military, uniquely, has to have a single, nation-wide command system (regional armies, by definition, would be ridiculous) means that the institutional question of how the military relate to the ministry has to be addressed. Depending on how that question is answered, military staff may be partially or even completely integrated with the civilian hierarchy, may work in a parallel hierarchy in the same organisation, or in another organisation completely.

Example 7.4: From parallel hierarchies to integrated staffing

During the apartheid era in South Africa, defence policy (and much security policy) was effectively made by the military. Defence HQ carried out the functions of a ministry, the latter having been abolished at the end of the 1960s. One of the electoral promises of the ANC in 1994 was to establish a proper 'civilian' ministry, which would 'control' the military, who, it was felt, had enjoyed far too much independence. This led to the creation of a defence secretariat, theoretically civilian, but often with retired or seconded military officers involved, since civilians did not have the necessary skills in the early days. The result was duplication of effort and institutional rivalry, and an enforced movement towards a more cooperative and integrated system which, in the author's observation, is continuing (see also Cawthra, 2005).

To provide clarity, two functions can be distinguished that military staffs perform for a government:

1. The military advice function
2. The command and control of forces function.

The first is part of normal policy-making. If the president asks about the feasibility of deploying a peacekeeping force abroad, much of the technical advice will inevitably come from the military. Just as with doctors or educational psychologists, there should be military experts in the ministry. The military, however, is a hierarchy in the sense that education is not, and there are also a host of policy and administrative questions relating to the military itself on which they will have a major (though not of course exclusive) contribution. It is thus common to have a Chief of Defence in the military, who heads staffs responsible for military advice and also the administration of the military themselves. Command and control, by contrast, is a coordination function, to be considered in a moment.

The coordinating level

'Coordination' means an intermediate level of organisation, command and control, to ensure that the institutions of the security sector which operate at ground level are properly organised, trained, equipped and led, and are given their orders to carry out. Institutions at this level are not concerned with making policy (though they might be consulted), but in turning that policy into actual security activities. This is the level of the national military HQ, any regional HQs, the level of police HQs, of intelligence agencies, and of the HQs of such units as coastguards and gendarmerie, if the country has them.

Example 7.5: Coordination in practice

Suppose that a militia group supported by a hostile neighbour has succeeded in taking control of a small area near the border rich in raw materials. The government's National Security Committee decides on a policy response, which is to expel them, and increase protection in the area thereafter. The national military HQ (NMHQ) draws up a plan which it submits for approval. Once that plan is agreed, the NMHQ identifies the units needed, appoints a commander with staff, and makes sure that equipment and training are up to standard. It may delegate day-to-day oversight of the operation to a regional Military HQ if there is one. In turn, other coordinating bodies identify support for the operation and its aftermath from the resources of the police and/or gendarmerie and the intelligence services. All of these forces are selected and tasked according to the objectives and limitations that have been laid down by the policy level. For example, ministers may have decided to try to force the militia units to disperse, with minimal violence, and they ask the NMHQ to prepare a force which will be sufficiently large and powerful that the militias will not try to oppose it. The military planners will seek to organise such a force, and present it to the political leadership for approval.

Most coordinating institutions are made up of specialists from the services concerned. A military HQ is, indeed, largely military, though these days it may well have civilians attached to manage budgetary issues, and provide legal, political and media advice to the senior commanders. It is also quite common to have liaison officers from police, gendarmerie and other organisations. The anomaly at this level is the organisation of intelligence services or, to be more precise, the intelligence function, which straddles the different levels.

   Governments need information if they are to deal with current problems and provide for future problems. Much of this information is freely available to anyone, and much more is available from other governments, or from embassies and similar sources. There remains, however, a hard core of information that is needed but is not easily available, either because of the target itself (transnational organised crime, for example), or the nature of the issue (a power-struggle between the chief of defence and the president, for example). Where ordinary methods cannot provide, extraordinary, secret ones must be used. This is all intelligence really is: it is a type of information that is gathered from people who do not want you to have it, without them knowing that you have done so. This is why, when the British set up their professional foreign intelligence service after the First World War, they called it the *Secret* Intelligence Service, a name it still bears. But intelligence is, in the end, just information obtained clandestinely.

Intelligence activities can be grouped under two headings: *collection* and *analysis*. The latter takes place at the policy level, often in specialised institutions reporting directly to the president or prime minister, and involving experts from the ministries who need the intelligence, and have often commissioned it. Collection on the other hand is done by specialised agencies operating at the coordinating level. They are executive institutions, and not policy-making ones. Their job is, by various human and technical means, to gather and process the information that the policy level needs to make decisions. Sometimes, these organisations may be directly subordinated to a ministry, or even formally part of it: an example would be a domestic intelligence service focused on counter-terrorism. Likewise, most defence ministries have a special intelligence department, which analyses the more technical aspects of defence-related subjects.

Conclusion

There are no security institutions that exist only at the lowest, implementation level. The police station, the military unit, the coastguard ship, the intelligence officer working undercover at an embassy, are all part of hierarchical chains leading up through the coordinating level, responsible for their organisation and tasking, to the policy level which sets the objectives against which they work. At least, a well-functioning system works this way, and units which seek too much independence (as Special Forces units notoriously do) risk damaging the orderly management of the whole system. Whilst some overlap between the levels is inevitable, as has been indicated, it is nevertheless helpful to keep them as conceptually and institutionally separate as is reasonably possible, if only to stop them trying to do each other's jobs.

Questions to consider

1. What security institutions exist in your country? Is the overall shape and constitution of the security sector as a whole clear?
2. Are the roles of different institutions in the security sector well understood and the limits respected? Is there any confusion of roles or institutional competition?
3. Do you think that the security sector of your country is appropriately structured for the security issues that your country faces?
4. Can you identify special historical, cultural or political factors that have influenced the structure and working of the security institutions in your country?

Suggested further reading

Omand, David (2010) *Securing the State*, London: Hurst.

Bearne, Susanna et al (2005) *National Security Decision-Making Structures and Security Sector Reform*, Brussels: RAND Europe, 2005. Available at https://www.rand.org/content/dam/rand/pubs/technical_reports/2005/RAND_TR289.pdf. [Accessed 5 December 2020].

Global Initiative Against Transnational Organised Crime. Available at: https://globalinitiative.net. [Accessed 5 December 2020].

References

Arsovska, Jana (2015) *Decoding Albanian Organized Crime*, Berkeley, CA: University of California Press.

Cawthra, Gavin (2005) 'Security Governance in South Africa', *African Security Studies, 14*, pp.95–105. DOI: 10.1080/10246029.2005.9627376

Clarke, Ronald V. (1997) *Situational Crime Prevention: Successful Case Studies*, 2nd ed., Boulder, CO: Lynne Reiner.

Rougier, Bernard (2020) *Les Territoires conquis de l'islamisme*, Paris: PUF.

United Nations Office on Drugs and Crime (2011) *Criminal Intelligence Manual for Analysts*, Vienna. Available at https://www.unodc.org/documents/organized-crime/Law-Enforcement/Criminal_Intelligence_for_Analysts.pdf [Accessed 5 December 2020].

8 Strategic management

Ifti Zaidi and Bryan Watters

Introduction

In today's fast-moving and complex world, strategic management (SM) is vital for organisational success. To remain viable, organisations in private, public and non-governmental sectors must continuously pursue strategies that enable them to generate value in the goods and services they provide to their customers and stakeholders. As noted in Chapter 1, managers transform and use their teams' talents to achieve organisational outputs. They attain this through planning, organising, controlling and directing organisational resources to achieve their corporate objectives. Adding the adjective 'strategic' to management implies the level, nature, and scope of managerial decisions and actions.

This chapter begins with a focus on the evolution and key developments in the field of SM. A discussion follows on the strategic managers' role as the coupling between strategic leadership and the senior management teams responsible for creating organisational outputs. The chapter concludes with a summary of key insights for strategic managers seeking to reconcile conflicting stakeholder demands in a volatile, uncertain, complex and ambiguous world.

Origins and evolution

SM as a field of study is relatively new and emerged as a sub-topic within scientific management in the latter half of the 20th century. The functions and activities that constitute contemporary SM practices, however, have historic origins in organisations such as the church, the military and other large public bodies (see Example 8.1). In the corporate world, SM became established as an organisational best practice in the 1950s and later developed into a science. Led by visionaries like Alfred Sloan, it quickly became an operational blueprint for progressive organisations (see Example 8.2), developing a broader scope, and becoming a sub-discipline in its own right (Joyce, 2015) and a function *sine qua non* for organisational survival.

As introduced in Chapter 1, Henri Fayol identified five key management functions and noted that business, industrial or corporate activities, regardless of sector, essentially divide into six functional categories (Fayol, 1949, pp.3–6):

- technical functions;
- commercial functions;
- financial functions;

DOI: 10.4324/9781003137061-8

- security or protective functions concerning people and assets;
- accounting functions which he described as stocktaking, maintaining balance sheets, costs, and generating statistical data; and
- managerial roles (these led to Fayol's management principles, namely: Planning, Organisation, Command, Coordination, and Control).

While these functional categories have remained relatively constant over time, the purpose of those functions and how they are performed has been the subject of almost continuous debate, with different schools of thought falling in and out of favour. There have, however, been certain constants: the connection between strategy and structure (Chandler, 1962), and that leaders should be cognizant not only of the inner workings and outputs of their organisations (Ansoff, 1968) but of the context in which those organisations operate (Mintzberg, 1981; Porter, 1983; Mintzberg & McHugh, 1985). Mintzberg and Porter (1983) also suggested a bi-directional relationship between strategy and structure. The concept of Strategic Management advocates a future-oriented approach. Successful SM depends on three elements: strategic analysis, systematically analysing an organisation's current operational context; strategic choice, which is about formulating a course of action based on that analysis; and strategy implementation, marshalling the resources required to ensure the strategy achieves the desired effect.

SM takes a whole system view of the organisation and entails two core functions: adding value to the organisational outputs and keeping the organisation competitive. It achieves these by analysing and interpreting organisational capabilities and the external trends that impact the organisation's mission and purpose, identifying what it ought to be doing, and developing strategies to bridge the gaps. Strategic managers ensure that the organisation is configured for efficient and effective delivery of its current and ongoing commitments and oriented to deal with over-the-horizon threats and opportunities. It is the 'art and science of formulating, implementing, and evaluating cross-functional decisions that enable an organisation to achieve its objectives' (David & David, 2016, p.33) and requires 'the identification of the purpose of the organisation and the plans and actions to achieve that purpose' (Lynch, 2018, p.9).

Example 8.1: Strategic management since Sun Tzu's *Art of War*

Sun Tzu's *Art of War* (ca. 6 BC) has inspired numerous studies of business strategy, its purpose and process (McNeilly, 2012; Gagliardi, 2012). Strategy, according to Sun Tzu, is two dimensional, inward (knowing oneself) and outwards (knowing one's opponents). His principle of authority (unity of command), heaven and earth (the permanent environment), organisation, control and logistics have relevance in statecraft, warcraft and business. Having studied the internal and external dimensions through the prism of these principals, one is able to make difficult choices; for example, whether to go on the offensive or the defensive. While Sun Tzu recommended that war be avoided, he also suggested that victory is not possible without the offensive (seizing the initiative). Many of Sun Tzu's teachings have laid the foundation for strategic theory and have been embraced by businesses.

The Prussian school of military thought applied modern principles such as strategy driving structure, functional specialisms, and divisional and hybrid structures as early as the 17th century. It also introduced strategy staff roles that would be akin to today's strategy advisors and strategy teams in organisations. In the 19th century, the industrial age military, particularly under Napoleon Bonaparte, demonstrated the added value of cross-functional management of the military system, coordinated strategy and synchronisation of operations on a mass scale. Embedding such practices brought Napoleon victories against larger and often better equipped competitors. Similarly, the Japanese defeat at the hands of US forces in 1945 had its origins in the 1800s when the US identified future competition over strategic zones of interest in the Pacific and recognised the need to defeat Japan through a naval campaign which culminated in War Plan Orange. This thinking formed the blueprint for the development of US military power, particularly the US Navy. War Plan Orange, with its conceptual origins predating World War One was executed in the Pacific theatre with minor changes due to unforeseen developments like air power and submarines (Miller, 1991).

Example 8.2: Alfred Sloan and General Motors

Under its founder William C. Durant, General Motors (GM) comprised a mixed bag of small manufacturing concerns brought together through random acquisitions in 1908. In 1923, Alfred Sloan took over as General Manager of what was then a small struggling organisation unable to compete with giants like Ford. Sloan identified a lack of coherence among the different units that formed GM and the markets in which it wanted to compete. While GM's senior managers were convinced that the company needed an engineering breakthrough to survive, Sloan's strategic and organisational genius looked for answers in business strategy, not engineering. Within a decade, GM became the largest single employer in the US and was making a profit. From a multitude of organisational innovations introduced by Sloan, was a compelling strategy built around a competitive culture that transformed GM (Sloan, 1963). Henry Ford may have put 'America on wheels' (*The Economist*, 1999), but it was Sloan who gave American enterprise a blueprint for strategic growth. Sloan put strategy first and structure followed to support that blueprint. Following GM's lead, other major enterprises followed suit and in the decades that followed, Sloan's innovations became the fundamental ingredients for success for enterprises around the globe. Analysing the growth of American Enterprise, Alfred Chandler (1962) concluded that structure follows strategy. However, as others caught up, GM's competitive advantage diminished and by the 1960s, the company was again struggling to add value in the face of quality advantage offered by some American, European and Japanese manufacturers. GM's organisational agility enabled it to adapt to its strategy and gain competitive advantage; however, an inability to create added value, through quality, which became increasingly important to the consumer in the decades that followed, led to strategic drift and decline.

Key concepts

The functions and tools that are at the heart of the role performed by strategic managers revolve around two key concepts; these are competitive advantage and value-added:

Competitive advantage

Competitive advantage is a company's comparative profitability against the average profitability of its competitors (Hill, et al., 2015, p.82). For commercial organisations, this may mean having a cost advantage over rivals producing similar products, having a unique differentiation, or a quality advantage over competitors. In the public sector competitive advantage is understood differently. As profit is not the purpose, the absence of external competition can take its toll on the quality of services, efficiency and effectiveness. Public organisations that fail to build and retain a competitive advantage over time also face decline, and ultimately failure. For example, there is active competition from entities that wish to create and exploit security vulnerabilities in the security sector. Without value-added and competitive advantage, security sector organisations would ultimately concede space to rivals who benefit from the resulting insecurity; for example, the strategy pursued by Fuerzas Armadas Revolucionarias de Colombia (FARC) in Colombia (Taylor II, 2020). Barney (1991) identified four qualities that become a source of sustained competitive advantage; these are referred to as the VRIO framework:

- Is the resource *valuable*? In a military sense, this implies the utility of the product, capability or service to the military in relation to what it already possesses or can potentially develop. Value is also applicable to spaces, for example, the comparative value of the Crimea to Russia.
- Is it *rare*? Can competitors easily acquire the building-blocks? Is there control of resources?
- Is it costly to *imitate*? Can competitors easily replicate the capability, thus achieving deterrence value, or produce substitutes, such as, countermeasures in a military sense? For example, cybersecurity technology.
- Is a firm *organised* to capture the value of the resources? Are the military's management systems, processes, structures, and culture able to capitalise on the resources and capabilities?

The explanations added to each of the questions above are intended to indicate how VRIO could be applied to a particular non-commercial context.

Value-added

Simply stated, value-added is the difference between the price of a product or service and the cost of producing it. Value-added, however, is a multidimensional construct. A value can be added to resources in many different ways and viewed through different perspectives. In commercial organisations, it may be an economic value or cash value to the organisation's activities. For decades, there has been an ongoing debate in the UK over the UK's Nuclear Deterrent's added value to the overall security construct. Those who politically support the idea, believe that the investment in a nuclear deterrent creates security, hence making a notional argument of value-added. On the other hand, those who oppose the need for a nuclear deterrent argue that investment in conventional capability and alliance building is a better alternative, hence making a contrary argument and a different focus for added-value towards the same end state – better security. Value-added is measurable as the difference between the cost of production of goods or services and their attained market value. There is a strategic linkage between value-added and competitive advantage. The objective of an organisational strategy is to gain a competitive advantage and create value-added. Commercial enterprises do this across various value-adding activities from raw material suppliers to the product's final consumers. On the other hand, the public sector (including defence) holds financial, corporate and physical assets in the pursuit of policy objectives and these are not solely for the creation of profit. Glendinning (1988) suggests that the public sector creates value in public spending through cost minimisation, output maximisation and the full attainment of the intended product or service. While there is implicit competition in public bodies for government funding, such competition is irrelevant from a government perspective, whereas value-added is of fundamental importance. For example, in providing security, value-added is the effective and efficient delivery of capability, freeing resources for other government initiatives.

The building blocks of strategy

SM seeks to attain and retain competitive advantage and value-added over time through organisational strategy. To do so, strategic managers analyse trends that affect an enterprise, from within and without and produce strategies aimed at steering the organisation to better navigate external influences and changes and prevent the organisation from drifting from its mission and purpose. As a concept, strategic drift reflects a static outlook over time, making the organisation increasingly distant from the reality of changing conditions in the economy, technology, and consumer demands (Johnson et al., 2017). The consequence of drift is a decline in competitiveness and value-added, leading to potential organisational failure. There are three main approaches to avoid drift: developing an early warning system, developing strategic resilience, and encouraging organisational flexibility.

In theory, organisations evolve either through small adaptive changes that can accumulate to produce significant change (the gradualist approach); or largescale changes at opportune moments (punctuated equilibrium approach). Figure 8.1 depicts an organisation's relationship with the external environment over time (t1 to t3); while the environment over this period changes from e1 to e2. The organisation's static outlook keeps it at e0 even though at t2, it could adapt and come close to the external rate

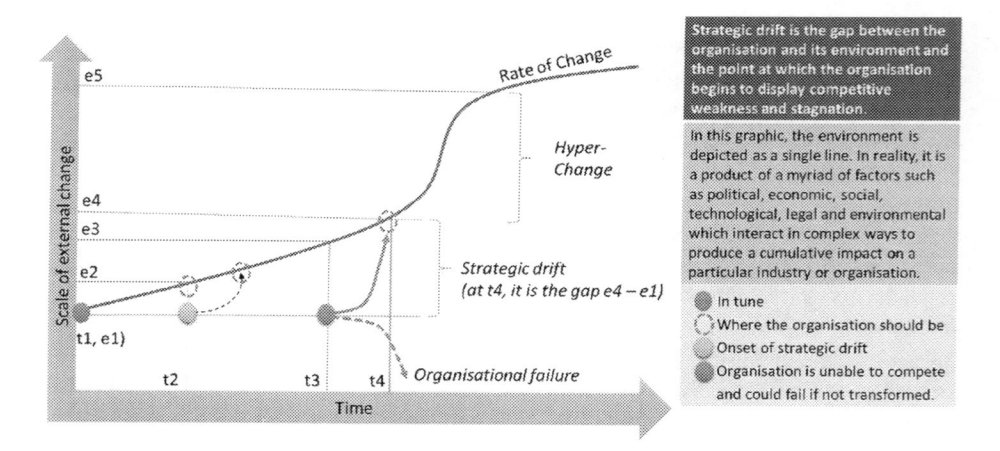

Figure 8.1 Strategic Drift
Source: adapted from Johnson et al. (2017)

of change. At t3, even a significant change leaves a large gap, making failure more probable.

Example 8.3: Strategic drift and its consequences

The photographic industry and telecommunications industry provide visible examples of strategic drift leading to product or brand failure due to the inability to embrace new technologies or the innovations resulting from their creative application. Digital photography, for example, marginalised Kodak because its leadership failed to recognise the future direction of the industry. Similarly, the smartphone affected enterprises that saw the mobile phone only as communication device (see also Example 8.5).

When an organisation makes a conscious effort to continuously realign and adapt to external change, making small corrections in its internal and external alignment, it is said to follow a gradualist approach. For the military, this may translate into mission-oriented training, regrouping, equipment refits, or the gradual adoption of new technologies, etc. The gradualist paradigm is suited only when the rate of external change is relatively low, and when external threats evolve slowly. In periods of hyper-change, flux occurs, where small, stepped changes consume time and effort but are insufficient for any meaningful alignment. Figure 8.2 depicts this approach.

The second approach is to actively pursue periods of stability while consolidating improvements and making block changes. When such changes are revolutionary, they potentially redefine the environment and may impact upon many associated industries. Figure 8.3 demonstrates this approach:

The punctuated equilibrium model may be a strategy or a constraint because of the nature of the industry. For example, the aviation industry (due to a highly regulated environment) and sport (due to the relatively fixed rules and bye-laws), compete within periods of regulatory stability interspersed by periods of rapid change, the punctuated equilibrium approach. They can maximise efficiency and effectiveness within

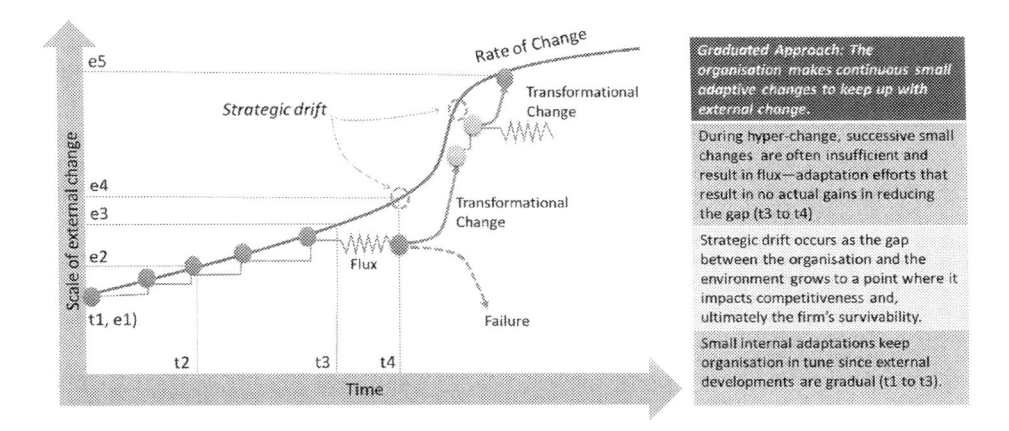

Figure 8.2 The Gradualist Paradigm
Source: Authors.

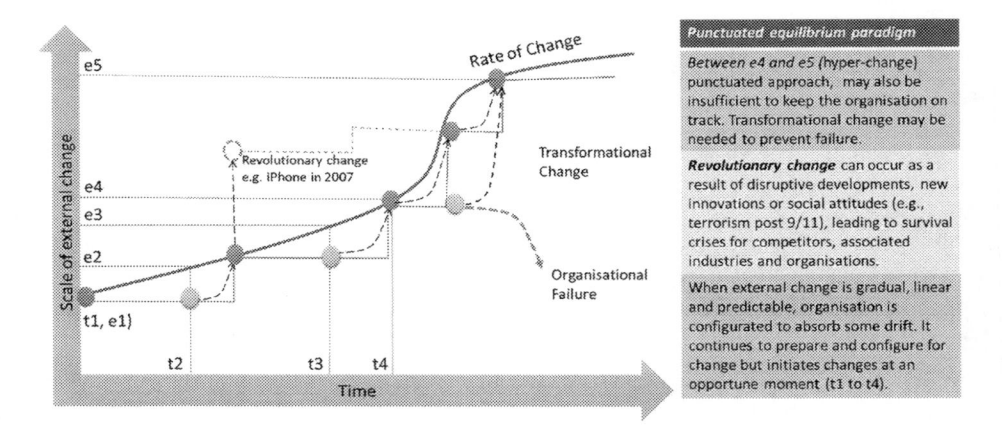

Figure 8.3 Punctuated Equilibrium Paradigm
Source: Authors.

both the regulatory environment and the dynamic environment in which they operate. The punctuated equilibrium paradigm is also common in the public sector since government institutions must quickly transition to delivering policy changes and new priorities in alignment with political change. A tactical dilemma for boards and top leadership is when and how to transition from stability to strategic change and what exactly needs changing (see Example 8.4).

Example 8.4 Incrementalism in foreign policy development

Observing evolutions in policy decisions, Dahl and Lindblom (1953) introduced the concept of incrementalism (stepped changes) as a mechanism for policy change (Howlett & Migone, 2017). The model dominated other approaches like the Rational Actor Model (Allison & Zelikow, 1999) till the 1990s. Lindblom observed that strategic change is the product of incremental changes that accumulate over time. In contrast, Allison argued that rational policy retains a long-term focus. Rational actors make decisions to achieve a relatively fixed strategic end. Since the 1990s, a new orthodoxy has emerged which aligns more closely with the Punctuated Equilibrium Paradigm where policy follows periods of strategic stability punctuated by upheaval and change. The US policy towards the Middle East since 1991 depicts such a pattern. Dahl and Lindblom warn that this orthodoxy does not supplant but supplements Incrementalism 'through 'atypical' or 'paradigmatic' change to the pattern of marginal or incremental change' that Lindblom et al. posited in the1950s.

Example 8.5: Shaping the environment

Apple introduced the iPhone in 2007 as its innovative offering in an already established smartphone market. The iPhone was a revolutionary development within an industry that followed a punctuated equilibrium paradigm and consequently left its competition far behind. Arguably, few industries or societies have been left unchanged by the impact of this innovation. These include: the IT industry by way of how software is created and used; the photographic industry by way of transforming photography from a hobby to a part of everyday life; social media and how media is consumed; and fuelling the rise of new social patterns and means of online shopping to name a few (Molla, 2017).

Contemporary organisations operate in what Barber (1992) described as a volatile, uncertain, complex and ambiguous (VUCA) world. Volatility is often the result of the pace of change, unexpected developments, instability and the unknown duration and impact of the phenomena that create it. Uncertainty results from the unknown cause and effect relationships, while complexity arises from the interconnected parts and variables that interact in a non-linear way. Ambiguity is the absence of antecedents that leads to unknown unknowns (Bennett & Lemoine, 2014). It is also a product of deceit, undisclosed intentions or veiled behaviours and actions of the actors. If we think of organisations as 'living entities' (Ansoff, 1979) or 'bio-social organisms' (Zipf, 1941), then we must consider the way in which operating environments affect, for good or ill, the well-being of that organisation. As discussed in Chapter 2, in a VUCA world, the pace of change necessitates organisational agility and the ability to adapt and become resilient to external changes (Barber, 1992; Zaidi & Bellak, 2019).

Example 8.6: Strategic management and the military system

Napoleon employed the possibilities of an industrial age to radically redefine the strategy and structure of the military. The adoption of the strategy of manoeuvre led to new military organisations and systems. Innovations such as *levée en masse*, the divisional system, and supply chain management allowed the French army to move at 120 paces per minute in contrast to its rivals who lumbered on at just 70 paces per minute. A system of information and intelligence and coordination was put in place. The situational awareness and ability to react quickly allowed Napoleon to get inside the opposition's decision loop and synchronise major operations and dispense with set-piece tactics of the time (Lefebvre, 1969).

Public organisations, including defence, may continue to survive despite strategic drift, poor strategic management or mislaid priorities. When these organisations fail, however, the consequences are often catastrophic. For example, the French revolution resulted in a military revolution and a revolution in military affairs that created a military system quite unlike any in Europe. Militaries and, in turn, countries that failed to understand what was going on, suffered the consequences (see Example 8.6).

Example 8.7: Tactical innovations and strategy

Similarly, in the opening years of the Second World War the German military developed and applied Blitzkrieg, a high tempo, coordinated form of mechanised warfare, to great effect. Blitzkrieg was an innovative conceptual leap that utilised existing technologies to create value-added in the delivery of combat power. The competitive advantage thus achieved was phenomenal as witnessed in the swift capture of Poland, France and the initial advance on Soviet Russia. The ideas that Blitzkrieg employed existed in literature in the writings of strategists like Tuchachevsky, Svechin, Basil

Liddell Hart and J. F. C. Fuller. Neither the Soviet Union nor Britain paid attention to these new ideas which explored the potential of mechanised warfare. The appeal to continuing with traditional and well-established military practices (static mindset) resulted in a strategic drift and the ultimate failure of French, Polish, British and Soviet militaries to cope (Liddell Hart, 1967). There is a caveat: tactical brilliance does not compensate for strategic blunders. The ultimate failure of Hitler's Germany was down to faulty grand strategy, not the strategy process or the balancing of ends, ways and means (Beverelli, 2020).

Example 8.8: Strategic drift – US/NATO failure in Afghanistan

With the end of the Cold War, the US focussed on airpower, precision targeting and remote warfare. This was based on a perception that the time of protracted wars and land battles involving heavy armour, infantry assaults had passed. NATO in general, with exception of Turkey and Greece, reorganised accordingly through the 1990s. After 9/11, the failure to seize military victory in Iraq or Afghanistan led to rethinking of counterinsurgency (COIN) doctrine (Farrell, 2014). Over six years, the US revised its COIN doctrine three times. Given the adoption cycle for new doctrines from concept to application is around six years (IGT&E, 2012), none of these new doctrines were ever fully effective. The result was confusion (flux) and continued strategic drift and a series of policy U-turns leading ultimately to negotiations with the Taliban, something the US had continuously ruled out for the first eight years in Afghanistan.

The building blocks of strategy are essentially an understanding of where the organisation is, how it got there, its current capabilities and vulnerabilities, and the threats and opportunities in the external environment. The 'what' and 'why' of strategy are a leadership concern; however, strategic managers are frequently involved in the process and must clearly understand the leadership's intent. SM then is used to deliver options and strategic plans to implement the strategic choice made by the leadership. An extensive suite of tools exists to help strategic managers understand the internal and external factors that aid strategy development. Strategy answers the questions 'why' and 'what', providing overarching guidance and roadmaps that lead to the 'who', 'how' and 'when' of change (see Chapter 14). While these tools were developed in the private sector, they are equally relevant across other sectors and for all types of organisations.

Exercise 8.1

Think about an organisation that you are familiar with and answer the following questions:

1. How does that organisation measure external change?
2. What strategies has it used in the last decade to keep up with change?
3. Does the organisation approach risk as something bad, neutral or an opportunity?
4. Will these strategies be valid in keeping the organisation on track for the next decade?

The strategy process

This section focuses on the SM process for the public sector and introduces a selection of associated tools to support managers in undertaking a systematic analysis of the internal and external environment: scenario building, positioning, and ultimately, developing and implementing strategies.

Strategic managers develop and apply strategies for the organisation's future direction and are responsible for ensuring business or service continuity. While continuity may entail critical and strategic decisions on the part of managers, the organisation's future direction is a more significant activity, fraught with risks and challenges associated with assumptions about the future. Determining possible futures, assessing threats and opportunities and positioning the organisation to succeed in a projected environment can be hazardous. Mintzberg and Walters' (1985) concept of emergent strategy as a realised pattern, not expressly intended is particularly relevant in a VUCA environment. They argue that deliberate strategies, albeit useful starting points, have little practical value. *'Futuring'* is a complex activity (van der Duin, 2016), requiring deliberate and detailed strategic analysis to make predictions. Nonetheless, organisations need to generate strategic choices based on how they seek to exploit opportunities, cope with threats, utilise their strengths, cover weaknesses, and deal with risks in pursuit of each of those futures. Importantly, option and choices are invariably a subjective undertaking and often connected with the key decision-makers' individual risk appetites (see Chapter 2). Major components of the SM process discussed above are shown in Figure 8.4.

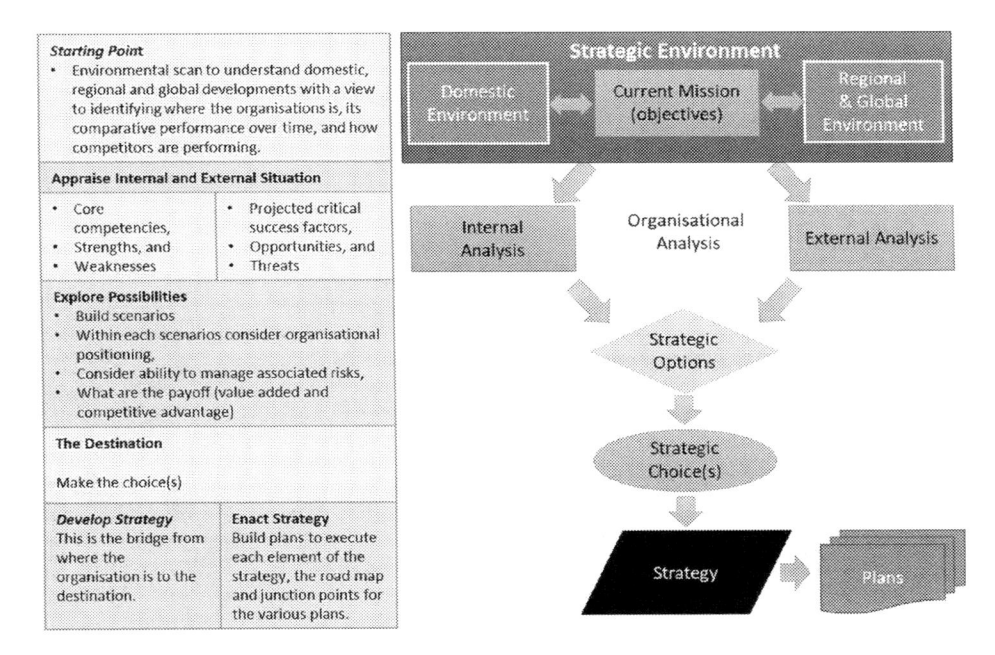

Figure 8.4 Strategic management process
Source: adapted from Zaidi (2009).

Strategic analysis: Towards a vision for the future

Strategic leadership is responsible for decisions regarding an organisation's purpose, a vision for its future and the core values that drive it. In all organisations, big or small, public or private, the members need purpose. In this regard, an organisational mission statement, vision, and future goals are central to SM as they ultimately influence strategy. In turn, strategy serves as the fountainhead, an overarching guidance for operational and tactical actions that drives the organisation.

Strategy delivers change. For this to happen, a clear understanding of the starting position and the destination are essential. Implicit in this is the nature of the change to be delivered and the gap that the organisation must cover from where it is today to where it intends to arrive at some point in the future. The PEST tool, or EPTS as it was originally called (Aguilar, 1967), provides a simple structure to undertake this analysis. PEST is an acronym for Political, Economic, Social and Technological factors that influence the environment within which an organisation sits. Two additional factors are frequently considered in this analysis; these are Legal and Environment (PESTLE). To focus the analysis further, the industry context can be added so that each of the six factors is seen through the prism of a context. For example, a National Security Council may add 'Security' or 'Military' as a focus.

When doing a PEST analysis, it is useful to look at the domestic, regional and global contexts as each may have an impact on the organisation. The output is an understanding of possible futures and the scenarios presented in each; typically expressed as hypotheses with the likelihood of occurrence and potential impact. This enables an initial understanding of the organisation's trajectory from

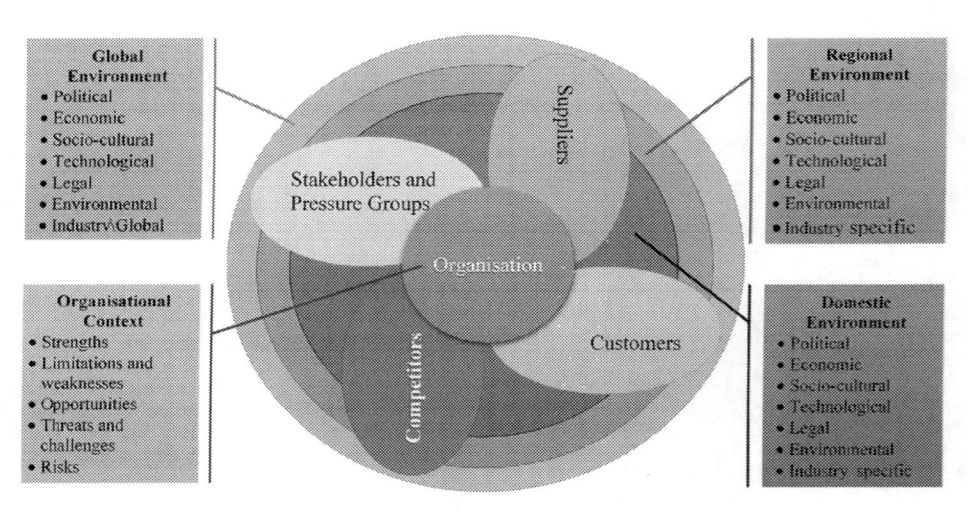

(Ifti Zaidi, 2019; adapted from Saylor Academy (2012) *Mastering Strategic Management*. Online: Creative Commons)

Figure 8.5 The Strategic Environment
Source: adapted from Zaidi (2009).

the present towards a particular convergence in the future. To what extent are its aspirations realisable, and how far it could drift or be pushed towards detrimental outcomes by external developments or active interference (indicated by the ovals)? For example, if a strategy in need of change is continued, the organisation will continue to drift away from its mission (strategic drift). Figure 8.6 represents a probable future:

A powerful tool for scenario building, contingency planning, and cause & effect analysis is Jerome C. Glenn's (1971) Futures Wheel analysis tool. The tool graphically presents the direct and indirect future consequences of a particular change or development. For scenario building, the analysis begins with a term describing a particular change placed in a circle in the centre and plotting the immediate or first-order consequences of that from the centre. The process is then repeated for each of the first-order consequences. The result is a series of connected circles flowing from the central change being investigated. The interconnections also allow relationships to be identified and crosslinked with other developments; the analyst can then build a set of possible scenarios. A futures-conscious perspective emerges. Finally, working from the outside inwards through each of the connected circles, contingency responses can be developed by answering the question 'so what?'.

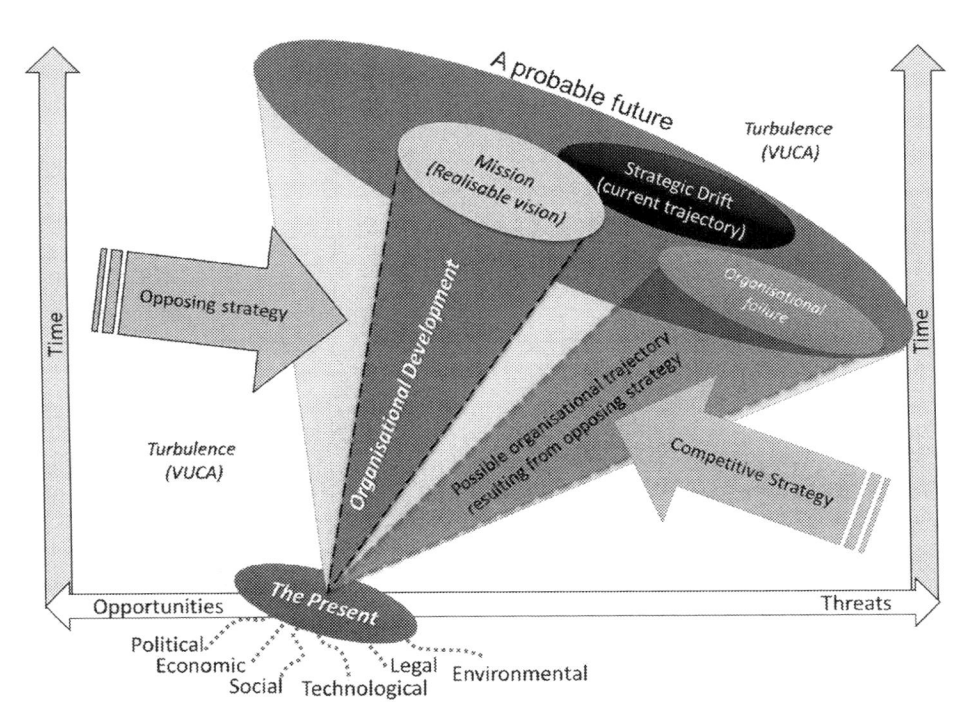

Figure 8.6 A Probable Future, Organisational Drift and Positioning
Source: adapted from Zaidi (2009).

However, with competition hastening detrimental outcomes (opposing strategy), the organisation could be marginalised or fail altogether (organisational failure). A competitive strategy that deals with external threats and helps the organisation develop internally will be needed to achieve a positive outcome (realisable vision). A competitive strategy achieves this.

Strategy deals with three primary resources (or currencies): time, space and relative opposing capabilities (RoC). Of these three, time is the only irrecuperable entity. The interpretation of space and RoC is context-dependent. For example, for an army, space represents the geographical space, the real estate, while RoC is the relative sum of the combat power, including morale and training. For a business, space could imply market capture and reach and RoC, the differential in resources like brand value, human capital, and financial strength available at a firm's disposal in relation to its competitors.

Organisational analysis

Several tools are available for qualitative and quantitative internal analysis of an organisation and its fit within its current environment (Evans, 2020). The SWOT tool, developed by Albert Humphrey in the 1960s, has become a quintessential planning tool. SWOT is an acronym for Strengths, Weaknesses, which are internal to an organisation, and Opportunities and Threats, which are external to the organisation. Being an abstract tool, the SWOT can be done in various ways, including qualitative, quantitative, visual or a combination of these.

Strategic options

Having completed the environmental, external and internal scans, narratives on possible futures emerge. Discussions among stakeholders and strategic managers are essential to inform policy, guide strategy and drive plans to propel the organisation in the desired direction. Orientating for the future is fraught with danger. All predictions and calculations of external interference have associated risks.

Risk analysis

Risk management has been covered in Chapter 2. The purpose of risk analysis in strategy is to inform emergent strategy in terms of the branches and sequels available to strategic leaders and strategic managers and to enable informed decisions.

Positioning

Having considered each option and associated risks, the strategic manager and the top leadership must decide where the organisation is to be steered in the future. Positioning of the organisation in the projected future is the redefining or retuning of the organisation's purpose, vision and mission and takes place when reviewing the strategic options available to the organisation together with associated risks and potential gains in each of the options. The infographic in Figure 8.7 presents the SM process overlaid with the tools discussed above.

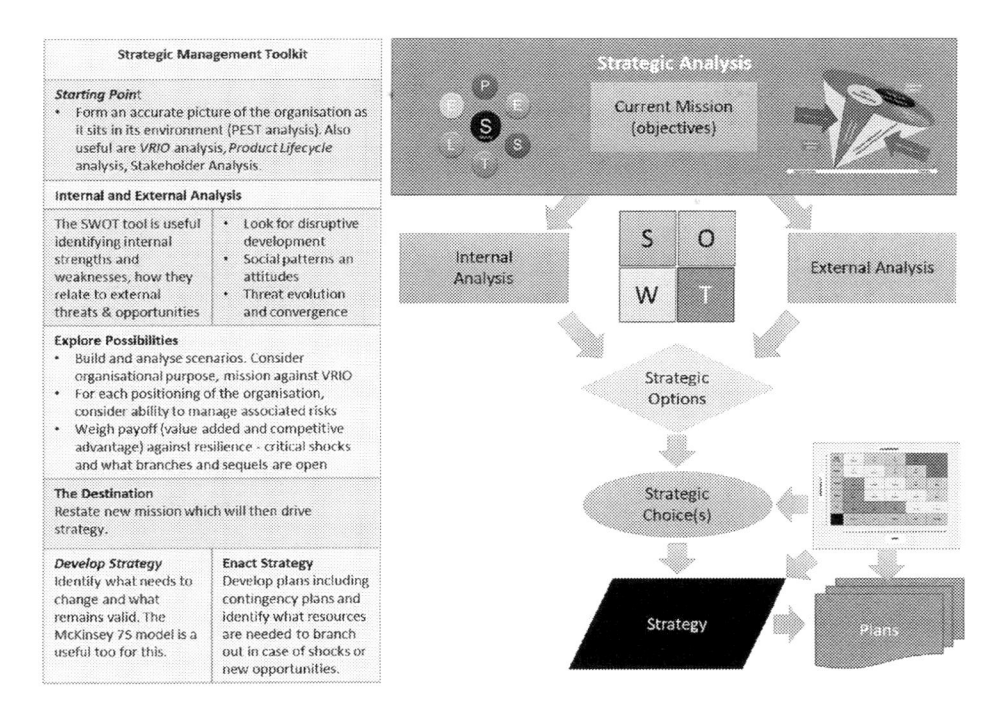

Figure 8.7 Strategic Management Process and Associated Analytical Tools
Source: adapted from Zaidi (2009)

Exercise 8.2

Take a moment to list your current goals and objectives (personal and professional). With this mission statement in mind go through the following steps:

- Do a SWOT analysis of yourself. Remember strengths and weaknesses are internal to you and linked with resources you control, and your skills and abilities. Whereas the opportunities and threats are external to you and sit in the social and professional environment that you operate in.
- Next, consider how the external environment might evolve over the next 10 years (the PEST tool is useful for this analysis).
- Once you have captured the main factors, answer the question *'so what?'*. You now have answers to how your current situation and the external environment impact on you and your current mission.
- Where do you see yourself in the next 10 years within each of those possible futures?

The answers provide you with building blocks of strategy, beginning with a set of choices. The next step is strategy development:

- Analyse each of these choices in the light of risks and payoffs associated with each of them.
- Make a choice based on where you can maximise your potential (positioning). Develop this into a vision and a mission statement.

- Once you know where you are and where you need to go, the resources available or needed to get there can be balanced against friction and the opposition visualised on the way.

Contemporary discourses in strategic management

Continuity and change

A common issue a strategic manager must deal with is how to balance continuity of service while producing change. The larger the scale of change, the more severe the challenge. When, for example, Western-Union transitioned from a communication company to a financial organisation, it was able to build new business units while phasing out the old. A common strategy for commercial organisations confronted with large-scale change is downsizing or refocussing products and services. Such choices are not usually open to public organisations such as the health services, or security sector organisations such as the police, the military and border forces.

Strategy and structure

Chandler's thesis that strategy drives structure, has dominated industrial thought for at least two decades. Mintzberg's concept of Emergent Strategy was a neat summation of how strategy must adapt as the organisation charts unexpected external threats or shocks. This approach is internalised in military thought and practice, as evidenced by the common adage, 'no plan survives first contact with the enemy'. In a VUCA world, there is a tenuous relationship between strategy and structure, requiring the former to also adapt to the latter. The result of this tension is a need for resilient structures and adaptive strategies. Ideas like Blue Ocean Strategy, which approaches strategy from a non-structural lens, has systematically reconstructed and reversed the structure-strategy sequence to some extent (Kim & Mauborgne, 2009).

Strategy as a function

Strategy is simultaneously concerned with continuity and change in the face of active competition and changing environments. It is rare, however, for public or private sector organisations to have dedicated strategic management teams who advise and coordinate all aspects of strategy from its development to execution, evaluation, and revision; military institutions being an exception. Despite the renewed interest in SM across industries and sectors, Zook and Allen (2001) observe that between 1988 and 1998, seven out of eight companies from a sample of 1,854 failed to create growth; whereas, companies with dedicated strategy teams performed better. Later, they re-iterated the need for dedicated leadership teams that form an epicentre of SM (2010). Adding strategy to Fayol's list of six primary organisational functions will be increasingly important for organisations to manage the impact of VUCA.

Example 8.9: Strategic management as a formal function

The UK Research and Innovation (UKRI), was established in April 2018 and is a non-departmental public body of the UK Government. UKRI brings together seven Research Councils, Research England and Innovate UK to support research within and across disciplinary domains. One of the key centralised functions introduced with the launch of the UKRI was the role of an Executive Director of Strategy with a dedicated team to support and advise senior leadership on a single strategy on behalf of all constituent parts of the UKRI. This centralised function is a significant step forward from mere coordination between the Research Councils (UKRI, 2020).

The UK Ministry of Defence (MOD) introduced a Director General Strategy to advise government on defence and oversee strategy implementation. This was later discontinued with the establishment of the National Security Council in 2010 (Devanny & Harris, 2014). An advisory function within the MOD now has a Directorate of Strategy and International. This body oversees policy on NATO, European Union and key bilateral defence relationships as well as strategic planning and strategic policy matters, e.g., nuclear deterrence, cyber security (UK Government, 2020).

At the state level, the establishment of a national security council (NSC) as a unified body charged with advising political leadership on security policy and strategy has become common around the world. The practice originated in the US when the Truman administration drafted the National Security Act of 26 July 1947. This was part of a general reorganisation of the US national security apparatus (Office of the Historian, 1997). Today, the NSC, chaired by the President, plays a central role in the coordination of foreign policy. Its composition and role, however, have changed several times due to myriad factors, most prominent being external developments or the needs and preferences of successive administrations. Over 50 countries now have similar entities. The UK is a relatively late adopter, having set up an NSC in 2010 (Devanny & Harris, 2014). What is important is not the existence of such high-level bodies but how they are used. This is often a very subjective debate contesting the role of agency over structure or strategy. Individual preferences of the chief executive often play a major role, as was noticeable in the US under President Trump. In principle, an NSC is a powerful coupling between political leadership, the security organisations, public bodies, industry, and other stakeholders, including the public.

Conclusion

SM is vital to the conduct of business and provision of services and has become an essential component for organisational success in today's fluid security environment. In the context of the public sector, strategic management provides a vital link between political leadership and the organisations that make government work. The requirement for dedicated strategy teams to advise senior executives and leadership is becoming increasingly important. Organisations that have formalised strategic management, whether public or private, have generally performed more cohesively, produced better goods and services, created value-added and remained more competitive. The greatest benefit for the public sector that SM offers is perhaps overcoming discontinuities that result from tenured leadership positions that can result in muddling through in the short term rather than taking an over-the-horizon perspective.

Questions to consider

1. How do the key SM concepts of Value-added and Competitive Advantage relate to your industry or organisation?

2. How would you generalise the relationship between strategy and structure in periods of hyper-change?
3. How can strategic management help break down industrial and organisational 'silos' in the defence and security sector?

Suggested further reading

Evans, V. (2020) *Key Strategy Tools: 88 Tools for Every Manager to Build a Winning Strategy*, 2nd ed., Harlow: FT Publishing.
Gray, C.S. (2010) *The Strategy Bridge: Theory and Practice*, Oxford: Oxford University Press.
Greene, R. (2006) *The 33 Strategies of War*, London: Profile Books.

References

Aguilar, F.J. (1967) *Scanning the Business Environment*, New York: Macmillan.
Allison, G. & Zelikow, P. (1999) *Essence of Decision: Explaining the Cuban Missile Crisis*, 2nd ed., New York: Longman.
Ansoff, I.H. (1968) *Corporate Strategy*, New Orleans: Pelican.
Ansoff, I.H. (1979) *Strategic Management*, New York: Wiley.
Barber, H.F. (1992) 'Developing strategic leadership: The US army war college experience', *Journal of Management Development*, 11, pp. 4–12.
Barney, J. (1991) 'Firm resources and sustained competitive advantage', *Journal of Management*, 17 (1), pp. 99–120.
Bennett, N. & Lemoine, J. G. (2014) 'Crisis management: What VUCA really means for you', *Harvard Business Review*, January–February, 92 (1–2).
Beverelli, L. (2020) *The Strategy Bridge*. Available at https://thestrategybridge.org/the-bridge/2020/4/7/the-importance-of-the-strategic-level-germany-in-the-second-world-war [Accessed: 10 December 2020].
Chandler, A.D. (1962) *Strategy and Structure: Chapter in the History of Industrial Empire*, Cambridge (MA): MIT Press.
Dahl, R. & Lindblom, C. (1953) *Politics, Economics and Welfare*, New York: Harpers.
David, F.R. & David, F.R. (2016) *Strategic Management: The Competitive Advantage Approach (Global Edition)*, 16th ed., Harlow: Pearson.
Devanny, J. & Harris, J. (2014) *The National Security Council: National Security at the Centre of Government*, London: Institute for Government.
Evans, V. (2020) *Key Strategy Tools: 88 Tools for Every Manager to Build a Winning Strategy*, 2nd ed., Harlow: FT Publishing.
Farrell, T. (2014) *Transforming Military Power since the Cold War: Britain, France, and the United States, 1991–2012*, Cambridge: Cambridge University Press.
Fayol, H. (1949) *General and Industrial Management*, 1st English ed., London: Sir Isaac Pittman and Sons Ltd.
Gagliardi, G. (2012) *Sun Tzu's The Art of War for the Business Warrior: Strategy for Entrepreneurs*, Seattle: Clearbridge Publishing.
Glendinning, R. (1988) 'The concept of value for money', *International Journal of Public Sector Management*, 1 (1), pp. 42–50.
Gray, C.S. (2010) *The Strategy Bridge: Theory and Practice*, Oxford: Oxford University Press.
Hill, C.W.L., Jones, G.R. & Schilling, M.A. (2015) *Strategic Management: Theory: An Integrated Approach*, 11th ed., Stamford: Cengage Learning.
Howlett, M. & Migone, A. (2017) 'Charles Lindblom is alive and well and living in punctuated equilibrium land', *Policy and Society*, 30 (1), pp. 53–62.
IGT&E (2012) *Guidebook for Doctrine Development*, Rawalpindi: GHQ Rawalpindi.

Johnson, G. et al. (2017) *Exploring Corporate Strategy: Texts and Cases.* 11th ed., Harlow: Pearson.

Joyce, P. (2015) *Strategic Management in the Public Sector,* Abingdon: Routledge.

Kim, C.W. & Mauborgne, R. (2009) 'How strategy shapes structure', *Harvard Business Review.* Available at https://hbr.org/2009/09/how-strategy-shapes-structure [Accessed 28 March 2021].

Lefebvre, G. (1969) *Napoleon: From 18 Brumaire to Tilsit 1799–1807,* New York: Columbia University Press.

Liddell Hart, B.H. (1967) *Strategy: The Indirect Approach.* 4th revised ed., New York: Faber & Faber.

Lynch, R. (2018) *Strategic Management.* 8th ed., London: Pearson.

McNeilly, M. (2012) *Sun Tzu and the Art of Business.* Revised ed., Oxford: Oxford University Press.

Miller, E. S. (1991) *War Plan Orange: The U.S. Strategy to Defeat Japan, 1897–1945,* Annapolis: United States Naval Institute Press.

Mintzberg, H. (1981) 'Organization design: Fashion or fit?', *Harvard Business Review,* January.

Mintzberg, H. & McHugh, A. (1985) 'Strategy formation in an adhocracy', *Administrative Science Quarterly, 30* (2), pp. 160–197.

Mintzberg, H. & Walters, J. A. (1985) 'Of strategies, deliberate and emergent', *Strategic Management Journal, 6,* pp. 257–272.

Molla, R. (2017) 'How Apple's iPhone changed the world: 10 years in 10 charts'. Available at https://www.vox.com/2017/6/26/15821652/iphone-apple-10-year-anniversary-launch-mobile-stats-smart-phone-steve-jobs [Accessed 16 December 2020].

Northouse, P. (2019) *Leadership: Theory and Practice,* London: Sage.

Office of the Historian (1997) *History of the National Security Council (1947–1997),* Washington (DC): US Department of State.

Porter, M.E. (1983) *Cases in Competitive Strategy,* New York: Free Press.

Sloan, A. (1963) *My Years with General Motors,* John McDonald with Catherine Stevens (eds.), New York: Doubleday.

Sun-Tzu, ca. 6 BC (2011) *The Art of War New Illustrated Edition,* London: Oxford University Press.

Taylor II, L. E. (2020) 'Case analysis: The FARC in Colombia', *Small Wars Journal, 3* (5).

The Economist (1999) 'Putting America on wheels', *The Economist Millenium Edition,* 23 December.

UK Government (2020) Available at https://www.gov.uk/government/organisations/ministry-of-defence [Accessed 6 December 2020].

UKRI (2020) 'Our structure'. Available at https://www.ukri.org/about-us/our-structure/ [Accessed 6 December 2020].

van der Duin, P. (2016) 'Introduction'. In: P. van der Duin, ed., *Foresight in Organisations: Methods and Tools,* Abingdon: Routledge, pp. 1–10.

Zaidi, I. (2009) 'Theory of war and strategy'. In: J. Ramday, I. Zaidi & U. Durrani, eds., *Operational Art,* Islamabad: NDU, pp. 11–39.

Zaidi, I. & Bellak, B. (2019) 'Leadership development for international crises management: The whole person approach', *Journal of Peacebuilding and Development, 14* (3), pp. 256–271.

Zipf, G.K. (1941) *National Unity and Disunity: The Nation as a Bio-social Organism,* Bloomington: Principia Press.

Zook, C. & Allen, J. (2001) *Profit from the Core: Growth Strategy in an Era of Turbulence,* 1st ed., Boston: Harvard Business School Press.

Zook, C. & Allen, J. (2010) *Profit from the Core: Growth Strategy in an Era of Turbulence,* 2nd ed., Boston: Bain & Co Inc.

9 Human resource management in the security sector

Roger Darby

Introduction

Contemporary analysis of security sector organisations highlights a central tenet involving the concept of *change*, namely, the *status quo is no longer acceptable*. This applies to the management of *people* – a major resource in any organisation. Consequently, the *employment relationship* encompassing *employee engagement* is increasingly recognised as crucial for the effective management of this key resource and an important variable in the success or failure of an organisation. Concomitantly, it is argued in this chapter that successful human resource management (HRM) must also consider the relevant factor of *situational context*. As public sector organisations (PSOs), defence and security forces are formally constituted by ownership, funding and authority; with the purpose of creating public value rather than profit maximisation (Knies & Leisink, 2020, Boxall & Purchell, 2011). Thus, any contemporary discussion of HRM will need to address the central issues of best fit and practice within the specific organisational context. An important question for security institutions in post-conflict, transitional and developing states is whether or not there is a single, identifiable way of managing human resources which is universally appropriate or if there is a need for an alternative contingent approach more suited to the local situational context.

The chapter begins by discussing the antecedents of HRM and is prefaced by the question, 'What is HRM?', to help provide a definition. From its emergence in the USA in the 1980s to a more current mature state, HRM now occupies an accepted central management role and has become a familiar global term. The increased emphasis placed on HRM reflects a broader interest in the relationship between HRM systems and organisational effectiveness. Dominant theories, such as a resource-based view (RBV) (Barney, 1991) and human capital theory (Wright & McMahan, 2011), suggest that valuable, finite and increasingly expensive resources (including people) contribute to organisational-level performance and service as well as economic value; thereby providing a major source of competitive advantage to an organisation. The mismanagement of such resources is seen to be inefficient, costly, and a potential waste of necessary limited *talent*.

The link between HRM and employee performance is a key factor addressed in this chapter. A behavioural perspective focuses on how HRM systems support organisations to achieve their goals (Jiang & Messersmith, 2018; Schuler & Jackson, 1987). Desired behaviours play a significant role in both challenging internal and external environments which are mediated between HRM systems and organisational outcomes. Also, it has a direct connection with the ability-motivation-opportunity framework

DOI: 10.4324/9781003137061-9

(AMO) (Jiang et al., 2012) which contributes to an individual's performance. The social exchange theory (Blau, 1964; Messersmith et al., 2011) has utility in understanding how HRM systems influence organisational performance by effecting behaviours and attitudes and is linked with reciprocity. For example, employers may use the reward system to provide benefits that are reciprocated with positive attitudes and behaviour by employees to support the exchange relationship.

Institutional theory is specifically relevant to public sector organisations as it addresses the processes by which structures, including schemes, rules, norms, and routines, become established as authoritative guidelines for social behaviour. It emphasises rational myths, legitimacy and isomorphism – which is a similarity of the processes or structure of one organisation to those of another: the result of imitation or independent development under similar constraints. Institutional theory also explains the influence of situational context on an organisation's adoption of HRM (Wright et al., 1994; Brinkerhoff & Brinkerhoff, 2015; Scott, 2008). Further, the theory provides an investigative framework to study the diffusion and adoption of organisational forms and HRM activities (Bjorkman, 2006; Rupidara & Darby, 2017).

The theory of New Public Management (NPM) (Hood, 1991; Schachter, 2014), which was developed during the 1980s in an attempt to make the public service more business-like and efficient through the application of private sector management models, is an example of the influence of isomorphism on public-sector management (Bordogna & Neri, 2011). Market liberalisation has made demands on moribund public services and created demands for the public sector to increase 'public value' (Kelly et al., 2002; Samaratunge et al., 2008; Painter, 2004). Traditionally, public sector management was based on a unitary model with bureaucratic, centralised, employment policy matching Weberian principles and practices of a rule-governed, rational notion. Employment was focused on career service, security of tenure and life-long employment directed by an over-arching powerful internal labour market. There were service-wide remuneration and conditions with little opportunity for variations in performance, and with financial reward based on job or position. Seniority or length of service was the basis for promotion. This unitary system came under pressure in the face of mounting criticisms of 'big government', and the application of NPM principles such as contracting-out services. Demands for a management approach that would lead to greater efficiency presaged more flexibility in staffing and recognition of the need for employee engagement. Recent research into post-NPM public sector reform has questioned the wisdom of shrinking government rather than improving the capability of government (Brinkerhoff & Brinkerhoff, 2015; De Vries & Nemec, 2013).

Defining HRM

HRM is distinct from the more traditional notion of *personnel management*, seen as an administrative and reactive process. Strategic HRM (SHRM) is a strategic and pro-active process, centrally linked to the overall strategic management of an organisation. Such an approach necessitates a change in how the HR function is viewed, from '…being reactive, prescriptive, and administrative to being proactive, descriptive and executive' (Budhwar, 2000: p.141).

This perspective is in line with the RBV approach which views people as a key resource worthy of investment, rather than as simply a commodity and cost to the organisation. Human resources have strategic importance as a necessary capability in the creation of competitive advantage, whether in the manufacturing of goods or the provision of services. Emphasis is thus placed on employee commitment, quality and flexibility rather than on employee compliance with rules and regulations, efficient organisational administration or standard performance and cost minimisation (Guest, 1991).

Concepts and framework

Numerous HRM models have been developed to support the management of human resources particularly in PSOs, to make them more economic, effective and efficient. These include: public values creation models (Wright & Nishil, 2013), the 'Ability, Motivation and Opportunity' (AMO) model (Sterling & Boxall, 2013), the Harvard model (Beer et al., 1984), the strategic partner model (Yusuf et al., 2017) and public sector motivation and administration (Scott, 2014).

Previously in this chapter, the importance of human capital theory to the antecedents of HRM was recognised. A significant issue is that human capital (including skills, knowledge and experience) is owned by individual employees and can be transferred to other organisations if they leave. For example, 'brain drain' presents a challenge to public sector organisations in many developing countries prompting the necessity to effectively manage key functions within HRM systems to retain the requisite human capital. These key functions are highlighted in Figure 9.1:

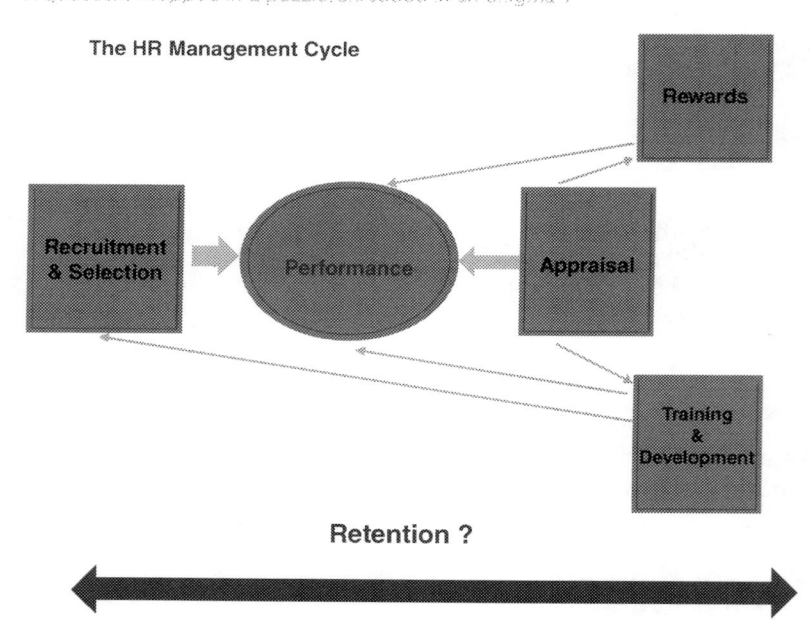

HRM - WHAT IS IT ?
  - *A question, wrapped in a puzzle, shrouded in an enigma ?*

The HR Management Cycle

Rewards

Recruitment & Selection

Performance

Appraisal

Training & Development

Retention ?

Figure 9.1 The HR Management Cycle
Source: Adapted from Alexandrou & Darby (2006).

The utility of the HR management cycle model is that it provides an insight into the definition of HRM by highlighting important functions, particularly from a transactional management perspective. It provides a framework that is transferable in most situational contexts and identifies the universal HR functions of resourcing, development, reward, appraisal and relations. All are integrated with the broader goal of employee and organisational performance, and are designed to support an organisation's strategic needs. It is a cyclical rather than linear design which propounds a continuous cyclic approach to be adopted for HRM rather than a one-off linear approach with a beginning, middle and end state to managing people.

Exercise 9.1

Using the HR Management Cycle, identify three key factors for every important function in the cycle when recruiting and developing Officers or Senior Civil Servants in a Ministry of Defence.

Resourcing

Commentators often discuss HRM as performing a *gate-keeping role*. This involves determining who to invite (recruit) into the organisation and who, on occasions, to encourage to leave (retirement, redundancy, dismissal). Recruitment practices serve to identify and attract potential employees. Selection involves identifying which applicant will best meet the demands of the job, as well as being the best fit with the work group and organisational culture. A fundamental role is to supply the organisation with people with the necessary knowledge, skills and experiences required to make it successful; often over an extended period, with management decisions ideally guided by an organisation's strategic plan. Recruitment and selection also involve a contractual issue involving a two-way relationship between the individual and the organisation aimed at satisfying the needs of both employer and employee. It is firmly linked to other employment issues such as sustaining interest and motivation. In both the armed forces and the civil service there is an assumption that those joining will commit themselves for several years of service. In the modern defence and security environment effective recruitment is even more important as many national forces are transitioning from conscript to volunteer forces. Therefore, a more strategic approach to recruitment is imperative.

One outcome of this shift to volunteer forces, particularly in the West, is that future forces may not necessarily be staffed by full-time employees. More flexible working practices may meet needs better by utilising reservists, consultants or subcontractors – on a variety of working contracts, from full-time, part-time, to casual labour force.

Training and development

Exercise 9.2

The UK MoD provides an interesting example of the need for SHRM in the future with its strategic defence plans for 'Future Force 2020' and beyond. What are the dilemmas faced when systematically reducing the size of a regular Armed Force to a reliance more on reservists and cyber security whilst strategically planning to maintain a global high-profile defence role?

As alluded to in the introduction, an over-arching factor covering all the key functions in the HR management cycle is the concept of *managing change*. Such change has prompted several important trends in training and development which are pertinent to defence and security institutions. Researchers have highlighted mega, macro and micro trends which are shaping organisations and their environment and require training and development responses by all organisations in every sector (Collings et al., 2019; Montealegre & Cascio, 2017). Three mega trends are globalisation, technology and demographic changes. At the macro level, there are increasing demands for personal and professional development by employees, the prevalence of digital technology at work, structural changes in labour markets and the importance of the employer's brand. Micro level trends include a better understanding of the process of learning, the role of digital learning, and options to bridge skills gaps. Within defence and security, these trends directly challenge traditional notions of capability management and capacity building. For example, those trends which have a direct effect on training and development highlight questions about defence institutions understanding, ability and willingness to change and influence the speed of learning, the transference of new knowledge and skills and adoption of new ways of learning. Training of Forces in many developing countries has too often been training for obsolescence, corrupt or self-serving for those in authority and with little benefit to support Force capability or relevant and required capacity building.

Exercise 9.3

The curriculum at many of the Staff Colleges in developing countries is borrowed from the UK, USA and France. Do the Armed Forces of the developing countries need to know how to fight and win a nuclear war? Or do they need to know how to counter insurgency? What factors should be considered when determining the curriculum?

However, all organisations face a dilemma. It would appear axiomatic to suggest training and development is a worthy and necessary process in any organisation and that development also increases productivity in most organisations. However, it is more difficult to provide a causal link between employee development and organisational performance. A key issue for defence and security institutions is their approach to the short-term versus long term perspective. The Defence and Security forces of countries transitioning from conflict or engaged in development need to take a long-term view when developing the competency and capacity of their personnel. Equally, those forces moving from a conscript to a volunteer force will face increased training and development costs. By necessity this requires clarity and a direct link between strategic need and training and development requirements.

Example 9.1: Leading and training for change

In 2003 senior managers at the Ethiopian Ministry of National Defence identified the need for training and development of officers and officials to bring about transformational change. A suitable programme was devised and taught by a foreign university. Among those attending the first course was the Chief of Defence Staff, the Minister of State and several other 1* and 2* officers. Their attendance said much more than any edict from their offices. Not only did they lead by example, they demonstrated their commitment to both the training programme and to the change that it was to facilitate.

Appraisal

Performance appraisal is a management process where managers assess employees' performance. Appraisal should consider the following objectives. First, it should be outcomes-based, with goal setting proving to be an effective enabler, challenging and focused on superior individual performance and on behaviour and learning. Second, it should identify performance ratings, which can be used for administrative purposes, such as decisions on pay or career development. Third, it should be recognised that appraisal is open to bias and can unduly affect performance ratings; this needs to be mitigated in the appraisal process. Andrews (2013) has argued more attention should be given to identifying contextual factors that influence managerial practices in PSOs. Given the political, institutional and cultural context of performance appraisal in different situational contexts attention to such contextual detail is appropriate.

Reward

At the heart of the employment relationship is the effort-reward bargain. Reward is a transaction involving benefits given by an employer to an employee in exchange for skills, knowledge, loyalty and labour. HRM involves aligning an organisation's reward system with its performance objectives. Concomitantly, decisions about reward also have major financial resource implications because money spent on people accounts for over 60% of an organisation's total costs (Hartley, 2018). The organisation therefore needs to manage finite financial resources and regulate costs. Within the bigger picture of financial and non-financial rewards (such as status, welfare or accommodation), the aim is to attract, retain and motivate employees to provide special effort, or to be more creative, so that their work adds value to the end product (or service). All of which is of mutual benefit to the individual and the organisation. However, reward trends change (or should change) as organisational strategy changes over time. Further, in more competitive labour markets reward management is crucial to attract and retain suitably qualified staff who are increasingly discerning about what they require from their employer. Pay is certainly a key motivator for most people, but it is also a short-term motivator, as acknowledged in the concepts Pay Plus and Total Reward. This is particularly relevant for defence and security forces within the public sector which cannot compete equally with the private sector on parity of salaries alone. This has necessitated a greater flexibility in providing additional benefits apart from salaries. A Total Reward approach considers benefits other than pay, but which are of value to the employee. These might include opportunities for career development, flexible working, pensions, healthcare, leadership, recognition, more voice and work–life balance. Defence and security institutions will increasingly have to manage the challenge of needing to recruit suitably qualified professional staff in a tight labour market without substantially increasing costs.

Example 9.2: Careers of last resort?

Although African economies were growing significantly before Covid-19, with Ethiopia, Kenya and Djibouti's economies being some of the fastest growing, individuals with low education levels and skills tended to gravitate towards the armed forces and police, because entry requirements are relatively low. The challenge is in recruiting and retaining better-educated individuals to fill officer positions.

Employee relations

As highlighted previously, the *employment relationship*, referring to the relationship between employee and organisation, is a crucial management concept. Consequently, an essential feature of HRM is the range of activities that are intended to uphold that relationship and prevent alienation between the employer and the employee. Effective management of employee relations occurs at both the individual and collective levels and includes the recognition of equity. Employee relations practice concerns the management of perception (and power) and necessitates effective communication between parties to maintain harmony and to achieve organisational objectives.

It can be argued that employee relations have seen a major transformation over the last 20 years, affecting both the private and public sectors. However, that change has not occurred at the same rate in both sectors. Here, the adage, 'the private sector leads, and the public sector follows' is apposite. Within the public sector (including defence and security institutions), more traditional models of employee relations have remained resistant to change despite successive government attempts at modernisation. However, traditional conflict between management and labour still exists with employee relations practices reflecting a wide variety of approaches around the world. For example, Employment Law is progressively playing a central role; aided by more collective calls for employee rights and protection, health and safety and more equal policies on managing diversity. Two contracts are central to the employment relationship: the formal, written, legal contract of employment; and the unwritten or psychological contract.

Trade unions have retained a role where public policy has offered a degree of protection, although in developing countries collective bargaining mechanisms remain weak and lack independence from management (Kim, 2008). The notion of 'voice' is of growing importance in organisations undergoing transformation (Ruck et al., 2017; Marchington, 2015). Employees like to express their voice both formally and informally, but it appears in different forms. For example, it has given rise to HR practices that include team building, involvement, employee participation and empowerment (Guest, 2011). These practices, however, require senior management receptiveness and an appreciation of employee views.

Exercise 9.4

Consider the role of 'voice' in your own defence and security institutions. What approach should be taken to support the employment relationship as it goes through necessary change and modernisation? Study the examples of the defence forces of Germany, the Netherlands and South Africa, which have instituted military unions or professional associations. What would be the advantages and disadvantages of having unions recognised in your country's defence and security forces? How could they support the closing of the civil-military gap and improve HRM?

Research has shown that high levels of engagement tend to correlate with high employee retention rates. It also raises the interesting question whether there are similar HR practices that are commonly associated with high levels of engagement and low levels of turnover. Furthermore, are such common initiatives likely to have similar positive effects in all situational contexts, in for example, PSOs as well as the private sector?

Performance

A general rule of thumb in HRM is the maxim, *'All roads lead to Performance'*. At the fulcrum of the HR management cycle is performance and all the other key functions are integrated and linked to that central role. Having the necessary quantity of personnel and quality of human capital becomes superfluous unless they are delivering the performance required. Performance management (PM) is a process aimed at maintaining and improving employee performance in association with an organisation's strategic objectives. Both formal and informal processes are crucial to effective PM. Planning objectives and linking them to organisational plans, and using appropriate metrics to define success are necessary. These are supported by performance reviews, and appraisals for example, annual reports, used in many defence forces. Informally, but equally important, it is about establishing a performance culture where individuals and groups take responsibility for their continuous improvement involving skills, knowledge and experiences; supported by line managers (officers).

It is argued in this chapter, what constitutes effective performance is inextricably related to situational context. For example, effective performance in a manufacturing firm in the private sector that produces engines is linked very clearly to financial profit. For defence and security forces in the public sector the onus is on providing a service not on profit maximization. It is much easier to equate the number of engines produced each year with profit or loss figures. More difficult to measure is the contribution of defence and security forces in often contradictory spaces for example, in a peace-keeping role or a counter terrorism or cyber defence context. NPM highlights the multiple and conflicting roles and outcomes now required of PSOs (Guo, et al., 2011). This has compelled PSOs to focus on transparency, accountability and efficiency to improve organisational and employee performance (Guest, 2011).

What is clear from the research is that national and organisational cultures impact on the performance-reward link, particularly in relation to pay. Therefore, each organisation should develop practices that are relevant to their specific organisational context and desired organisational culture; ideally flexible enough within the system to take account of the different ways teams, forces, e.g., an army, navy and air force within a national defence force, or functions operate in a single organisation.

Retention

The issue of retention, identified in Figure 9.1, highlights a formidable challenge for defence and security forces undergoing major change. Retention of key staff is linked with the notion of 'employee engagement' (Purcell, 2014). Retention is normally measured by labour turnover rates, but these are multi-faceted and include, for example, resignations, retirements, dismissals, and redundancies. It is particularly relevant for volunteer forces to avoid the negative impact of labour turnover given their reliance on a (limited) pool of talent who volunteer and are not conscripted to join an armed force. Therefore, it is crucial for defence and security institutions to continually monitor the reasons behind turnover in order to reduce costs, maintain capacity and improve capability.

Exercise 9.5

In several countries around the world, defence and security forces are moving from conscript to volunteer forces. This means a transition from quantity to quality of its services supported by the skill, knowledge and experience of its human capital – that process faces continual change and requires constant updating of knowledge and skills to maintain its capability whilst sustaining its capacity. What are the critical success factors (CSFs) to achieve this transition?

Strategic HRM

In support of Chapter 8, any analysis of the functional nature of HRM needs to be viewed through the prism of strategic management; which includes analysis of external environments, internal structures and processes of an organisation (Knies & Leisink, 2018). Gratton et al provide a useful starting point for defining strategic HRM (SHRM), stating that:

> ....it is the creation of linkage or integration between the overall strategic aims of the business and the human resource strategy and implementation [and] .... managing the various human resource interventions, such as selection, training, reward and development, so that they complement each other.
>
> (Gratton et al. 1999: p.7)

Budhwar (2000) notes that one of the central features of the debate on HRM has been the importance placed on integrating HRM with organisational strategy, concentrating on how and when HR issues are considered in the formulation of that strategy. In terms of SHRM's conceptual framework, the key principles can be linked with issues related to organisational design and the development of strategy and structure (Hedlund, 1996); the development of integrative contingency frameworks based on the need to differentiate and integrate HRM policies; and the focus on life-cycle models linked to the notion of fit between the stages of operations and HRM (Schuler et al., 2005). Figure 9.2 identifies the important link between strategic and functional HRM.

Furthermore, SHRM emphasises what can be termed 'vertical fit' – integration between the organisational HR strategies and 'horizontal fit' – integration among the various HRM practices. This is illustrated in Figure 9.3:

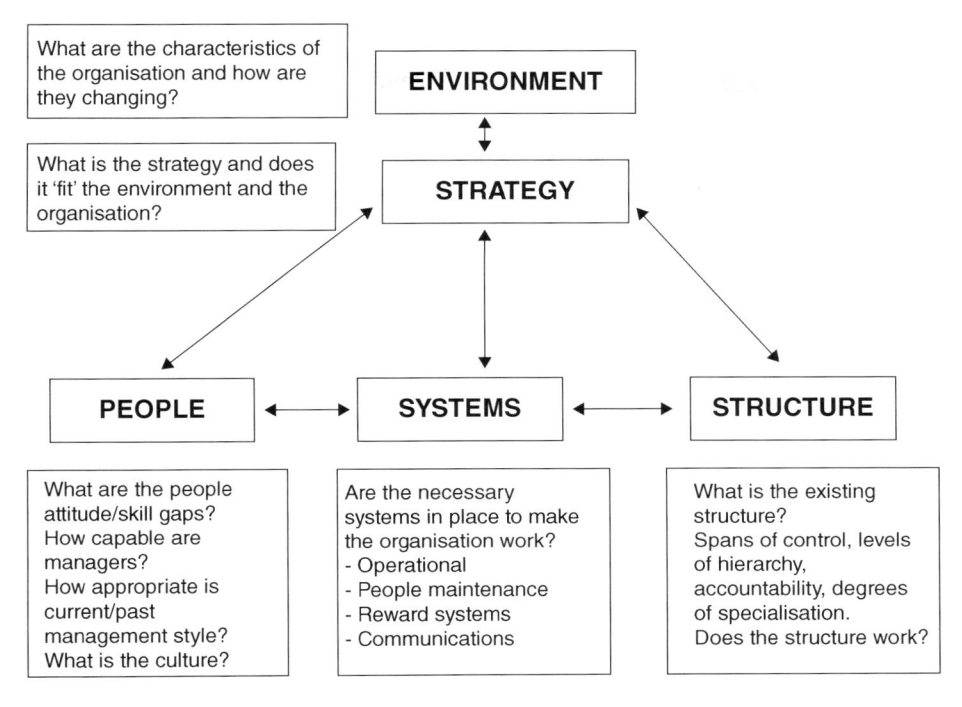

Figure 9.2 The External Environment and HRM
Source: Alexandrou & Darby (2006)

Figure 9.3 Integrated HR Sub-strategies
Source: Author.

Developing and implementing SHRM

To illustrate how to achieve the application of SHRM, Schuler et al. (2005) developed a Four Task Model, which has utility for contemporary defence and security forces. Each task has a set of questions.

Managing employee assignments and opportunities

- What number and type of employees are needed, and with what qualifications?
- Where are they needed, and when?
- Where will they come from?
- What opportunities for growth, development, and reward will attract them to the organisation?

Managing employee competencies

- What competencies do employees have now?
- What competencies will be needed in the future?
- What competencies will be less important in the future?
- Which specific employees need which specific competencies?
- Can/should needed competencies be purchased or developed?

Managing employee behaviour

- What behaviours does the organisational culture value?
- What behaviours are detrimental to the strategy and need to be eliminated or modified?
- How do employees' behaviours affect customers' buying patterns and satisfaction?

Managing employee motivation

- How much more effort are employees willing and able to give?
- What is the optimal length of time for employees to stay with the firm?
- Can production costs or customer service be improved by reducing absence and tardiness?

International and cross-cultural contexts in developing countries are as relevant today for the defence and security sector as any other sector (Horwitz & Budhwar, 2015). The importance of an international perspective has enhanced the development of SHRM; the main driver has undoubtedly been the multinational corporations (MNCs) and their influence on international, cross-cultural management.

The impact of international, cross-cultural management on SHRM is relevant to the consideration of two key issues confronting the defence and security forces of countries in transition. Both issues relate to force structure planning. The first issue pertains to the inclusion of former combatants into security services as part of a peace settlement (the case of Nepal is a recent example). The second issue relates to the inclusion of women into the security services as part of the broader gender mainstreaming agenda arising from the UN's Sustainable Development Goals. These are core people management issues and the adoption of SHRM approach will be required to assist countries in addressing these requirements.

Exercise 9.6

BAE Systems is a key player in the global defence industry and is influential in the partnership between business and defence. Its sphere of influence, by necessity, includes the rapidly changing issue of innovation and the need for strategically managing human capital to continually provide new knowledge, skills and experience in the workforce. There is often a 'knowledge gap' between the business and the security service when buying new equipment. What problems does this pose for the security forces and how can this gap be managed?

Of similar importance within the defence sector is the growing number of defence alliances, force coalitions and the use of multi-national forces. What is significant for this chapter is the increasing number of independent variables acting to influence international HRM. Within HRM, the implications of cultural diversity on management include key issues such as organisational loyalty, the focus of control, rewards and performance, risk, time frames for planning commitment, communication and decision making. Military personnel who have served in multinational peace keeping forces for example, will be aware of the different demand's cultural diversity places on their management of not only the defence space but also the increasingly important business space in the changing 21st century defence environment.

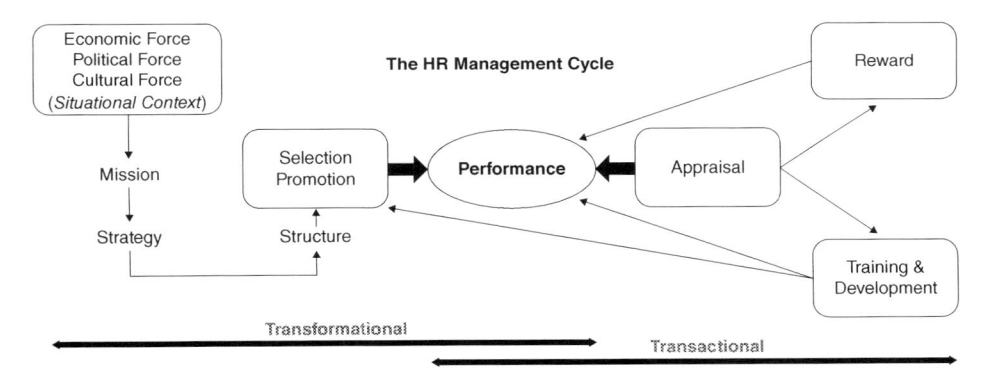

Figure 9.4 The Human Resource Cycle and 'Fit' with Organisational Strategy
Source: Alexandrou &Darby (2006).

HRM in the defence and security spaces

It is contended in this chapter that defence and security organisations are (belatedly) coming to terms with the concept of HRM, and not before time. This connotes a change of mindset in institutions that now acknowledge that *people* are a key asset; whilst also recognising the need for employee engagement to ensure staff are managed more effectively, efficiently and economically. Consequently, relevant, updated HR management and leadership skills are of paramount importance in the process of modernisation of defence and security forces. The demand for more relevant updated HR management and leadership capability has occurred in many Forces around the world where defence budgets have fluctuated but demand for security services remain constant if more complex and, in some instances, contradictory. The contemporary reality facing defence and security forces in those countries includes experiencing rationalisation, restructuring and increasing complexity in all the *spaces* managed by such forces. Figure 9.5 identifies the key spaces:

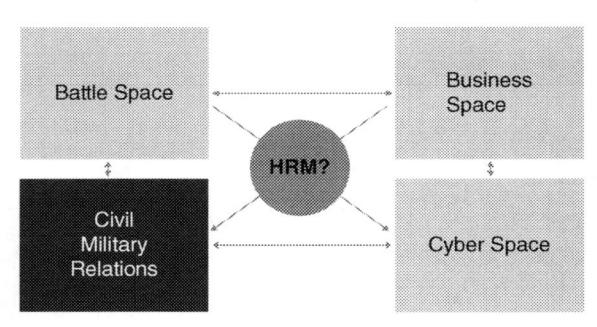

Figure 9.5 Managing Spaces in Defence and Security
Source: Author.

For example, defence and security forces will have to continuously invest in new technology, augment reduced forces with larger numbers of unmanned platforms, face the unprecedented challenges of cyber security and prepare for conflicts wholly unlike those in the past 20 years. Consequently, contemporary security personnel include cyber-soldiers, satellite controllers and software engineers. From an HRM perspective, there are two issues. First, the central role of human capital needs to be acknowledged in any future strategic reviews and defence plans. That includes the correct 'quantity' of personnel (juxtaposing a possible decreasing number of permanent staff with increasing number of reservists) to suit a multiplicity of spaces and situational contexts. Second, there is a long-term requirement for strategic planning and resourcing to ensure the availability of 'quality' staff with the necessary skills, knowledge and experience to be flexible and agile enough to meet the changing requirements within short, medium and long-term time frames.

The employment contract in defence and security

The importance of employee engagement to HRM was identified earlier in this chapter. There is a potential division in most organisations, between the aspirations of individuals and the needs of their organisation. Effective HRM maintains a delicate balance or bridge between these two key protagonists in the employment relationship. Central to maintaining this equilibrium is the importance of two significant contracts. Firstly, there is the formal, legal, normally written employment contract. This sets out the terms and conditions of employment, remuneration, and the rules that govern the employment relationship. Secondly, and fundamental to the efficacy of HRM, is the *psychological contract* (Guest & Conway, 2000, 2001). This refers to the expectations that employees have about their role and what the employer is prepared to give them in return. Furthermore, as external and internal environments inevitably change over time, so do the psychological contracts – placing more pressure on organisations to manage the change in employee relationships in order to overcome attitudinal and behavioural drift as its workforce reacts to the constant variability in direction to meet fluctuating organisational objectives.

Conclusion

As in all sectors, defence and security face an uncertain future. That uncertainty will inevitably affect key management practices like HRM. Various critical questions about human capital requirements, suitably trained staff and financial cost will continue to emerge in conjunction with future national and international challenges to a country's economic, social, political, cyber and security environments. This chapter has highlighted fundamental HRM concepts challenged by the notion of *change*. From its derivation and the influence of its antecedents to a more contemporary role involving fluid, flexible, yet more high-profile, approaches to managing the key resource of *people*. This is compounded by the issue of situational context incorporating organisational architecture as a key component in future HRM; influenced by transactional and transformational management issues involving strategy, structure and control in all types of organisations. Organisational design often determines how HRM functions, both negatively as well as positively. As future demands point to the need for the security sector to be more flexible, adaptable and responsive to more complex needs incorporating the enabler of SHRM; so too must organisations be designed to engage with and manage those changes.

In practical terms, the HR function within defence and security services will still need to address the 'cradle to grave and beyond' philosophy, as they seek to cultivate, obtain, retain, sustain and remember their crucial human capital. This will require more understanding and management of the importance of the psychological contract or military covenant. In the past, human resource planning was mainly about determining size (quantitative); now emphasis is placed on a more qualitative approach. HR strategies will need to enable existing or reduced workforces (both permanent and part-time) to carry out diverse tasks that may emerge in the future. This in turn requires a more flexible workforce with transferable skills to meet the needs of the different defence 'spaces' and changing requirements in a multiplicity of locations and diverse and often contradictory environments.

HRM has gained prominence in its strategic management thinking over the last 20 years. The theoretical and empirical advancement of the subject has highlighted the importance of the relationship between HRM, performance and organisational effectiveness. Nevertheless, it is argued, defence and security institutions are only belatedly coming to terms with the concept of HRM. Many defence organisations still have a prevailing cultural heritage where the predominance of personnel management is viewed as a reactive, administrative function rather than seeing HRM as a strategic pro-active, executive function.

A crucial question raised in this chapter is whether there is a single, identifiable way of managing human resources that is universally appropriate in transitional defence institutions. It is argued that there is a need for an alternative contingent approach, taking into consideration cross-cultural factors, and more suited to local situational context. Isomorphism, using the example of NPM, was identified as an exemplar of the influence on PSOs in the developing world. NPM incorporating imitation or independent development was shown to be a key variable in using similar (HRM) processes and structures. However, it was argued a paradigm shift in HRM in the public sector is required to accommodate much needed intended reforms with the centrality of 'situational context' still paramount in all management decision making.

One final point to highlight in this conclusion regards talent management (TM), a major issue for all defence and security forces in the future. Important questions about how and where organisations concentrate their investment in talent in order to function effectively will be crucial strategic decisions in the years ahead. PSO and private-sector organisations face the same challenges in terms of how to manage different types of human capital development from the individual to the unit, and then to the organisation level, to build a range of sustainable talent. It can be argued that creating a meritocracy developed from HRM using succession management will be one of the most valuable long-term strategic decisions a defence organisation can make.

This chapter has offered an à la carte rather than a prescriptive menu for an understanding of the importance of HRM in all organisations including those in the defence and security sector. As has been emphasised throughout, situational contexts will determine management choices, whether a country is developed or developing. The over-arching theme in this chapter has been that *'people'* are the most important asset in any organisation. Normally, however, they are the most expensive and usually the most poorly managed. To continue the cycle of waste and misuse of talent is an example of bad management practice. No organisation, including those in defence and security, can afford such bad management practice if it wishes to maintain its capability and sustainability in the future and remain relevant in a fast-changing, complex and uncertain global security environment.

Questions to consider

1. What role does HRM play in the defence and security sector? Using the HR Management Cycle model, identify how all the key functions are integrated and should contribute to the overall performance of an organisation.
2. In relation to the strategic demands of your organisation in the next five years, using the Four Task Model identify the strengths, weaknesses, opportunities and threats (SWOT) facing the organisation.
3. Give examples in your organisation of the potential benefits of employee engagement to both the organisation and its personnel. How can the Psychological Contract play a significant role in improving employee engagement?
4. Considering the future, identify how specific changes in Talent Management supported by an effective HRM system could be utilised to support capacity-building and the improved capability of a defence and security force.

Suggested further reading

Torrington, D., Hall, L., Taylor, S. & Atkinson, C. (2017) *Human Resource Management*, 10th ed., London: Pearson.

References

Alexandrou, A. & Darby, R. (2006) 'Human resource management in the defence environment'. In: Cleary, L. & McConville, T. (eds) *Managing Defence in a Democracy.* Abingdon: Routledge.

Andrews, M. (2013) *The Limits of Institutional Reform in Development: Changing Rules for Realistic Solutions,* Cambridge: Cambridge University Press.

Barney, J. (1991) 'Firm resources and sustained competitive advantage', *Journal of Management, 17*: pp. 99–120. DOI:014920639101700108

Beer, M., Spector, B., Lawrence, P., Quinn Mills, D. & Walton, R. (1984) *Managing Human Assets,* New York: Free Press.

Bjorkman, I. (2006) 'International human resource management research and institutional theory'. In: G.K. Stahl & I. Bjorkman (eds.), *Handbook of Research in International Human Resource Management,* Cheltenham: Edward Elgar, pp. 463–474, DOI:10.4337/9781845428235.

Blau, P.M. (1964) 'Justice in social exchange', *Sociological Inquiry, 34* (*2*), pp. 193–206, DOI:10.1111/j.1475–682X.1964.tb00583.x

Bordogna, L. & Neri, S. (2011) 'Convergence towards an NPM programme or different models? Public service employment relations in Italy and France', *The International Journal of Human Resource Management, 22* (*11*), pp. 2311–2330, DOI:10.1080/09585192.2011.584393

Boxall, P. & Purcell, J. (2011) *Strategy and Human Resource Management,* London: Macmillan International Higher Education.

Brinkerhoff, D.W. & Brinkerhoff, J.M. (2015) 'Public sector management reform in developing countries: Perspectives beyond NPM orthodoxy', *Public Administration and Development, 35* (*4*), pp. 222–237. DOI:10.1002/pad.1739

Budhwar, P.S. (2000) 'Evaluating levels of strategic integration and development of human resource management in the UK', *Personnel Review, 29* (*2*), pp. 138–153.

Collings, D.G., Mellahi, K. & Cascio, W.F. (2019) 'Global talent management and performance in multinational enterprises: A multilevel perspective', *Journal of Management, 45* (*2*), pp. 540–566. DOI:10.1177%2F0149206318757018

De Vries, M. & Nemec J. (2013) 'Public sector reform: an overview of recent literature and research on NPM and alternative paths', *International Journal of Public Sector Management 26* (*1*): pp. 4–16. DOI:10.1108/09513551311293408

Gratton, L., Hope Hailey, V., Stiles, P. & Truss, C. (1999) *Strategic Human Resource Management,* Oxford: Oxford University Press.

Guest, D. (1991) 'Personnel management: The end of orthodoxy?', *British Journal of Industrial Relations, 29* (*3*), pp. 149–175. DOI:10.1111/j.1467–8543.1991.tb00235.x

Guest, D.E. (2011) 'Human resource management and performance: Still searching for some answers', *Human Resource Management Journal, 21* (*1*), pp. 3–13. DOI: 10.1111/j.1748–8583.2010.00164.x

Guest, D. & Conway, N. (2000) *The Psychological Contract in the Public Sector,* London: CIPD.

Guest, D. & Conway, N. (2001) *Public and Private Sector Perceptions on the Psychological Contract,* London: CIPD.

Guo, C., Brown, W., Ashcroft, R., Yoshioka, C. & Deng, H. (2011) 'Strategic human resources management in non-profit organizations', *Review of Public Personnel Administration, 31* (*3*), pp. 248–269.

Hartley, K. (2018) 'Defence Budgets'. In: *Routledge Handbook of Defence Studies,* D.J. Galbreath & J.R. Deni eds., Abingdon: Routledge.

Hedlund, G. (1996) 'The hypermodern MNC – A heterachy?', *Human Resource Management, 25* (*1*), pp. 28–43.

Hood, C. (1991) 'A public management for all seasons?', *Public Administration, 69* (*1*), pp. 3–19. DOI:10.1111/j.1467–9299.1991.tb00779.x

Horwitz, F. & Budhwar, P. eds. (2015) *Handbook of Human Resource Management in Emerging Markets*, London: Edward Elgar Publishing.

Jiang, K., Lepak, D.P., Hu, J. & Baer, J.C. (2012) 'How does human resource management influence organizational outcomes? A meta-analytic investigation of mediating mechanisms', *Academy of Management Journal, 55 (6)*, pp. 1264–1294. DOI:10.5465/amj.2011.0088

Jiang, K. & Messersmith, J. (2018) 'On the shoulders of giants: A meta-review of strategic human resource management', *The International Journal of Human Resource Management, 29 (1)*, pp. 6–33. DOI:10.1080/09585192.2017.1384930

Kelly, G., Muligan, G. & Muers, S. (2002) *Creating Public Value: An Analytical Framework for Public Service Reform*, London: Strategy Unit, Cabinet Office.

Kim, P. (2008) 'How to attract and retain the best in government', *International Review of Administrative Sciences, 74 (4)*, pp. 637–652. DOI: 10.1177/0020852308098472

Knies, E. & Leisink, P. (2018) 'People management in the public sector'. In: C. Brewster & Cerdin, J-L., eds., *HRM in Mission Driven Organizations*, London: Palgrave Macmillan, Cham, pp. 15–46. DOI: 10.1007/978-3-319-57583-4_2

Knies, E., Leisink, P. & van de Schoot, R. (2020) 'People management: Developing and testing a measurement scale', *International Journal of Human Resource Management, 31 (6)*, pp. 705–737. DOI:10.1080/09585192.2017.1375963

Marchington, M. (2015) 'The role of institutional and intermediary forces in shaping patterns of employee involvement and participation (EIP) in Anglo-American countries', *The International Journal of Human Resource Management, 26 (20)*, pp. 2594–2616, DOI:10.1080/0958 5192.2014.1003088

Messersmith, J.G., Patel, P.C., Lepak, D.P. & Gould-Williams, J.S. (2011) 'Unlocking the black box: Exploring the link between high-performance work systems and performance', *Journal of Applied Psychology, 96 (6)*, p. 1105. DOI:10.1037/a0024710

Montealegre, R. & Cascio, W.F. (2017) 'Technology-driven changes in work and employment', *Communications of the ACM, 60 (12)*, pp. 60–67. DOI:10.1145/3152422

Painter, M. (2004) 'The politics of administrative reform in East & South East Asia: From gridlock to continuous self-improvement', *Governance, 17 (3)*, pp. 361–386, DOI:10.111 1/j.0952–1895.2004.00250

Purcell, J. (2014) 'Disengaging from engagement', *Human Resource Management Journal, 24 (3)*, pp. 241–254. DOI:10.1111/1748–8583.12046

Ruck, K., Welch, M. & Menara, B. (2017) 'Employee voice: An antecedent to organisational engagement', *Public Relations Review, 43 (5)*, pp. 904–914.

Rupidara, N. & Darby, R. (2017) 'Institutional influences on HRM in the Asian business environment: The case of Indonesia', *Journal of Asia Business Studies, 10 (3)*, pp. 1–16, DOI:10.1108/JABS-07–2015–0110

Samaratunge, R., Alam, Q. & Teicher, J. (2008) 'The new public management reforms in Asia: A comparison of South and Southeast Asian countries', *International Review of Administrative Sciences, 74 (1)*, pp. 25–46. DOI: 10.1177/0020852307085732

Schachter, H.L. (2014) 'New public management and principals' roles in organizational governance: What can a corporate issue tell us about public sector management?', *Public Organization Review, 14 (4)*, pp. 517–531. DOI:10.1007/s11115-013-0242-y

Schuler, R.S. & Jackson, S.E. (1987) 'Organizational strategy and organization level as determinants of human resource management practices', *Human Resource Planning, 10 (3)*, pp. 10–17.

Schuler, R.S., Jackson, S.E. & Storey, J. (2005) 'HRM and its link with strategic management'. In: J. Storey, ed., *Human Resource Management: A Critical Text*, 2nd ed., London: Thomson Learning.

Scott, W.R. (2008) 'Approaching adulthood: The maturing of institutional theory', *Theory and Society, 37 (5)*, p. 427. DOI:10.1007/s11186-008-9067-z

Scott, W. (2014) *Institutions and Organisations: Ideas, Interests, and Identities*, 4th ed, Thousand Oaks, CA: Sage Publications.

Sterling, A. & Boxall, P. (2013) 'Lean production, employee learning and workplace outcomes: A case analysis through the ability-motivation-opportunity framework', *Human Resource Management Journal*, 23 (3), pp. 227–240. DOI:10.1111/1748–8583.12010

Wright, P. & McMahan, G. (2011) 'Exploring human capital: Putting 'human' back into strategic human resource management', *Human Resource Journal*, 21 (2), pp. 93–104, DOI:10.1111/j.1748–8583.2010.00165.x

Wright, P., McMahon, G. & McWilliams, A. (1994) 'Human resources and sustained competitive advantage: A resource-based perspective', *International Journal of Human Resource Management*, 5 (2), pp. 312–328. DOI:10.1080/09585199400000020

Wright, P.M. & Nisbet, L.H. (2013) 'HRM and performance: The role of effective implementation'. In: J. Paauwe, D. Guest & P. Wright (eds), *HRM and Performance: Achievements and Challenges*, Chichester: John Wiley & Sons.

Yusuf, R.M., Fidyawan, S. & Wekke, I.S. (2017) 'Ulrich model on practices of human resource strategic roles', *Journal of Engineering and Applied Sciences*, 12 (6), pp. 1657–1661. DOI:10.31227/osf.io/ysnu8

10 Cyber security and knowledge management

Roger Darby, Lorraine Dodd and Jeremy Hilton

Introduction

In recent years, digital transformation and internet connectivity have provided unprecedented opportunities for both public and private organisations. The resulting price paid for such transformation by defence and security organisations is vulnerability to a growing number of cyber risks and threats. The adoption of reactive approaches to combatting the burgeoning range of potential assaults is proving ineffective. Physical attacks, like 9/11, and natural disasters, involving tsunamis and pandemics, have prompted governments to adopt new strategies for dealing with risk and threats; however, similar intrusions and shocks in the digital sphere (e.g. digital theft, disruption, sabotage and political warfare), have not been met with a commensurate strategic, organisational response. This is exacerbated by increasing cyber-attacks, which have undermined state security; including for example, in 2009 the malware attack against the Iranian nuclear industry, Russia's attacks against Estonia in 2007 and Georgia in 2008, interference in the 2016 USA and 2017 French presidential elections, and the Norwegian parliament in 2020. It is contended here that states are not only experiencing information warfare, but also cognitive warfare where hostile forces seek to undermine what nation states understand to be true and false. The public and private sectors are equally vulnerable to attack from state, non-state actors and terrorist proxies. It is argued in this chapter that effective cyber defence and security require not just a whole-of-government, but a whole-of-society approach.

It is also contended in this chapter that the fundamental concepts of cyber security need to be better understood by organisations if cyber resilience and security are to be achieved. The ability to understand and anticipate your organisation's part in an increasingly complex operating environment is key to its survival. Defence and security organisations need to cultivate a culture of cyber-resilience and develop an appropriate security framework. One key asset highlighted in this chapter is the utility of knowledge in fostering vital shared understanding. It is axiomatic that knowledge sharing has many comparable benefits for organisations and individuals. So, the management of this key resource is critical to an organisation's success or failure regarding cyber security, defence and resilience.

It is argued that systemic risk and cyber threats challenge existing paradigms for managing data, information and knowledge, and that a more radical approach to creating, capturing and sharing knowledge is required if security institutions are to remain agile and responsive. Further, if the security sector acknowledges data, information

DOI: 10.4324/9781003137061-10

and knowledge as strategic assets, it needs to be more aware of systemic risk methods and the advantages in Knowledge Management (KM), placing these at the centre of a strategic management approach that can then be enhanced, rather than impeded, by powerful IT systems.

Technical terminology

First, it is necessary to define the concepts central to cyber security and defence, starting by drawing a distinction between the terms 'security system', and 'defence system'. The term 'system' in the context of this chapter has a particular meaning:

> ... the concept of 'system' is used not to refer to things in the world but to a particular way of organising our thoughts about the world... We consider the notion of 'system' as an organising concept ....
>
> (Flood & Jackson, 2004: p.16)

Thus a 'security system': is organised to prevent, or block-out, latent (or potential) threats to self.

This definition stands in contrast to that of defence system, which assumes that there is a threat actor, or perpetrator, with whom the defending system has a relationship (usually assumed to be adversarial). In this context, a defence system effects capability in response to a patent threat to self. This distinction is important because the way in which any capability (i.e. as a security system or a defence system) is then developed and exploited, needs to take the different purposes into account; in particular, when determining what constitutes important and relevant knowledge that needs to be managed and shared for the varied purposes of cyber security and cyber defence. *Cyber security*, which often also encompasses information security, refers to the establishment of systems to ensure the integrity, confidentiality, and availability of information (Caravelli et al., 2019). These cyber security systems comprise an evolving set of tools and technologies, risk assessment approaches, specialised skills training, and best practices in organisational knowledge management designed to protect networks, devices, programmes, and data from unauthorized access. On the other hand, *Cyber defence* (Darko et al., 2017) focuses on preventing, detecting and providing timely responses to attacks or patent threats.

Exercise 10.1

It may be helpful to think about the ways in which an organisation would *secure* its physical premises and compare those with the ways in which it would *defend* its premises. These ways would necessarily be different. They would also be different from the ways in which an organisation would need to *protect* its premises.

Write down the activities you would envisage taking place against each of the three purposes of *securing*, *defending* and *protecting* your organisation's premises. This may necessarily involve assumptions about the different natures (e.g., accidental or deliberate) of risk, threat, attack and hazard.

There are three interrelated verbs that relate to cyber security and defence: *secure*, *defend* and *protect*. While often used interchangeably, they actually involve different activities for varied purposes, as Exercise 10.1 illustrates.

As highlighted in Chapter 2, the terms threat, risk, impact and vulnerability are crucial concepts in the lexicon of defence and security. For example, *Threat* connotes an intimidation and menacing potential cause of an unwanted incident, which is intended to result in harm to a system or organisation and tends to have a more deliberate intent. Whilst *Risk*, generally, is calculated according to probability and impact. *Impact*, can be seen as a realised outcome or consequence, that can be negative or positive, direct (e.g., financial) or non-direct (e.g., reputational). *Vulnerability*, is a systemic weakness due to an asset or control that can be exploited by one or more threats (ISO: 27001, 2017; The National Cyber Security Centre (NCSC), 2020).

To aid in the understanding of these important concepts, Figure 10.1 illustrates the interrelationship of concepts. This Concept Map can be used to highlight where key areas might need to be strengthened; for example, in terms of where knowledge management and information security need to be focused in specific organisations concerned with different aspects of business or security contexts.

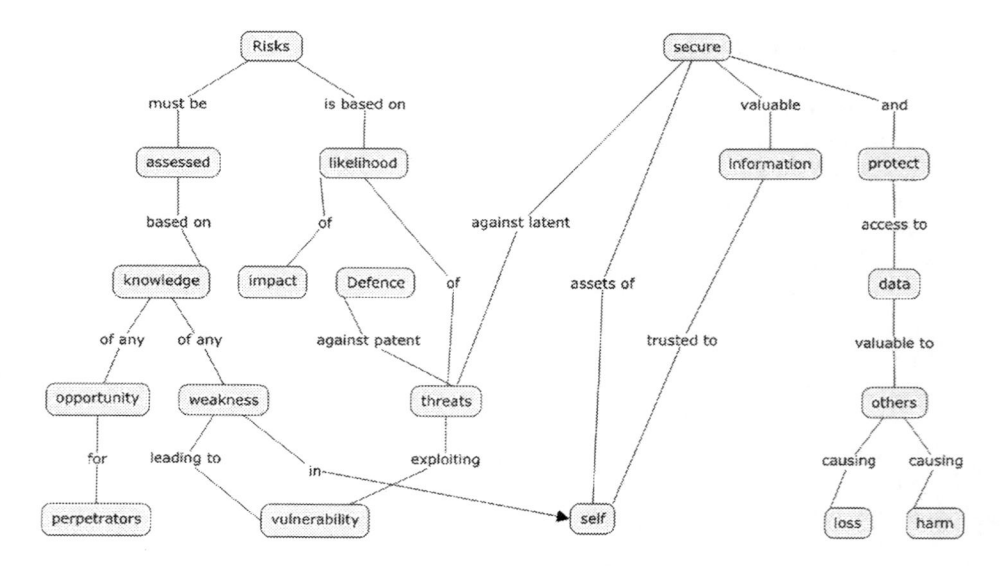

Figure 10.1 Concept Map Showing the Concepts Relating to Cyber Defence and Security
Source: L. Dodd.

Exercise 10.2

Extend the concept map in Figure 10.1 to develop the concepts relating to cyber risk assessment and the importance of sharing knowledge, where knowledge can often be based on unchecked assumptions.

Concept maps were developed at the Institute for Human-Machine Cognition (Novak & Canas, 2008) to empower users to construct, navigate, share and criticise knowledge models. Their strength lies in the connections between named concepts; for example, in Figure 10.1, in relation to risks and being secure, the concept of 'weakness' is specifically mapped in terms of any weakness that leads to vulnerability, which could be exploited via patent threats. This also points to the importance of risk assessment being dependent on knowledge.

As discussed in Chapters 1 and 2, managing risk is a critical part of the Defence and Security business. In this chapter, we are specifically concerned with assessing cyber risk. The ability to understand and anticipate your organisation's part in an increasingly complex operating environment plays a key role in its continued survival. As discussed in Chapter 2, we endeavour to objectively analyse the external and internal risk environments, conscious of the fact that risks may emerge from hidden (possibly incorrect) assumptions. This internal extension into perspectives on risk is what is meant by systemic risk. It is then natural to ask: Where might the major contribution to systemic risk come from?

Exercise 10.3

Can you elaborate on the aspects of risk that begin to embrace systemic risk, for example:

*   Your own and your organisation's hidden and or unspoken assumptions and beliefs about what might be facing you in the future.
*   Your tacit acceptance of constraints and restraints being placed on parts or all your organisation's degrees of freedom of manoeuvre or choice; importantly where managerial control structures may be impeding vital functional structures.

Any more?

Much of the systemic risk resides within one's own assumptions (Dreyer et al., 2018); also, within systems of governance (e.g., points of agency, lines of authority, responsibility and accountability). Therefore, another contributor to systemic risk is the nature of the interrelationships and the intricacy of organisational interdependencies. These two key factors lie at the heart of systemic risk. Examples of major systemic failures tend to stem from behaviours that are bounded by an organisation's focus of interest (e.g., focus on the 'bottom-line' at the expense of lost potential value and damage to reputation), unspoken beliefs (e.g., hidden assumptions) and unacknowledged preferences (e.g., preferred ways of working).

Viable System Model for diagnosing organisational cyber resilience

To think through these systemic challenges, it is important to diagnose the organisation for its cyber vulnerabilities using, for example, the Viable System Model (VSM) (Espejo & Gill, 1997). The VSM is frequently used as a diagnostic tool to improve the cyber resilience and continued viability of organisations. It is, however, quite a challenging methodology to grasp as it does not consider organisations in the usual, organogram way, but from a functional management perspective, viewed in a recursive hierarchical manner. The value of VSM is that it considers not only the different focus of each layer of management, but also how the organisation joins up across the layers and what coheres the organisation. It is ideally suited to explore the functional aspects of cyber risk, cyber vulnerability and risk management.

VSM is derived from a neuro-cybernetic analogy based on the human system. Quite simply, our organisations have a brain and a coherent, collaborative set of functional organs, and they operate in and interact with an environment. This leads to the three main elements of the VSM as shown in Figure 10.2: the management and operational elements, with the environment sitting to one side.

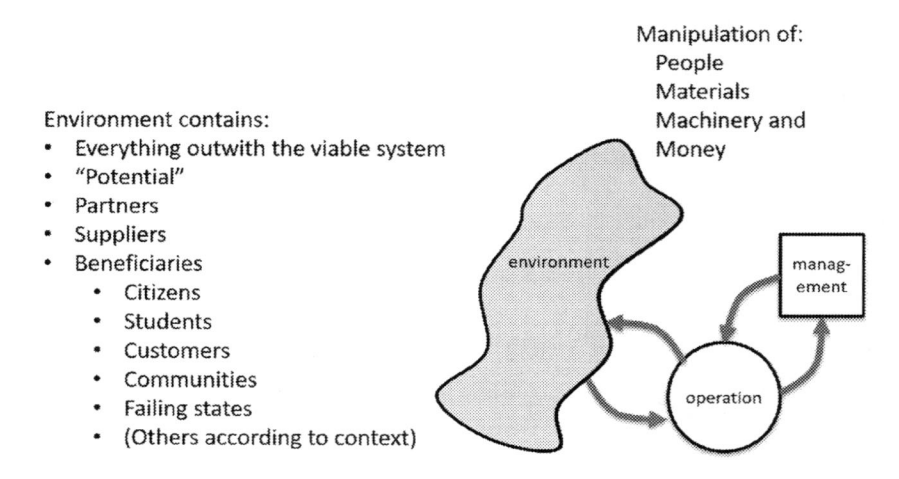

Figure 10.2 Basic Elements of VSM
Source: J. Hilton derived from (Beer, 1985).

The management element comprises strategic direction and value-setting; an externally focused 'horizon-scanning' element; and day-to-day internally focused management. The operations element comprises the parts of the organisation that add value. From an institutional perspective, these would be the front-line service providers: defence forces, police, etc.

The VSM is nested, which is necessarily complex (Conant & Ashby, 1970), and can be applied at any level in society. For example, from a cyber perspective, one can consider the government-level (National Cyber Security Centre) development of cyber policies and best practice, down through an organisation's board-level consideration of cyber risk, to a senior leadership team's development of policy and auditing compliance, to operational units' implementation and management of controls. Each layer can be considered separately, but importantly, the VSM encourages consideration of the links and channels between the layers. It enables one to ask questions and to diagnose issues and challenges resulting in a more resilient and cyber-secure organization.

The VSM (see Figure 10.3) looks quite complicated. System 5 includes the leadership and strategic management; System 4 is the future-looking and research aspect; and, System 3 is the day-to-day management (including System 3* which includes periodic reviews of the operating elements that bypass the local operational-level management). An ongoing dialogue between System 4 and System 3 is important as it is this relationship that ensures the organisation continues to be viable, adapting to ongoing changes in the environment in a timely, effective way. System 2, a key aspect of day-to-day management, includes the essential coordination and conflict resolution across the operation's arms of the business or service.

The operating units in System 1 are the parts of the organisation that add value. System 1 needs to be able to operate in its environment as freely as possible. The remaining systems are there to support and direct System 1. Consequently, each operating unit will have its own internal policy, development, operational control, coordination and monitoring, hence the recursive nature of the model. System 1 needs to be viable, but as sub-units within the organisation, they are subject to organisational policies and direction. Within the context of Cyber Security, the System 4 function should be monitoring the cyber risks, national policy and other business guidance and discussing with the System 3 what policies and controls should be put in place. These should then be issued across the organisation via the System 2 function, and periodic audits of compliance would be undertaken by the system 3* function.

Exercise 10.4

Within your organisation, identify who undertakes the function of researching outside the organisation to determine risks, cyber security best practice and relevant guidelines. The next step is to identify who undertakes an appropriate risk assessment and develops appropriate controls issued through organisational policies and procedures. Finally, who in your organisation will decide the appropriate controls and, if necessary, cyber security-focused IT solutions. Then try to construct a VSM.

Although Figure 10.3 is a complicated diagram, it is a useful framework for asking questions about who in your organisation is taking responsibility for cyber security and vulnerability and how. The links between the functions are important here as

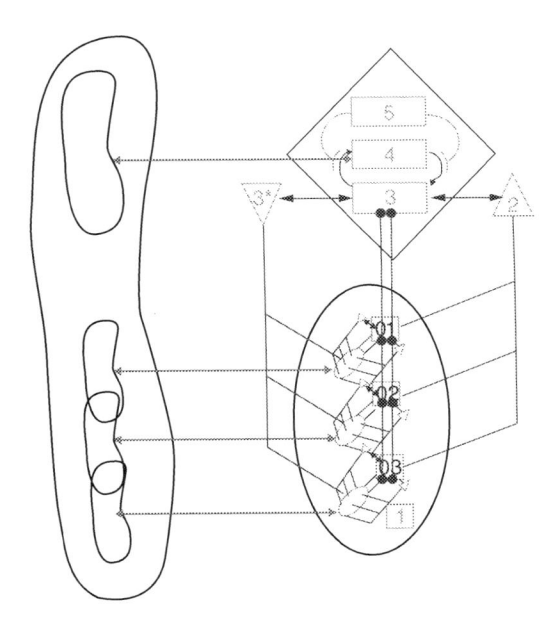

Figure 10.3 The Systems of the VSM
Source: J. Hilton derived from (Espinosa et al., 1991).

you must consider these links in terms of information and knowledge flows, processes and/or specific technology. Furthermore, it is essential to identify and clarify who operates the various functions and links, especially as some of these may be by parties contracted by the organisation. In these circumstances, it is important to realise that defence and security organisations will always retain the liability for any cyber risks even if services and operations are outsourced.

Example 10.1: The importance of IT governance

In September 2018, British Airways (BA) notified the Information Commissioners Office (ICO) that it had suffered a breach of customer data from its website and mobile app. The compromised data included customers' full names, email addresses and financial details (such as credit/debit card numbers, their expiry dates and CVV numbers). The breach was said to have involved user-to-BA transactions being diverted to a fraudulent site. This would appear to involve the perpetrators having gained access to BA's website and modifying the underlying code to run a 'data-skimming function' such that any customer information typed into an affected webpage could be sent directly to a server operated by the perpetrators, before it could be collected and stored by BA, whose customers would see no obvious signs that their data was being collected by anyone other than BA. The perpetrators must have gained access to the necessary code on the servers, which suggests a more systemic issue of IT governance, rather than an isolated vulnerability.

The functional organisation is represented as a VSM at Figure 10.4. The System 5 function is represented by the Service Sponsor in the top box of the diagram. The Service Sponsor is responsible for ensuring the service remains up to date, operates securely and meets the business and service needs. They are responsible for ensuring the System 3 and 4 functions are in constant communication to ensure the service remains fit for purpose.

The System 4 is represented by the Development box. It will ensure cyber security breach notifications are received and acted on, as well as ensuring code updates; also, that software patches are acquired and applied through a controlled software update process within the organisation.

System 3 day-to-day management of the service will include the system administrators, system operators and service operations teams. They will be informing the development team of the current state and performance of the system and will receive relevant tested code updates for the operational systems. These code updates will be passed to the relevant Systems 1.

Systems 1 are for illustration purposes and do not represent a complete system. They include the key elements of the service such as the web application itself, the analytics algorithm incorporated in it, the code and data storage component and the software development function. There is a dependency between some of them, shown by the zigzag lines, and the information or data that passes along the links is identified.

The System 2 ensures the coordination and conflict resolution between the operational systems. This includes workflow in code, business processes, security procedures and the rules-based model for the AI element. This is aimed at enabling as much autonomy at the System 1 level as is desired.

Within System 1, the software development function has developed the web application and this is operating in the web application system. The customer is sitting in the environment and has a form presented to them by the web application providing data from storage. They will enter data regarding the flight or service they wish. This is transferred to the AI system which pulls in additional data from the environment according to the algorithm needs. The AI algorithm will then return a response to the web application which will contain a decision and, depending on the service, a price tailored to the specific individual. The web application will also pull customer data from storage, incorporate the AI-generated response, and present this to the enquirer in the form of a quote, and so on. The enquirer may accept and pay. The simple flows are shown in blue.

The red lines indicate a malicious attack. If the web service and other code in use is not kept up to date regarding security updates and code patches vulnerabilities may be present in the code. By exploiting vulnerabilities in the web code, an attacker may be able to alter the code to insert additional code to intercept the data flows and collect customer data. This could be personal information, including financial data which the attacker sits back and collects for future exploitation.

The VSM organisational diagnosis indicates the presence of vulnerabilities in the website software configuration and the web application developed by (or on behalf of) BA, the lack of effective defence against a threat exploiting the vulnerability. One might argue that the valuable information was not effectively secured against a latent vulnerability, but the data storage server most likely was protected. The BA website would have been given the necessary data access privileges and so was a trusted application. Insufficient development, testing and management of the web server software enabled a breach. Therefore, there may have been issues in the development of the web site software, or in the configuration and maintenance of the web site server and application in its operational state.

Here, there may have been an insufficient risk assessment undertaken, or insufficient controls put in place. There may not have been an appropriate software development standard, or no monitoring of current breaches leading to software security patches being applied. From the VSM, several departments and individuals must all play their part. All of these need to be considered systemically and be monitored and audited as a coherent system to ensure there are no 'cracks' in the system that can be exploited.

The BA ICO principles make clear that *every conceivable aspect* of data and information processing must be covered by the organisation's security procedures. This means that every area of the BA business must be paying attention and be open to seeking out, managing and sharing knowledge relating to all aspects of physical, logical, device and website security.

If the problem 'system' is seen simply, and technically, as 'one compromised script' it could be treated as a technicality with blame placed at technical levels; however, the technical vulnerability in the third-party script used by BA was known about more generally and yet this *knowledge had not been managed or shared*. Therefore, there had been no responsibility or regard taken to do the costly, time-consuming updates, suggesting a more systemic problem at the level of knowledge sharing for risk assessment, pointing to IT governance at BA.

The VSM diagram at Figure 10.4 provides a whole system view that can be used to ask if cyber security management and operation is integrated.

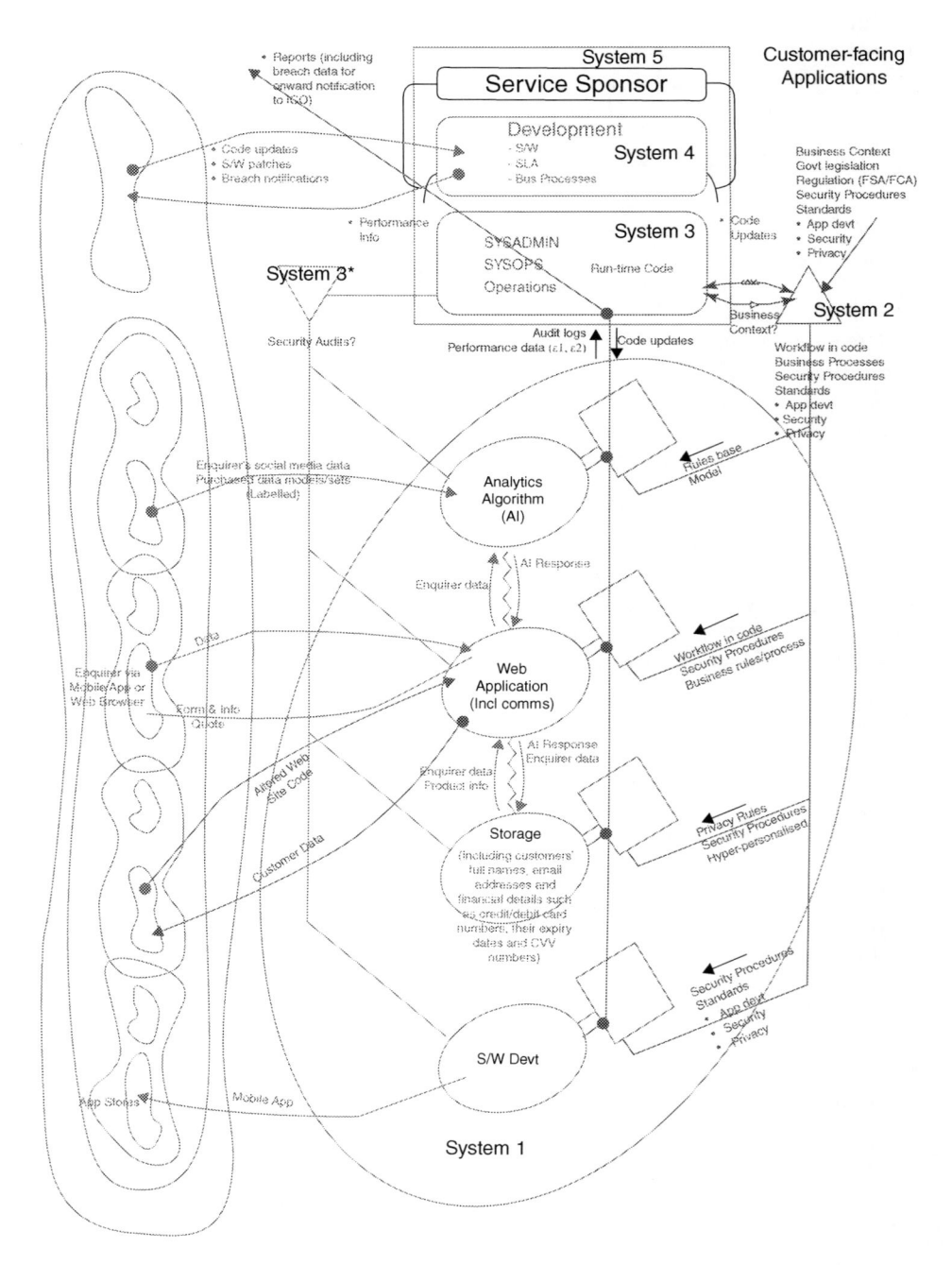

Figure 10.4 VSM of BA Case Study
Source: J. Hilton.

That there is a function that keeps up to date with cyber security issues, and that applies relevant security patches, is important; however, none of this is effective unless there is also a corporate cyber security policy that is enforced appropriately and is periodically audited. Software development processes must incorporate cyber security aspects. Regulatory and legislative requirements must be known and complied with, particularly regarding payment protection and data protection. Vulnerabilities here, if exploited, can have a significant impact on the future viability of the organisation, as regulatory non-compliance can lead to significant fines and, in extremis, cessation of trading.

The significant amount of knowledge in people across the organisation must be kept up to date and made available to relevant parts of the organisation. Also, the requisite set of cyber-related information must be kept current and coherent; and, any changes in policy, or new vulnerabilities or potential attack methods must be made available to relevant parts of the organisation in order to update policy and implement technology. Consequently, knowledge management is essential in maintaining a cyber-secure viable organisation.

Knowledge management

In the introduction to this chapter, we emphasised the utility of knowledge in understanding and anticipating increasingly complex operating environments. Knowledge sharing, and the management of that exchange, can provide comparable benefits for organisations. In this section, the relevance of KM for meeting emerging challenges and opportunities linked to Cyber Security is addressed. That examination is framed with reference to the question:

In what ways might knowledge be acquired, shared and managed to meet 21st century security challenges?

It is acknowledged that there is a paradox here, for, as knowledge boundaries become wider the need grows for more secure boundaries.

Exercise 10.5

Answer the following questions:
1. What is knowledge?
2. Why is knowledge important in the Defence and Security sector?
3. What is knowledge management?
   - What is the process?

Characteristics of KM best practice

It is useful to characterise knowledge according to the different perspectives on managing it. Building on Exercise 10.5 above, the aspects of knowledge referred to across academic literature are characterised as:

- A resource (i.e., as any other type of asset or resource that needs to be managed);
- A support to (and content thereof) managerial processes (i.e., seen as what needs to flow and be shared to support a KM process);

- A fundamental requirement for decision superiority and effective operational impact (i.e., necessary to carry out an activity, course of action or a decision);
- A contribution (i.e., auditable element contributing to the achievement of objectives);
- A service (i.e., knowledge provided as a service to be acquired, e.g., search engines);
- A capability dependent on competencies (i.e., adding to the organisation's capability);
- A 'weapon' to be used to good or bad effect.

These characteristics are inextricably linked to knowledge superiority in defence operations which require dominant defence space awareness and visualisation. For example, as the defence space changes and the speed of conflict increases, the pace of information creation and decision-making also multiplies. Modern defence relies on information from many sources that must be assessed and compiled for immediate use. The timelines are shorter, and the individuals more significant in their roles. This type of conflict requires superiority at all levels of command and control. It demands situational awareness tools that are superior to those of opponents for anticipating their reactions, for sense-making, for problem solving and for superior decision-making.

Data, information and knowledge management

This chapter also highlights a key conundrum faced across corporate and public sectors, including defence, regarding the distinction between data, information management (IM) and knowledge management (KM). Some researchers have argued that the difference between data, information and knowledge must be made as many people believe that they are synonymous (Girard, 2004; Davis et al., 2006). Figure 10.5 provides an illustration of the differences.

If knowledge is about the gathering and interpreting of information, then knowledge management is about the process through which that is done. Rumizen (2002) for example, defines KM as: 'The systematic processes by which knowledge needed for an organization to succeed are created, captured, shared and leveraged'. Collison and Parcell (2004) in turn suggest that KM: '…is about capturing, creating, distilling, sharing and using know-how'. Frappaolo (2006) draws a distinction between information and knowledge management, arguing that:

> …the primary repository for knowledge is people's heads (at least until we agree that machines have intelligence). Electronic and paper-based knowledge repositories, then are merely intermediate storage points for information enroute between people's heads.
>
> (p.5)

This difference highlights the important distinction respectively between 'explicit and implicit (tacit)' knowledge (Polanyi, 1962). Harnessing both explicit and implicit (tacit) knowledge is an increasing and necessarily important challenge to support organisational knowledge creation. One of the fundamental aims of utilising KM is to understand the importance of tacit knowledge and have the skills and tools to convert tacit knowledge into explicit knowledge (Allee, 2002). For it is suggested that when explicit and tacit knowledge interact innovation occurs (Prusak, 1996; Nonaka et al., 2008).

It could be argued, however, that neither data, information nor knowledge is a bounded and discrete entity to be managed. Rather they form a dynamic symbiotic relationship and are seen in the data and information, as raw materials that enter an

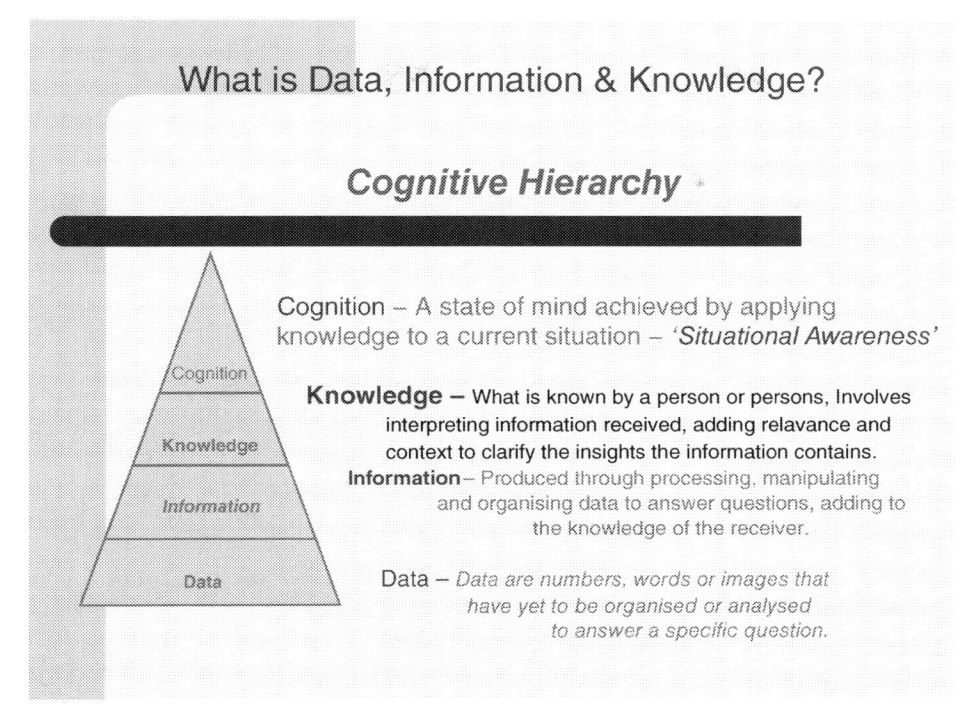

Figure 10.5 Cognitive Hierarchy
Source: R. Darby.

organisation by any means (for instance, physical, electronic or social) and knowledge, which is the organisationally constructed meaning of that data and information that is stored as a resource (physically, organisationally or personally) (Choo, 2006). Furthermore, in the untidiness of the lived experience in any organisation the boundaries between knowledge, information and data are not always clearly distinguished in organisational practice. KM is rooted in practice, action and social relationships with an important interplay between the individual and collective levels in an organisation (Stroh & Caligiuri, 1998; Davenport & Prusak, 1998).

Knowledge sharing

Exercise 10.6

How does your organisation:

- Create knowledge?
- Capture knowledge?
- Transfer knowledge?
- How could your organisation improve the whole KM Dynamic?

It is self-evident that knowledge sharing has many comparable benefits for organisations and individuals; playing a major role in the process of knowledge management and as a key contributor to organisational success (Bouthillier & Shearer, 2002; Marr et al., 2003; Debowski, 2006). However, knowledge sharing can be perceived as difficult mainly due to the complex interactions between organisations and individuals that are affected by human factors as well as technical imperatives (Dalkir & Wiseman, 2004). Previous studies have highlighted the KM problems and technology adoption difficulties drawn from experts' practices embedded in the work context (Hsiao et al., 2006, 2012) and is associated with what Darby (2012: p.525) identifies as the 'dynamic of KM' involving knowledge creation, capture and transfer in organisations.

Further research has highlighted relevant issues regarding the dissemination of knowledge, locating knowledge holders and exploiting existing knowledge (Hubert et al., 2001; Sambamurthy & Subramani, 2005). Two pertinent issues arise from these studies. First, little consideration is given to knowledge attributes when analysing KM problems (Alavi & Leidner, 2001). Second, and more pertinently for this chapter, although previous studies have mainly examined how knowledge barriers can be mitigated to achieve better technology acceptance, they are generally insensitive to exploring how work contexts may affect KM problems (Purvis et al., 2001; Hubert et al., 2001). This highlights a challenge to previous research which appears to treat knowledge barriers as universal and acknowledges that different expert groups (including those in defence) may adopt different types of knowledge within different contexts (Gherardi, 2000; Orlikowski, 2002; Bogenrieder & Nooteboom, 2004). Knowledge in such contexts may reside in physical processes, social communities and service or industrial settings (Hsiao et al., 2012; Tyre and von Hippel, 1997; Lam, 1997).

Knowledge management in the defence sector

It is argued in this chapter that KM in defence does not differ in theory from corporate versions, but in terms of *context, content and pace*. Corporate KM tools can depend on a more sedentary infrastructure, whilst operational settings in defence often require mobile solutions with corresponding questions of security, bandwidth, robustness and reliability; with varying content, and often more targeted to the particular operation. Most corporate situations do not need the comparable, quick reaction time required in conflict situations. Consequently, KM in the military context requires: knowledge processes that are robust and reliable within operational contexts; content and intellectual assets that are focused, precise, reliable, with suitable recall levels; and knowledge creation and conversion processes that match the pace of operations.

Concomitantly, modern-day 'information overload' is one of the greatest technical challenges facing national security communities. The ongoing, exponential increase in digital data necessitates the use of more sophisticated analytical tools to effectively manage risk and proactively respond to emerging security threats. Constantly contending with the certainty of uncertainty at the strategic and operational levels, the provision and leveraging of knowledge resources, much like intelligence, can be a key enabler to deriving better outcomes in defence processes as well as with current and planned future outputs (see Chapter 2). However, defence organisations usually tend to be part of extremely large institutional structures designed along rigid hierarchies and reinforced by a top-down 'chain of command' culture. Security is a constant theme across defence operations and processes, taking many forms – operations security, communications security, information security and cyber security, for example – which strongly instil a 'need to know' basis and a conservative attitude towards disclosure or sharing of data, informational and even knowledge resources. Therefore, the management of data, information and knowledge in the defence sector stands at an interesting juncture. Key dilemmas facing the defence sector are on the one hand, identifying and effectively using the increasing potential of technical interoperability; on the other hand, the need for new management practices juxtaposed with the escalating global challenge to security to counteract the rise of emerging threats (Darby, 2012). Consequently, governments are increasingly identifying their digital infrastructure as a strategic national asset that also needs to be better protected.

It is argued in this chapter, that such threats to the defence sector challenge existing paradigms for managing data, information and knowledge and suggest a more radical approach to gaining knowledge superiority is a requirement to remain agile in the fast-moving, technologically advanced wider defence and security sector. Further, if the defence sector acknowledges data, information and knowledge as strategic assets it needs to be more aware of the advantages of KM and place it at the centre of the strategic management approach (Sveiby, 2001; Dalkir, 2005).

But what of the human component? The necessary body of people who must understand and operate these more sophisticated systems? As changes multiply, the need to manage change more effectively becomes even more important. It is self-evident that sense-making, problem solving, and decision making are more complex and more vital in military situations than ever before. New technologies have resulted in increasingly dynamic, unpredictable and complex operations that require people to filter and analyse information from multiple sources. Concomitantly, know-how, expertise and interoperability are equally important key factors in a defence sector organisation's ability to create knowledge superiority (Gold & Arvind Malhotra, 2001; Malhotra, 2004). Command and control are taking on new dimensions and the role of military personnel is evolving; some would suggest they are becoming knowledge workers (Adler, 2007; Starbuck, 1992). It can be further argued that as organisations gain access to even more advanced technology the impetus behind successful global organisations (including those in the defence sector) to maintain competitive advantage is dependent upon the development of knowledgeable employees (and multi-level and multi-cultural relationships).

Exercise 10.7

In a defence acquisition management context, project teams could be creating new knowledge about clients, costing, suppliers, legal and statutory issues, procedures or technical matters, which will not be effectively captured, transferred or related to future projects once the project team disbands. While KM in permanent organisations can focus on knowledge silos that exist within departmental or divisional constructs, organisational routines or organisational memory are unlikely to emerge at all in project-based teams or organisations. How can Defence manage the 'organisational memory' in these temporary working constellations more effectively to meet changing defence needs in the next five years?

Example 10.2: The Huawei case

The British Government's original contentious decision to use the Chinese firm Huawei to provide a significant part of the UK's 5G telecommunications system caused alarm and heated debate related to the security implications. Huawei has risen from a small importer of foreign telecoms equipment to one of the world's largest makers of 5G mobile networks. A number of countries including the USA, Australia and Japan raised concerns that the kit may come with 'back doors' – deliberate security holes that can act as conduits for Chinese spies or cyber-saboteurs. On the other hand, many believed Huawei should be allowed to compete in new markets. Its products are high-quality and cheap. Excluding it would be costly and risks delaying 5G.

It is suggested the risks are real although countries can adopt three broad strategies to mitigate them:

1. *Technical* – Encouraging encryption would ease spying concerns, since intercepting data would produce only gibberish. Networks need to be defended in depth. Britain intended to exclude Huawei from sensitive parts of the network, though geography may limit that approach elsewhere. Because accidental bugs can be as dangerous as deliberate back doors, having several suppliers and spare capacity is a good idea. Redundancy and resilience are the watchwords.
2. *Encouraging Existing Industry Trends Towards Openness* – Present telecom networks are built with proprietary products. In future they will become just another piece of software running on off-the-shelf computers. That should allay worries about compromised hardware and make it easier for new entrants to compete. Open-source is in fashion and an alliance of tech companies is keen on open-source versions of antennae and masts that make up a mobile network's outer edge. Having code and devices open for inspection makes it easier to find security holes, and harder to hide back doors.
3. *International Co-operation* – Britain had already stripped down and inspected all Huawei kit. Sharing the results and experience more widely would make more scrutiny possible to keep Huawei honest. In the longer term, an international inspection body, modelled for example, on the International Atomic Energy Agency, could be a good idea.

Computer security, like all security is about trade-offs, not absolutes. Back doors are a concern, but most hackers make do with the accidental flaws. Russia, for example, has no domestic electronics industry to speak of, and therefore no ability to insert back doors. Designing robust networks, building them with checkable equipment and sharing knowledge and expertise should make it harder for hackers from all countries, not just China.

Exercise 10.8

1. Analyse the debate about the British Government's initial intention to use Huawei in the installation of a 5G network. Was the UK government's final decision not to use Huawei right or wrong? Give your reasons.
2. What security concerns are raised by the Huawei case when a government is planning for the latest SDSR which may involve a decision about installing a 5G network provided by a foreign supplier?

3. Discuss the three strategies in the case to mitigate possible risks to national security. Are they resilient enough?
4. What strategies could be added to them to support the further mitigation of security risks?

Conclusion

This chapter has highlighted a pivotal issue in the contemporary security and defence milieu; namely, the ubiquitous role that cyber security and defence play in all societies across the world. Digital transformation and web connectivity now provide unprecedented opportunities for individuals and organisations. This technological transformation has created vulnerability to an unparalleled, burgeoning range and scope of cyber risks and attacks on individuals and organisations alike. Governments, no matter how big or powerful, are not protected or immune from such cyber risks and attacks. Indeed, security and defence forces face a bewildering array of state-based and non-state actors, and terrorist proxies, which add to the complexity that state agencies are forced to manage with increasing difficulty. It is argued in this chapter that as the scale of cyber threat and risks is exponentially increasing, there is a real need to think and work systemically. Consequently, governments increasingly need to identify their digital infrastructure as a strategic national asset that needs to be better protected. This includes being systematic about what we take cyber concepts to mean; also, being systematic about cyber resilience by using cybernetic organisational diagnosis to check for cyber vulnerability. Furthermore, effective cyber defence and ultimate security require not just a whole-of-government, but a whole-of-society approach.

Not all governments are successful in managing rapid complex change, especially where there are tensions between what must remain commercial and what needs to be regarded as sovereign stewardship or guardianship (Jacobs, 1992). There are additional challenges for those governments engaged in post-conflict recovery and development, as they often do not have commensurate strategic organisational responses to common digital disruption, theft, sabotage and political warfare occurring in the area of cyber security. This chapter has emphasised the need for a deeper understanding of cyber resilience and security within an organisationally focused security framework.

Several emerging themes have been raised in this chapter in relation to KM and Cyber Security in complex environments. One theme highlighted is the basis on which knowledge is shared as well as managed. For example, if knowledge is being treated as a resource, then questions need to be asked whether it would be more appropriate (and operationally effective) to treat knowledge as a support to strategy, a contribution to objectives and, with knowledge sharing, being a defined capability in its own right.

Another emergent theme is that of context, both operational and organisational contexts, within which KM is happening. For KM, the operation tends to form the immediate context for knowledge (e.g., KM within a HQ), which then forms the context for the organisation and its people and processes responsible for managing and sharing and protecting knowledge.

Further, KM principally supports access to new knowledge and sharing of knowledge. A traditional KM lifecycle tends to be represented as an end-to-end process; starting with creation of 'information-based' knowledge and ending with a composed, collated view of 'the situation out there'. So, in a KM lifecycle, the movement from knowledge acquisition to learning outcomes (e.g., 'lessons identified' captured in managed knowledge bases) sits within a context of constraints consisting mainly of extant organisational ways of thinking and ways of working (which may be outdated and outmoded).

The new context for KM, will tend to be formed first by individuals involved, according to their prior knowledge and experience, then by the organisation and finally by the operational environment (about which much of the knowledge will be gained and formed). As such, the organisation (and individuals) tend to form the immediate context, within which the operational setting forms the framing context for the use of knowledge to support understanding and decision-making. However, as highlighted in Chapter 9, the significant amount of knowledge in people across the organisation must be kept up to date and made available to relevant parts of the organisation. Also, the requisite set of cyber-related information must be kept current and coherent; and, any changes in policy, or new vulnerabilities or potential attack methods must be made available to relevant parts of the organisation in order to update policy and implement technology. Consequently, KM is essential in maintaining a cyber-secure viable organisation.

Adopting an end-to-end process view can neglect the open-ended nature of 21st-century defence and security challenges, where feedback and effective learning must form a key part of an essential framework. Here is where shared knowledge techniques open-up new ways to re-frame and then to gain new knowledge; and where cybernetic models such as VSM become essential organisational diagnostic tools to ensure cyber resilience. Technology solutions to KM tend to focus principally on the 'texts' in the form of content of the knowledge. Non-technology KM good practice would suggest the need to look outwards to contexts and self-wards to organisational constraints.

What can be inferred from this chapter is that the future for Cyber Security is very uncertain and difficult to predict. This can be exemplified by some of the current trends and threats faced by security forces across the world today; including, threats to *digital security*, which comprise the use of polymorphic malware that adapts its identifiable characteristics to evade detection, or the automation of social-engineering attacks to target individuals. Palpable threats to *political security* include the use of 'deep fake' technology to generate synthetic media and disinformation, with the objective of manipulating public opinion or interfering with electoral processes; leading to what was identified in the introduction as the threat of 'cognitive warfare'. Threats to *financial security* are of immediate concern. Furthermore, increased adoption of the Internet of Things (IoT) technology, artificial intelligence (AI), autonomous vehicles, 'smart cities' and interconnected critical national infrastructure will create numerous cyber vulnerabilities which could be exploited to cause damage or disruption. Additionally, emerging from the novel research areas (see *US Defense Advanced Research Projects Agency (DARPA))* are biomimetic nature-imitating weapons, which cannot be ignored as a techno-military fantasy. This could lead to the danger of lethal autonomous 'swarm' weapon systems and the question of laws to control such arms.

This chapter also links to the interesting question related to international humanitarian law, which is highlighted in Chapter 4. Key ethical principles of warfare have covered discrimination and proportionality that require aggressors to distinguish between combatants and civilians. In the modern defence space, soldiers and cyber-warriors could face many difficulties in distinguishing neutrals from enemies and pose greater risks when robotic weapon systems are increasingly utilised.

Of course, it should never be forgotten that the weapons industry has always been very big business, as discussed in Chapter 11. The military-industrial complex supporting cyber defence and security has accelerated an arms race including research and development into, for example, the lucrative world of AI. This all produces a double-headed hydra allowing for burgeoning domestic use as well as external foreign use of AI surveillance with nebulous apparatuses of control.

The final point links with Chapters 1 and 2 in this volume; namely, how do governments and leaders respond to new weapon technology? A simple binary choice between ban or regulate may not suffice because new 'cyber weapons' can be deployed without discernible attribution and they can operate 'below the legal radar' to create disruption. A more measured discourse is needed around the issue of reform, and the importance of accountability within the *real-politik* of cyber warfare and the use of autonomous weapons. The fog-of-war is often used as an excuse. However, national governance and international legal systems must impose more accountability and responsibility on states and forces who use such weaponry that has the potential to cause untold civil damage in the future.

Questions to consider

1. What skills sets are required for cyber warriors to be effective today and in the future?
2. Identify the different ways in which non-state actors might pose cyber threats in future?
3. How might the sensitivities around cyber vulnerabilities be navigated to allow for more sharing of knowledge about how to remain cyber resilient?
4. How would you regulate the control of the use of autonomous weapons in your country's security forces?

Suggested further reading

Choo, W., & Bontis, N., eds., (2002) *The Strategic Management of Intellectual Capital and Organizational Knowledge*, Oxford: Oxford University Press.

Hislop, D., Bosua, R. & Helms, R. (2013) *Knowledge Management in Organizations*. 3rd ed., Oxford: Oxford University Press.

References

Adler, P. (2007) 'The future of critical management studies: A Paleo-Marxist critique of labour process theory', *Organization Studies*, 28, pp. 1313–1345, DOI:10.1177F0170840607080743

Alavi, M. & Leidner, D. (2001) 'Knowledge management and knowledge management systems: Conceptual foundations and research issues', *MIS Quarterly 25 (1)*, pp. 107–136. DOI: 10.2307/3250961

Allee, V. (2002) *The Future of Knowledge: Increasing Prosperity Through Value Networks*, Newton, MA: Butterworth-Heinemann.

Bogenrieder, I. & Nooteboom, B. (2004) 'Learning groups: What types are there? A theoretical analysis and an empirical study in a consultancy firm', *Organization Studies*, 25 (2), pp. 287–313. DOI:10.1177/0170840604040045

Bouthillier, F. & Shearer, K. (2002) 'Understanding knowledge management and information management: The need for an empirical perspective', *Information Research*, 8 (*1*), paper no. 141.

Caravelli, J., Jones, N. & Kozup, J.C. (2019) *Cyber Security: Threats and Responses for Government and Business*, London: Praeger.

Choo, Chun Wei (2006) *The Knowing Organization: How Organizations use Information to Construct Meaning, Create Knowledge, and Make Decisions*, 2nd ed., Oxford: Oxford University Press. DOI: 10.1093/acprof:oso/9780195176780.001.0001

Collison, C. & Parcell, G. (2004) *Learning to Fly. Practical Knowledge Management from Leading and Learning Organizations*, Chichester: Capstone Publishing Limited.

Conant, R.C. & Ashby, R.W. (1970) 'Every good regulator of a system must be a model of that system', *International Journal of Systems Science*, 1 (*2*), pp. 89–97.

Dalkir, K. (2005) *Knowledge Management in Theory and Practice*, Oxford: Elsevier.

Dalkir, K. & Wiseman, E. (2004) 'Organizational story-telling and knowledge management: A survey', *Storytelling, Self, Society*, 1 (*1*), pp. 57–73, DOI:10.1080155053404094902 58

Darby, R. (2012) 'Cyber defence in focus: Enemies near and far – or just behind the firewall. The case for knowledge management', *Defence Studies*, 12 (*4*), pp. 523–538. DOI:10.1080/147 02436.2012.745964

Darko, G., Darko, M. & Guberina, B. (2017) 'Cybersecurity and cyber defence: National level strategic approach', *Automatika*, 58 (*3*), pp. 273–286, DOI:10.1080/00051144.2017.1407022

Davenport, T. & Prusak, L. (1998) *Working Knowledge: How Organizations Manage what they Know*, Boston, MA: Harvard Business School Press.

Davis, J., Miller, G.J. & Russel, A. (2006) *Information Revolution: Using the Information Evolution Model to Grow your Business*, Hoboken, New Jersey: John Wiley & Sons, Inc.

Debowski, S. (2006) *Knowledge Management*, Wilton, Australia: Wiley.

Dewar, J. (2002) *Assumption-based Planning: A Tool for Reducing Avoidable Surprises*, New York: RAND Corporation and Cambridge University Press.

Dreyer, P., Jones, T., Klima, K., Oberholtzer, J., Strong, A., Welburn, J.W. & Winkelman, Z. (2018) *Estimating the Global Cost of Cyber Risk: Methodology and Examples*, Santa Monica, CA: RAND Corporation. DOI:10.7249/RR2299

Espejo, R. & Gill, A. (1997) 'The Viable System Model as a framework for understanding organizations'. In: Y. Malhotra, ed., *Knowledge Management and Virtual Organizations*, Idea Group Publishing, 2000, pp. 350–364.

Espinosa, A., Harnden, R. & Walker, J. (2006) Structural design for sustainability: Cybernetic Theory and Practice'. In: *Proceedings of the 50th Annual Meeting of the ISSS-2006*, Sonoma, CA, USA.

Flood, R.L. & Jackson, M.C. (2004) *Creative Problem Solving: Total Systems Intervention*, Hoboken, NJ: Wiley.

Frappaolo, C. (2006) *Knowledge Management*, Chichester: Capstone Publishing Limited.

Gherardi, S. (2000) 'Practice-based theorizing on learning and knowing in organizations', *Organization*, 7 (*2*), pp. 211–223, DOI: https://doi.org/10.1177/135050840072001

Girard, J. (2004) 'Defence knowledge management: A passing fad', *Canadian Military Journal*, Summer, 2004, pp. 17–28.

Gold, A.H. & Arvind Malhotra, A.H.S. (2001) 'Knowledge management: An organizational capabilities perspective', *Journal of Management Information Systems*, 18 (*1*), pp. 185–214, DOI:10.1080/07421222.2001.11045669

Hsiao, R., Dun-Hou Tsai, S. & Lee, C.F. (2012) 'Collaborative knowing: The adaptive nature of cross-boundary spanning', *Journal of Management Studies*, 49, pp. 463–491. DOI:10.1111/j.1467–6486.2011.01024.x

Hsiao, R., Dun-Hou Tsai, S. & Lee, C.F. (2006) 'The problems of embeddedness: Knowledge transfer, coordination and reuse in information systems', *Organization Studies*, 27 (*9*), pp. 1289–1317, DOI:10.11772F0170840606064108

Hubert, C., Newhouse, B. & Vestal, W. (2001) 'Building and sustaining communities of practice'. In: *Knowledge Management, Enabling Business Processes*, Houston, USA.

International Standards Organisation (2017) *ISO 27001 Information Technology-Security Techniques-Information security management systems-requirements.* Available at https://www.iso.org/isoiec-27001-information-security.html [Accessed 11 October 2018].

Jacobs, J. (1992) *Systems of Survival*, New York: Random House.

Lam, A. (1997) 'Embedded firms, embedded knowledge: Problems of collaboration and knowledge transfer in global cooperative ventures', *Organization Studies, 18 (6)*, pp. 973–996. DOI: 10.1177/017084069701800604

Malhotra, Y. (2004) 'Why knowledge management systems fail: Enablers and constraints of knowledge management in human enterprises'. In: *Handbook on Knowledge Management, 1,* Berlin Heidelberg: Springer, pp. 577–599.

Marr, B., Gupta, O., Pike, S. & Roos, G. (2003) 'Intellectual capital and knowledge management effectiveness', *Management Decision, 41 (8)*, pp. 771–781.

NCSC (2020) Available at https://www.ncsc.gov.uk/information/understanding-vulnerabilities [Accessed: 1 November 2020].

Nonaka, I., Toyama, R. & Hirata, T. (2008) *Managing Flow: A Process Theory of the Knowledge-based Firm*, London: Palgrave Macmillan.

Novak, J. D. & Cañas, A. J. (2008) 'The theory underlying concept maps and how to construct and use them, technical Report IHMC CmapTools 2006–2001 Rev 01–2008', Florida Institute for Human and Machine Cognition. Available at http://cmap.ihmc.us/Publications/ResearchPapers/TheoryUnderlyingConceptMaps.pdf [Accessed: 1 November 2020].

Orlikowski, W. (2002) 'Knowing in practice: Enacting a collective capability in distributed organizing', *Organization Science 13 (3)*, pp. 249–273, DOI:10.128713.3.249.2776

Polanyi, M. (1962) *Personal Knowledge*, Chicago: University of Chicago Press.

Prusak, L. (1996) 'The knowledge advantage', *Planning Review, 24 (2)*, pp. 6–8.

Purvis, R., Sambamurthy, V. & Zmud, R. (2001) 'The assimilation of knowledge platforms in organizations: An empirical investigation', *Organization Science, 12 (2)*, pp. 117–135. DOI:10.1287/orsc.12.2.117.10115

Rumizen, C.M. (2002) *The Complete Idiot's Guide to Knowledge Management*, Washington: Alpha Publishing.

Sambamurthy, V. & Subramani, M. (2005) 'Special issue in information technologies and knowledge management', *MIS Quarterly, 29 (1)*, pp. 1–7. DOI:10.2307/25148665

Starbuck, W. (1992) 'Learning by knowledge-intensive firms', *Journal of Management Studies, 29*, pp. 713–740. DOI:10.1111/j.1467–6486

Stroh, L. & Caligiuri, P. (1998) 'Increasing global competitiveness through effective people management', *Journal of World Business, 33 (1)*, pp. 1–16, DOI:10.1016/S1090–9516(98)80001-1

Sveiby, K.E. (2001) 'A knowledge-based theory of the firm to guide in strategy formulation', *Journal of Intellectual Capital, 2 (4)*, pp. 344–358.

Tyre, M. & von Hippel, E. (1997) 'The situated nature of adaptive learning in organizations', *Organization Science, 8*, pp. 71–83, DOI:10.1287/orsc.8.1.71

11 Defence acquisition

John McCormack and Tim Burnett

Introduction

Defence acquisition is the process of investing in the technologies, goods and services, which are required for a nation to deliver its national security objectives. Often confused with the term procurement, acquisition is a broader concept focused on achieving strategic objectives, while procurement deals with managing the technical processes of obtaining desired products from external suppliers. In this chapter we will be discussing the part that acquisition plays in helping nations develop and maintain the capabilities that are essential to the protection of their citizens, their economies, and national interests in an increasingly complex, global, and decentralised environment.

This distinction is important, because while *procurement* is concerned with ensuring taxpayer resources are spent efficiently and that the product or service received complies with the required standard, an *acquisition* approach requires organisations to view their decisions, systems and goals in a holistic and systematic way. This includes procurement but also focuses on the decision-making processes around the procurement activity, understanding that the decisions made at the early stages of the project selection and design phases can have significant consequences later in the life cycle of the project and the final product. It is therefore about looking at which projects should be selected and why, reviewing alternative solutions and processes for optimising the development, delivery and total product life cycle. As stated throughout this book, the effective use of resources is particularly significant in the defence and security environment due to the critical nature of the activities involved as well as the cost, scale and technical complexity of many of the programmes and long project life cycles. Whether it is developing a next generation fighter, a new aircraft carrier or an IT system, defence budgets tend to involve a disproportionate number of large and complex projects. In the UK, for example, although the defence budget constitutes 2.1% of the national budget, it contributes 25% of the projects, included in the Government Major Project Portfolio (deemed to be of the highest complexity and risk) (Infrastructure Projects Authority, 2019).

Leaders involved in acquisition need to consider all aspects of the administrative and bureaucratic processes and systems controlling the development and oversight of the activities, ensuring not only quality and compliance but continuing alignment with the organisational goals and objectives.

DOI: 10.4324/9781003137061-11

Strategic defence acquisition

Governments looking at equipment need to communicate a clear statement of the military requirement to their supply chain. This is not as simple or straight forward as it sounds; with an extensive array of stakeholders, complex and often competing needs and interests, it is vital that leaders are able to define strategic priorities. However, given the inherent intricacy of the task, and sometimes-conflicting pressures, it is not always clear which goals or needs are the top priorities – leaving development choices potentially subject to unclear scope or poor definition. With limited resources, it is necessary to identify and qualify key objectives so that resources can be allocated as efficiently and rationally as possible. At the same time identification and ultimately cutting spending on activities that no longer serve the current set of strategic goals and objectives is important. As with private organisations, this is handled through a structured decision-making process, where the key decision makers conduct a needs analysis as part of their strategic planning activities which they will want to communicate appropriately across their development systems. For many nations, this takes the form of a published Defence Industrial Strategy (DIS).

Industrial strategies are useful because they communicate intentions and allow involved stakeholders to plan and make their own decisions about their budgets and desired objectives. It also acts as an anchor for future decision-making, allowing managers across the organisation to make better-informed and coordinated decisions. In effect, it is a road map for planning and coordination between policy makers and the diverse competent elements of the delivery supply chain.

The United Kingdom has developed and communicated its DIS through a series of government white papers, with, at the time of writing, the National Security Strategy and Strategic Defence and Security Review (SDSR) in 2015 being the most recent. These documents lay out the high-level national security objectives, with expanded explanation on the underlying priorities in policy development and construction. The three objectives identified in the current 2015 strategy are:

1. Protect our people – at home, in our Overseas Territories and abroad, and to protect our territory, economic security, infrastructure and way of life.
2. Project our global influence – reducing the likelihood of threats materialising and affecting the UK, our interests, and those of our allies and partners.
3. Promote our prosperity – seizing opportunities, working innovatively and supporting UK industry (HM Government, 2015).

This list is noteworthy as it illustrates that, for the policy makers, security is not only seen as the provision of fighting forces, but includes a broader definition of what it means, such as the ability to support the economy, maintain technological sovereignty, encourage innovation, help project influence, and defend national interests. Some other nations view their spending on defence as a way of creating influence, others view certain stocks, like tanks, as national prestige markers, while others prioritise involvement in cutting edge development activities to encourage development of identified industrial sub-sectors. Added to this is the changing nature and scope of the activities with which the defence community is called upon to deal. The rise of asynchronous warfare, cyber threats, peacekeeping and disaster recovery activities challenge the notion of traditional threats from overtly hostile nations in the minds of strategists and planners.

As a result, defence policy will by necessity look very different from country to country, matching the various interests of each nation and its leaders, but the clear trend is toward viewing defence spending as a much more nuanced tool for goal attainment, with the expectancy that expenditure will return more benefit than before. Many countries are in search of 'value for money', where value of goods or service is determined by individuals and organisations based on the benefit they receive from it.

This view is a far cry from the Cold War view of defence where military spending was largely self-contained within a narrow community of 'in house' resources and a select community of 'national champion firms' such as BAE systems in the UK or Lockheed Martin, Boeing or Raytheon in the US.

Nations such as the United States, France and the United Kingdom who have large domestic defence industries have long relied on these constructs to help broaden the value they get for their defence expenditure. However, increasingly, smaller nations are recognizing the ability to integrate their defence spending with other objectives around industrial and technology development (see Chapter 12).

Most countries have some form of DIS, but how it is formulated, used and communicated can vary significantly. States such as the UAE and Saudi Arabia have begun using their DIS to try to encourage domestic armoured vehicle industries, where their role as client and budget holder allows them to require participation of local firms in the production supply chains (Aljeeran et al., 2019). Nations without significant domestic defence industries have traditionally been limited in how they could use their defence spending to support their domestic economic, social or technological interests, as the spending represented a one-way outflow of capital.

The changing nature of the post-Cold War defence industrial sector has, however, made the use of carefully constructed policies more vital than ever before. The increasingly fragmented and outsourced nature of defence research, development and delivery networks has allowed a much more nuanced use of industrial policies by nations of all sizes. For example, Turkey, South Korea, and Malaysia have sought to compete with the likes of the United States, China and Europe to supply the global demand (Li and Matthews, 2017).

Exercise 11.1

1. Does your country have a published industrial strategy?
2. Does your country have a published defence industrial strategy?
3. Do these two documents clearly relate to each other and to broader national security objectives?

The structure of policy and how clearly it is communicated and integrated into the industrial production base and supply chains clearly varies significantly depending on factors such as the relative importance of the domestic defence industrial base, the operational role of the defence forces, or treaty obligations. This policy, written or otherwise expressed, serves as the starting point for decision making about what is to be acquired and why.

There has been relatively little research done into the decision-making processes behind defence acquisition, particularly in smaller and developing nations. Most work looks at the economic impact of the arms trade (Grimmett, 2005). Therefore, this chapter will discuss the role of decision making, especially as a process that happens within an organisation, linking strategy, systems and standards with human factors.

Change and inertia in defence acquisition

'Ministries of Defence in both London and Paris have highly effective "immune systems", notorious for rejecting new ideas. It can be challenging enough to embed change within the confines of a single department, never mind across different departments in two different countries. It is only natural that such a process will meet resistance from those who will tend to protect their functions and be cautious of different ways of working'.

(Jones, 2011)

Defence acquisition is rarely a straightforward exercise and needs to be considered as a dynamic process, characterised by long-term goals and relationships with suppliers, and shifting conditions and priorities. Combined with the nature and complexity of defence acquisition, this means that a critical issue in acquisition decisions is that of inertia, also known as a status quo bias or (in the case of supplier–buyer relationships) incumbency advantage. Inertia can affect numerous aspects of acquisition, including procurement decisions, where future purchasing decisions are governed or influenced by past purchases, and also the tendency to fall back on existing processes and ways of doing things.

Conventionally, within complex purchasing or commissioning decisions for products or services with multiple inputs (such as defence), one expects that decisions are taken to ensure compatibility between the various inputs – known as horizontal dependency. Such compatibilities include more obvious aspects such as ensuring one piece of equipment is interoperable with another, and also the idea that decisions are made which take into account the training, skills, and knowledge of users.

However, status quo bias adds a second dependency between past and future acquisition decisions. This temporal aspect is manifested in two ways:

- Relatively homogeneous products or services can become heterogeneous in the eyes of buyers accustomed to a particular supplier, meaning that existing suppliers have an advantage over new entrants or rivals.
- Horizontal compatibility concerns can 'lock' commissioners and purchasers of defence-related goods and services into long-term de-facto relationships with existing suppliers or current product/service specifications.

There are a number of reasons and theories why such inertia exists, most of which sit at the nexus of human cognitive factors, and those related to the nature and characteristics of the product:

- Risk of regret: First put forward by Loomes and Sugden (1982), Regret Theory posits that individuals may exhibit excessive caution when making choices, which exhibit a potential downside. This avoidance of regret is one reason why individuals responsible for acquisition or procurement may stick to 'known quantities' at the expense of contracting for revised product specifications, or with new providers. Avoidance of regret can be accentuated where the consequences of the realisation of negative outcomes are tangible and/or particularly severe, even where the probabilities of such realisations are very small.

- Switching costs: There is a branch of literature which considers economic (financial) and cognitive costs associated with switching a provider for a good or service, which lead to inertia when making repeat purchases. In a well-developed bank of theoretical literature, Nilssen (1992) segregates these costs into two distinct categories:
  - Transaction costs: Transaction costs are the financial costs that are directly associated with the switch of supplier or process, rather than the cost of the product or service itself. These may be one-off expenses associated with terminating an existing agreement, costs associated with changes to supply chains or overcoming compatibility issues between existing equipment and a proposed purchase.
  - Learning costs: These are psychological costs which are borne when moving from a known product or process toward one which is unknown, or about which a commissioner has limited experience. Unlike transaction costs, which are borne every time a switch of supplier takes place. Such learning costs are often the underlying motive for habit formation and brand loyalty, even where underlying products are very similar.
- Heuristic thinking: In defence acquisition which exhibits a high degree of product complexity and swift pace of technological change, there is the risk that purchasers fall back upon heuristic thinking. Put forward by Tversky and Kahneman (1974), heuristics are mental shortcuts individuals make when confronted with new information. Though it is posited that heuristics and similar modes of 'fast thinking' are evolutionary survival mechanisms, associated with concepts such as intuition and 'hunches', they are also associated with suboptimal decision making in the face of complexity; such 'fast' decision making is therefore likely to favour incumbent providers.

These different sources of inertia should not be considered in isolation, but rather should be correctly seen as a system that serves to lock commissioners, purchasers, and stakeholders into existing arrangements and increase the tendency to maintain the status quo. Many of these do not occur in isolation, and inertia can often be seen to be *locally* rational (in respect of the immediate decision being made) with regard to the avoidance of immediate cognitive and financial costs.

Unfortunately, considered more holistically, status quo bias can result in a range of negative outcomes:

- Inertia, status quo bias, and incumbency advantage enjoyed by suppliers, results in the formation of market power – irrespective of whether the supplier in question has deliberately acted to protect their incumbency. Typically associated with the idea of monopoly pricing, such market power can also result in diminished quality or other negative impacts. In general, suppliers are aware of the power afforded to them via their incumbency advantage and can accentuate or create costs that serve to reinforce a status quo bias.
- The tendency to favour existing processes, or incumbents in procurement, has been shown to hinder the adoption of innovative or improved technologies in

several different settings, especially where new technological approaches are challenging existing standards.

- The risks associated with inappropriately awarding contracts (to incumbent suppliers or otherwise) are amplified where it is costly to retender.

As stated at the start of this chapter, defence acquisition carries a host of competing priorities and challenges around diplomacy, self-sufficiency, and technological change (amongst others). With complex demands, there may be a host of 'unknown unknowns' which lead to risk aversion on the part of buyers. Similarly, where there are learning costs associated with new or unproven products or services, operational considerations may warrant remaining with an existing supplier. Defence acquisition must balance these concerns against the costs associated with inertia and inappropriately maintaining a status quo.

Exercise 11.2

Inertia, and its consequent status quo bias and incumbency advantage, is usually the result of unconscious thought processes. Given that bidders will frequently propose slightly different specifications in their proposals for defence contracts, it is often difficult, ex-post, to determine the extent that a status quo bias has impacted on the award of a contract.

In October 2018 the UK Ministry of Defence (MoD) awarded a contract worth £357 million to the incumbent Cammel Laird for the maintenance of five naval vessels (full details at https://www.navylookout.com/mod-awards-1-billion-royal-fleet-auxiliary-ship-support-contracts/).

Reflect on the following questions:

1. How can we apply the reasons for inertia in acquisition outlined earlier (Regret Theory, Switching Costs, Heuristics) to this example?
2. What other reasons might the MoD have for favouring Cammel Laird over competitor bids?
3. What might be the risks associated with inappropriately favouring an incumbent in this situation?

Programme acquisition strategy

In order to link the broad organisational strategy to an individual project or programme it is necessary to construct an acquisition strategy. This is an integrated plan which is produced during the project's planning phase. It covers the range of activities affecting the business, technical, and support elements needed to satisfy strategic objectives and identify and manage associated risks. It acts as a roadmap for effective completion across the whole project life cycle and should communicate and clarify the relationship between the different activities and their consequences; identifying what is linked to key milestones, decision points, gateways, tests, or reviews. This should be a living document which recognises the changes in the project environment and strategy of the project so that everyone involved has a clear idea of what is going on. How this is done varies by country, but generally relies upon a centralised and documented processes of stakeholder engagement and benefit definition, where the final plan is communicated across the sector (Aljeeran et al., 2019)

Procurement

Once an organisation has decided on what it wants to do, it is then necessary to decide upon how to get it. There are two basic options, to make the product or buy it from an external agency. Obviously, it is not always as clear cut as this with many a continuum of possible configurations, with one extreme being buying products off the shelf, ready made with no customisation and the other extreme representing a totally bespoke solution whole produced in house, and the full range in between of customisation to common platforms, partnered development or technology transfer.

The reasons to select one option or the other are also varied. Buying products off the shelf tends to have several advantages; it is often less expensive, available quickly, performed by teams with economies of scale. In effect you are buying from an expert who has experience building the item, improving predictability of quality and lowering uncertainty and associated risk. On the other side, buying in has downsides. Loss of control over development, potential issues with coordination or conflict, or the need to share information or technology with outside actors can provide other forms of risk.

Example 11.1: South Africa and Armscor

In 1968 South Africa revised its national defence policy to account for the UN arms embargo on the state due to its apartheid system. In order to preserve a now isolated defence sector the state developed the Armaments Development and Production Corporation, or Armscor as a unified defence procurement agency. Armscor's structure allowed South Africa to develop one of the most advanced arms industries of any developing or newly industrialising economy in the world.

It allowed the regime to provide for its defence and security requirements, as well as developing for industrial technology, and providing jobs to the Afrikaans workforce who were the government's political power base. When the Apartheid system was finally dismantled, the new government, which needed a much smaller defence and security apparatus, found this system inefficient and expensive.

As a result, Armscor was restructured to better serve the needs of a society which was now able to partner with global firms and nations and wanted to better distribute the investment value of the sector across its society. This meant, in some areas, sacrificing sovereign capability for fiscal concerns. The result is that South Africa today has a much reduced defence industry, but one which is more complementary to the nation's social and economic wellbeing.

Adapted from Dunne (2006)

Choosing to build in house has added advantages like allowing the funds involved to be channelled into local firms helping the organisation, or the nation to develop or retain key skills and abilities, helping key domestic industries, and supporting sovereign capabilities and lessening dependence on foreign countries or firms.

The selection of the appropriate products or structures, as discussed previously, is the result of a decision-making activity. The choice of what that product will be is partly made by the leadership team, but many of the details and specification will be developed through the organisation's acquisition processes and across the life of the project. Therefore, it is important to think about life cycles and their impact on the costs, risks and final nature of the acquired items as well as its enduring fit with the organisation's emergent strategy.

There are two major types of approaches to acquisition life cycle, Evolutionary and 'Big Bang'. There are variations of each type with their own strengths and weaknesses. In this section we will discuss what they are and how they help inform the organisation's decision making about product and delivery structure.

Big Bang approach

The Big Bang strategies are constructed around what project managers refer to as a waterfall life cycle. This is what many managers consider the traditional acquisition model; decide what you want, plan, execute and deliver. This is a deliberate and linear approach that has the advantage of focusing the efforts of the staff to deliver, as close as possible, precisely what the client asks for. It identifies requirements, conducts detailed up-front planning and then works on executing on the plan through to completion.

Waterfall tends to be requirements led, meaning that the acquisition project is organised into activity phases, such as concept design, product design, development and construction, utilisation, decommissioning.

Many real world models, such as the UK's CADMID model or the Acquisition System in the United States, Figure 11.1, are customised to fit the needs, processes and interests of their host nation, but the basic waterfall structure of the approach is generally consistent.

The CADMID is a mnemonic acronym for initial letters of its six phases, Concept, Assessment, Demonstration, Manufacture, In-Service, Disposal/Termination.

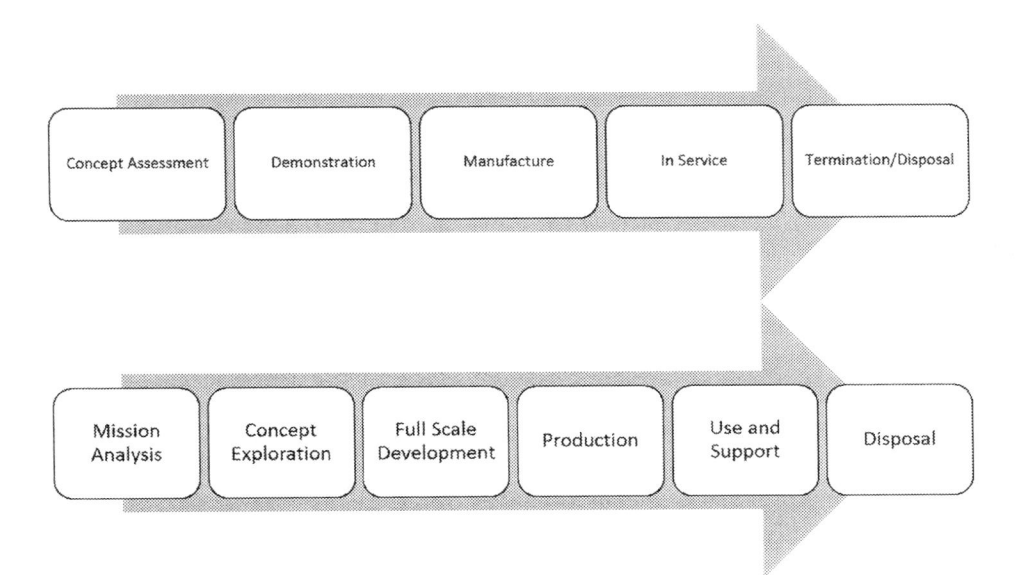

Figure 11.1 Requirements Based Models
Source: Authors.

The US DoD Acquisition Life Cycle is also six phases but differently named and with slight variations in the process assumptions, but the approaches are effectively the same. Other nations have their own versions of these requirement-based models, designed to organise their acquisition activities in ways that fit their own ethos and situation but work in essentially the same way.

Traditionally this meant drawing up a statement of requirements. It is assumed that the buyer knows what they want and understands the underlying technologies, and that the requirements, specifications and technologies are unlikely to change significantly between commission and delivery. Acceptance happens upon an evaluation of the product to ensure compliance with the requirements which were defined up front.

These are fundamentally linear structures, where key decisions are at the start and then efforts are made to deliver to the agreed plan as closely as possible. Periodic milestone approval points, such as phase reviews or gateways, are planned around transitions between the identified activity states.

These structures assume the system requirements, technologies and product specification are well understood, and that the operating environment will remain sufficiently stable across the development life cycle. If this is the case, and the predictions that underpin the planning assumptions hold true then the waterfall or 'big bang' approaches can be very efficient.

The downside is that it can be more expensive and logistically difficult to change or cancel mid-project, consequently limiting the ability of the team to adjust the scope of work to emerging needs or conditions. This requirements-led approach has fallen out of favour recently due to its relative inflexibility and focus on the product, features and functions rather than on the benefit the product is intended to deliver. The size, technical complexity and unusually long development times associated with the defence sector has resulted in defence acquisition agencies shifting to more evolutionary strategies, which are better at identifying and responding to change.

For example, India's Defense Research Development Organisation developed its Missile Technology Control Regime (MTCR) for its BrahMos missile system in a remarkably short time and has been widely viewed as a case of a well-run project. Largely because it clearly understood its requirements and technologies. Unlike its T-90 Main Battle Tanks (MBTs), where the need for an integrated air conditioning system was overlooked in the initial planning stages, and has proven almost impossible to fix, even after more than 20 years and tremendous financial investment (Singh & Das, 2020).

Evolutionary approach

The evolutionary approach is where existing products are iterated, upgraded or built upon across their life cycle. Often shifting focus from rigid upfront planning and de-emphasising the requirements and increasing focus on the capability or benefit that needs to be realised. This often results in a fundamentally different way of thinking of workflow, decision making, and how power is distributed across an activity. There are several evolutionary approaches to acquisition that can be used to accomplish this. Three of the most common will be discussed here; Incremental, Spiral, and Agile.

Incremental development utilises numerous, relatively small, adjustments to existing systems. It can be fast, flexible and allows the team to leverage their existing products. It works best where a known end state is well defined, and available and mature technology can be deployed and modified to deliver the desired product. The risks tend to be low due to the use of known technologies and material. This is often used for modifications of existing systems or to make numerous low risk adjustments to large product development processes. A classic example might be a road, where the first leg of the entire road is completed, connecting just the first two towns, it is opened up to the public, and then continued to the next leg of the work and so on until the entire road is completed. This allows for central, up-front planning but also allows products to be released for use before the entire project is completed.

Spiral is used when an ideal end state can be identified, but the tools or technology are not yet available. It is based around the development of prototypes, where each iteration is marginally closer to the desired product and may be composed of a number of sub-projects that focus on a limited number of features being developed in each iteration. This approach is used when risk management is particularly important. It provides a greater degree of flexibility to change due to the work focusing on a limited and focused set of objectives for each iteration, with the next work set being developed after reviewing the work to date and comparing it against current needs. Although Spiral may use a waterfall model for each iteration it allows for more adaptation of product specification as the technology or the mission changes over the course of the product development. The Spiral methodology was formally defined in the 1980s as a software development model, it evolved out of classic defence procurement project development techniques used to develop aircraft and missile platforms in the 1950s and 1960s.

The Agile acquisition strategy is also adapted from a software development methodology. It is still most frequently used in software projects but can be integrated into many different contexts. The basic concept turns the waterfall approach on its head by shifting the emphasis from the final end product being delivered through structured phases, and instead tries to focus on developing individual component elements of the final work, and blending the phases into time constrained pieces of work, often called sprints, which may last only 30 days at a time. The short time period means the risk exposure is limited, and therefore organisations can reduce the amount of 'ceremony', contracts, documentation and formal approvals processes. It also allows teams to shift focus very quickly at the end of each sprint, as the next sprint represents a new project and therefore may focus on whatever piece of work is seen as most essential. This fluid workflow allows for rapid evolution of work and may cut production time and costs significantly. The approach tends to work best in smaller teams and smaller projects, although there are methods for applying the standards to larger activities and programmes. An example of this is where SAAB Aeronautics reorganised its Gripen E multi-role fighter jet development project using an agile approach (Furuhjelm et al., 2017).

Agile systems are ideal for high uncertainty environments where planning needs to be constantly evolving rather than front-loaded as in waterfall. It is also particularly useful in situations where the actual end state of the product under development is uncertain. This is common in projects with significant uncertainty, whether this is in terms of the means of development, applying cutting-edge technologies or technologies not yet developed, dependent on creative input, or other questions about the means of production. It is also useful as an approach when the desired end state of the product itself may not be clear, and needs to evolve, as some other factors become known.

Exercise 11.3

Think about your own experiences with acquisition. How have the projects you have seen been developed? Have they been big bang projects, with the leaders defining requirements and planning up front, or evolutionary, developing over time as the needs and conditions are identified? How might a different life-cycle approach have affected the success or failure of a key project with which you have been involved?

To be successful this approach requires fundamental changes to the way the organisation works. It requires empowerment of members of the team to make decisions and changes, within their limited project sprint time. It needs teams to focus on informal communication and flat organisational power structures focused on skill sets rather than seniority. This is frequently challenging to large institutional organisations such as those in many defence ministries who have, evolved rigid, high bureaucratic procurement systems over a long period.

The capability view

> If we manage an IT project, then what we get is IT. If we manage an IT project which has some organizational outcomes, then we may get some organizational deliverables. If, however we concentrate on project managing the benefits, we can create a value, which may incidentally have an IT component.
>
> (Association Of Project Management, 2006)

Capability management is a more recent evolution, emerging in the past decade, which seeks to improve the value production in acquisition and allow systems to be more flexible to change by emphasising operations and uses, or the capabilities that the product will support rather than the engineering of equipment. It is based on the 'theory of the firm' which views organisations as a collection of their capabilities that can be used to achieve their goals (Park et al., 2010). In this approach, the most efficient use of existing capabilities is the key to long-term success rather than just considering resources, it allows a broader perspective. It de-emphasises control of physical resources like equipment and cash and places a higher value on knowledge, expertise and know-how and encourages organisations to focus on balancing the goals and interests of multiple stakeholders. It does this by establishing and executing a governance process that balances the interests of various individuals and groups with the need for operational agility to make trade-offs among cost, schedule, and scope as the conditions, environment and objectives change over a project's life (The MITRE Corporation, 2014). This encourages a much more holistic view of the firm and its resources but can allow for a much more focused application of strategy, and greater 'bang for the buck' with increasingly constrained resources (Leonard-Barton, 1995).

Within the context of Defence Acquisition, an approach based on a capability management perspective seeks to integrate some of the flexibility and ability to adapt or change projects from the incremental approaches into the acquisition. It does this by conceptualising the entire organisation, its staff, equipment, special advantages and strategic context as a portfolio of capabilities that serve the organisation in order to execute its strategy, rather than a set of product requirements that a product needs to satisfy acceptance criterion.

For instance, consider a tank. There are many forms of tank. However, understanding what we want a tank to do will inform the requirements we select for any tank we wish to acquire. The tank, on its own, is a product of limited use. It is only when it is packaged with appropriate logistical support, trained crews, ammunition, and fuel and transport that it is able to deliver benefit to the organisation that owns it.

When we seek to understand how to weigh the benefit that is delivered, against the cost it is important that we have a holistic understanding of the costs of the benefit. Not only considering the cost of procurement, but also through life costs such as sustainment and disposal, which can be as much as 200% of the purchase cost of the tank, and we are forced to consider our choices more carefully.

Shifting the organisation's focus from engineering a product to delivering benefits and value shifts planning, decision-making and activity integration across a broader range of concerns. Effectively forcing the organisation to consider its equipment planning in a more holistic way.

The Republic of Korea's defence ministry identified significant inefficiencies in its acquisition system following a defence review in 2010, specifically related to poor programme integration between agencies and services, acquisition of overlapping or redundant systems, poor prioritisation of requirements, and ineffective needs analysis in the acquisition system. It decided to adopt a variation of the Joint Capabilities Integration and Development System (JCIDS) designed by US Secretary of Defence Donald Rumsfeld that had proposed a new process for linking and categorising requirements in acquisition in the US defence procurement system (Park et al., 2010). One which would consider the full and integrated set of needs across the services and try to create a context for cataloguing and linking them together to improve decisions about procurement, logistics and support.

The process starts with bringing cross service specialists together to develop joint integrating concepts and the capabilities they support or imply. The process is divided into three phases: a functional area analysis (FAA), a functional needs analysis (FNA), and a functional solution analysis (FSA). The functional area analysis finds and defines the work, conditions and standards that need to be in place to achieve the identified objectives. The functional needs analysis assesses the ability of current and desired capabilities to accomplish the tasks identified in the functional gap analysis. The functional solutions analysis looks at the whole range of possible solutions. It should then be possible to make a rational comparison of options. The value of this process is not only in identifying gaps or redundancies but also in encouraging the organisation and its staff to consider alternative approaches. It challenges them to be very clear with themselves about what in their delivery systems is most important, and why. This allows for more focused and nimble adaptation to scope creep events, strategic adjustments, or technology shifts. Thereby making it clearer what features and functions are necessary to keep or enhance, and which can be reduced or removed (Department of Defence, 2008). In the case of the tank, mentioned previously, this model now forces us to consider not only what we want the tank for but whether something else could accomplish the same objective better, cheaper or faster. Could we use a drone, a computer programme, or handheld weapon system instead?

The United Kingdom, France and most other nations with large acquisition activities have their own version of this process, but the intent and underlying structure is

Table 11.1 The Capability View

Step	Functional Area Analysis (FAA)	Functional Needs Analysis (FNA)	Functional Solution Analysis (FSA)
What it does	Identifies operational tasks, conditions, and standards for achieving the effects needed to accomplish military objectives.	Assesses the ability of current and programmed capabilities to accomplish the FAA-identified tasks, under the full range of operating conditions and to the designated standards.	Develops and assesses potential DOTMLPF approaches to solving one or more capability gaps identified in FNA.
Output	Tasks to be reviewed in FNA.	Prioritised list of capability gaps.	Potential solutions to needs.

Source: Authors.

essentially the same. What this does is effectively wrap the requirements management process into a broader framework. Linking strategy to operations more explicitly and helping firms avoid the temptation to focus on the engineering or procurement aspects of the acquisition and instead consider whole strategy. One difficulty of this approach is in its complexity. The broader range of considerations in planning and operational delivery requires significantly more work, not only up front but throughout the project life.

The other difficulty is that working in this way is not something that an organisation can simply choose to do, it requires strategic fit. Fit in this sense means that the hierarchy, culture, processes and systems in the firm need to be able to work together this way. If the organisation is used to doing things one way, getting to fit would mean making major changes to the way the group works. For most large firms who have strongly established functional structures and practiced habits of thinking this can be an enormous challenge. In fact, this type of change management activity is one of the most difficult, contentious and high-risk activities that an organisation will undertake.

As will be discussed in detail in Chapter 14, there are a number of contingent factors that contribute to an organisation's ability to change: size and age, technical systems, environment and nature of control/power (Mintzberg, 1980). It is the interplay of these factors that provides an indication of whether an organisation will be receptive or resistant to change, but we should not assume that they are the only factors that matter. Leaders of a defence organisation also need to acknowledge the distinctive nature of the staff, both uniformed and civilian, who work there, because their attitudes and behaviours will also have a bearing on the nature of change.

The military tradition of intensive acculturation, team building, and a bottom-up career management progression model, creates a social and psychological contract, much stronger than that found in most other types of organisations (Vigoda-Gadot, Baruch & Grimland, 2010). The military is one of the most 'greedy' professions, demanding unusually strong institutional identification, devotion and loyalty 'that is as strong as or even stronger than that towards the family' (Vuga and Juvan, 2013). Coser (1974) proposed the term greedy institution, referring to an organisation's effective colonisation of member's personal lives, time, and commitment and engagement. In this type of environment, it is common for loyalty to service, firm, protocol and processes to be linked, and change resistance is a human factor issue as well as one of adjusting formal processes, systems or organisation charts.

This resistance to change along with institutional inertia make nimble and adaptive working particularly difficult to cultivate. Change, organisational and procedural is required, however, if the kind of knowledge sharing and communication needed to implement a fully functional capability management system are to be affected (Ministry of Defence, 2018).

One of the key adaptations used by defence ministries is that of the matrix structure. Often referred to as a 'two managers' structure, it allows the division of control between functional line managers and specialist, cross business groups. This allows specialist talent and knowledge to be pooled across the operation and allows the programme or strategy to be seen and understood in a more focused way by subject matter experts rather than generalist functional managers. The United Kingdom refers to these cross functional groups as Defence Lines of Development (DLOD) and includes specialist groupings in Training, Equipment, Personnel, Information, Doctrine and Concepts, Organisation, Infrastructure, and Logistics. Figure 11.2 shows how other countries have organised their equivalent matrixed groups in order to better focus their specialist skills and knowledge to capability development.

United Kingdom Defence Lines of Development (DLOD)		Australia Fundamental Inputs to Capability	United States DOTMLPF		South Korea
T	Training	Command and Management	D	Doctrine	Doctrine
E	Equipment	Organisation	O	Organisations	Organisation
P	Personnel	Major Systems	T	Training	Education, Training
I	Information	Personnel	M	Materiel	Weapon, Equipment, Material
D	Concepts and Doctrine	Supplies	L	Leader development	Human Resources
O	Organisation	Support	P	Personnel	Facilities
I	Infrastructure	Facilities	F	Facilities	
L	Logistics	Collective Training			
		Industry			

Figure 11.2 Capability Focused Models
Source: Authors.

P3M

Many defence acquisition projects are big, and are increasingly developed across traditional organisational boundaries, and delivered through complex supply chains often involving staff from hundreds of firms. Functions which were traditionally done in house have been outsourced, and it is no longer feasible for defence agencies to expect compliance with bespoke, in house working standards. In order to facilitate this type of work many agencies have adopted Project, Program and Portfolio Management (P3M) to establish common standards and working practices so that people and organisations across different operational systems, technical specialties and work cultures can work together. Professional associations like the Project Management Institute (PMI) in the United States, the Association for Project Management (APM) in the UK or the International Project Management Association (IPMA) in Europe have created bodies of knowledge to create a standard set of terms, tools and assumptions of best practice.

Partnering with groups like the APM to co-develop their body of knowledge allows agencies in defence, as well as across the public sector more generally, to tap into these common frameworks which, in many ways, act like a common language and make it easier to manage across organisational borders. They can guide the different teams through the complex processes by capturing lessons from previous experience and established best practice in a mutually agreed set of procedures.

Conclusion

This chapter focuses on acquisition in defence, with a specific emphasis on the importance of decision making to successful acquisition. The defence sector has gone through profound changes in recent years, and the rate of change looks only to increase as traditional threats are replaced by new ones. Technology is advancing at unprecedented rates and traditional public defence acquisition models are increasingly criticised for being out-dated and in some cases obsolete.

Recognising acquisition requires a broader and more holistic view of the system of product delivery, so organisations can better understand the range of elements that can affect their ability to provide and sustain the capabilities they need to protect their sovereignty and deliver on their strategic objectives.

Questions to consider

Consider the development of a particular defence-focused product or service (in particular, one which you are close to or is currently being considered by your organisation):

1. How long is the development of the product or service likely to take, and what changes are likely to occur over this time?
2. How certain are you about what your organisation needs, and how certain are you that the equipment you are ordering will satisfy this need?
3. Are your systems and processes ready for changes at any point during the programme's life cycle?
4. What else is needed in order to make a product (or service) into a successful capability?

Suggested further reading

Department of Defence (2008) *Defence Acquisition Guidebook*. DoD Instruction Number 5000.02. Available at https://www.dau.edu/tools/dag [Accessed 16 January 2021].

Heidenkamp, Louth & Taylor (2011) *The Defence Industrial Ecosystem Delivering Security in an Uncertain World*, RUSI. Available at https://rusi.org/sites/default/files/201106_whr_the_defence_industrial_ecosystem_0.pdf [Accessed 12 January 2021].

Ministry of Defence (2018) *Mobilising, Modernising & Transforming Defence*, pp. 1–28. Available at https://assets.publishing.service.gov.uk/government/uploads/system/uploads/attachment_data/file/765879/ModernisingDefenceProgramme_report_2018_FINAL.pdf [Accessed 17 January 2021].

The MITRE Corporation (2014) *Systems Engineering Guide*. Available at www.mitre.org [Accessed 15 January 2021].

Tversky, A. & Kahneman, D. (1974) *Judgment under Uncertainty: Heuristics and Biases*, DOI: 10.1126/science.185.4157.1124

References

Aljeeran, I., Antil, P. & McCormack, J. (2019) 'A strategy for self sufficiency', *Defence Procurement International* (Winter 2018/2019), pp. 61–66.

Association Of Project Management (2006) 'APM Body of Knowledge', *Journal of Lesbian Studies*. DOI:10.1080/10894160.2010.508411

Coser, L.A. (1974) *Greedy Institutions*, New York, NY: Free Press.

Department of Defence (2008) *Defence Acquisition Guidebook*. DoD Instruction Number 5000.02. Available at https://www.dau.edu/tools/dag [Accessed 13 January 2021].

Dunne, J.P. (2006) 'The making of arms in South Africa', *The Economics of Peace and Security Journal, 1 (1)*. DOI:10.15355/epsj.1.1.40

Furuhjelm, J. et al. (2017) *Owning the Sky with Agile: Building a Jet Fighter Faster, Cheaper, Better with Scrum*, pp. 1–4. Available at https://www.scruminc.com/wp-content/uploads/2015/09/Release-version_Owning-the-Sky-with-Agile.pdf [Accessed15 January 2021].

Grimmett, R.F. (2005) *CRS Report for Congress Conventional Arms Transfers*, pp. 1997–2004.

HM Government (2015) *National Security Strategy and Strategic Defence and Security Review 2015*. Available at https://www.gov.uk/government/uploads/system/uploads/attachment_data/file/478933/52309_Cm_9161_NSS_SD_Review_web_only.pdf [Accessed 12 January 2021].

Infrastructure Projects Authority (2019) 'Major projects portfolio report 2018/19', *White Paper*, p. 40. Available at https://assets.publishing.service.gov.uk/government/uploads/system/uploads/attachment_data/file/817654/IPA_AR_MajorProjects2018-19_web.pdf [Accessed 13 January 2021].

Jones, B. (2011) *Franco-British Military Cooperation: A New Engine for European Defence? European Union Institute for Security Studies - Occasional Paper*. DOI:10.2815/21700.

Leonard-Barton, D.A. (1995) *Wellsprings of Knowledge: Building and Sustaining the Sources of Innovation*, Boston: Harvard Business School Press.

Li, L. & Matthews, R. (2017) '"Made in China": An emerging brand in the global arms market', *Defense and Security Analysis*, Routledge, *33 (2)*, pp. 174–189. DOI:10.1080/14751798.2017.1310700

Loomes, G. L. & Sugden, R. (1982) 'Regret Theory: An alternative theory of rational choice under uncertainty', *The Economic Journal, 92 (368)*, pp. 805–824 [Accessed 17 January 2021].

Ministry of Defence (2018) 'Mobilising, modernising & transforming defence', pp. 1–28. Available at https://assets.publishing.service.gov.uk/government/uploads/system/uploads/attachment_data/file/765879/ModernisingDefenceProgramme_report_2018_FINAL.pdf [Accessed 15 January 2021].

Mintzberg, H. (1980) 'Structure in 5's: A synthesis of the research on organizational design', *Management Science, 26 (3)*, pp. 322–341. DOI:10.1287/mnsc.26.3.322

Naval Lookout (2018) 'MOD awards £1 billion royal fleet auxiliary ship support contracts', 7 October 2018. Available at https://www.navylookout.com/mod-awards-1-billion-royal-fleet-auxiliary-ship-support-contracts/

Nilssen, T. (1992) 'Two kinds of consumer switching', *The RAND Journal of Economics, 23 (4)*, pp. 579–589. DOI:10.2307/2555907

Park, S.-G. et al. (2010) 'Integrated framework and methodology for capability priority decisions', *Information & Security: An International Journal, 25*, pp. 78–98. DOI:10.11610/isij.2509

Singh, A. & Das, P. (2020) 'The long list of misses, and few hits, in India's defence acquisitions', *The Print*. Available at: https://theprint.in/opinion/the-long-list-of-misses-and-few-hits-in-indias-defence-acquisitions/474226/ [Accessed: 15 January 2021].

The MITRE Corporation (2014) *Systems Engineering Guide*. Available at: www.mitre.org. [Accessed 12 January 2021].

Tversky, A. & Kahneman, D. (1974) 'Judgment under uncertainty: Heuristics and biases', *Science*, *185 (4157)*, pp. 1124–1131. DOI:10.1126/science.185.4157.1124

Vigoda-Gadot, E., Baruch, Y. & Grimland, S. (2010) 'Career transitions: An empirical examination of second career of military retirees', *Public Personnel Management*, *39 (4)*, pp. 379–404. DOI:10.1177/009102601003900405.

Vuga, J. & Juvan, J. (2013) 'Work-family conflict between two greedy institutions – The family and the military', *Current Sociology*, *61 (7)*, pp. 1058–1077. DOI:10.1177/0011392113498881

12 Generating value through offsets in international defence procurement

Kogila Balakrishnan

Introduction

This is a chapter about how to generate value through offsets or industrial collaboration in international defence procurement. To understand why this is a vital subject, we need only look at recent global statistics about offsets growth. An OECD report quoted that offsets enjoy a compound annual growth of 3–5%, with obligations expected to rise by 36% between 2012 and 2021 reaching a cumulative total of more than \$425billion (Broecker & Beraldi, 2017). The explosion in offsets figures is mainly attributed to the increasing number of countries practising offsets. As of 2020, approximately 80 countries encourage offsets. Offset is a non-conventional policy tool tied to large international public procurement, initially promoted in the defence sector as a means of acquiring self-sufficiency in industrial, technological and military capability. Recently, offsets have also been extended to other strategic sectors such as aerospace, energy, critical infrastructure and transport as part of national industrial strategies to support state-led industrial growth and economic development.

Offsets, as a sub-field of defence economics, are pursued for various political and economic reasons, mainly for developing indigenous capability contributing to security of supply and national resilience effort but also as an economic stimulant for employment creation, exports and capturing global markets through supply chain penetration (Martin, 1996: pp.1–14). Despite the growth in offsets value and activities globally, they have received little academic attention until recently. Interest in offsets policy has risen from four separate, but related, groups, those emanating directly from the government, those in the business sector, those related to academic scholarship and those related to the wider community concerned over the real value of offsets to defence industrialisation and economic growth. Research evaluating the effectiveness of offsets has been supported by governments and universities, but most of these studies have struggled to obtain data that clearly illustrates economic impact and associated challenges. This failure is due to issues of commercial sensitivity and personal interest in concealing information (Skons, 2004: p.150). Studies conducted on the defence sector, an industry renowned for secrecy, highlight a lack of transparency and alleged corrupt practice. As a result, offsets are claimed to be tainted by poor management practice, so increasing the costs of procurement, causing unnecessary delay to completion of projects resulting in a less attractive business model with a poor return on investments (Brocker and Beraldi, 2017). Further, there is endless debate on how offsets policy is resourced and who has responsibility for the costs of offsets. Thus, despite the increasing popularity of offsets, the money invested into implementing them

DOI: 10.4324/9781003137061-12

and compelling reluctant original equipment manufacturers (OEMs) to still undertake offsets obligation, overall the results have been disappointing.

This chapter argues that the current offsets model does not work due to the high rate of offsets project failure (Cowshish, 2020b), and there is a compelling need to review the existing offsets management framework. The purpose of this chapter is fourfold: 1) to define the concept of offsets; 2) to outline the relevance of offsets in the current environment; 3) to evaluate why offsets projects fail; and, 4) to propose a new model, the Triple Offsets Value (TOV) framework, which enumerates the key components that are vital to delivering value through offsets in international defence procurement. The framework is not a 'one size fit all' model and must be aligned and read in context to suit national objectives and intended socio-economic outcomes.

Exercise 12.1

1. What do you understand by the term offsets in relation to defence procurement?
2. What are the advantages of offsets to a country's defence force going through transition from post-conflict to development?
3. What are the disadvantages of offsets to a country's independence and self-reliance?

Conceptualising offsets

What are offsets?

Both the definition and value of offsets are subject to continuous debate. In this chapter, offsets are defined as a policy tool used by purchasers (government) to obtain additional benefits from sellers (industry), primarily technology, work packages, licensing, export opportunities and knowledge-transfer. Offsets can be clustered into three distinctive categories of definition, first an economic compensatory practise, second a contractual obligation and third a policy tool for economic development. Academics such as Markowski and Hall (1998), Brauer and Dunne (2004), Skons (2004), Dunne and Lamb (2004), and Martin (1996) view offsets as compensation or a form of coercion imposed on sellers that distorts the market; and is economically inefficient if not implemented properly. OECD and trade associations such as the Global Industrial Cooperation Association (GICA), Aerospace and Defence Society as well as the European Club for Countertrade and Offsets (ECCO) view offsets as a trade or mandatory contractual obligation, ancillary to government procurement contracts in international defence business when entering into dealing with foreign governments. Others such as Matthews (2019), Balakrishnan (2019), Behera (2009), and Bitzinger (2009) take an economic development perspective, leveraging offsets to generate industrial and technological benefits and spin-offs. A clearer definition of offsets combines all three perspectives, which then makes offsets inclusive but challenging as a policy instrument. A key question is why a sale should involve additional benefit when a direct transaction involves payment in the form of hard currency for the product and services purchased. This sounds like a corrupt practise yet continued and legalised through policy intervention. The following section explores why offsets continue to be employed as an element of international defence procurement.

Why are offsets popular in the defence sector?

Prior to offsets, the more popular means of trade transaction was countertrade. The most ancient practise being barter followed by switch, swap, clearing arrangements and counter purchase (Balakrishnan, 2019: pp.21–24). These activities became less popular post 1992 when the World Trade Organization (WTO) labelled countertrade and associated activities as unlawful and distorting of the free market. Yet, offsets are regulated under the WTO's Government Procurement Agreement, including available exceptions for developing countries, national security, and general public interest matters (Collins, 2018). The current modern offsets practice is an American invention introduced in the 1940s after the Second World War. Offsets at that time were presented to European NATO member countries by encouraging US defence contractors to offer offsets as a means of rebuilding their allies' defence industrial base. Offsets slowly evolved as a supply side economics tool, gaining popularity when US defence companies were clearly encouraged to use offsets as a differentiator in an already competitive defence market during the Cold War. However, the end of the Cold War in 1989, was followed by a pattern of increased mergers and consolidation within the defence industry and a thriving buyers' market turned offsets into a demand-side economic tool, used to leverage industrial and technological prowess in arms production for stronger military deterrence and self-reliance. In the present environment, defence offsets still remain a government-led policy tool imposed on foreign suppliers as a condition of sale although sellers still reluctantly provide offsets as part of the sales offering with the primary motive of winning a contract (Balakrishnan, 2019: pp.36–37).

Recently, there have been immense efforts by a few countries such as Malaysia, Oman and Thailand to extend offsets to the civil sector. Although this is possible, it will be disastrous to copy and apply the defence offsets model holistically into a civil industry environment. Offsets is more commonly applied to a linear non-competitive procurement bid in monopsony-monopoly buyer–supplier relationship, where the government is directly involved in overseeing the investment and growth of strategic industries critical to the nation's interests. In this case, governments have a stake in the development of critical industries and there may only be one or a few players in the market identified as technology recipients. Further, sellers establish a special relationship and seek approval from their governments in relation to export control, intellectual property right (IPR) and other restrictions. Equally important to note is that the commercial market is generally very different, where governments take a hands-off approach, embrace a market-driven process and allow a more business-to-business transaction to take place. In such instances, a more effective offsets strategy in the civil sector should embrace a more flexible industrial strategy policy that outlines national industrial strategy, objectives and priority sectors.

Unique features of offsets

Offsets are complex for several reasons. Firstly, offsets policy is heterogenous and cuts across a wide range of interests from defence policy, international relations, politics, economics, business management, supply chain, science and technology policy and engineering. Secondly, there are numerous variations to offsets practice, from structured institutionalised written offsets policy to non-written unstructured offsets policy. A written offsets policy offers guidance to implementation and process. However, written offsets policy could also be prescriptive and punitive leaving less scope for creativity and innovation. A written offsets policy normally incorporates detailed technical terms such as direct and indirect offsets, threshold, multipliers, banking of credits, penalty and pre-offsets credits. This means offsets negotiators must grasp the terminologies and be able to use them effectively during negotiation (Balakrishnan, 2019: pp.37–43). Countries like Saudi Arabia, Malaysia, Indonesia and Oman practice written offsets policies, as do Nordic countries such as Sweden, Denmark, Finland and Norway (Hagelin, 2004). In an environment where the offsets requirement is not explicit or local industrial partnership is mandatory, the sellers may assume that the procurement deal should include some form of offsets or industrial partnership activities. In such circumstances, it is vital to develop a high degree of technical and business knowledge in negotiating for offsets. Countries like Japan, Singapore, the United Kingdom and Australia have unwritten offsets policies. In either case, both written and unwritten policies are seeking to maximise defence procurement for technology transfer.

Third, Table 12.1 illustrates that offsets have so many labels including industrial participation, industrial collaboration, economic engagement and partnership for development (Collins, 2018: pp.301–322).

Table 12.1 Labels of Offsets Practised By Different Countries

Number	Label	Description
1	Offsets	Additional benefits offered by an OEM as part of a sale to the purchaser. Offsets can be direct (specifically related to the purchased equipment) and indirect (any other activities). Offsets has a cost and covers a broad spectrum of economic activities. Offsets is mandatory and forms part of the main contract. Examples include Indonesia, India, UAE.
2	Industrial Participation or collaboration	Industrial activities that require the participation of OEM in developing the capability of local companies through activities such as licensing, co-production, licensing and sub-contracting. It can be voluntary and not tied to the main contract. There are general guidelines without penalties. Examples include Malaysia, Canada, Kingdom of Saudi Arabia.
4	Industrial engagement	Similar to industrial participation but purely on 'voluntary basis' without monitoring. The onus is on the OEM to prove in-country industrial and technology transfer activities and to produce reports for purposes of track record. Examples include the United Kingdom.
5	Partnership for Development (PfD)	Offsets type activities that are focused on economic development for the purchaser country in both defence and non-defence sector. Activity is mandatory and includes penalty and other multipliers. Examples include Oman.
6	Industrial capability development	Offsets activity that is focused mainly on building defence industrial capability in-country by incorporating local content, value-add, through collaboration, flexible, not part of the main contract but there is an expectation that the OEM will embark on industrial collaboration and technology transfer as part of the sale. Examples include Australia.
7	Economic enhancement	Similar to PfD but a broader remit with emphasis on indirect offsets that cover investments, private financial investments, public–private partnership and other alternative financing models. Examples include Kuwait in the past.

Source: Author.

The labels change as states change their offsets policy objectives to align with their overall political economic environment. For example, as nations increase their technology growth, they upgrade their offsets threshold requirement from seeking basic technology transfer, such as sub-contracting and training, to a more sophisticated approach comprising licensed production, co-production and joint research and development (R&D). For example, Malaysia moved away from offsets policy which was introduced in 2005 to the situation in post 2020 called the Industrial Collaboration Programme (ICP). Similarly, Australia's offsets policy evolved into the Industrial Participation Programme and finally to the Industrial Capability Plan in 2016. Canada's offsets policy has also evolved since the 1970s and as of 2018 is now framed as Industrial and Technological Benefits Policy. In 2010 the UK also changed its offsets policy label from Industrial Participation to Industrial Engagement; under the new strategy offsets are deemed a voluntary activity on the part of the OEM to encourage work in the UK. Even the US disguises offsets under the label of 'Buy America Legislation' (1933), where foreign contractors must prove that 50% of programme content is produced in the US (Matthews, 2019).

Exercise 12.2

Which of the above labels of offsets fit those practiced by your defence ministry? And why?

Costs and benefits of offsets

A clear argument made by purchasers is that the primary benefit from an offsets policy is acquisition of technology aimed at gradually developing an indigenous defence industrial base that supports military capability and total national resilience. The ancillary benefits expected from offsets include economic multipliers such as employment creation, export opportunities, skills development, and new prospects for industries to gain industrial competitiveness and enter the global supply chain. However, buyers often fail to acknowledge that there is a cost to an offsets policy, which is borne by the overall procurement contract. Thus, buyers must argue rationally for why resources are allocated to an offsets policy as opposed to other impending socio-economic requirements. In such instances, it is in the interest of the buyer to invest in programmes that will deliver maximum impact and returns on investments. For example, jointly investing in a cutting-edge research and development centre may result in product or process innovation, that could be monetised, the development of skills through technology partnership in a cutting-edge field, and the generation of skilled employment and resulting in patents and further joint business opportunities for the OEM and local companies.

For sellers, the primary benefit is where offsets can be used as a differentiator in an international defence sale, when technical capability and price alone are not sufficient to secure a sale. Of late, offsets have captured increasing attention as a part of company corporate strategy and are incorporated into discussions at the company executive level. Although there is lack of hard evidence to prove that offsets were the catalyst to clinch a deal, they are nevertheless being given increasing consideration by states engaged in international tenders for procurement.

Example 12.1: The costs of offsets

Dehoff, Dowdy and Sung Kwon (2014) reported that during Korea's assessment of bidders for its F-X III fighter programme in 2013, offsets and technology-transfer arrangements accounted for 17% of the total evaluation 'score' while transaction of the acquisition costs accounted for only 15% of the score meaning offsets were given higher weighting (Dehoff, Dowdy & Kwan, 2014).

Further, international relations and foreign policy dictates defence sales. Seller countries have an interest in developing defence industrial and technological capabilities of ally states. During the Cold War, countries like the UK, Japan, South Korea and Turkey hugely benefited from US technology transfer as part of weapons deals. Similarly, the former Soviet Union was transferring technology to India, China and Iran. Even today, US companies, supported by the government, continue to foster the efforts of countries like Singapore, Australia and Canada as they build their defence industrial capability through technology transfer. In Europe, there is a concerted effort among EU members to build a consolidated defence industrial base through EU procurement with the help of larger and more technologically advanced countries like France, the UK and Germany. However, offsets come as a huge burden to sellers if they are not core business of an OEM. This means there is a sizeable administrative cost to plan and implement offsets projects, which sometimes extend beyond the life cycle of the main contract. Offset projects are of high risk and require skilled managers and negotiators who understand the defence environment and have contractual and business management knowledge. It should be acknowledged that introducing a new offsets programme could distort existing supply chains, negatively impact employment in the seller country, and may generate competition through new entrants.

Example 12.2: The benefits of offsets

South Korea which obtained the technology for landing gear for the T50 trainer from Lockheed Martin to KAI is today a major competitor to the US fighter trainer aircrafts capturing almost all the Asian market. Similarly, Turkey, a major recipient of US technology has through its local companies such as Haselsan, Avelson, Roketson and Otakar successfully captured defence export market worth US$2.035bn in 2019. BMC's *Kirpi* 4x4 patrol vehicles have been sold to Tunisia and Turkmenistan, while Otokar's *Cobra* 4x4 armoured personnel carrier is now in service with countries such as Bahrain, Bangladesh, Mauritania and Rwanda (Chang, 2019).

OEMs constantly face compliance and export control issues when dealing with overseas technology transfer as the approval process is often convoluted and tedious. For example, US contractors face huge challenges and battle with the Congress and State Department to obtain export licenses for defence articles and services.

Why are offsets still relevant?

Despite the reservations expressed about offsets they remain relevant for defence industrial strategy and technological enhancement. There are five reasons for why they remain the preferred option.

Building indigenous defence industrial capability for defence self-reliance

The first reason relates to autonomy in defence and security. Most countries aspire to develop some level of in-country defence industrial base, starting with establishing a basic capability to support procured equipment and extending to securing high-end manufacturing and R&D, where offsets are used for this purpose. The ultimate objective of most nations is to attain autarky, though that is impossible even in the case of the US which still imports parts and components, the need for in-country industrial capability and resilience is enforced by a few recent developments in geopolitics. First, incidences such as Brexit in the UK, the Trump administration's isolationist policy and China's imposition of new national security law on Hong Kong are just a few examples of rising nationalist sentiments, gradually eroding globalisation and inter-dependence. These trends are prompting inward-looking trade policies and import substitutions.

Example 12.3: European defence industrial base: Nationalism v. integration

A classic example is how European Union countries tried to navigate around offsets when it was announced as unlawful under Directive 2009/81EC with exemptions for protection of critical and strategic technologies in-country (Balakrishnan, 2019: p.6). National protectionism still exists within Europe, covered by Article 346 where countries are wary of harmonisation and unwilling to give up technological lead nor the commercial sector want to lose their competitive edge. In fact, the ban has pushed offsets to go underground to avoid punitive EC laws.

Second, there is an increasing lack of buy-in from nations to multilateral platforms. Prior to COVID, the US and China had already entered into a trade war and the US decision to withdraw from the Trans Pacific Partnership (TPP) came as a blow to regional multilateral trade cooperation. Although the Comprehensive and Progressive Agreement for Trans-Pacific Partnership (CPTPP) was then set up to salvage the situation, most countries still prefer bilateral platforms for trade negotiations including technology transfer deals. Finally, in 2020 COVID-19 further exacerbated and exposed the challenges of globalisation, rising inequality and economic disparity. COVID-19 has unfortunately revealed some of the vulnerability of being solely dependent on a single or limited supply chain, with increased disruption and escalation of supply chain costs and highlighted the overwhelming risks associated with high dependence on a complex global supply chain. The reaction from the US and Japan in decoupling and de-risking their supply chain and re-shoring or diverting their supply chain elsewhere is a case in point (Liang, 2020). As the world enters into a revisionist policy era, tools such as offsets will become even more critical.

Supporting industrial strategy

Offsets feature as an important component of defence industrial strategy. For example, the UK's SDSR 2015, the refreshed Defence Industrial Policy (2017) and the Defence and Security Industry strategy review (2020), all alluded to the importance of promoting and incorporating the defence industry supply chain and exports as part of the UK prosperity agenda. Hence, where competition is not possible, long-term collaboration through industrial engagement will be vital to retain in-country capability. Similarly, Australia is developing its defence industrial base through its defence industrial capability plan. Indonesia's Committee for High Technology and Strategic Industries (KAIN), which reports directly to the President of Indonesia, has made offsets a key policy component for industry development. Offsets has also contributed to the distribution of regional development as in the case of Canada's regional programme criteria as part of its policy. South Africa took a similar approach in using offsets for regional development in the past (Haines, 2004: pp.299–313). France has used the south as a regional hub for the development of defence maritime capability including submarines, sonar systems and other underwater capabilities. In the UK, Glasgow in Scotland and Plymouth in the south of England are still the epicentre of the defence maritime industry in the UK. South Korea has used defence procurement to develop the maritime defence industry through a collaboration of OEMs with Korean companies such as Daewoo Shipbuilding and marine engineering as well as Hyundai Heavy Engineering in the south of the Korean peninsula (Chang, 2019).

However, moving forward, offsets policy cannot work in isolation but has to be incorporated into the wider industrial strategy. This is due to the changes in the future of warfare, shifting from primarily conventional to digital technologies such as artificial intelligence, cyber warfare and autonomous vehicles that require much more integration and collaboration between civil and military technology. Further, this means a more collaborative defence – civil industrial strategy that incorporates small to medium enterprises (SMEs) and start-ups that are more agile and innovative to work with than large defence primes. However, the danger is that offsets normally feature as part of a defence industrial strategy and sit within the defence sphere in most countries. Offsets policy and its possible benefits are not reflected in the wider industrial strategy, questioning whether it is only marginally adding low return on investments. In the digital tech era, the defence and civil sector must integrate to ensure resources are maximised to build in-country industrial capability.

Technology acquisition through offsets

Offsets were traditionally used to acquire critical technologies that cannot be bought off-the-shelf. That was the reason for inclusion of the condition for proof of 'additionality' and 'causality' when recognising an offsets project. In the past, offsets have supported technological spin-offs such as radar, sonar, computers and autonomous vehicles. But offsets have also been instrumental in generating technological spin-on through US transfer of technology into countries like Japan in areas such as semiconductor, electro-optical devices, microwave and automation. Offsets have also been useful to smaller countries with a limited industrial base to build capability in dual-use technologies that have better potential to generate more economies of scale. For example, Malaysia in the 1990s used offsets heavily to build its composite technology capability and later became part of the global supply chain in producing composite parts and components for Boeing and Airbus aircrafts. But the future of technology acquisition through offsets will be much more challenging as nations have to face multiple threats and actors. This is not easy as countries embark on the 'third offsets strategy' that pushes them to invest in state-of-the-art military technologies (Bolder & Kool, 2020). The United States is already on this path of defence innovation through its Buy America Act. Another development is the rise of selective collaborative activities, away from the traditional offsets model such as the A400M, F35 and the Eurofighter projects, which is based on 'just retour' and equal distribution of work though these models come with their own challenges. The most recent example is collaboration between BAES of Britain, SAAB of Sweden and Leonardo Italy to develop air combat capability (Adamczyk, 2020).

Alternative models are purely transactional

There are other policy instruments that can be used to build in-country industrial and technology capability. Governments have used instruments such as tariff barriers and subsidies to protect local industries, mainly arguing that infant industries need to be given preferential treatment or protected through government policies before they can attain sufficient competitiveness to enter the international market. For example, import substitution policies have been used to impose heavy excise duty on imported cars to protect the local automotive manufacturing industry. In the past, local companies have become complacent and used protectionism as a crutch, failing to develop competitiveness. Foreign direct investments (FDIs) have also been used as a catalyst for technology transfer by transnational companies, as an incentive to obtaining tax exemptions in exclusive economic zones (EEZs). Again, there is no real evidence of substantive technology transfer especially into the high technology sectors. Most of these companies operate on a non-committal basis and move their factories elsewhere. Even in the 1980s and 1990s, when US companies were transferring huge amounts of work into the electronics industry through FDIs into Asia, the transfer was only limited to assembly and production, keeping the high-end R&D, design and IPR in the host country. In the case of Apple, the IPR and high-end knowledge remains in the US and Europe, with only the lower-end of the technology being transferred to Taiwan and China. In recent years, despite China's huge investments in FDIs through the Belt and Road initiative into countries like Sri Lanka and Malaysia, there was almost no local transfer of technology, skills development or involvement of local companies in the projects (Wignanaraja et al., 2020). In such instances, offset policy has built a robust long-term strategic partnership between foreign suppliers and local companies, especially as there is direct government involvement and support in follow-through and monitoring of technology transfer. Offsets also cut through bureaucracy and red-tape as commitments to project completion are supported at the strategic level.

What are the reasons for offsets project failure?

Two volumes of books on offsets have produced case studies that discuss project failures. The first book published in 1996 by Stephen Martin entitled *The Economics of Offsets: Defence Procurement and Countertrade* consisted of 14 case studies across the US, Europe, Africa and Asia. The majority of the cases reported project failures due to various reasons. The second book produced in 2006, co-edited by Jurgen Brauer and Paul Dunne entitled, *Arms Trade and Economic Development: Theory, Policy and Cases in Arms Trade Offsets* comprised 19 country case studies, again with most of the projects failing. However, it is evident that most of these case studies were written by economists who had evaluated the project outcomes on the basis of economic logic and metrics. What are the reasons for why offsets projects fail? Listed here are four main reasons why projects fail followed by two brief case studies. These studies date back to the 1990s and 2000s, hence the need to undertake empirical research to write up new offsets case studies in the future.

The first reason for project failure relates to the offsets strategy. There may be a lack of clarity in shaping objectives, which are then not in alignment with finance, infrastructure and industry absorptive capability. It is harder for smaller states to be able to afford their own limited defence industrial base. Ambition and aspirations have to be redefined with realistic expectations. For example, Norway and Denmark ended up paying an additional $125–150 million for obtaining subcontracts for engineering and manufacturing development phase as part of the Joint Strike Fighter programme (Hagelin, 2004). Second, a particularly important gap arising in the offsets management process is a lack of skills in translating policy into practise and the shifting of the goal post. Offsets become an afterthought, and are not given due consideration nor are they seen as the core business in a bidding and procurement process. The incentives, usually in the form of multipliers attached to offsets, are viewed as less attractive than other types of incentives such as tax exemption for investments in the exclusive economic zone areas (EEZ). At other times, the contractual terms are too punitive, implying harsh punishment for non-performance. In such instances, sellers become risk averse and limit commitment to business innovation. The third reason relates to culture which may include poor leadership, lack of political will to see through project completion, poor relationship management with the OEM and lack of engagement and buy-in from the different stakeholders including end-users, local companies, SMEs, research think-tanks, universities and other related organisations. Often, the offsets management authority lacks resources such as funding, skilled manpower and supporting tools to implement and monitor projects through successful completion. The fourth reason relates to governance, such as the lack of a transparent organisational structure for selection, evaluation, approval, and monitoring of offsets projects (Balakrishnan, 2019: pp.120–129). For example, Joanna Spears in a RUSI blog commented that India's monitoring of offsets policy was inadequate, failing to recover penalties due to non-fulfilment of annual offsets obligation (Spears, 2013). Below are two brief case studies on failed projects selected from secondary sources.

Example 12.4: South Africa offsets policy

South Africa has had one of the most controversial offsets programme in international defence procurement history. Its Defence Industrial Policy (DIP) was developed in 1996 from the National Industrial Policy (NIP). DIP was meant to retain and create jobs, abilities and capabilities and allow a sustainable defence industrial capacity with strategic logistics support capabilities, promote value-added exports, technology transfer and joint-ventures as well as maintain skilled indigenous manufacturing capabilities (Dunne and Lamb, 2006). All DIP activities were managed by ARMSCOR and non-military portions by the Department of Trade and Industry (DTI) in accordance with NIP. Apartheid policy and arms embargoes drove the country to build its own defence industrial base to develop military self-sufficiency. The most intriguing offsets programme in South Africa was the $5 billion arms trade deal under the Strategic Defence programme, which included countertrade, DIP and NIP. The paper by Henz Kirchewehm argued that Denel, the largest RSA defence company did not make any profit at all from the contracts (Kirchwehm, 2014). The RSA parliament committee reported that offsets projects earned low growth and employment. It was also reported that many of the defence companies' set-up were not sustainable and not competitive by OEM standards. These companies also lost capability including skilled workers, mainly in the shipbuilding industry. The cost of per employment generated was at R1.6 million was claimed to be extremely high. It was reported that the joint venture Snecma Turbomeca was a failure due to the lack of business acumen on local sourcing of raw material for the projects (Kirchwehm, 2014). Further, many contracts with companies like Eurocopter, Agusta and SAAB had to be rewritten as there was lack of government financial support for infrastructural development. Other reasons included lack of transparency and governance in how the projects were managed and the reports contradicted between what was reported and the actual project achievements. In the indirect offsets category, which involved investments into mineral and energy sector in regions such as province of Kwazulu Natal, Western Cape and Eastern Cape, projects were deemed highly dubious (Kirchwehm, 2014).

Example 12.5: Malaysia's ACV 300 Adnan Procurement Deal with FNSS Savunna

Although Malaysia has practised offsets since the early 1990s, the official defence offsets policy was only introduced in 2005 by the Ministry of Defence. It has been revised a few times and the 2018 version is labelled the Industrial Collaboration Policy (ICP). ICP covers both defence and civil offsets and is implemented by six key organisations, including the Ministry of Defence. Malaysia has had mixed results when it comes to impact. A specific offsets project that was controversial is the 8 by 8 ACV 300 procurement deal between the government of Malaysia and FNSS, Turkey. The major local technology partner was DEFTECH, a subsidiary of DRB HICOM. The deal was to assemble 66 out of the 214 vehicles in-country, generating technology transfer, work packages, training and future export opportunity as part of FNSS's supply chain. There were huge investments by the Malaysian government into building infrastructure, test track, tools in Pekan, Pahang where the DEFTECH assembly plant was located. However, the project cost escalated as the main contractor was dependent on a third party for technology and upon the completion of the project, there were no future orders or sales till 2009. Despite the huge investment, there was minimal return as the facilities and equipment were underused, workers lost their skills and there was no future work for the factory. Hence, in this case, a one-off project without a long-term business plan was a catastrophe (Balakrishnan and Matthews, 2009: pp.341–358).

Based on the poor records of offsets, how can offsets evolve to deliver value? To answer this question, an Offsets Value Framework (OVF) has been developed that illustrates the composition of factors that is needed to deliver value. The next section explains what value in the context of offsets is followed by a description of the OVF framework.

How to deliver value through offsets policy?

It is not the purpose of this chapter to discuss the concept of value at length, but an understanding of the concept is required if we intend to measure it. Throughout the chapter we have attempted to draw attention to the importance of associating offsets management to value and provide a conceptual framework on how offsets could deliver value. The intention is not to measure value but to describe drivers to deliver it through offsets.

At the core of economic thinking, value is defined as price set by supply and demand. Hence, when an activity results in a payment or price discovery, this is seen as value. Value can also be seen as an intermediary process or 'flow', such as adding value to a manufacturing supply chain or creating new knowledge bases (Porter, 1998). Then there are further riddles in how these outputs are produced, how they are shared across society, whether production is useful and what is done with subsequent earnings. Measuring the value derived through defence spending is even more suspicious when the marketplace is a battlefield. Defence is often considered an opportunity cost dilemma, with some suggesting it has limited direct economic benefits. In this context, offsets, often considered an afterthought and given less prominence in defence, is taken less seriously as to its value through defence spending. A McKinsey paper in 2014 highlighted the value of offsets despite defence companies looking at them as a burden in international sales (Dehoff, Dowdy & Kwon 2014). Instead, stakeholders consider offsets' value as trivial and unimportant in the overall defence impact. Value can be explained using three pillars, strategy, innovation and governance, shown in Figure 12.1:

The first pillar of value describes strategy, where offsets policy should distinctly identify primary, secondary and tertiary level of value. In this context, the primary focus of offsets is to support the activities directly related to the procurement, including technology, work packages, developing skills and any other related activities

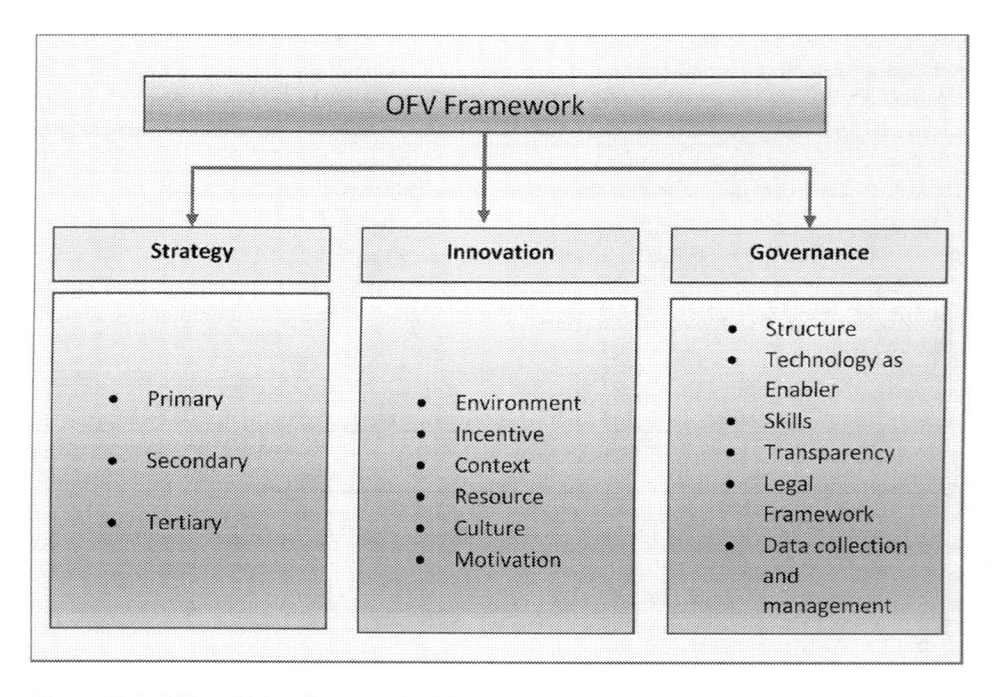

Figure 12.1 Offsets Value framework (OFV)
Source: Author.

to build in-country capability to be able to sustain the purchased equipment. The secondary strategy of offsets is to obtain economic derivatives from activities such as setting-up joint-ventures, luring FDI and capturing exports. The third strategy is to obtain know-how and knowledge transfer mainly in the area directly related to the procurement and related technology space, but also other related knowledge through training and education.

The second pillar of value describes innovation as a foundation to offsets projects, mainly in demonstrating 'additionality' and 'causality', demonstrating that offsets pave the way for disruptive product or process innovation. Offsets policy should incorporate attractive incentives beyond mere subjective and dubious multipliers. It is also important that the offsets culture embrace the precise environment, context and motivation for innovation to flourish. For example, innovation cannot flourish if the offsets policy sets a rigid and prescriptive policy, which is not attractive for business growth.

The third pillar for value relates to governance. A policy committee of experts on offsets and industrial policy should be set-up to outline the parameters for an offsets programme and what it should achieve. It is vital that there is a transparent offsets structure consisting of an oversight committee that monitors and evaluates offsets policy impact. This committee should be independent of the policy committee in order to provide check and balance. At the committee level, a first tier executive committee of CEOs and Ministers at Board level should set direction, strategy and vision; at the second tier, a strategic committee of senior management, managing directors of industries and one board member is to provide an oversight of projects and institute projects, auditing and risk management; at the third tier, a technical committee to undertake day-to-day operations, specify technical aspects of offsets, negotiate offsets contracts, and for the resourcing and financing of projects. An independent joint committee such as an Industry Development and Innovation Committee to be formed with a government representative from the Ministry of Finance, Trade and Industry, Science and Technology, Human Resources and other relevant agencies and industry members to discuss the impact of offsets and create a transparent measure to make offsets work. Both sellers and purchasers should consider assembling a pool of personnel skilled in offsets strategy, negotiations and implementation for a level playing field, to build trust and long-term relationships. However, this is hard to achieve as offsets does not take priority for most organisations. Offsets projects are managed over a very long period which requires sustainable trustworthy partnerships. Further, it is important to develop a clear legal framework including offsets contracts, compliance rules and regulations around business ethics and corruption which can ensure less suspicious projects. Finally, offsets management must include a better measurement process and embrace a technology enabler such as block chain technology and data science to capture accurate data for transparent reporting (Stone, 2019).

Conclusion

It has been argued in this chapter that offsets are crucial to progress as countries aim to move away from transactional international procurement especially for strategic items, and focus more on acquiring in-country capability. Furthermore, offsets will remain if nations continue to emphasise autonomy, independence and self-sufficiency. The contentious 5G technology development is a case in point. The incidences around COVID-19, the disruption of supply chains and over dependence on a single market are important illustrations that indigenous capability is crucial despite globalisation and the trust on interdependence. COVID-19 has come as a sudden shock and acted as a catalyst for many states and businesses to build resilience and reconsider self-sufficiency, even if it is at a higher cost. However, limited resources in the current economic climate would require nations to be more innovative about how to acquire technology and build industrial capability and skills. Self-sufficiency is expensive and requires meeting competing goals, thus not all countries can be fully self-sufficient. Therefore, for smaller states, strategic alliances and international collaboration is increasingly important, where offsets are then imperative. The current offsets model, however, is no longer relevant; it is expensive, inefficient and does not feature the most attractive incentives. In order to transform offsets, we argue that three critical steps are necessary.

First, policy makers must be brutal about strategic priorities, meaning the offsets budget holder must be given the authority to decide which are the most important capabilities for what offsets should be used. For example, if the Ministry of Defence is the custodian, then offsets should be prioritised for specific defence capability or be used to develop a technological capability that has a dual-use purpose. Second, if offsets are to stay relevant, yielding the benefits and impact as a result of investment, the current business model must change. Procurement and sales should not be the sole drivers for offsets; commitment to sustainability, innovation and business continuity processes should also be considered as significant factors. OEMs must adjust from seeing offsets as a condition of sale only, to viewing them as providing viable business opportunities and enduring relationships. For this to happen, the host country government must also work hard to lure investments through attractive incentives. Third, offsets activities must be transparent. Despite the sensitivity around offsets programmes, governance should be enforced through audit reports, published documents on outcomes and research to be conducted on impact. Finally, this chapter argues that the new model should be based on clearly defined strategic priorities, robust cost-benefit analyses, highly attractive and incentivised business model and a transparent governance process.

Questions to consider

1. Using OFV as a guideline, develop an offsets strategy for your country in the next five years.
2. Why do offsets projects fail? Compare and contrast your answers with colleagues from other defence organisations in different countries.
3. What are the key drivers to generating a successful offsets policy and programme? What are the potential resistors to such a policy and programme?

Suggested further reading

Balakrishnan, K. (2019) *Technology Offsets in International Defence Procurement*, London: Routledge.

Balakrishnan, K. & Matthews, R. (2009) 'The role of offsets in Malaysian defence industrialization', *Defence and Peace Economics*, 20(4), pp. 341–358. DOI:10.1080/10242690802333117

Brauer, J. & Dunne, P. (2004) *Arms Trade and Economic Development: Theory, Policy and Cases in Arms Trade Offsets*, Abingdon: Routledge.

Martin, S., ed., (1996) *The Economics of Offsets: Defence Procurement and Countertrade*, New York: Routledge.

References

Adamczyk, E. (2020) 'Britain, Sweden, Italy to collaborate on combat aircraft', *Defence News*. Available at https://www.upi.com/Defense-News/2020/07/22/Britain-Sweden-Italy-to-collaborate-on-combat-aircraft/6041595436255/ [Accessed 11 August 2020].

Balakrishnan, K. (2019) *Technology offsets in International Defence Procurement*, London: Routledge.

Balakrishnan, K. & Matthews, R. (2009) 'The role of offsets in Malaysian defence industrialization', *Defence and Peace Economics, 20 (4)*, pp. 341–358. DOI:10.1080/10242690802333117

Behera, L.K. (2009) 'India's defence offset policy', *Strategic Analysis, 32 (2)*, pp. 242–253.

Bitzinger, R. (2009) *The Modern Defence Industry: Political, Economy and Technological Issues*, Santa Barbara. CA: Praeger Security International.

Bolder, P. & Kool, D. (2020) 'Third offset strategy: Reacting to risk or becoming blindsided?', *The Hague Centre for Strategic Studies*. Available at https://hcss.nl/report/third-offset-strategy-reacting-risk-or-becoming-blindsided [Accessed 11 August 2020].

Brauer, J. & Dunne, J.P. (2004) *Arms Trade and Economic Development: Theory, Policy and Cases in Arms Trade Offsets*, London & New York: Routledge.

Brocker, E. & Beraldi, F. (2017) 'Offsets in public-sector procurement: Tools for economic development or avenues for corruption', *2017 OECD Global Anti-Corruption & Integrity Forum*. Available at https://www.oecd.org/cleangovbiz/Integrity-Forum-2017-Beraldi-Broecker-offsets-public-procurement.pdf [Accessed 7 August 2020].

Chang, F.K. (2019) 'The rise of South Korea's defence industry and its impact on South Korea foreign relations', *Institute of Foreign Policy*. Available at https://www.fpri.org/article/2019/04/the-rise-of-south-koreas-defense-industry-and-its-impact-on-south-korean-foreign-relations/ [Accessed 7 August 2020].

Collins, D. (2018) 'Government procurement with strings attached: The uneven control of offsets by the World Trade Organization and Regional Trade Agreements', *Asian Journal of International Law, 8 (2)*, pp. 301–322. Available at https://www.cambridge.org/core/journals/asian-journal-of-international-law/article/government-procurement-with-strings-attached-the-uneven-control-of-offsets-by-the-world-trade-organization-and-regional-trade-agreements/9FB28D1F244BCE97A0E15C7D46813019 [Accessed 7 August 2020].

Cowshish, A. (2020b) 'Should MoD persist with defence offsets?', *IDSA Comments*. Available at https://idsa.in/idsacomments/should-mod-persist-with-defence-offsets-acowshish-070820 [Accessed 7 August 2020].

Dehoff, K., Dowdy, J. & Sung Kwon, O. (2014) 'Defence Offsets: from contractual burden to competitive weapon', 1 July 2014, Mckinsey report in https://www.mckinsey.com/industries/public-and-social-sector/our-insights/defense-offsets-from-contractual-burden-to-competitive-weapon.

Dunne, J.P. & Lamb, G. (2004) 'Defence participation: The South African experience'. In: Brauer, J. & Dunne, P.J., eds., *Arms Trade and Economic Development*, London: Routledge, pp. 284–298.

Hagelin, B. (2004) 'Nordic offset policies: Changes and challenges'. In: J. Brauer & P.J. Dunne, eds., *Arms Trade and Economic Development*, London: Routledge, pp. 137–148.

Haines, R.J. (2004) 'Defence offsets and regional development in South Africa'. In: J. Brauer & P.J. Dunne, eds., *Arms Trade and Economic Development*, London: Routledge, pp. 299–313.

Kirchwehm, H. (2014) 'Why failed so often the offsets part of a South Africa procurement deal? A case study of based examination', *Business Management and Strategy, 5 (2)*.

Liang, Y. (2020) 'The US, China, and the perils of post-COVID decoupling', *The Diplomat*. Available at https://thediplomat.com/2020/05/the-us-china-and-the-perils-of-post-covid-decoupling/ [Accessed 7 August 2020].

Markowski, S. & Hall, P. (1998) 'Challenges of defence procurement', *Defence and Peace Economics, 9 (1–2)*, pp. 3–37. DOI: 10/1080/10430719808404892

Martin, S., ed. (1996) *The Economics of Offsets: Defence Procurement and Countertrade*, New York: Routledge.

Matthews, R., ed. (2019) *The Political Economy of Defence*, Cambridge: University Printing House.

Porter, M.E. (1998) *Competitive Advantage: Creating and Sustaining Superior Performance*, New York: Free Press.

Skons, E. (2004) 'Evaluating defence offsets: The experience in Finland and Sweden'. In: J. Brauer & P.J. Dunne, eds., *Arms Trade and Economic Development*, London: Routledge, pp. 149–163.

Spears, J. (2013) 'The implementation of India's defence offset policy', *RUSI*. Available at https://rusi.org/commentary/implementation-indias-defence-offset-policy [Accessed 7 August 2020].

Stone, J.C. (2019) 'Defence procurement offsets and their economic value in Canada', *CDA Institute*. Available at https://cdainstitute.ca/defence-procurement-offsets-and-their-economic-value- [Accessed 7 August 2020].

Wignannaraja, G., Panditaratne, D., Kannangora, P. & Hundlani, D., eds. (2020) 'Chinese investment and the BRI in Sri Lanka', *Chatham House*. Available at https://www.chathamhouse.org/publication/chinese-investment-and-bri-sri-lanka?utm_source=Chatham%20House&utm_medium=email&utm_campaign=11728875_New%20Template%20-%20Asia-Pacific%20July%20Newsletter&dm_i=1S3M,6ZE23,YKDIW,S4D7Y,1 [Accessed 7 August 2020].

13 Strategic leadership
Concept, theory and practice

Bryan Watters and Ifti Zaidi

Introduction

Throughout this book the authors have stressed the importance of analysing the strategic context and have introduced methods for doing so (see Chapters 2, 5 and 8). In this chapter we relate those prior arguments and practices to strategic leadership. Our discussion of leadership encapsulates the key themes of this book: change is a constant, context matters, conceptual clarity is crucial and experiential learning valuable. Like so many concepts addressed within this book, leadership is a contested phenomenon; it is as conceptually diverse as human nature. 'Leadership is one of the most observed and least understood phenomena on earth' (Burns, 1978: p.2).

We begin this chapter with a brief outline of the evolution of the conceptual and theoretical framework of leadership. We then focus on strategic leadership and present philosophies and models that illustrate the demands of leading at the strategic level. Finally, we explore Adaptive Leadership, formulated to address challenges that have no solutions, such as the strategic challenge of national security.

The concept of leadership

> To an extent, leadership is like beauty: It's hard to define, but you know it when you see it.
>
> (Bennis, 2003: p.1)

What do we mean when we speak of leadership? Writing in 1974, Ralph Stogdill, opined, 'There are almost as many different definitions of leadership as there are persons who have attempted to define the concept' (Stogdill, 1974: p.7). He astutely encapsulated our problem, there is no universally accepted definition of leadership. In 1991, Rost (1991) noted 221 definitions of leadership. Bass (1990: pp.19–20) in seeking to present his own authoritative definition cited 7,500 references on leadership; his own became another statistic. The absence of a universally accepted definition makes it difficult to measure the occurrence of leadership with any accuracy or consistency. For the purposes of this chapter, we turn to etymology, for a conceptual meaning, of leadership. The Oxford English Dictionary Online (2008) gives the origin of the word from Old English *lædan*, of Germanic origin, meaning to cause to go with one. The Dictionary also provides multiple interpretations of the word lead and leader as both nouns and verbs. Whilst lead (leader) has its origins in ancient language, leadership is

DOI: 10.4324/9781003137061-13

a more contemporary term. The addition of the suffix 'ship' (scipe) in old and middle English was used to denote 'the state of being' and therefore, leadership is the state of being a leader. We describe strategic leadership, as the practice of 'organisational' leadership in the strategic environment. In our experience strategic leaders have a vision of the organisation's future state and the trust of the organisation to guide them on the strategic journey, obtaining the necessary resources and developing the required competences over the long term.

Before we proceed with a review of leadership theory it is important to draw a distinction between leadership and management. Lead and manage are etymologically distinct but leaders and managers are often conflated. In 2004 the Defence Leadership Centre, part of the UK's Ministry of Defence (MOD) was asked to write the MOD's first leadership Doctrine. As part of this Doctrine, they were tasked with differentiating between Command, Leadership and Management and explain their relationship. In Leadership in Defence (MOD, 2004: p.7) *Command* is explained as the whole complex business (of Commanding) and a position enshrined in law. Management and Leadership are described as the two sides of the Command coin. *Management* it argues brings order and consistency to complex organisations involving planning and budgeting. *Leadership* is described as setting direction, developing a vision of the future, and developing strategies for developing the vision. Management, when compared to leadership's lines of vision, inspiration and communication, may look dull and mechanical, but no organisation can hope to survive without proper husbandry and housekeeping (MOD, 2004).

This differentiation of management and leadership is derived from the work of John Kotter (1990: pp.3–8) who argued that management produces order and consistency through planning and budgeting, organising, and staffing, controlling and problem solving. Leadership however produces change and movement through establishing direction, aligning people and motivating and inspiring. The UK MOD recognised that some Commanders may have a leadership or management bias and would thus need to compensate through personal development and the selection of suitably skilled staff (MOD, 2004: p.7). This perspective of differentiating leadership and management is generally supported by authors on the subject. (Kotter, 1990; Bennis and Nanus, 1997; Rost, 1991; Simonet and Tett, 2012).

Leadership: The evolution of theory

If beauty, and leadership, are in the eye of the beholder then we need to recognise that leadership theory and practice is socially constructed. This is reflected in many of the theories that have been propounded over the last century. Chester Barnard (1948: pp.97–98) argued: 'Leaders, I think, are made quite as much by conditions and by organisations and followers as by the qualities and propensities that they themselves have'. There are almost as many leadership theories as there are theorists. Yukl and Gardner (2020: pp.31–32) provide a useful table of key variables (Table 13.1) within their five research approaches which are:

1. The trait approach: Is based on an assumption that leaders are born not made. Between 1904 and 1947 hundreds of studies sought to identify the elusive qualities of leadership, but failed to identify traits that would guarantee leadership success (Bass, 1990). There has been renewed interest in Trait theory, with studies

suggesting that an individual's leadership potential is the result of a complex product of genetic and environmental influences (De Neve et al., 2013).

2. The behaviour approach: dates from the early 1950s following disenchantment with the Trait approach. Its focus was on manager behaviour (the terms 'leader' and 'manager' were conflated) and it examined correlations between leadership behaviour and indicators of leadership (in)effectiveness.

3. The power influence approach: Initially focused on the leader alone, research was broadened to include wider relationships between the leader, follower, peers, superiors, and wider stakeholders outside the organisation. This field of study further evolved into 'Participative Leadership', examining power-sharing between leaders and followers and the empowerment of followers, leading to the theory of Distributed Leadership or as described in the military, Mission Command.

4. The situational approach: This approach emphasised the contextual factors that influence leadership interactions such as: characteristics of followers, the nature of work, the type of organisation and the nature of the external environment. The assumption being that different attributes will be effective in different situations and equally a particular attribute will not be effective in all situations. Theories describing the relationship between attributes and situations are often called Contingency Theories. Contemporary research, often in the information or digital economy, examines an extreme situational approach, described as leadership substitute where conditions make traditional hierarchical leadership superfluous or redundant (see Chapter 10).

5. The integrative approach. This final approach is a catch all and explains leadership research that increasingly involves two or more of the key variables explained in Figure 13.1. Yukl and Gardner (2020: p.32) capture the breadth of factors that influence perspectives and, in turn, definitions. In Figure 13.1 we add to this set of variables the tacit influence of external and internal liberties and constraints that bias perceptions. An example cited by Yukl (2013: p.303) is House's (1971) theory of charismatic leadership.

Exercise 13.1: Reflection on leadership experience

When introducing Strategic Leadership to senior Defence and Security Practitioners on the UK MOD's Senior Leadership Programme the authors began with a deceptively simple exercise, we encourage the reader to undertake now.

1. Reflecting on your career think about the leaders you have known. Recall your experience of their leadership.

2. Begin with what you would describe as good leadership experiences. Describe what made them good in your view. Having written down the key constructs of this good leadership experience reflect on how it made you feel. Write down the description of your feelings. Do this about five times.

3. Now think about bad leadership experiences. Write down your description of what made them bad and reflect on how those experiences made you feel. Do this for every bad leadership experience you have had.

4. You now have your leadership experiences classified as good and bad and the associated feelings or emotional responses. This is a very personal reflection and in terms of good leadership serves to illustrate Bennis' argument that you know leadership when you see it.

5. The bad leadership experience serves to describe the concept of 'Toxic Leadership', which will be discussed in detail.
6. Keep this list and continue to update it from memory and new leadership experiences. You might find it shapes and influences your own leadership.

As we noted above, there are a plethora of theories on leadership: which implies that there are no truths only paradigms. Table 13.1, provides a summary of the influential theories, with example contributors, that have guided research to the present day.

Building and sustaining relationships is a critical and defining aspect of leading at the strategic level. In addition to Adaptive Leadership, discussed here, we should highlight the pertinence of the relational approach to strategic leaders. The Relational Approach falls into the category of schools that bridge theory and practice. It has a direct impact on our discussion of definitions; as all relationships are unique (Yukl,

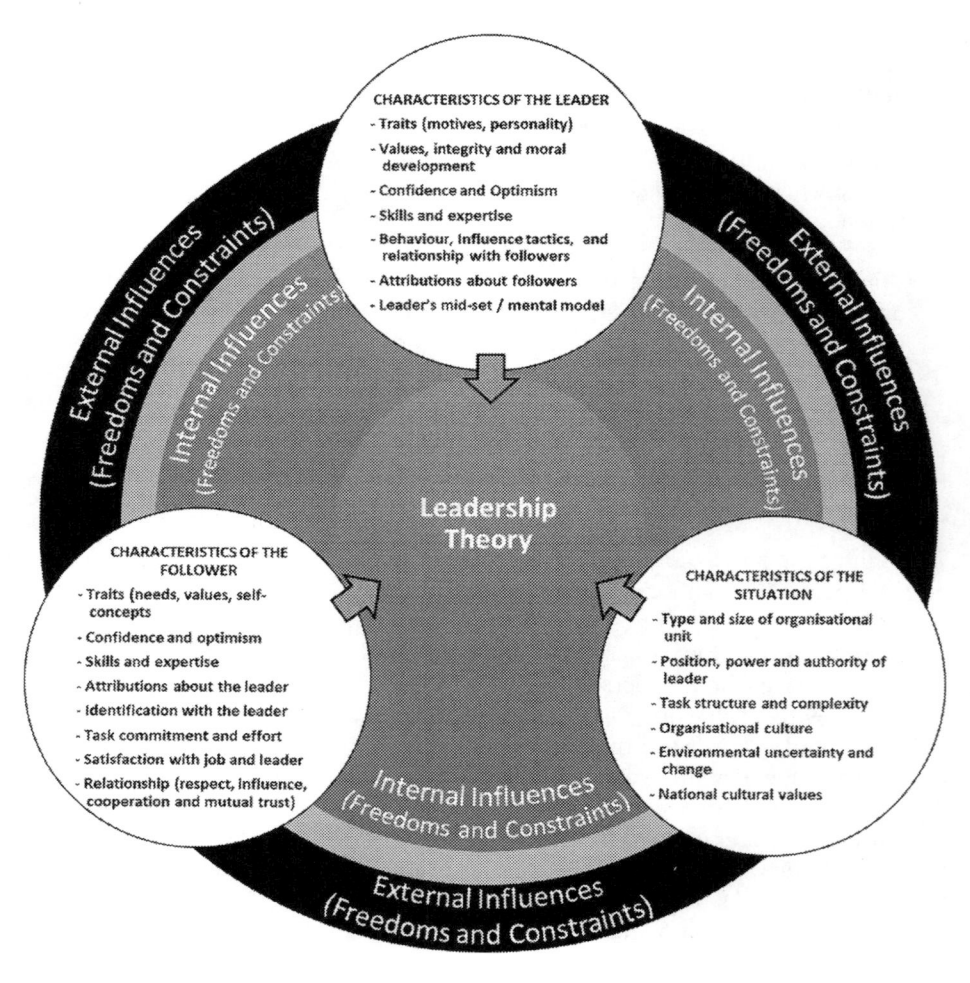

Figure 13.1 Key Variables in Leadership Theories
Developed form Yukl and Gardner (2020: p.32).

Table 13.1 Leadership Theories and Approaches

Influential Leadership Theories

Theory	Date	Example Contributors
The Ancients	A long time ago	Homer, Asoka, Confucius, Sun Tzu, Plato, Aristotle, Marcus Aurelius, Machiavelli
Great Man Theory	19th century	The history of the world is the history of great men (James, 1880). Carlyle's (1841) essay on 'Heroes and Hero Worship' was influential. Sir Francis Galton (1869) Heredity Genius
Trait Approach Trait Theory	20th century to present day	Stogdill (1974), Lord et al. (1986), Zaccaro et al. (2018)
Skills Approach Skills Model	20th century to present day	Katz (1955), Mumford et al. (2000) Yammarino (2000)
Behavioural Approach Ohio State University Studies University of Michigan Studies Blake and Mouton's Managerial (Leadership) Grid	20th century	Hemphill (1950), Stogdill (1963, 1974), Cartwright and Zander (1970), Katz and Kahn (1966) Likert (1967), Blake and Mouton (1985), Blake and MCanse (1991)
Situational Approach Situational Leadership Model	20th century to present day	Hersey and Blanchard (1996) Blanchard, Zigarmi and Zigarmi (2013).
Path Goal Theory	20th century	House (1971) House and Mitchell (1974)
Contingency Theory	20th century	Fiedler (1967), Fiedler & Chemers (1974)
Leader Member Exchange Theory (LMX)	20th century to present day	Bakar and Sheer (2013) Omilion-Hodges, Ptacek and Zerilli (2015)
Transactional and Transformational Leadership	20th century to present day	Burns (1978) Bass (1990) Bass and Avolio (1993) Avolio (1999) Kouzes and Posner (2017) Bennis and Nanus (1997) Notgrass (2014)
Authentic Leadership	21st century	George (2003) Gardner, Avolio and Walumbwa (2005) Eagly (2005) Anderson et al. (2017)
Relational Leadership	20th century to present day, With roots in the 20th-century LMX Theory, Relational Theory takes a distinct direction in the 21st century.	Uhl-Bein (2006); Cunliffe and Eriksen (2011); Epitropaki, Martin, and Thomas (2018).
Servant Leadership	20th century to present day	Greenleaf (1977) van Dierendonck (2011) Coetzer, Bussin and Geldenhuys (2017)
Adaptive Leadership	20th century to present day	Heifetz (1994) Heifetz, Linsky and Grashow (2009) Thygeson Morrissey and Ulstad (2010)
Followership	20th century to present day	Meindl (1995) Chaleff (2009) Kellerman (2008) Carsten, Harms and Uhi-Bien (2014)

(Continued)

Table 13.1 (Continued)

Influential Leadership Theories

Theory	Date	Example Contributors
Leadership and Ethics	Ancients to the present day	Aristotle (340 BC- 2009) Kant (1785) Bentham (1789) Ciulla (2014) Johnson (2017) Wilson and McCalman (2017)
Distributed and Team Leadership	20th century to the present day	Spillane (2006) Bolden (2011)
Gender and Leadership	20th century to the present day	Kanter (1977) Eagly and Wood (2013) Eagly (2013)
Culture and Leadership	20th century to the present day	Hofstede (2001) House, Hanges, Javidan, Dorfman and Gupta (2004)

Source: Adapted from Bass (1990), Northouse (2019) and Antonakis and Day (2018).

2013: p.23), the only definition that matters is the one given by the person defining it. Human relationships are never constant, leaders have a dynamic influence on relationships and the collective activity within an organisation (Uhl-Bein, 2006; Antonakis & Day, 2018: p.8).

One question asked by our students is why are there so many theories of leadership? The answer is that, as a field of academic scholarship, leadership studies embrace multiple disciplines in the social, management and military sciences. The practice of leadership changes in response to changing circumstances, for example, from peace to war, from economic prosperity to a recession. Bolden et al. (2011) provide a useful reference for those interested in discovering more about the arguments and philosophies surrounding the phenomenon of leadership.

The practice of strategic leadership

What makes leadership strategic? Arguably, leadership is leadership, but some aspects of the strategic environment may change the leader's focus. Joyce P. (2016) undertook a functional analysis of the role of strategic leaders and suggested three broad areas of activity: strategy development, planning, and communication. From this perspective, there is potential for overlap between strategic leadership and management (see Chapter 8). However, leadership and management remain separate systems of action; and when both functions are performed, the decisions highlight which system of action prevailed (Zaidi and Bellak, 2019).

Strategic leadership implies an organisational and positional perspective; decisions taken impact the entire organisation. Historically in the Defence and Security domains reference has been made to Strategic, Operational and Tactical levels of activity. The advent of cyberspace and the proliferation of social media and enabling technologies has blurred these demarcations, contributing to the contemporary VUCA environment (Barber, 1992). The strategic context of any country is made more challenging by the competing agendas of numerous and diverse stakeholders, thus giving credence to Clausewitz's dictum: 'War is the continuation of politics by other means'.

Gardner's (2000) theory of multiple intelligences provides a useful framework when reflecting on the required qualities and behaviours of strategic leaders. In positing eight distinct intelligences (linguistic, logical/mathematical, spatial, bodily-kinaesthetic, musical, interpersonal, intrapersonal and naturalist) Gardener challenged the traditional emphasis placed on cognitive ability alone. Relational Leadership Theory draws Gardener's inter and intrapersonal intelligence to address how to gain and sustain influence. We would argue that it is this 'Emotional Intelligence' (Goleman, 1996) that might be the defining characteristic of successful strategic leaders.

Example 13.1: Emotional intelligence defined: Eisenhower

An examination of the personalities of General Dwight D. Eisenhower (affable, gregarious, and a decent, honourable man who quietly inspired confidence and commanded respect) and General Bernard Montgomery (arrogant, unlikeable, but ultimately successful. He famously lacked diplomacy and tact when dealing with others) illustrates that sheer ability can take you so far. Had Montgomery been more like Eisenhower who knows what he might have achieved. On the other hand, Montgomery's bête noire, Field Marshall Erwin Rommel was also deeply respected by his troops and his enemies. Rommel demonstrated the breadth of leadership intelligences and the occasional toxic traits as biographed by Butler (2015).

Acquiring and developing strategic leadership skills

Based on a study of 20,000 executives, Schoemaker et al. (2013) identified six essential skills that, when synergised, allow leaders to think strategically and effectively navigate the unknown. These are the abilities to anticipate, challenge, interpret, decide, align, and learn. The empirical set of strategic skills that Schoemaker et al. list, align with Adaptive Leadership. We build on this research, having carefully considered its provenance from the corporate world and the authors' experiences in the military context to give the reader a model of strategic leadership skills and the building blocks of a personal development plan. We do this recognising that leadership learning and development never stops; the higher one rises the more intense and pressing the need. The result is our Six +1 model of essential skills, illustrated below:

The Six +1 essential skills of strategic leadership are:

Anticipate

Most organisations and leaders are poor at detecting ambiguous threats and opportunities on the periphery of their business. The Strategic Drift Theory and Futures Wheel discussed in Chapter 8, are tools to improve you and your organisation's ability to anticipate. Talk to your subordinate organisations, equipment suppliers, national partners, and allies to understand their challenges. Conduct analysis and simulation exercises to understand potential adversaries' perspectives, gauge their likely reactions to new initiatives or weapon systems, and predict potential counter measures. Use diverse thinkers to do scenario planning to imagine various futures and prepare contingency plans for the unexpected. Look at emerging potential adversaries and examine actions they are taking. List mistakes the organisation has made and examine what caused the mistakes. Attend diverse conferences and events in related and unrelated disciplines/organisations.

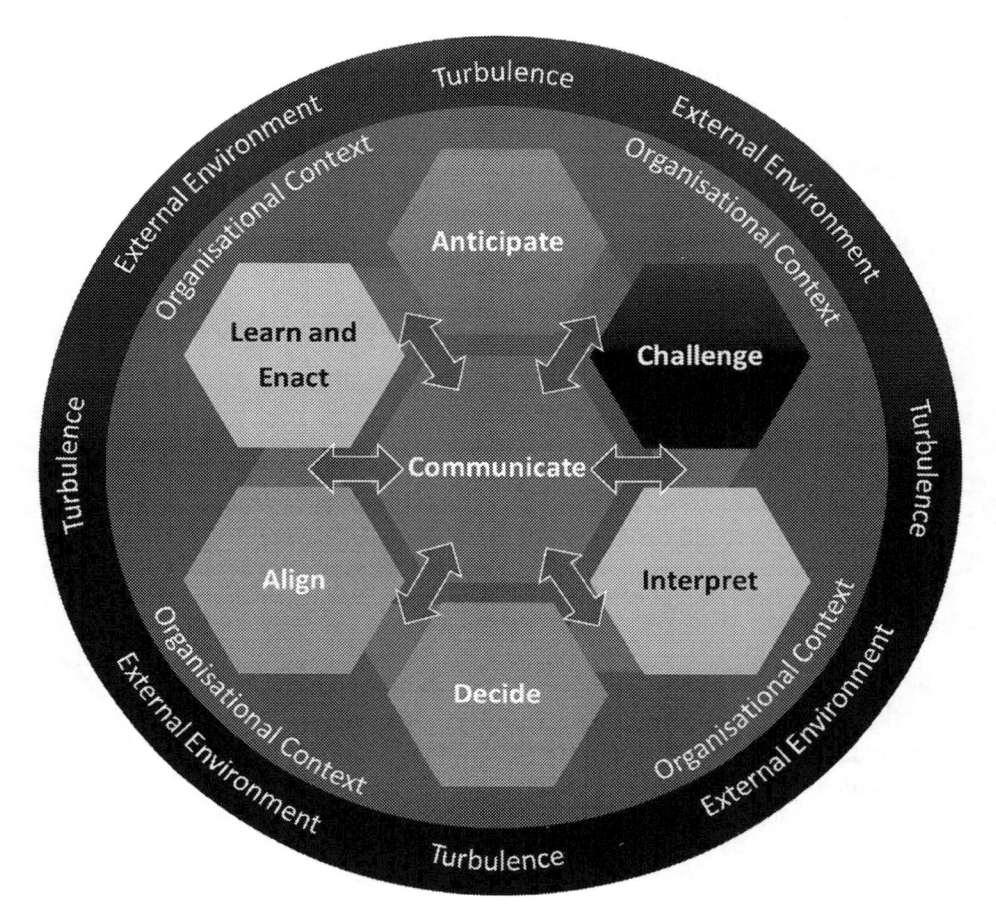

Figure 13.2 Six+1 Model of Essential Leadership Skills at the Strategic Level
Source: adapted from Schoemaker et al. (2013).

Challenge

As a strategic thinker, you need to challenge the status quo, including your own and others' assumptions and encourage divergent views. Only after careful reflection and examination of a problem through many lenses do you take decisive action. This requires patience, courage, and an open mind. Focus on the root causes of a problem rather than be deflected by more easily understood symptoms. Create a rotating 'red team' leader for the express purpose of questioning the status quo. Capture input from people not directly affected by a decision who may have a good perspective on the repercussions.

Interpret

Leaders who challenge in the right way invariably elicit complex and conflicting information. You'll need to recognise patterns, push through ambiguity, and seek new insights. When analysing ambiguous data, list at least three possible explanations for what you're observing and invite perspectives from diverse stakeholders. Force yourself to zoom in on the details and out to see the big picture (we will expand on this when we look at Adaptive Leadership). Actively seek to challenge or disprove your hypothesis. Supplement observation with quantitative analysis. Step away and relax, stepping away prompts the subconscious mind to engage, our most powerful part of the brain.

Decide

In uncertainty, decision makers may have to make difficult choices with incomplete information, and often they must do so quickly. At the strategic level you need to insist on multiple options and avoid simplistic go/no-go choices (Peltonon, 2019). Strategic leaders do not act in haste but follow a disciplined process that balances rigor with speed, considers the trade-offs involved, and takes both short- and long-term goals into account. In the end, strategic leaders must have the courage of their convictions, informed by a robust decision process. Reframe binary decisions by explicitly asking your team, 'What other options do we have?'. Divide big decisions into component parts, seek and analyse potential unintended consequences. Tailor your decision criteria to long-term versus short-term projects. Let others know where you are in your decision process. Are you still seeking divergent ideas and debate, or are you moving toward closure and choice? Determine who needs to be directly involved and who can influence the success of your decision. Consider pilots or experiments instead of big bets and make staged commitments.

Align

Strategic leaders must be adept at finding common ground and achieving buy-in among stakeholders who may have disparate views and agendas. Success depends on proactive communication, trust building, and frequent engagement. Reach out to resisters directly to understand their concerns and then address them. Be vigilant in monitoring stakeholders' positions during the rollout of your initiative or strategy, recognise colleagues who support team alignment.

Learn

Strategic leaders are the focal point for organisational learning. This is achieved by promoting a culture of inquiry, searching for the lessons in both successful and unsuccessful results. They study failures, their own and their teams, in an open, constructive way to find the hidden lessons. A culture of experimentation inevitably produces failure, these need to be condoned, celebrated, and learnt from. Learning must also translate into organisational advantage in performance and through development. An enduring lesson from the defence and security sector is that 'lessons learnt' on their own are not lessons enacted. For the security context, we would enhance Schoemaker et al.'s (2013) skill of *'learn'* with *'learn and enact'*.

Communication

This is critical as the leadership, the stakeholders (external and internal) as well as the followership must be engaged as necessary through each of the six progressions. Communicate early and often to combat the two most common complaints in organisations:

'No one asked me' and 'No one told me.' For leaders, delivering strategies that propel the organisation towards the shared realisable vision (see Chapter 8) and getting buy-in to that vision through communication is critical.

Exercise 13.2: Are you a strategic leader?

To find out if you think and act like a strategic leader from the point of view of your position, function or organisation, answer these questions:		*1 = Rarely* *5 = Almost always*				
How often do you…		*1*	*2*	*3*	*4*	*5*
Anticipate	*Gather information from a wide network of experts and sources both inside and outside your function, organisation or industry?*					
	Communicate with your team, experts and across industry to visualise potential challenges?					
Challenge	*Reframe a problem from several angles to understand root causes?*					
	Share your own interpretations with others?					
Interpret	*Demonstrate curiosity and an open mind?*					
	Discuss hypothetical developments with senior team members and other stakeholders through formal or informal forums?					
Decide	*Balance long-term investment for growth with short-term pressure for results?*					
	Anticipate forces against change and reach out to create a community of interest across the organisation and external stakeholders?					
Align	*Assess stakeholders' tolerance and motivation for change?*					
	Ensure that a system of monitoring, evaluation and feedback is in place for every level and up the chain to you?					
Learn	**Learn** *Communicate stories about success and failure to promote institutional learning?*					
	Correct course in the face of discounting evidence, having taken a decision?					
	Act *Translate learning into organisational performance by taking corrective actions across systems, processes as well as structure and strategy*					
	Interpret over the horizon events and initiate actions to make your function and organisation future ready?					
	Take risk and act, having considered a change that is unconventional, unpopular or unforeseen?					

	Ensure exchange of ideas on experiences, lessons learnt, and that outcomes feed into the short-term performance related actions, as well as long-term strategy, ready for the next cycle of anticipation – action?					
	Total all scores and compare with our guideline below: **<50 = Managerial mind-set; 50–74 = Transitional; 75–100 = Strategic mind-set**					

Source: adapted from Schoemaker et al. (2013).

Adaptive leadership

> The single most common source of leadership failure we've been able to identify – in politics, community life, business or the non-profit sector- is that people, especially those in positions of authority, treat adaptive challenges like technical problems.
>
> (Heifetz and Linsky, 2017: p.14)

The increasing speed of change in the private and public sectors and the challenge facing leaders to lead and manage this change inspired Ron Heifetz's distinctive theory of 'Adaptive Leadership'. He differentiates *Technical Problems* (problems with solutions) and *Adaptive Challenges* (problems with no solutions) and explores how leaders can guide their organisations through multiple changes to enable them to 'thrive' in the new context created by the Adaptive problem (Heifitz, 1994).

Heifetz and his colleagues suggest 'Adaptive Leadership is the practice of mobilising people to tackle tough challenges and thrive' (Heifetz et al. 2009: p.14). In explaining these tough challenges, he describes what he calls situational challenges and divides them into three: technical problems, challenges that are both technical and adaptive and adaptive challenges. These are briefly discussed.

Technical problems

Technical problems are easily identified and lend themselves to solutions that self-evidently solve the problems. The solution will sit within the expertise of an acknowledged expert or authority. Heifetz describes these as people who have a 'repertoire' of skills or procedures based on current knowledge. We are generally receptive to technical problems because we can see the logic of the solution even if we ourselves cannot solve the problem, we can find the expert within the organisation or buy in the expertise from outside. Technical problems can be complex, for example the redesign of a modern jet airliner after repeated failures, think about the crashes of two Boeing 737 Max aircraft five months apart killing 346 people. Another example is the British Army's rifle. The L85A1, often referred to as the SA80, was introduced in 1985 and proved to have several design and manufacturing faults leading to poor reliability. In 1998, the German company Heckler and Koch received a contract to modify L85A1s to the L85A2 standard. The rifle is now reliable and has the confidence of British soldiers. It was a technical problem with a technical solution, the solution self-evidently solved the problem.

Adaptive challenges

Adaptive challenges or problems are difficult to identify and easy to deny. When leaders are engaging with adaptive challenges, they need to think systemically to understand the whole array of actors involved, and the root causes which require committing time and energy. Understanding the adaptive challenge is an adaptive challenge in itself. Take for example the challenge of providing national security. National Security Councils and involved Ministries have not found a solution to national security, you might say they manage national insecurity whilst mitigating the impact of that insecurity on the nation state. As with other adaptive challenges the people with the problem, the responsible ministries and associated stakeholders, need to work to address the problem, which may require changes to values, beliefs, roles, and relationships, taking a whole system approach. The problem, and possibly the solution, rests with these key actors developing relations of trust as they work across organisational and, possibly, national boundaries to develop new approaches. The evolution of relationships and approaches will in turn create new and unexpected dimensions. These adaptive challenges present leaders with additional dilemmas: there will always be national insecurity, so what values, beliefs, roles and relationships are the nation willing to change to enhance national security? As Heifetz argues, the leader needs to give the work back to the people. COVID-19 provides us with an example of an adaptive challenge within the sphere of public health. Every nation would prefer COVID-19 to be a technical problem rather than an adaptive challenge. The reader might like to think about how national leaders have changed values, beliefs, roles and relationships as they attempt to control COVID-19, while scientists experiment to find a solution. For, without a technical solution COVID-19 will remain an adaptive challenge.

As Heifetz points out, not all problems come labelled technical or adaptive, many problems are adaptive with technical components as illustrated above. As leaders we need to identify the technical problems, mobilise resources to tackle them, whilst simultaneously engaging the adaptive problem. Technical problems can be seductive diverting the strategic leader from the VUCA nature of the adaptive challenge.

Heifetz (1994: pp.250–276) described a range of leadership skills he calls 'the Personal Challenge' required for tackling adaptive challenges. The first and most fundamental he calls 'getting on the balcony', an analogy for maintaining the strategic perspective and avoiding getting swept up by the events surrounding and involving us. This is illustrated with reference to the dance floor: whilst dancing our attention is captured by the music, our partner and interaction and deconfliction with the other dancers. We are part of the dance. To understand the larger patterns of the dance floor, who is dancing with who, who is not dancing to certain tunes, we need to stop dancing and get on the balcony to gain the balcony perspective. The second skill is to be able to identify the adaptive challenge, described as the gap between the shared values of people and the reality of their lives. This conflict induces distress, which is the diagnostic principle of an adaptive challenge if it cannot be alleviated through technical know-how and existing procedures. Again, think of the impact of the COVID-19 pandemic before the prospect of a potential technical solution; we all certainly felt distress. As the prospect of a technical solution emerged that distress diminished slightly. The third skill is that of regulating distress. To maintain the capacity to tackle an adaptive challenge the leader needs to create a balance of distress, too much and the organisation burns out, too little and they stop engaging with the adaptive challenge. Heifetz called this productive area the zone of disequilibrium and cautioned that each community and culture have their limits of tolerance for productive distress. The role of the leader, cognisant of their community and culture's tolerances, is to maintain this zone of disequilibrium by regulating distress to create the conditions for the community to tackle the problem. He offered further guidance on 'regulating distress' and 'directing disciplined attention to the issue'. Think of how governments maintained a tolerable degree of distress about COVID-19, placing us in a 'zone of disequilibrium', that enabled us to change values, beliefs, roles and relationships, whilst endeavouring to thrive in the new context. The last skill is 'giving the work back to the people'.

Heifetz (1994: p.262) further explained how a community's dependency on authorities to avoid distress, responsibility and pain can result in a failure to adapt values, beliefs, roles and relationships. Authority figures can collude in this dependency culture attempting to shield people from pain, treating the adaptive challenge as a technical problem. This is a natural leadership trait but enabling people to avoid distress allows 'work avoidance' and within the typology of adaptive challenges leads to leadership failure. The 'balcony' enables the leader to gain a broad perspective, but it is not a retreat. The involvement on the 'dance floor' ensures the leader remains anchored in the reality of the distress and regulates it to ensure tolerance and a productive rather than destructive 'disequilibrium'. Whilst strategic leaders can propose technical solutions to control the COVID-19 pandemic, it is the people who have to make the adaptive challenge by taking responsibility for enacting the required changes.

Writing two decades earlier two professors of the science of design and city planning, Rittel and Webber, described their problem typology as tame (technical) and wicked (adaptive). They proposed 'that it becomes morally objectionable for the planner to treat a wicked problem as though it were a tame one, or to tame a wicked problem prematurely' (Rittel and Webber, 1973: p.161). This pre-echoes Heifetz's observation at the beginning of this section, on Adaptive Leadership, that the single most common source of leadership failure is that people, treat adaptive challenges like technical problems.

Example 13.2: The Vance-Owen Peace Plan (1993)

A vivid example of planners treating an adaptive (wicked) problem as a technical (tame) problem occurred in 1993 during the Civil War in Bosnia Herzegovina when Bryan Watters was serving as a UN Commander (Watters, 2019). In early January 1993, the United Nations Special Envoy, Cyrus Vance and European Community representative Lord David Owen began negotiating a peace proposal with the leaders of Bosnia's warring factions. The proposal, which became known as the 'Vance-Owen peace plan', involved a series of measures including the division of Bosnia into ten semi-autonomous regions, and received the backing of the UN (Vance Owen, 1993). On 30 April 1993, the plan was signed by Radovan Karadžić, the President of the Republic of Srpska, Alija Izetbegović, Chairman of the presidency of Bosnia Herzegovina and Mate Boban, President of the Croatian Democratic Union of Bosnia and Herzegovina. However, on the 6 May, the National Assembly of Republika Srpska rejected it, and on 18 June, Lord Owen declared that the plan was 'dead'. Vance and Owen had proposed a technical (tame) solution to the adaptive (wicked) problem, of Bosnia's civil war, one consequence of the plan was the Bosnian Croat initiated ethnic cleansing along Bosnia's Lasva Valley including the massacre of over 100 Bosnian Muslims in the Village of Ahmici (UN ICTY, 1996). The Vance-Owen plan did not recognise the historical culturally motivated grievances, differences and aspirations of the warring factions that only they could address through strategic changes in their values, beliefs, roles and relationships, and be willing to accept the loss this change would involve. The 'frozen war' is still unresolved and will possibly take many more decades if not centuries for these divided communities to resolve their differences – a truly adaptive (wicked) problem.

Conclusion

In this chapter on strategic leadership, we have attempted to establish some conceptual clarity on what leadership is and what makes leadership strategic. In describing the evolution of leadership scholarship, we have acknowledged the bewildering array of concepts, theories and practices, and have sought to identify those elements that may be of greatest use when reflecting upon and developing one's own leadership style. Those working in and hoping to lead the security sector need to be cognisant of the myriad challenges contained within the broader strategic context: longer time frames, manifold uncertainties, multiple actors with their own agendas, increasingly blurred boundaries between levels, and the impact of and need to integrate within the political dimension. Based on our own eighty combined years of practicing, researching and teaching in this field we believe that the Six +1 model (anticipate, challenge, interpret, decide, align, learn and enact and communicate) and the concept of Adaptive Leadership are useful frameworks through which to explore the strategic context and the role of the strategic leader. An Afghan proverb provides a pertinent close to this chapter, 'If you think you're leading, and no one is following you, then you're only taking a walk' (Anon).

Questions to consider

1. 'Leadership is one of the most observed and least understood phenomena on earth'. Discuss why this quote is of relevance to a security force going through change in the 21st century.
2. Identify the differences between Strategic Leadership and Strategic Management. How can the two concepts be defined to create more synergy in a professional security force?
3. Consider the Six+1 model of essential leadership skills. Give examples of how a modern security force could train and develop such skills for new officers.

Suggested further reading

Antonakis, J. & Day, D. (2018) *The Nature of Leadership*, 3rd ed., London: Sage Publishing.
Yukl, G. & Gardner, W. L. (2020) *Leadership in Organisations*, 9th ed., London: Pearson.

References

Anderson, H.J., Baur, J.E., Griffith, J.A. & Buckley, M.R. (2017) 'What works for you may not work for (Gen) me: Limitations of present leadership theories for the new generation', *The Leadership Quarterly*, 28 (1), pp. 245–260.
Antonakis, J. & Day, D. (2018) *The Nature of Leadership*, 3rd ed., London: Sage Publishing.
Avolio, B.J. (1999) Full Leadership Development: Building the Vital Forces in Organizations, Thousand Oaks, CA: Sage.
Bakar, H.A. & Sheer, V.C. (2013) 'The mediating role of perceived cooperative communication in the relationships between interpersonal exchange relationships and perceived group cohesion', *Management Communication Quarterly*, 27, pp. 443–465.

Barber, H.F. (1992) 'Developing strategic leadership: The US army war college experience', *Journal of Management Development, 11 (6)*, pp. 4–12.

Barnard, C. (1948) 'The Nature of leadership'. In: Grint, K. ed., *Leadership, Classical, Contemporary, and Critical Approaches*, Oxford: Oxford University Press, pp. 89–111.

Bass, B.M. (1990) *Bass and Stogdill's Handbook of Leadership, Theory, Research and Managerial Applications*, New York: The Free Press.

Bass, B.M. & Avolio, B.J. (1993) 'Transformational leadership: A response to critiques'. In: M.M. Chemers & R. Aymen, eds., *Leadership Theory and Research: Perspectives and Directions*, Academic Press. San Diego. CA: Northouse (2004).

Bennis, W.G. (2003) *On Becoming a Leader*, Cambridge, MA: Perseus Pub.

Bennis, W.G. & Nanus, B. (1997) *Leaders, Strategies for Taking Charge*, 2nd ed., New York: Harper Collins.

Bentham, J. (1789) 'An Introduction to the Principles of Morals and Legislation'. In: J.H. Burns & H.L.A. Hart, eds., *The Athlone Press*, (1970), pp. xliii, 343. Reprinted in paperback with new introduction by F. Rosen, Oxford: Clarendon Press (1996).

Blake, R.R. & Mouton, J.S. (1985) *The Managerial Grid III: The Key to Leadership Excellence*, Houston, TX: Gulf Publishing Co.

Blake, R.R. & McCanse, A.A. (1991) *Leadership Dilemmas – Grid Solutions*, Houston, TX: Gulf Publishing Co.

Bolden, R. (2011) 'Distributed leadership in organizations: A review of theory and research', *International Journal of Management Reviews, 13*, pp. 251–269.

Bolden, R., Hawkins, B. Gosling. J. & Taylor, S. (2011) *Exploring Leadership Individual, Organisational and Societal Perspectives*, Oxford: Oxford University Press.

Burns, J.M. (1978) *Leadership*, London: Harper and Row.

Butler, D.A. (2015) *Field Marshal: The Life and Death of Erwin Rommel*, Oxford: Casemate Publishers.

Carlyle, T. (1841) *Heroes and Hero Worship, and the Heroic of History*, Edited by Michael K. Goldberg, Joel J. Brattin & Mark Enge. Berkeley, CA: University of California Press, 1993.

Carsten, M.K., Harms, P. & Uhl-Bien, M. (2014) 'Exploring historical perspectives of followership: The need for an expanded view of followers and the follower role'. In: L.M. Lapierre & M.K. Carsten, eds., *Followership: What is it and Why do People Follow?*, Bingley: Emerald Group Publishing, pp. 3–26.

Cartwright, D. & Zander, A. (1970) *Group Dynamics Research and Theory*, 3rd ed., New York: Tavistock.

Chaleff, I. (2009) *The Courageous Follower: Standing Up To and For Our Leaders*, 3rd ed., San Francisco, CA: Berrett-Koehler.

Ciulla, J.B. (2014) *Ethics, the Heart of Leadership*, 3rd ed., Santa Barbara, CA: Praeger.

Coetzer, M.F., Bussin, M. & Geldenhuys, M. (2017) 'The functions of a servant leader', *Administrative Sciences, MDPI, Open Access Journal, 7 (1)*, p. 1, February.

Cunliffe, A.L. & Eriksen, M. (2011) 'Relational leadership', *Human Relations, 64 (11)*, pp. 1425–1449.

Eagly, A.H. (2005) 'Achieving relational authenticity in leadership: Does gender matter?', *The Leadership Quarterly, 16*, pp. 459–474.

Eagly, A.H. (2013) 'Women as leaders: Leadership style versus leaders' values and attitudes'. In: *Gender and Work: Challenging Conventional Wisdom*, Boston, MA: Harvard Business School Press.

Eagly, A.H. & Wood, W. (2013) 'The nature–nurture debates: 25 years of challenges in understanding the psychology of gender', *Perspectives on Psychological Science, 8(3)*, pp. 340–357.

Epitropaki, O.; Martin, R. & Thomas, G. (2018) 'Relational Leadership'. In: Antonakis, J. & Day, V.D. (2018) *The Nature of Leadership*, 3rd ed., London: Sage Publishing, pp. 109–137.

Fiedler, F.E. (1967) *A Theory of Leadership Effectiveness*, New York: McGraw-Hill.

Fiedler, F.E. & Chemers, M.M. (1974) *Leadership and Effective Management*, Glenview, IL: Scott, Foresman and Co.

Galton, F. (1869) *Hereditary Genius*, London: Macmillan and Co.

Gardner, H.E. (2000) Intelligence Reframed: Multiple Intelligences for the 21st Century, London: Hachette.

Gardner, W.L., Avolio, B.J. & Walumbwa, F.O. (2005) 'Authentic leadership theory and practice: Origins, effects, and development', *Monographs in Leadership and Management, 3*, Bingley: Emerald Group.

George, B. (2003) Authentic Leadership: Rediscovering the Secrets to Creating Lasting Value, San Francisco, CA: Jossey-Bass.

Greenleaf, R.K. (1977) Servant Leadership: A Journey into the Nature of Legitimate Power and Greatness, New York, NY: Paulist Press.

Heifetz, R.A. (1994) *Leadership Without Easy Answers*, Cambridge, MA, Belknap Press of Harvard University Press.

Heifetz, R.A. & Linsky, M. (2017) *Leadership on the Line: Staying Alive through the Dangers of Leading*, Boston, MA: Harvard Business School Press.

Heifetz, R.A., Linsky, M. & Grashow, A. (2009) *The Practice of Adaptive Leadership*, Boston, MA: Harvard Business Review Press.

Hemphill, J.K. (1950) *Leader Behavior Description*, Columbus: Ohio State University, Personnel Research Board.

Hersey, P. & Blanchard, K.H. (1996) 'Great ideas revisited: Revisiting the life cycle theory of leadership', *Training Development Journal, 50 (1)*, p.42.

Hofstede, G. (2001) Culture's Consequences: Comparing Values, Behaviors, Institutions, and Organizations Across Nations, 2nd ed., Thousand Oaks, CA: Sage Publications.

House, R.J. (1971) 'A path-goal theory of leader effectiveness', *Administrative Science Quarterly, 16*, pp. 321–328.

House, R.J. & Mitchell, T.R. (1974) 'Path goal theory of leadership'. *Journal of Contemporary Business, Autumn*, pp. 81–97.

House, R.J., Hanges, P.J., Javidan, M., Dorfman, P.W. & Gupta, V., eds. (2004) *Culture, Leadership, and Organizations: The GLOBE Study of 62 Societies*, Thousand Oaks, CA: Sage Publications.

James, W. (1880) 'Great Men, great thoughts, and their environment', *Atlantic Monthly, 46*, pp. 441–459. Available at https://www.uky.edu/~eushe2/Pajares/jgreatmen.html [Accessed 2 January 2021].

Johnson, C.E. (2017) *Meeting the Ethical Challenges of Leadership*, 6th ed., Thousand Oaks, CA: Sage Publications.

Kant, I. (1785) *Groundwork for the Metaphysic of Morals*. Copyright © Jonathan Bennett 2017. Available at https://www.earlymoderntexts.com/assets/pdfs/kant1785.pdf [Accessed: 10 January 2021].

Kanter, R. (1977) *Men and Women of the Corporation*, New York: Basic Books.

Katz, R.L. (1955) 'Skills of an effective administrator', *Harvard Business Review, 33 (1)*, pp. 33–42.

Katz, D. & Kahn, R.L. (1966) *The Social Psychology of Organisations*, New York: J. Wiley and Sons.

Kellerman, B. (2008) Followership: How Followers are Creating Change and Changing Leaders, Boston, MA: Harvard Business Press.

Kouzes, J.M. & Posner, B.Z. (2017) The Leadership Challenge: How to Get Extraordinary Things Done in Organizations. 6th ed., San Francisco, CA: Jossey Bass.

Likert, R. (1967) The Human Organisation: its Management and Value, New York: McGraw Hill.

Lord, R.G., DeVader, C.L. & Alliger, G. M. (1986) 'A meta analysis of the relation between personality traits and leadership perseptions: An application of validity generalisation procedures', *Journal of Applied Psychology, 71*, pp. 402–410.

Meindl, J.R. (1995) 'The romance of leadership as a follower centric theory: A social constructionist approach'. *The Leadership Quarterly, 6 (3)*, pp. 329–341.

MOD (2004) *Leadership in Defence*, Shrivenham: Defence leadership Centre, Defence Academy of the UK.

Mumford, M.D., Zaccaro, S.J., Connelly, M.S. & marks, M.A. (2000) 'Leadership skills: Conclusions and future directions', *The Leadership Quarterly*, *11 (1)* pp. 155–170.

Notgrass, D. (2014) 'The relationship between followers' perceived quality of relationship and preferred leadership style', *Leadership and Organisation Development Journal*, *35 (7)*, pp. 605–621.

Omilion-Hodges, L.M., Ptacek, J.K. & Zerilli, D.H (2015) 'A comprehensive review and communication research agenda of the conceptualized workgroup: The evolution and future of leader-member exchange, coworker exchange and team-member exchange'. In: E.L. Cohen, ed., *Communication Yearbook*, *40*, New York, NY: Routledge, pp. 343–377.

Oxford English Dictionary Online. (2008) Available at http://www.oed.com [Accessed: 12 December 2020].

Peltonon, T. (2019) Towards Wise Management. Wisdom and Stupidity in Strategic Decision Making. Case Study 1, Stuttgart: Palgrave Macmillan, pp. 69–102.

Rittel, H.W.J. & Webber, M.M. (1973) 'Dilemmas in a general theory of planning', *Policy Sci*, *4*, pp. 155–169. Available at https://www.jstor.org/stable/4531523?origin=JSTOR-pdf&seq=1 [Accessed 5 January 2021].

Rost, J.C. (1991) *Leadership for the 21st Century*, Westport, CT: Praeger.

Schoemaker, P. J. H., Krupp, S. & Howland, S. (2013) 'Strategic leadership: The essential skills', *Harvard Business Review*, *91 (1–2)*, pp. 131–134.

Simonet, D.V. & Tett, R.P. (2012) 'Five perspectives on the leadership-management relationship: A competency-based evaluation and integration'. *Journal of Leadership and Organisational Studies*, *20 (2)*, pp. 199–213.

Spillane, J.P. (2006) *Distributed Leadership*, San Francisco, CA: Jossey-Bass.

Stogdill, R.M. (1963) *Manual for Leader Behavior Description Questionnaire – Form X11*. Columbus, OH: Ohio State University, Bureau of Business Research.

Stogdill, R. M. (1974) Handbook of Leadership, A Survey of Theory and Research, New York: The Free Press.

Thygeson, M., Morrissey, L. & Ulstad, V. (2010) 'Adaptive leadership and the practice of medicine: a complexity-based approach to reframing the doctor–patient relationship', *Journal of Evaluation in Clinical Practice 16 (5)*, pp. 1009–1010.

Uhl-Bein, M. (2006) 'Relational leadership theory: Exploring the social processes of leadership and organizing', *Leadership Institute Faculty Publications*, *19*. Available at https://digitalcommons.unl.edu/leadershipfacpub/19 654–676 [Accessed 12 January 2021].

UN ICTY (1996) 'Nine more persons indicted for attacks on Muslins in Lasva River Valley'. Available at https://www.icty.org/en/press/nine-more-persons-indicted-attacks-muslims-lasva-river-valley [Accessed 12 January 2021].

Van Dierendonck, D. (2011) 'Servant leadership: A review and synthesis', *Journal of Management*, *37 (4)*, pp. 1228–1261.

Vance Owen (1993) *The Vance Owen Plan*. Available at https://www.peaceagreements.org/wview/606/The%20Vance-Owen%20Plan [Accessed 5 January 2021].

Watters, B.S.C. (2019) 'Leadership in the "Wicked" problem of Bosnia's civil war: A case study examining ethical decision making under duress', *Leadership*, *15 (1)*, pp. 3–26.

Wilson, S. & McCalman, J. (2017) 'Re-imagining ethical leadership as leadership for the greater good', *European Management Journal*, *35 (2)*, pp 151–154.

Yammarion, F.J. (2000) 'Leadership skills: Introduction and overview', *The Leadership Quarterly*, *11 (1)*, pp. 5–9.

Yukl, G. (2013) *Leadership in Organisations*, 8th ed., London: Pearson.

Yukl, G. & Gardner, W.L. (2020) *Leadership in Organisations*, 9th ed., London: Pearson.

Zaccaro, S.J., Dubrow, S. & Kolze, M. (2018) 'Leader traits and attributes'. In: J. Antonakis, D.V. Day, eds., *The Nature of Leadership*, 3rd ed., London: Sage, pp. 29–55.

14 Change management

Roger Darby

Introduction

> The definition of insanity is doing the same thing over and over again and expecting a different result.
>
> Albert Einstein

This quote attributed to Albert Einstein, provides a salutary reminder for those contemplating and managing change. Throughout this book, it has been argued that learning from experience and adapting peoples' behaviours is central to resilience and ultimately security. States and their security organisations are operating in an increasingly volatile, uncertain, complex and ambiguous (VUCA) world. To survive and thrive within that context will undoubtedly require reform within and of national security sectors. As has been argued in previous chapters, SSR is fundamentally about change: institutional, sectoral, political and social. Yet SSR does not occur within a controlled environment, but within conditions of dynamic complexity; often individuals, organisations and situational contexts are in a state of flux, making change difficult to control. This is a significant factor in why the failure rate of reform of security sectors is so high. Whether change is called reform, evolution, revolution or transformation, the clear message for the security sector is that the *status quo is no longer deemed acceptable, desirable or even realistic.* To improve success rates those engaged in reform need to have the skills to manage change within specific situational contexts, albeit there is no universal formula for managing change.

This chapter addresses fundamental questions related to the requirements for change, the types and methods of change, and the variables that can influence the outcomes of a change initiative. This chapter draws together a number of themes that have been addressed throughout this book. It is in the development and implementation of change programmes that we realise just how important situational context (national and organisational), strategic analysis and planning, people and the management of their knowledge are to determining success or failure. It is argued that organisations that remain heavily reliant on culture and practices that assume machine-like regularity, are in danger of allowing homeostasis to be the norm; and are at risk of continuing to manage obsolescence. This chapter concludes by introducing tools and techniques for the management of change within the security sector.

DOI: 10.4324/9781003137061-14

Current themes in change management

Why change?

Change management represents a paradox: at one level, issues and concepts may appear easy to comprehend and understand, but their application is extremely complex. There is universal consensus amongst experts in this field that the vast majority of change programmes fail, with a 70% failure rate regularly cited (Al-Haddad & Kotnour, 2015). This rate applies to both private and public organisations. This raises a question: if most change programmes fail, why attempt to change? Do organisations change willingly, reluctantly or under duress? Of course, the answer can be all three – and there lies the problem that there is no uniform way to effectively manage change. Therefore, the leading assumption that practices of change management are universal should be challenged (Gunder, 2010; Whittington, 2006). Most organisations are slow to react to change, particularly those in the public sector, and security institutions are often the worst. For these organisations change is frequently initiated to address problems encountered in the past, rather than the ones they anticipate confronting in the future. That makes the quote attributed to Marshall McLuhan particularly apposite: 'We look at the present through a rear-view mirror. We march backwards into the future ' (Ciastellardi & Patti, 2011: p. 5).

While the processes, implementation, leadership and consolidation of change have been given significant attention over time (Schreyögg & Sydow, 2011; Van de Ven & Sun, 2011), there has been a lack of consistency in empirical evidence, theories and approaches to change management (By, 2005). Schwarz and Stensaker's (2016) review of organisational change over a 60-year period concluded there was little consolidation or integration in this field of study. So, how can we make sense of organisational change? An understanding of change management can be supported by focusing on the major schools of thought identified by Burns (2004: p. 262), for example:

- Individual perspective
- Group dynamics
- Open systems.

Hughes (2006: p. 15) built upon Burns' typology and created a useful classification that conjoins the related disciplines of change management with organisational behaviour and management.

To provide more clarity, it is argued here that managing change can be approached through the lens of *universality* (commonly applicable) or *particularity* (locally applicable) (Fyvberg, 1998). For example, all armed forces are expected to defend the nations that they serve, yet they do so in different ways depending on the specific nature of their civil-military relationship and their general operating spaces, as highlighted in Chapter 9 (e.g., battle, civil-military, business and cyber). Viewing organisational change through the lens of universality often results in the overemphasis of techniques and the underemphasis of contextual factors and cultural, rhetorical, and discursive norms. As has been argued throughout this book, situational context matters. Jansson (2013) has argued that 'rules, tools, methods, meetings, socio-material practices and discursive practices' all contribute to socially constructed contexts. Efforts to apply

Table 14.1 Overview of Mainstream Theoretical Perspectives to Understanding Organisations

Structural functionalism	– change structure and functions in order to reduce conflict.
Human relations	– facilitate change to more easily meet needs of individuals.
Psychodynamic	– facilitate the individual to realise the implications of defensive behaviour.
Systems theory	– change will have systemic effects on the other parts of the organisation as a whole.
Contingency theory	– change the contingencies within the system to develop the most appropriate management system and structure.
Action frame of reference	– change the rules which inform behaviour to change and transform the meaning of the organisation for the individual.
Cultural, ethnographic, and metaphorical	– change the meaning of the symbols within the culture of the organisation.

Source: Adapted from Hughes (2006).

'universal practices' without acknowledging the social context in which change is occurring is likely to result in the failure of the initiative. Example 14.1 provides illustrations of the different reasons for change affected by contextual factors.

Example 14.1: Different cases of contextual change

1. The Republic of Kosovo provides an example of how external determinants have the potential to influence change. Between 1996–1999 the Kosovo Liberation Army (KLA) engaged in armed insurrection, challenging Serbia's control of Kosovo. Between 1998–1999 that struggle intensified, and it was only with the support of NATO that Kosovo was able to achieve a ceasefire and create the conditions to enable it to eventually declare independence in 2008. Kosovo's legal and symbolic status as a state, however, remains subject to external influence. As of January 2020, 97 out of 195 countries in the world recognised Kosovo's statehood. Kosovo, however, does not have universal support from NATO and EU members. Given that both institutions have been extremely influential in shaping the structures and remits of the Kosovo Security Force (KSF), the Kosovo Police, and justice systems this is a significant issue for Kosovo's long-term status within Europe.
2. In the case of Sri Lanka, we see a mixture of external and internal drivers for defence reform. Between 1983 and 2009 Sri Lanka was engaged in a bitter civil war against the Liberation Tigers of Tamil Eelam (LTTE). It has been estimated that 100,000 people were killed during the course of the conflict (BBC, 2020), with 40,000 of those deaths attributed to the final offensive in 2009 (BBC, 2018). Following the conclusion of the war, little effort was made to restructure or reduce the size of the armed forces. That changed in 2015 with the Premiership of Ranil Wickremesinghe, a change in Sri Lanka's strategic context and the publication of the UNHCR's report into Human Rights abuses during the war. The armed forces were reoriented to an internal peacetime security role and efforts were made to increase the capability of the Navy and Air Force to patrol the littoral waters. The Army, as a result, was reduced in size. As a consequence of the UN report, Sri Lanka was pressured to address the shortcomings of the Armed Forces internal accountability mechanisms as well as improve civilian oversight of those forces.

3. Lesotho has had a long history of political instability and security challenges, which means that it has also been subject to an extended period of foreign intervention. In 2014 the South African Development Community (SADC) established an observer mission (SOMILES). In 2017 the Commander of the Lesotho Defence Forces (LDF), Lt. General Khoantle Motsomoto was assassinated, which led to the deployment of a SADC Standby Force. Reform of Lesotho's security sector was recommended by SADC, SOMILES and the Commonwealth Secretariat. In November 2017 the Government published its programme for national transformation. The objectives of the reforms were to promote long-term national stability, unity and reconciliation; to create professional, functioning and effective institutions for the efficient management of public affairs, service delivery and development; and to create the consensus for constitutional reform (Government of the Kingdom of Lesotho, 2017). To achieve those objectives reform of the Armed Forces, Police, Civil Service, Justice sector, legal system, and legislative oversight system were all deemed necessary.

Planned versus emergent change

Types of change

Organisations considering change face a dilemma: change may be required, but the process of change may fundamentally transform the organisation and sever ties with the past, both literally and psychologically. Kurt Lewin (1951) was prominent in advocating the concept of planned change leading to a *gradualist approach.* Numerous definitions have been advanced, which can be summarised as a process consisting of a sequence of phases, which are monitored and guided by change agents (senior officers), and through which intended outcomes can be achieved. (De Caluwe & Vermaak, 2003; Wilson, 1992).

However, as argued in Chapter 8, the gradualist approach is only suited when the rate of external change is relatively low, and when external threats slowly evolve. While it is useful to think about change as a series of actions rather than one sweeping one, there has been some criticism of the planned change model because of the factors that it does not adequately address. Van de Ven and Sun (2011) have argued that the process of planned change can be attributed to human and social factors, emotional responses, sense making and the nature of the organisational discourse. Therefore, organisational change is challenging due to the combination of human, structural and procedural factors that need to be encompassed within a new pattern of social and behavioural norms. We see within the literature an increased focus on the emotional context of change (Garg, 2017; Rafferty, Jimmieson & Armenakis, 2013) and the impact of sense making on implementation including within a team context (Steigenberger, 2015: Guiette & Vandenbempt, 2013). Ellis, Margalit and Segev (2012), identified organisational-level influences on mental models of change and that organisational learning mechanisms improved receptivity in future change. Middle managers were also shown to play a key role in influencing the process of sense making by employees experiencing change (Balogun & Johnson, 2005; Rouleau, 2005). Further research has been undertaken to understand how the use of language and discourse within an organisation affects how change is formulated, articulated, and engaged (Jaynes, 2015; Grant & Marshak, 2011; Marshak & Grant, 2008).

An alternative approach to planned change is that of emergent change. Within this model change is viewed as unpredictable, sometimes serendipitous, and often shaped by inter-relationships involving a range of variables. It focuses on bottom-up rather than top-down approaches, with an open-ended and continuous process of adaption to changing conditions. An example was alluded to in Chapter 8, identifying the punctuated equilibrium model, where policy follows periods of strategic stability punctuated by upheaval and change. This is common in the public sector, where public bodies need to deliver speedy policy changes and new priorities in directions that are closely aligned with political change. This can create a dilemma for senior management involving when and how to enforce the transition from stability to strategic change.

As has been argued throughout this book, the environments in which defence and security forces operate are complex and growing more so. Contemporary management theory, based as it is on a combination of cognitive psychology, focusing on motivational behaviour and goals, and scientific methods that emphasise task organisation, project management and process engineering, rarely acknowledges complexity. That has begun to change; complexity science has entered the lexicon of change management. Complex systems are ones with the following characteristics: an inherent underlying structure in the system; feedback in the system; nonlinearity, where things do not happen in a cause and effect way; emergence as an outcome of the system without planned intent; no central control; and a non-reducible system where one cannot understand the system's behaviour just by looking at a single part (Miller and Page, 2009). These characteristics are anathema for many security forces because they challenge traditional working practices, deep and embedded cultures, outmoded organisational structures, rigid hierarchies and systems of control. However, whether by design or default, modern defence and security forces operate within increasingly complex systems; to be successful they need to update and learn new ways of managing complexity and change. It is prescient at this point to note a word of caution when polarising a gap between planned and emergent change:

> Rather than seeing the argument between the planned and emergent approaches to change as a clash of two fundamentally opposing systems of ideas, they can be better viewed as approaches which seek to address different situational variables (contingencies).
>
> (Burns, 1996: p. 16)

Exercise 14.1

1. Consider the necessity of a nascent state going through transition after civil war that wishes to transform its Armed Forces from a conscript to a professional force. How would you plan to manage that successfully over a short-, medium-, and long-term period?
2. Imagine you were the CEO of an airline managing the consequences of COVID-19 on your business. All your planned change had been ruined by those events. How would you manage the future of your service?

Individual response

Any discussion about the success or failure of change management will inevitably focus on the primary importance of the individual. For, it has often been stated that the biggest resistors to change are *people*. In managing change we need to manage people as the following quotes attest:

> Organisations don't change - people do. Change happens person by person, and you cannot change people; they change themselves.
>
> (Quirke, 1996: p. 106)

> Organisations as we know them are the people in them: if the people do not change, there is no organisational change.
>
> (Gustavsson & Harung, 1994: p. 94)

> Change in behaviour is considered a primary criterion for effectiveness by organisational development researchers and practitioners.
>
> (Argyris, 1999: p. 67)

Generally, it can be argued that people are wary of or dislike change. Even after all the rational arguments have been put forward, usually some natural opposition remains. Individuals are commonly more motivated by avoiding losses than they are of making gains and improvements. It is much simpler not to take risks, retain the *status quo* as it is, than to alter it entirely. Those promoting change in their organisations face the Cassandra-syndrome (Cassandra in Greek mythology was cursed by the Gods. She could see the future, but no one would believe her). They may believe there is a requirement for change, yet they are confronted by excessive resistance when the initiative is announced. If success is to be achieved, then resistance must be overcome and that is done through clear and consistent communication. The reason for, the method and intended benefits of change and the efforts that will be made to reduce risk and disruption all need to be clearly explained.

Structural change has an impact on and is influenced by the psychological transitions people experience. Learning initiatives and knowledge acquisition involve changes in behaviours and working practices, therefore the psychological process needs to be managed as the organisation transitions. We cannot automatically assume that everyone in an organisation views it or the context in which it operates in exactly the same way. Cameron and Green (2019) provide a useful four-factor guide to individual change in Table 14. 2.

Table 14.2 Four Approaches to Individual Change

Factors	Action	Descriptors
1. Behavioural	**Changing behaviours** Guideline for managers (officers): Get your reward strategies right	Focus on how one individual can change another's behaviour using reward and punishment. However, little attention may be given to improving processes or relationships or increasing involvement in goal setting. There may be no interest in how individuals experience the change.

(Continued)

Table 14.2 (Continued)

Factors	Action	Descriptors
2. Cognitive	**Achieving results** Guidelines for managers (officers): Link goals to motivation	Cognitive theory based on the view that our emotions and our problems are a result of the way we think. Concerned with the internal processes in an individual's brain. These are internal processes which behavioural psychology did not concentrate on. By changing individual's thought patterns can change how they respond to situations. Advocates the use of goals and building a positive mental attitude supported by demanding goals. However, has a lack of recognition of the inner emotional world of the individual and its effect on managing change.
3. Psychodynamic	**The inner world of change** Guideline for managers (officers): Treat people as individuals and understand their emotional states as well as your own	The notion that individuals go through an internal psychological process during change. Useful for managers (officers) who want to understand the reactions of their staff during a change process and deal with them. Gain an understanding of why people react the way they do. However, it can be a complex process. Individuals don't always know when they are going through different stages with no clear beginnings or ends.
4. Humanistic	**Maximising potential**	A holistic approach where people exist within a social and cultural context. Importance of individuals taking responsibility for their own situations with an element of choice in how they think, feel and act. Emphasis on self-actualisation. Belief in development and growth and exploiting potential. However, people do not experience change in a consistent or uniform way.

Source: Adapted from Cameron and Green (2020).

Organisational response

Exercise 14.2

Bridges (2009) highlights the distinction between *planned change* and *transition. Transition* is about leaving the past behind and accepting new thinking and ways of behaving. *Planned change* is seen more as physical movement – re-structuring, moving location, introducing new technology into the workplace. The suggestion is that transition lags behind planned change. Change is situational and can be planned; whilst transition is psychologically driven and harder to manage.

Identify an example of the distinction between planned change and psychological transition in your organisation; and give two examples of why the change initiative may have failed?

The second key factor in managing change is the organisation itself. Morgan (1986) developed a typology of organisations through reference to eight metaphors: machines, organisms, brains, cultures, political systems, psychic prisons, flux and transformation and instruments of domination. Table 14.3 highlights four more common metaphors used with reference to the defence and security sectors.

What this discussion has sought to illustrate is that the theories of change are as varied as the practices of change. Strategies, structures, systems and resources, particularly human resources, all have a bearing on whether a change programme is successful. The consequences of failure are also variable. Typically, if a private sector organisation fails to change effectively, the very survival of the company may well be at stake. Most public sector organisations do not necessarily have this threat, if they fail to deliver change and, as a result their performance suffers, it usually results in an enquiry being held, some of the senior management being replaced, the department being restructured, and told that the mistakes must not happen again – until the next

Table 14.3 Selected Examples of Metaphors Used in Different Approaches to Managing Change

Metaphor	*How Change is Managed*	*Whose Responsibility*	*Main Guiding Principles*
Machine	Senior managers set targets and timescales. Consultants advised on techniques. Training emphasises behavioural change.	Senior management	Change can be driven from the top. Resistance can be managed. Targets set at beginning of the process and set course of travel.
Political System	Led by a powerful group in coalition with a new guiding principle. New people take power who control resources.	Those with power	There will be winners and losers. Change requires new coalitions and negotiations.
Organisms	Begins with research phase. Data presented to and analysed by those making decisions. Full involvement and collaboration to find a solution is sought. Training given to those who need to make changes.	Service/ Business improvement/ HR/OD managers	Participation and involvement are key. Awareness of the need for change is crucial. People need to be fully supported through change.
Flux & Transformation	Emergent change is a key topic and driver. Someone with authority takes the initiative to create 'discussion' which can be initially unstructured but well supported. Forums are democratic and involve anyone with an interest who sees the need for change. A plan how to handle change emerges.	Someone with authority to take action.	Change cannot be managed, it merges. Conflict and tension give rise to change. People are part of the process that need to be managed. It is key to highlight gaps and contradictions.

Source: Adapted from Morgan (1986).

time. Failure within a ministry of defence is much the same but if the failure impacts on operations this can for example, result in the loss of life in conflict situations. This was the case in Nigeria in 2018, where a demoralised and underequipped army was blamed for slow progress against Boko Haram militants in the northeast of the country who killed, tortured, or starved civilians. Despite multiple declarations of victory by the state, Boko Haram while significantly degraded, continued to slaughter soldiers and citizens across northeastern Nigeria and in neighbouring Niger, Chad and Cameroon.

Incremental and transformational change

How to manage change

So, how do we manage change? The answer is dependent upon the type of change we wish to pursue: incremental or transformational. The hallmarks of each are detailed in Table 14.4.

Table 14.4 Summary of Research into the Characteristics of Incremental and Transformational Change

Author	First order change (incremental)	Second order change (transformational)
Management theory Wilson (1992) Whittington (2006) Pettigrew et al. (2002) Ramaprasad (1982)	Branch change: a series of small, incremental changes that gradually move away from the current situation, step-by-step, by small degrees. Executive change: gives effect to policies by maintaining the course of affairs in line with governing relations, norms, and standards. Normal change: a constant tinkering of the various dimensions of the organisation, to try to improve the fit between the organisation and its environment. Minor change: simply improving current operations in attempts to boost efficiency.	Root change: A rational comprehensive approach, building from the ground up, starting from fundamentals each time, only relying on the past when experience is embodied in a theory. Policy-making change: establishing the overarching principles that will create and communicate a new culture and system of values. Paradigm change: concerns many or all dimensions of culture, reflecting a radical change in either the world or the world view. Revolutionary change: a redefinition of the entire system, which may occur at the conceptual, structural, or process level, or at some combination of the three.
Creative thinking De Bono (1971)	Vertical change: seeks to establish links between different aspects of the organisation, so that one thing will follow logically from another.	Lateral change: Breaks from the past and tries to find new patterns by restructuring.
Planned change Burns (2004) De Caluwe & Vermaak (2003)	Evolutionary change: Gentle adjustments, aimed at maintaining growth while retaining the same overall pattern of management. Rational change: retains internal structures because it does not question the underlying assumptions.	Revolutionary change: major alteration, abandoning past management practices and establishing a new set of organisational practices as the basis for the next phase of evolutionary growth. Radical change: a system change bringing a whole new cultural paradigm.

Organization theory Lewin (1951)	Homeostasis: sees current forces, internal and external, as close to equilibrium so managers work to short-term goals, largely maintaining existing systems.	Radical change: likened to caterpillars turning into butterflies; large scale change operations ... high speed, large-scale processes are initiated, to bring about transfiguration of the organization.

Source: Adapted from Lira (2004).

Exercise 14.3

What metaphors listed in Table 14.3 accurately describe the security institutions in your country and why? Do they provide a useful framework in which to contemplate change? If so, how? If not, why?

Culture and change management

Culture, both national and organisational, can be either a help or hindrance to the management of change. The challenge is that culture is intangible, invisible and pervasive. The metaphor of the 'iceberg' shown in Figure 14.1 illustrates the depth of cultural influence. Within the armed forces rituals and stories are important because they bind those who serve together. Those rituals and stories, however, are reflective of much deeper beliefs, values, attitudes, and ideologies.

In the same way that a scientist would not assess an iceberg based on the visible surface area alone, we should not judge the viability and effectiveness of an organisation based on observable activities alone. Whether the aim is planned change or transition, there will be a requirement to address employee attitudes and behaviours and organisational culture.

Figure 14.1 The Organisational Iceberg
Source: Author.

Exercise 14.4

Drawing on the key points in this chapter, consider the reward strategy employed in your organisation to encourage successful change management. What aspects of this strategy sends the right messages and encourage employees to perform better whilst accepting change? How can the reward strategy be improved particularly in respect to the links between performance culture and change management?

Current reward strategy

*   Tools
*   Benefits/Problems
*   Issues

Changes

*   Tools
*   Benefits
*   Issues

Tools and techniques for managing change

How to change?

In this section, the process of *how to change* is addressed. As highlighted in Chapters 2 and 8, for an organisation to remain viable, the starting point requires an analysis of the strategic context involving the identification of what needs to change. This includes the development of a strategy for change identifying key stakeholders and a continuous communication about the change process by an effective leadership (see Chapter 13). Change tools and techniques fit more with a planned rather than emergent approach to change. However, both are still popularly employed with an emphasis on successful use being selected and adapted according to the specifics of the situation; how they are used is as important as the tools or technique which are selected. Several change tools have been used over time with a varying degree of success. These have included, at the more macro level, for example: learning organisations, lean production, total quality management and high-performance work organisation (Graetz et al., 2002). Whilst mindful of the previous emphasis in this chapter on *particularity* over *universality* in managing organisational change, I have concentrated more on the micro level so as to overcome a more prescriptive approach and have highlighted three useful diagnostic and intervention tools and techniques. These include a Force-Field Analysis, the Pre-requisites for Success Model, and Managing Resistance to Change Equation; all are transferable and can be utilised in many situations faced by defence and security.

Force-field analysis

Kurt Lewin's (1951) force-field analysis is a useful technique for first identifying all the forces for and against change. By carrying out an analysis at the beginning of the change process a plan can be made to strengthen the forces supporting a decision and reduce the impact of the opposition. It identifies the forces that both *help and hinder* from closing the gap from where you are now and where you want to be in the future; and identifies possible action areas to input into a plan for implementation. It is also a useful tool for resource management of finite resources which can help identify potential wastage and costly use of precious tangible and intangible resources. Figure 14.2 provides two examples of change management: first, where senior managers want to improve the overall morale of their organisation and improve the performance of the staff. Second, an example of the need to recruit and maximise new talent into a professional force.

Resistance to change – The Force Field Analysis

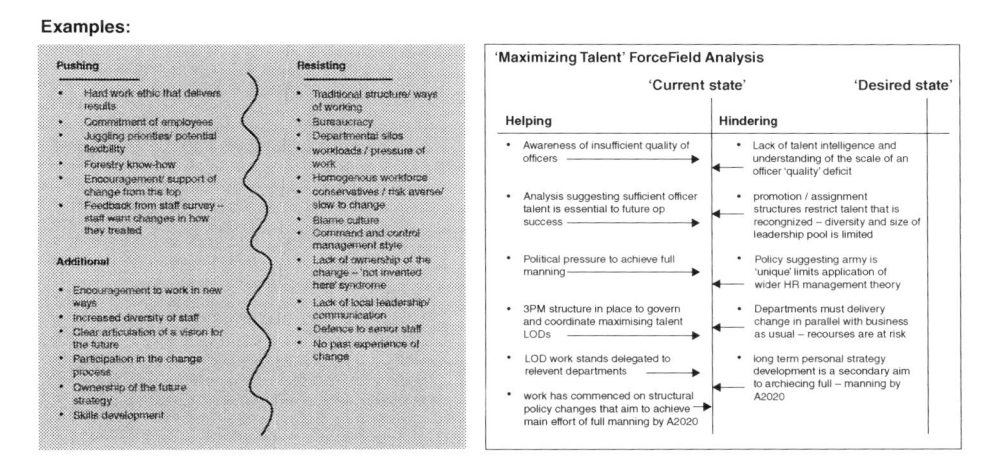

Figure 14.2 Force-Field Analysis
Source: Adapted from Lewin (1951).

Exercise 14.5

Identify a potential change initiative in your organisation that would benefit from using a Force Field Analysis at the start of the process. Draw a force field identifying present and future states, helping, and hindering forces and the end state or objective of the change.

The process of effective change management involves a comprehensive and integrated effort from all levels of management involving the consideration of several factors. The literature on change management contains numerous pre-requisites for successful change. Figure 14.3 condenses a few success factors into a useful tool called the Pre-requisites for Success Model, highlighting four key pre-requisites.

Exercise 14.6

Reflect on a change programme that you have either been involved in or observed. To what extent were the four key pre-requisites for successful change management evident?

Pre-requisites for Success

| Commitment |

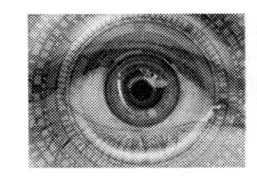

| Clear Vision |

| Strong, visible leadership |

| Good, two-way communication |

Figure 14.3 Pre-requisites for Successful Change Management
Source: Author.

Managing Resistance to Change Equation

$$C = (A\ B\ D\ ) > X$$

C = Change
A = Dissatisfaction with the status quo
B = Desirability of the proposed change
D = Practicality of change (minimum risk/disruption)
X = Cost of changing

Figure 14.4 Managing Resistance to Change Equation
Source: Adapted from Harris and Beckhard (1987).

By having a much broader view of an organisation, managers often identify the need for change far earlier than employees. This can cause resistance to the change initiative and, as previously identified, lead to individuals generally favouring the *status quo* and organisations maintaining *homeostasis*. The Harris-Beckhard Change Equation Tool shown in Figure 14.4, provides a simplified and concise way of capturing the process of change and identifying the factors that need to be prominent for change to take place and help analyse the potential success or failure of a change initiative within the workplace. It can be used at any time in the change process to evaluate progress.

Exercise 14.7

Using the Change Equation, identify a recent example of a change initiative in your organisation that you could have used this tool to have managed the change more successfully. Give examples for each factor to illustrate your example.

Change management in defence and security

The character of conflict and military science are constantly evolving. In just over a century we have seen an astounding transformation in the ways of war, from industrialisation to digitisation and miniaturisation. While traditional platforms, weapons and methods continue to have utility they are being used increasingly in combination with more modern capabilities, e.g., cyber and unmanned vehicles, to generate heightened levels of anxiety and to attack opponents without resorting to all-out war. The incorporation of these platforms and methods has resulted in changes to doctrine, the theory of military science, the application of international humanitarian law (IHL) (see Chapter 4) and paradigms for leadership and management (see Chapter 13). Those changes in turn have led to a requirement to reskill and upskill personnel at all levels of the armed forces.

That trend is likely to continue, with changes to military human capital being influenced by changes in the global security environment and within national security sectors and defence institutions. Researchers have posited several interesting scenarios, which will have a bearing on future change management in defence and security. The first challenge is to the battlespace, with it becoming opaquer and more chaotic. In the last quarter of a century observers have closely watched the Western way of war, which has involved amassing large forces, dominating land, sea and air. Conventional wisdom, for example, has supported concentrating forces and replacing infantry with long-range rockets and promulgating 'area denial'. Potential enemies, be they state or non-state actors, have developed ways to counter that strategy: dispersing forces in smaller, cellular units that are very mobile and involve faster decision-making processes. This in turn has led to a requirement to fight on both the physical and digital fronts.

The second challenge concerns the development and employment of autonomous platforms with the freedom to rove, swarm and fire. Allowing the next generation of drones and ground vehicles to be better at navigating with GPS allowing for greater span and autonomy; with smarter software permitting weapons to identify and select targets with minimal human input. However, although the defence industry boasts some of the most advanced technology to-date, supported by governments with big budgets and military research and development projects, it is notorious for long-lead times for delivery. Allowance must be made for an array of contradictory forces including bureaucracy, competition, lawsuits, and rapidly evolving requirements. Furthermore, defence companies are often reluctant to change with their culture highlighted as one of the most resistant to advancing intelligent enterprise.

The third issue is the pharmacological research into the development of neurotransmitters and the use of drugs to boost physical and mental performance (NRC, 2009). For example, the use of neuroscience in future Army applications including overcoming sleep deprivation (Groeger et al., 2011; Viola et al., 2007), anabolic hormones to repair muscles; amphetamines to sustain pilots on long missions; recent research into LSD to help intelligence analysts; memory suppressants to tackle PTSD (Hoge et al 2008; Bliese et al., 2008) or enhance aggression in the infantry.

Finally, the continuing importance of military deception with habits developed through previous years of experience. Military deception, which is closely connected to operations security (OPSEC), is an attempt by a military unit to gain an advantage by misleading adversaries into taking actions detrimental to themselves. This is usually achieved by creating or amplifying confusion via psychological operations, information warfare, visual deception, or other methods. As a form of disinformation, it overlaps with psychological warfare. This also draws links between communication theory, game theory and cognitive factors with on-going deception theories (Brams, 2011; Rrushi, 2011). Three further important assumptions when undertaking military deceptions at the strategic level involves large numbers of individuals and organisations including national command authorities. Also, they involve relatively long-term deceptions and finally, the stakes are very high and can affect the outcome of large-scale wars as opposed to tactical deceptions affecting the outcome of local battles or engagements (Daniel & Herbig, 2013). With increasing deception and anti-deception built into the contemporary planning process.

However, as timely reminder of the importance of *particularity*, defence and security forces who have well-established capabilities and reasonably sized budgets will need to invest in new technology, augment reduced full-time forces with larger numbers of unmanned platforms and prepare for conflicts wholly unlike those fought in the past decades. Conversely, those states forces representing a larger majority who have limited capability, comparatively small budgets, out-dated technology, and smaller reserves of trained human capital face even more uncertain and challenging futures. The differential remains great between those two camps with the potential for the chasm between them to grow even more dangerously wider in the future.

Conclusion

This chapter has highlighted the ubiquitous and dominant role change plays in contemporary organisations including those in defence and security. Change is inevitable and must be managed in the future. Whether change is called evolution, revolution, security sector reform (SSR), transformation the clear message for the security sector is that the *status quo is no longer acceptable.* This has prompted security organisations to address the fundamental question: *why and how to change?* However, high failure rates in managing change were shown to be a constant statistic with the corollary over time, for homeostasis to become the norm, which has been the general default setting for many in defence and security.

The previous chapters in this book have supported the centrality of change in both the theory and practice of SSR. Constituting a 'new normal' that requires a step-change in defence and security in terms of having different mindsets and practical applications to those previously adopted. The individual and the organisation were identified as two key players and fundamental to the change management equation. Both are fused with the crucial concepts of national and organisational culture which was shown to be all pervasive and often a reactionary force when bringing about much needed change.

In terms of *how* to manage change, three themes were shown to be of relevance: firstly, as highlighted in Chapter 8, a strategic plan involving clarity of management intentions in relation to the change initiative. Secondly, a balanced view of the expectations and outcomes for stakeholders. Thirdly, attention to the structure associated with implementation (ownership, governance, leadership competence, and human resource management (HRM) involving employee participation). Cross-case analysis indicated that embedding change in mindset and behaviour is particularly important; balancing planning and adaptation is also necessary throughout implementation to maintain relevance; and a sense of change fatigue as well as the varying pattern of emotional responses to change, will need particular attention.

Furthermore, organisational research suggests the following: ensure that there is a clear line of sight to an explicit organisational objective and keep returning to this even when the implementation remains clear. One or more key individuals or 'change champions' need to sustain attention and ownership in relation to the change initiative well beyond the launch and early stages. They also need to take responsibility for learning about what is working and what is not by refining the approach and sustaining communication about the benefits and values. Change agents need to be proactive in responding to changes in the organisational environment to sustain relevance and alignment with the overall organisational objectives. Effective governance processes also need to be established to evaluate progress, refine the approach, and ensure implementation.

Embedding change initiatives often involves changes in behaviour (e.g., conscript to professional force), new team dynamics (e.g., in inter-agency working) or the adoption of different processes or technologies (e.g., cyber security) that have an impact on well-established working practices and organisational culture. Inserting change involves a new state of mind, as well as shifts in behaviours and working practices. Ultimately, it is the shifts in mindsets that determine whether something has been embedded. This human dimension means a simple project management approach is unlikely to be enough. Change management means paying attention to the wider implications of an initiative, and the consequences for the people involved, the most expensive asset and usually the most poorly managed.

Questions to consider

1. What does change mean to you? Describe two successful and two failed examples of change in your organisation. What made them successful? What made them fail?
2. What problems are created for organisations by managing change?
3. What are the key points to note in the relationship between culture and change?
4. Do you think the culture(s) within your national defence sector need to change? If so, why, to what and how?
5. How would you set about introducing new types of desired behaviour to manage change in the defence and security sector?

Suggested further reading

Cameron, E. & Green, M. (2020) *Making Sense of Change Management: A Complete Guide to the Models, Tools and Techniques of Organisational Change*, 5th ed., London: Kogan Page.
Hughes, M. (2006) *Change Management: A Critical Perspective*, London: Chartered Institute of Personnel & Development.

References

Al-Haddad, S. & Kotnour, T. (2015) 'Integrating the organisational change literature: a model for successful change', *Journal of Organisational Change Management*, 28 (2), pp. 234–262. DOI:10.1108/JOCM-11-2013-0215
Argyris, C. (1999) *On Organizational Learning*, Malden, MA: Blackwell.
Balogun, J. & Johnson, G. (2005) 'From intended strategies to unintended outcomes: The impact of change recipient sensemaking', *Organisation Studies*, 26 (11), pp. 1573–1602. DOI: https://doi.org/10.1177/0170840605054624

BBC (2018) 'Sri Lanka War: I wanted "my side" to lose'. Available at https://www.bbc.co.uk/news/world-south-asia-45347956 [Accessed 19 February 2021].

BBC (2020) 'Sri Lanka Civil War: Rajapaska says thousands missing are dead'. Available at https://www.bbc.co.uk/news/world-asia-51184085 [Accessed 19 February 2021].

Bliese, P.D., Wright, K.M., Adler, A.B., Cabrera, O., Castro, C.A. & Hoge, C.W. (2008) 'Validating the primary care posttraumatic stress disorder screen and the posttraumatic stress disorder checklist with soldiers returning from combat', *Journal of Consulting and Clinical Psychology*, 76 (2), p. 272. DOI: 10.1037/0022–006X.76.2.272

Brams, S.J. (2011) *Game Theory and Politics*, Massachusetts, USA: Courier Corporation.

Bridges, W. (2009) *Managing Transitions: Making the Most of Change*, Boston, MA: Da Capo Press.

Burns, J.M. (1996) 'No such thing as…a 'one best way' to manage organizational change', *Management Decision*, 34 (10), pp. 11–18. DOI:10.1108/00251749610150649

Burns, J.M. (2004) *Transforming Leadership: A New Pursuit of Happiness, 213*, New York: Grove Press.

By, T.R. (2005) 'Organisational change management: A critical review', *Journal of Change Management*, 5 (4), pp. 369–380. DOI:10.1080/14697010500359250

Cameron, E. & Green, M. (2019) *Making Sense of Change Management: A Complete Guide to the Models, Tools and Techniques of Organizational Change*, London: Kogan Page Publishers.

Ciastellardi, M. & Patti, E. (2011) *Re-cognizing McLuhan's Critical Thought*, Milan: Research Publications at Politecnico di Milan.

Daniel, D.C. & Herbig, K.L. eds., (2013) *Strategic Military Deception: Pergamon Policy Studies on Security Affairs*, London: Elsevier.

De Bono, E. (1971) *The Use of Lateral Thinking*, London: Penguin.

De Caluwe, L. & Vermaak, H. (2003) *Learning to Change: A Guide for Organization Change Agents*, London: Sage.

Ellis, S., Margalit, D. & Segev, E. (2012) 'Effects of organizational learning mechanisms on organizational performance and shared mental models during planned change', *Knowledge and Process Management*, 19 (2), pp. 91–102.

Flyvbjerg, B. (1998) *Rationality and Power: Democracy in Practice*, Chicago: University of Chicago Press.

Garg, N. (2017) 'Workplace spirituality and employee well-being: An empirical exploration', *Journal of Human Values*, 23 (2), pp. 129–147. DOI: 10.1177/0971685816689741

Government of the Kingdom of Lesotho (2017) *The Lesotho We Want: Dialogue and Reforms for National Transformation*, Maseru.

Graetz, F., Rimmer, M., Lawrence, A. & Smith, A. (2002) *Managing Organisational Change*, Chichester: John Wiley & Sons. UK.

Grant, D. & Marshak, R.J. (2011) 'Toward a discourse-centered understanding of organizational change', *The Journal of Applied Behavioral Science*, 47 (2), pp. 204–235. DOI: 10.1177/0021886310397612

Groeger, J.A., Lo, J.C., Burns, C.G. & Dijk, D.J. (2011) 'Effects of sleep inertia after daytime naps vary with executive load and time of day', *Behavioral Neuroscience*, 125 (2), p. 252. DOI:10.1037/a0022692

Guiette, A. & Vandenbempt, K. (2013) 'Exploring team mental model dynamics during strategic change implementation in professional service organizations. A sensemaking perspective'. *European Management Journal*, 31 (6), pp. 728–744. DOI:10.1016/j.emj.2013.07.002

Gunder, M. (2010) 'Planning as the ideology of (neoliberal) space', *Planning Theory*, 9 (4), pp. 298–314. DOI: 10.1177/1473095210368878

Gustavsson, B. & Harung, H.S. (1994) 'Organizational learning based on transforming collective consciousness', *The Learning Organization*, 1 (1), pp. 33–40. DOI:10.1108/09696479410053421

Harris, R.T. & Beckhard, R. (1987) *Organizational Transitions: Managing Complex Change*, Reading, MA: Addison-Wesley Publishing Company.

Hoge, C.W., McGurk, D., Thomas, J.L., Cox, A.L., Engel, C.C. & Castro, C.A. (2008) 'Mild traumatic brain injury in US soldiers returning from Iraq', *New England Journal of Medicine*, *358* (5), pp. 453–463. DOI: 10.1056/NEJMoa072972

Hughes, M. (2006) *Change Management: A Critical Perspective*, London: Chartered Institute of Personnel & Development.

Jansson, N. (2013) 'Organisational change as practice: A critical analysis'. *Journal of Organisational Change Management*, *26* (6), pp. 1003–1019. DOI:10.1108/JOCM-09–2012–0152

Jaynes, S. (2015) 'Making strategic change: A critical discourse analysis', *Journal of Organisational Change Management*, *28* (1), pp. 97–116. DOI: 10.1108/JOCM-04–2013–0053

Kofman, F. and Senge, P.M., (1993) 'Communities of commitment: The heart of learning organizations', *Organizational dynamics*, *22*(2), pp.5–23. DOI:10.1016/0090–2616(93)90050

Lewin, K. (1951) *Field Theory in Social Science*, New York: Harper & Brothers.

Lira, L. (2004) *'To change an army: Understanding defense transformation'*. Paper presented to ISSS. ISAC Annual Conference, 28–30 October 2004.

Marshak, R.J. & Grant, D. (2008) 'Organisational discourse and new organisation development practices', *British Journal of Management*, *19*, S7–S19. DOI:10.1111/j.1467–8551.2008.00567

Miller, J.H. & Page, S.E. (2009) *Complex Adaptive Systems: An Introduction to Computational Models of Social Life*, Princeton, CA: Princeton University Press.

Morgan, G. (1986) *Images of Organization*, Newbury Park, CA: Sage Publications.

National Research Council (NRC) (2009) *Opportunities for Neuroscience for Future Army Applications*, Washington, DC: The National Academy Press.

Pettigrew, A., Thomas, H. & Whittington, R., (2002) 'Strategic management: the strengths and limitations of a field', *Handbook of Strategy and Management*, *3*, London: Sage.

Quirke, J. (1996) *Communicating Corporate Change: A Practical Guide to Communication and Corporate Strategy*, New York: McGraw-Hill Business.

Rafferty, A.E., Jimmieson, N.L. & Armenakis, A.A. (2013) 'Change readiness: A multilevel review', *Journal of Management*, *39* (1), pp. 110–135. DOI:10.1177%2F0149206312457417

Ramaprasad, A. (1982) 'Revolutionary change and strategic management', *Behavioral Science*, *27* (4), pp.387–392. DOI:10.1002/bs.3830270406

Rid, M. (2019) *Active Measures*, New York: Farrar, Strauss & Giroux.

Rouleau, L. (2005) 'Micro-practices of strategic sensemaking and sensegiving: how middle managers interpret and sell change every day', *Journal of Management Studies*, *42* (7), pp. 1413–1441. DOI:10.1111/j.1467–6486.2005.00549.x

Rrushi, J.L. (2011) 'An exploration of defensive deception in industrial communication networks', *International Journal of Critical Infrastructure Protection*, *4* (2), pp. 66–75. DOI:10.1016/j.ijcip.2011.06.002

Schreyögg, G. & Sydow, J. (2011) 'Organizational path dependence: A process view', *Organization Studies*, *32* (3), pp. 321–335. DOI: 10.1177/0170840610397481

Schwarz, G.M. & Stensaker, I.G., (2016) 'Showcasing phenomenon-driven research on organizational change', *Journal of Change Management*, *16* (4), pp. 245–264. DOI:10.1080/1469701 7.2016.1230931

Steigenberger, N. (2015) 'Emotions in sensemaking: A change management perspective', *Journal of Organizational Change Management*, *28* (3). pp. 432–451.

Van de Ven, A. & Sun, K. (2011) 'Breakdowns in implementing models of organisational change', *Academy of Management Perspectives*, *25* (3), pp. 58–74. DOI:10.5465/amp.25.3.zol58.

Viola, A.U., Archer, S.N., James, L.M., Groeger, J.A., Lo, J.C., Skene, D.J., von Schantz, M. & Dijk, D.J. (2007) 'PER3 polymorphism predicts sleep structure and waking performance', *Current Biology*, *17* (7), pp. 613–618. DOI:10.1016/j.cub.2007.01.073

Whittington, R. (2006) 'Completing the practice turn in strategy research', *Organization Studies*, *27* (5), pp. 613–634. DOI: 10.1177/0170840606064101

Wilson, D.C. (1992) *A Strategy of Change: Concepts and Controversies in the Management of Change*, London: Routledge, Cengage Learning, EMEA.

15 Managing security
Continuity and change

Laura R. Cleary and Roger Darby

Introduction

When we began scoping this project in 2019, we had a specific purpose in mind. We wanted to reflect upon how our understanding of and approach to teaching security governance and management had changed over time. That desire was fuelled by a recognition that the interests and concerns of our students had subtly changed over the years. In many cases they were less concerned with the reform *of* the security sector than they were with reform *in* the security sector. They wanted to know how to improve the efficiency, effectiveness and the economic management of security institutions so that they could address immediate challenges, be those serious organised crime, insurgency, terrorism, cyber-attack, or hybrid warfare. This distinction between the reform *of* the security sector and reform *in* the security sector is an important one to make, because the scale of a proposed change has implications for the manageability of that change. Our students recognised that security sector reform (SSR) while necessary was perhaps too ambitious for their governments because it could take generations to implement, the scale of the change would be beyond their financial means, and it would demand a degree of direction and coordination beyond the existing skills set of government. So, our students – mid-ranking to senior level officials – sought to identify what they could change within their departmental or service context and how that change could be affected. The topics addressed within this book are the ones which underpin, and may be the subject of, reform within security institutions.

We have endeavoured to frame our discussion of those topics with reference to four themes: change is a constant, context matters, conceptual clarity is crucial and experiential learning is key. Our authors also have sought to address five central questions: How does the state conceptualise its security? What are the perceived risks to attaining that vision? For whom does the state wish to provide security? What is the best way of doing so? Who is ultimately responsible for its provision? Over the following pages we offer some final thoughts on these themes and questions.

Security in the 21st century: What does the future hold?

We contend that the fundamental understanding of security has not changed, nor do we anticipate that it will do so in the foreseeable future. Peoples and nations will continue to define security as 'freedom from fear, want or threat' (Buzan, 1991). Whether we consider the individual or state as the referent object of security that definition will remain accurate. What will continue to change are the sources of insecurity; those

DOI: 10.4324/9781003137061-15

issues, events and actors that generate fear, want and threat. Previous chapters have highlighted the myriad risks and threats the world currently faces: shifting global power dynamics, finite tangible and intangible resources, contradictory legal and ethical positions, corruption and a lack of accountability, terrorism, economic inequality and poverty, AI, cyber insecurity, arms races, global warming, pandemics and unpredictable human behaviour. The extent of the risk posed by any one of these will ebb and flow and will be felt in different ways depending on situational context.

That situational context may be influenced in part by geographical context, but only in part. What has become evident in the first two decades of the 21st century is the speed with which defence and security are being decoupled from physical space. Armed forces may be constituted to defend the territory of a given state and they may do so by patrolling borders, protecting seaways and Exclusive Economic Zones (EEZs), or monitoring airspace, but increasingly they are being drawn into the protection of cyberspace and space. They are not the only security providers operating within these domains. Police may still patrol the streets of local communities, but in their efforts to counter serious organised crime or terrorism they will be operating in the digital space as much as the physical one. The same holds true of the intelligence services as they are called upon to support the efforts of the police or to deter industrial or political espionage. As David Chuter suggested in Chapter 7, there may be no fixed template for how to organise the various security institutions, but there is a degree of commonality with respect to the roles they play and how those roles are evolving.

For the foreseeable future we will see a mixed picture in terms of activities and domains. The armed forces of industrialised states will seek to demonstrate that they can operate effectively in all five operational domains: land, maritime, air, cyber and space. To do so will require partnering with other security services, industry and academia, and innovation in terms of restructuring of existing institutions, the establishment of new organisations, and the development of new ways of working. Other states will observe what is happening and try to keep up, compete, or collaborate, specifically through manufacturing within their defence industries. As Kogila Balakrishnan argued in Chapter 12, for many countries investment in the defence industry must be seen to drive the development of the economy as a whole, thus the strategy of offsets will continue to be of interest to those states seeking to catch-up economically and militarily with the hegemons. We will continue to see a hierarchy of military and broader security capabilities across the world, but with increasing efforts at partnership between the civilian and security sectors as they endeavour to limit or close the gap with their competitors.

In Chapter 2, Edith Wilkinson and Laura Cleary, argued that given the complexity and interconnectedness of the risks the world faces it is perhaps advisable to couch our responses in terms of resilience, rather than security. During the course of 2020–2021 it was interesting to note the frequency with which the term resilience and its underlying principles were employed when individuals, corporations, and countries outlined their plans for the post-COVID-19 age. There was a perceived requirement to develop the resilience of individuals, healthcare systems, supply chains and economies; the aim being to 'build back better'. In some cases, the plans for developing resilience are expressed in terms of the (re)nationalisation of agricultural and industrial supply (Pilling et al., 2021: p.9). This has caused concern in some quarters as it is viewed as evidence of a return to economic nationalism, a policy that proved destructive in the

1930s. This agenda, however, can be viewed in a different light, as evidence of a desire to build national resilience. As Wilkinson and Cleary argued in Chapter 2, the resilience of any system is dependent upon the resilience of its individual components. A point that was reiterated by Dodd, Hilton and Darby in their examination of cyber security in Chapter 10. If we want to achieve global resilience, we may need to start with the development of national resilience. That in turn may require the promotion of whole-of-government and whole-of-society approaches to the risks we face.

Resilience is ultimately about agency, adaptive capacity, capability, risk and change management; themes with which all of our authors have been concerned. As Wilkinson and Cleary posited, individuals and nations will continue to live with uncertainty, and thus with insecurity. Therefore, in planning for resilience, it is advisable to characterise the types of uncertainty that we face into three domains: the 'foreseeable', the 'cross-scale' and the 'out of the blue' domains (p. 25). The response at each level will require different types of information, knowledge, strategies and management processes. As a number of authors have argued within this volume it is one thing to identify a risk, responding to it requires a very different mindset and skills set. Ultimately, resilience and security are linked to the overall quality of our governance and management systems.

Governing security

As was argued in Chapter 1, there is a symbiotic relationship between governance and management. As defined by Haynes (2006: p.17), governance is about the process of decision-making and the manner by which those decisions are put into practice (or, in some cases not put into practice). Governance is in essence about *content* – what do we want to do – and management is about *process* – how do we want to do it. Given the risks nation states and their security services face we argue that the governance and management of security need to be considered in tandem.

While risk identification and assessment may be precursors to policy formation, policy implementation is dependent upon the identification and use of appropriate resources. An example provided by students on a cyber security course illustrates the way in which the failure to act exacerbates existing vulnerabilities. Over the last decade there has been growing recognition that individuals, corporations and states are increasingly vulnerable to cyber surveillance and attack. Declaratory policy in the form of executive directives or national security policies may identify the risk and prioritise a response, but rhetoric does not match reality. Students on that course indicated that despite the urgent requirement to shore up cyber defence, budgets either had not been allocated or were insufficient, there was no cyber security policy in place and thus little coordination of state ministries. Further, the equipment available to those engaged in cyber defence was outdated, public sector wages were lower than those in the private sector, and politicians did not truly understand the nature of the threat or how it could be combatted. As one student declared, they didn't just have one arm tied behind their back, but both legs as well.

The experience of those students is undoubtedly common across all nations, and amongst those dealing with a range of security issues, not just those originating in the cyber domain. The standard by which we judge governments, and the quality of governance may not have fundamentally changed over the years, but the range of issues to which we want government to respond and against which we will subsequently judge it has grown exponentially. The 'securocratic' approach referred to in Chapter 5, has implications for governance. As a result, it will prove ever more challenging to achieve high levels of satisfaction across a polity, but we need to be aware that the political community is itself changing. Analysis of modern techno-politics, for example, has highlighted that the further development of networking platforms and AI will generate new populations of users and politics, new laws, ethics, standards and governance systems.

As Turns and Van Engeland indicated in Chapter 4, the existing legal framework that defines the role and enables and constrains the use of defence and security forces is predicated upon traditional concepts of security, peace and war. If the purpose of law is to create order through regulation, then we may need to assesses whether the current legal framework (national and international) is sufficient for current and future security requirements. That assessment should in turn prompt a review of our systems of accountability. As Cleary concluded in Chapter 6, systems of accountability should mirror our systems of power. Over the last several decades we have witnessed shifting power dynamics, with political, economic and military power flowing between states and economic and political power from states to global corporations. While accountability mechanisms are organic, changing over time, it is evident that those mechanisms evolve more slowly than the systems of power they seek to check. Evolve they must, however, if governments are to retain their authority and be perceived as legitimate and effective in the eyes of the citizenry.

Managing security

It has been the contention throughout this book that governments need to think and act strategically. Given the nature of the security risks that they face, a reactive posture is inappropriate. Thinking and acting strategically is challenging for all forms of government. In the case of democracies, however, the strategic timeframes are often defined solely in terms of the electoral cycle. As has been noted by academics and officials alike, governments appear to be losing the capacity to think strategically (Cornish & Dorman, 2009; Strachan, 2009; Newton, Colley & Sharpe, 2010). How can this trend be reversed? It can be countered through the effective management of people, skills, knowledge and resources.

National security strategies and defence policies regularly proclaim that 'people are the greatest asset', or words to that effect. If that is truly the case, and we would argue that it is, then that asset needs to be managed strategically. All organisations, including those within the security sector, will eventually need to address the quantity v. quality conundrum. Traditionally, quantity, or mass in military parlance, has been viewed as a critical enabler in the attainment of effect. For example, the Russian approach to warfare, from the age of Imperialism onwards, was to rely on the number of men, rather than the quality or availability of equipment. The Russian army might be out-gunned by its enemy, but it was unlikely to be outnumbered. Its reserves of human capital were the key to victory, as was proved in the Second World War. In the modern era, governments around the world still publicly equate mass with effect. 'If we have more men or more missiles, we will be more effective in war'. With respect to domestic security, emphasis is placed on increasing the number of police on patrol as a means to increase overall levels of security. As has been argued in the preceding chapters, the nature of the risks we face means that scale will be less important than capability in the future. An argument that has been made recently within British National Security Strategies and Capability Reviews (HM Government, 2015; HM Government, 2018; HM Government, 2021).

The development of capability requires strategic management and strategic leadership. As argued in Chapter 8, strategic management seeks to add value to organisational outputs and keep the organisation competitive. Strategic leadership is concerned with setting the vision of that organisation and defining what value looks like. All security institutions are faced with the questions of how they add value to the security of the state and how they can remain competitive against their enemies, be those states or non-state actors. We would argue that to be able to do this requires us, in a sense, to go back to basics, meaning that we need to be able to plan, organise, command, coordinate, and control.

We recognise that the context in which those basics will be applied is changing. We have made reference above to changing dynamics within the security environment, but it is also worth noting the changes that have occurred within organisational contexts as a result of the promotion of liberal political and economic agendas. As Cleary and Collantes-Celador identified in Chapter 3, participation and inclusiveness are two of eight characteristics of governance. Within the business space the equivalent characteristics are classed as voice and engagement. As Darby detailed in Chapter 9, as employees come to view themselves and are viewed by their employers as knowledge workers the more the balance of power shifts from the organisation to the individual. Institutions need to work harder to obtain and retain their employees. This is as true in the public sector as it is in the private sector. We have seen in a number of countries across Africa, Asia and Latin America the difficulties that security services have in retaining well-trained and capable staff leading to brain-drain. Those institutions may have access to a wide pool of applicants, and be able to recruit the best among them on the basis of promises of access to education and training, but once trained those individuals may feel frustrated by the lack of opportunity to express their voice or to advance through the ranks or to earn a comparable salary to those in the private sector.

The requirement to operate within new security domains may lead to the creation of new institutional structures, which in turn will require the acquisition of new knowledge. The security professional of the future will look very different from the security professional of today. We contend, therefore, that a better understanding of the psychological contract, incorporating employee engagement, will be a key factor in whether security forces add value and remain competitive in the future. The value of human capital needs to be more than simply acknowledged. It needs to be understood, sustained and regularly enhanced.

The final point that we would make is that defence and security are no longer the sole purview of those in uniform. For several decades in the West, we have observed the blurring of the demarcation line between the military and civilian spheres, as a result of changes in the security environment. A strict division of labour between the military experts and statesmen, as argued by Samuel Huntington in *The Soldier and the State* (1957), is not practicable (Nielsen & Liebert, 2020: p.11). This change has been driven by adaptations in the nature and objectives of security operations (Gordon, 2006: p.339), the legal contracting of military personnel, the employment of civilian contractors, and in some instances their deployment alongside military personnel. Some of these trends are evident also with regards to policing. The promotion of the community policing model has led to greater engagement and collaboration between those in uniform and those they are meant to protect. We believe that this trend will continue and accelerate as governments seek new ways to provide security across physical, cyber and spatial domains.

In light of this trend, we have suggested that the way in which civil-military/civil-security relations are conceived needs to change. In far too many countries the relationship is viewed in adversarial terms; us (civilians) v. them (security services). We advocate a recalibration of that relationship, couching it not in terms of control, but in terms of cooperation and partnership in the delivery of the ultimate public good – security. We recognise that the rebalancing of relationships takes time and that trust is based on an assessment of actions. Trust is also more likely to occur when there is clarity and consistency in communication. Hence our desire within this book to clarify concepts and contribute to the security literacy of those engaged in the reform of their security institutions.

In closing

It is a complex, dynamic and difficult task to provide security, and it will always be so. What is effective and acceptable in one time or place, will not be so in another. Anyone who says that there is a single best way to govern and manage security should be treated with caution.

Our experience of working in countries in transition is that the concerns and desires of those engaged in the provision of security are common, as are many of the challenges that they face. The solutions to those challenges, however, will be unique to each country. Our aim in this volume has not been to prescribe a way of governing and managing security, but to provide a baseline from which those issues can be considered. We have sought to share commonly agreed principles, to provide examples of good practice, and to highlight the challenges that may be encountered when seeking to apply those principles. We recognise that we have not been able to provide a comprehensive review of the subject of security. It would have been impossible to do so. We hope, however, that our treatment of the issues is sufficient to encourage those engaged in the reform of security institutions to reflect on what they are doing and how to effect positive change in the future.

We have argued throughout this book that change is a constant, but it is important to stress that change is not consistent. The pace and pattern of change is variable between countries, within countries and within institutions. There will be different levels of desire for and engagement in reform. Resistance to change can be mitigated in part by communicating a clear vision for why that change is necessary. The vision of 'what might be' will be unique to institutions and nations, and determined by social, economic, political and technological factors. There is no single best way of providing security, but as we have attempted to demonstrate throughout this book, there is another way.

References

Buzan, B. (1991) *Peoples, States and Fear: An Agenda for International Security Studies in the Post-Cold War Era*, 2nd ed., Boulder, CO: Harvester Wheatsheaf.

Cornish, P. & Dorman, A. (2009) 'Blair's wars and Brown's budgets: From strategic defence review to strategic decay in less than a decade', *International Affairs*, 85 (2), pp. 247–261.

Gordon, Stuart (2006) 'Exploring the civil-military interface and its impact on European strategic and operational personalities: "Civilianisation" and limiting military roles in stabilisation operations?', *European Security, 15 (3)*, pp. 339–361. DOI:10.1080/09662830601097389

Haynes, J. (2006) 'The principles of good governance'. In: L. Cleary and T. McConville, eds., *Managing Defence in a Democracy*, Abingdon: Routledge.

HM Government (2015) *National Security Strategy and Strategic Defence Review.* Available at https://assets.publishing.service.gov.uk/government/uploads/system/uploads/attachment_data/file/478933/52309_Cm_9161_NSS_SD_Review_web_only.pdf [Accessed 31 March 2021].

HM Government (2018) *National Security Capability Review.* Available at https://assets.publishing.service.gov.uk/government/uploads/system/uploads/attachment_data/file/705347/6.4391_CO_National-Security-Review_web.pdf [Accessed 31 March 2021].

HM Government (2021) *Global Britain in a Competitive Age: the Integrated Review of Security, Defence, Development and Foreign Policy.* Available at https://www.gov.uk/government/publications/global-britain-in-a-competitive-age-the-integrated-review-of-security-defence-development-and-foreign-policy [Accessed 31 March 2021].

Newton, P., Colley, P. & Sharpe, A. (2010) 'Reclaiming the art of British strategic thinking', *The RUSI Journal 155 (1)*, pp. 44–50. DOI: 10.1080/03071841003683435

Nielsen, Suzanne C. & Liebert, Hugh (2020) 'The continuing relevance of Morris Janowitz's *The Professional Soldier* for the education of officers', *Armed Forces & Society.* DOI:10.1177/0095327X20960480

Pilling, D., Inagaki, K., Dempsey, H. & Campbell, P. (2021) 'A creaking global economy', *The Financial Times*, 27/28 March 2021, p. 9.

Strachan, H. (2009) 'The strategy gap in British defence policy', *Survival, 51 (4)*, pp. 49–70.

Index

Note: References to figures are indicated in *italics* and references to tables in **bold**.

Printed in the United States
by Baker & Taylor Publisher Services